The European Union as a Leader in International Climate Change Politics

Climate change poses one of the biggest challenges facing humankind. The European Union (EU) has developed into a leader in international climate change politics although it was originally set up as a 'leaderless Europe' with decision-making powers spread amongst EU institutional, Member State and societal actors.

The central aim of this book, which is written by leading experts in the field, is to explain what kind of leadership has been offered by EU institutional, member state and societal actors. Although leadership is the overarching theme of the book, all chapters also address ecological modernisation, policy instruments, and multi-level governance as additional main themes. The book chapters focus on the Commission, European Parliament, European Council and Council of Ministers as well as member states (Britain, Germany, France, the Netherlands, Poland and Spain) and societal actors (businesses and environmental NGOs). Additional chapters analyse the EU as a global actor and the climate change policies of America and China and how they have responded to the EU's ambitions.

This book will be of interest to students and scholars of environmental politics, EU politics, comparative politics and international relations as well as to practitioners who deal with EU and/or climate change issues.

Rüdiger K. W. Wurzel is Reader and Jean Monnet Chair in European Union Studies in the Department of Politics and International Studies at the University of Hull where he is director of the Centre for European Union Studies (CEUS).

James Connelly is Professor of Politics at the University of Hull and is the Director of the Institute of Applied Ethics.

Routledge / UACES Contemporary European Studies

Edited by Federica Bicchi, London School of Economics and Political Science, Tanja Börzel, Free University of Berlin, and Roger Scully, University of Wales, Aberystwyth, on behalf of the University Association for Contemporary European Studies

The primary objective of the new Contemporary European Studies series is to provide a research outlet for scholars of European Studies from all disciplines. The series publishes important scholarly works and aims to forge for itself an international reputation.

The European Union as a Leader in International Climate Change Politics

**Edited by
Rüdiger K. W. Wurzel and
James Connelly**

Routledge
Taylor & Francis Group

LONDON AND NEW YORK

First published 2011
by Routledge
2 Park Square, Milton Park, Abingdon, Oxon OX14 4RN

Simultaneously published in the USA and Canada
by Routledge
270 Madison Avenue, New York, NY 10016

*Routledge is an imprint of the Taylor & Francis Group, an
informa business.*

Typeset in Times by RefineCatch Limited, Bungay, Suffolk
Printed and bound by the MPG Books Group in the UK

British Library Cataloguing in Publication Data
A catalogue record for this book is available from the British Library

Library of Congress Cataloging in Publication Data
The European Union as a leader in international climate change politics / edited by
Rüdiger K. W. Wurzel and James Connelly.
    p. cm. – (Routledge / UACES contemporary European studies ; 15)
Includes bibliographical references and index.
1. Environmental policy–European Union countries.   2. Climatic changes–Government
policy–European Union countries.   3. European Union.   I. Wurzel, Rüdiger.
II. Connelly, James.
GE190.E86E97 2010
363.738'74526–dc22

                                                                    2010018493

ISBN 13: 978–0–415 58047 2 (hbk)
ISBN 13: 978–0–203–83995–9 (ebk)

To Alfred, Kelsey, Ruth and Tom

Contents

x   *Contents*

List of figures, tables and boxes

Figures

Tables

Boxes

List of contributors

Guri Bang is Senior Research Fellow at the Center for International Climate and Environmental Research, Oslo (CICERO). Her work on climate change politics in the United States and the interface between domestic politics and developments in the international climate change negotiations was recently published in journals such as *European Journal of International Relations, International Studies Perspectives, Energy Policy, Review of International Studies* and *Global Environmental Change*. Bang is currently researching low carbon energy policy development in the United States, the European Union, Norway and China.

Pamela M. Barnes is Jean Monnet Chair *ad personam* in European Political Integration, Law School, University of Lincoln. She has written on various aspects of the EU's environmental policy including on enlargement and EU environmental policy, the EU environmental management and audit legislation, the environmental impact of CAP reforms, EU institutional developments and their impact on the EU's environmental decision making process.

Kathrin Birkel studied Political Sciences and Modern History at the University of Hamburg, graduating with a thesis on EU leadership in international climate change politics. From 2005 to 2009 she was a junior researcher/Ph.D. candidate at the Department of the Political Sciences of the Environment at Radboud University Nijmegen. Kathrin is managing a project on sustainable food and labelling at the Netherlands Nutrition Centre, The Hague.

Charlotte Burns is a research fellow in the School of Politics and International Studies at the University of Leeds. She works on EU institutions and EU environmental policy with a particular focus upon the European Parliament.

Neil Carter is Professor of Politics at the University of York. His main research interests are environmental politics and policy, and British politics. He is the author of *The Politics of the Environment* (2nd edition, Cambridge University Press, 2007) and he is joint editor of the journal, *Environmental Politics*.

James Connelly is Professor of Politics at the University of Hull and Director of the Institute of Applied Ethics. He has published widely in environmental politics, political theory and the philosophy of R.G. Collingwood. He is the author (with G. Smith) of *Politics and the Environment: From Theory to Practice* (2nd edition, Routledge, 2003) and *Method, Metaphysics and Politics: the Political Philosophy of R.G. Collingwood* (Imprint Academic, 2003).

Oriol Costa Fernández is Lecturer in international relations at the Autonomous University of Barcelona and researcher at the Observatory of European Foreign Policy. He was a postdoctoral researcher at the Centre for European Integration of the Free University of Berlin 2007–9. He has published in refereed journals on environmental and international relations issues.

Xiudian Dai is Senior Lecturer in the politics and political economy of the new media, with particular reference to the European Union and China, at the University of Hull. He is author of *The Digital Revolution and Governance* (Ashgate, 2000) and *Corporate Strategy, Public Policy and New Technologies* (Pergamon, 1996) and co-editor of *The Internet and Parliamentary Democracy in Europe* (Routledge, 2008).

Zhiping Diao is Professor of Philosophy in the Faculty of Humanities and Social Sciences at Beijing Jiaotong University. She was visiting scholar at the University of Hull during 2007–8. Her main research interests include the relationship between consumption and ecology and the ecological impact of science and technologies. She is author of *Science and Technologies: A Historical Materialist Perspective* (China Social Publishing, 2004).

Claire Dupont is a Research Fellow at the Institute for European Studies (IES) at the Vrije Universiteit Brussels (VUB). Her research is focused on EU climate policies, and she has co-authored with Sebastian Oberthür on EU Leadership in International Climate Policy (*International Spectator,* 2008).

Wyn Grant is Professor of Politics at the University of Warwick. He has written on a number of topics in environmental policy including the effectiveness of EU policy, the relationship between climate change policies and social exclusion, substratospheric air pollution and the interface between agriculture and the environment.

Martin Jänicke is Professor and a former Director of the Environmental Policy Research Centre at the Freie Universität Berlin (1986–2007). He was the Vice-President of the German government's Expert Council on the Environment (2000–2004), is a member of the International Advisory Board of the *Wuppertal Institut* and on the Board of the *Deutsche Bundesstiftung Umwelt.* He has been chosen as a review editor for the fifth IPCC report. His books on state failure, ecological modernisation, and best practice in environmental policy have been translated into several languages.

Karolina Jankowska is a Ph.D. candidate at the Environmental Policy Research Centre at the Free University in Berlin working on the Polish transition from coal-based manufacturing to renewable oriented society. She worked as a teaching assistant at the Free University in Berlin within the scholarship STIBET Program of the German Academic Exchange Service (DAAD, 2009–10). From 2006 to 2010 Karolina was a member of the National Council of the Polish Green Party, Zieloni 2004.

Andrew Jordan is Professor of Environmental Politics at the University of East Anglia in Norwich, UK. He is particularly interested in the governance of environmental problems in different political contexts, but especially the European Union. He is a Managing Editor of the journal *Environment and Planning C (Government and Policy)* and has published many papers and books, including *The Coordination of the European Union* (Oxford University Press, 2006), *Governing Sustainability* (Cambridge University Press, 2009) and *Climate Policy in the European Union* (Cambridge University Press, 2010).

Duncan Liefferink is a Senior Researcher in the Department of Political Sciences of the Environment at Radboud University Nijmegen, the Netherlands. His main research fields are European and comparative environmental politics, with a particular interest in the dynamic interrelationship between national and EU environmental policy making. His recent publications include the textbook *Environmental Politics in the European Union* (Manchester University Press, 2007 with Christoph Knill).

Sebastian Oberthür is Academic Director of the Institute for European Studies (IES) at the Vrije Universiteit Brussels (VUB). He is a renowned expert on international and European environmental and climate policy and law. He recently co-edited, with Marc Pallemaerts, a volume on the *New Climate Policies of the European Union* (VUB Press, 2010).

Tim Rayner is a senior research associate at the Tyndall Centre for Climate Change Research at the University of East Anglia. He is a political scientist with a long-standing interest in environmental policy, including the role of appraisal and evaluation practices therein. From 2010 he is working on the EU-funded RESPONSES project, which examines the relationship between mitigation and adaptation in EU climate policy.

Miranda Schreurs is Director of the Environmental Policy Research Center of the Free University of Berlin, Professor of Comparative Politics, a member of the German Advisory Council on the Environment (SRU), and vice-chair of the European Environment Advisory Councils. She was selected to be the Fulbright New Century Scholar Program's Distinguished Leader for 2009–10. Her recent books include *Transatlantic Environment and Energy Politics* (co-edited with Stacy VanDeveer and Henrik Selin, Ashgate 2009), *The Environmental Dimensions of Asian Security* (co-edited with In-taek Hyun, USIP Press, 2007), and *Comparative Environmental Politics* (in Japanese, Iwanami Press, 2007).

Joseph Szarka is Reader in European Studies in the Department of European Studies, University of Bath, England. His research interests are in environmental, climate and energy policy. He has published widely in international journals and his monographs include *The Shaping of Environmental Policy in France* (Berghahn, 2002) and *Wind Power in Europe: Politics, Business and Society* (Palgrave Macmillan, 2007).

John Vogler is Professor of International Relations at Keele University UK. He has published work on the global commons and the international relations of the environment as well as on the EU as a global actor. He is convenor of the British International Studies Association Environment Group and is currently a member of the ESRC Centre for Climate Change Economics and Policy.

Rüdiger K. W. Wurzel is Reader and Jean Monnet Chair in European Union Studies at the University of Hull where he is Director of the Centre for European Union Studies (CEUS). He has conducted a large number of grant funded research projects and published widely on European environmental policy, EU and German politics and new modes of governance.

Preface and acknowledgements

Climate change poses one of the biggest challenges facing humankind. Averting climate change or at least mitigating its negative effects will require sustained innovative political leadership by a wide range of actors at different levels of governance. The European Union (EU) has developed into a leader in international climate change politics although it was originally set up as a 'leaderless Europe' in which decision-making powers are spread amongst a wide range of EU institutional, Member State and societal actors. The central aim of our book, which takes an actor-focused perspective, is to explain what kind of leadership has been offered by EU institutional, member state and societal actors in EU climate change policy. All chapters in our book will therefore analyse who exercises what kind of leadership, how and when.

Although leadership is the overarching theme of our book, all chapters also address the additional main themes of ecological modernisation, policy instruments, and multi-level governance. Climate change poses not only a threat but also the opportunity to develop a low-carbon future through what, at least in Europe, is widely referred to as ecological modernisation which claims that ambitious environmental policy measures can be beneficial for both the environment and economy. Moreover, innovative low-carbon technologies (such as renewable energy) may also reduce Europe's dependence on oil and gas imports and thus increase its energy security. The use of 'old' and 'new' environmental policy instruments is needed to bring about what amounts to fairly fundamental (EU climate change) policy changes which must take place at different levels of governance including the Member State, EU and international level and across different policy sectors.

Our book grew out of a workshop at which the authors presented and discussed early versions of their chapters. The workshop formed part of a two-day event on 'The European Union as a Leader in International Climate Change Politics' which appropriately took place in the conference centre of The Deep, a spectacular Submarium on the banks of the river Humber, and at the University of Hull in September 2008. It was co-funded by the Commission (grant number 30CE02089680038) to whom we are extremely grateful. We would like to thank Dominic Brett and in particular Christine Harland from the Commission's London office for their support. More information about the event can be found at the University of Hull's Centre for European

Union Studies' (CEUS) website at <http://www2.hull.ac.uk/fass/politics/news-and-events/past-news-and-events/eu-climate-change-conference.aspx>.
    Our thanks also extend to Sarah Hoffman who helped us with the organisation of the two-day CEUS event. The chapters in this book benefited greatly from the lively workshop discussions and the excellent comments provided by Ian Bailey, Pamela Barnes, Neil Carter, Jenny Fairbrass, Jack Hayward, Simon Lightfoot and Anthony Zito who all acted as discussants. We would also like to thank our editors at Routledge, Heidi Bagtazo and Hannah Shakespeare, as well as the editorial assistant Harriet Frammingham and the former editorial assistant Lucy Dunne for their support and patience. We are grateful to two anonymous referees for very useful comments. Tanja Börzel, the UACES series editor, provided many extremely perceptive and constructive comments which helped us greatly to improve the manuscript. All remaining errors and/or omissions are the sole responsibility of the chapter authors and/or us, the editors.
    Rudi owes a huge debt to Ita and our two boys for their patience and tolerance during the completion of this book. James would like to express his gratitude to Eylem for her endless patience and support. The book is dedicated to our children.

R W and J C.

List of abbreviations

ACEA	*Association des Constructeurs Européens d'Automobiles* (European Automobile Manufacturers Association)
BASIC	Brazil, America, South Africa, India and China
C	Celsius
CAN	Climate Action Network
CCS	Carbon capture and storage
CFSP	Common Foreign and Security Policy
CLIM	European Parliament's Temporary Committee on Climate Change
CO_2	Carbon dioxide
COP	Conference of the Parties
DG	Directorate-General (of the European Commission)
EAP	Environmental Action Programme
EC	European Community or European Communities
ECJ	European Court of Justice
EEA	European Environmental Agency
EEB	European Environmental Bureau
ENGOs	Environmental Non-Governmental Organisations
EP	European Parliament
ETS	Emissions trading scheme
EU	European Union
FoE	Friends of the Earth
G8	Group of Eight
G20	Group of Twenty
GHG	Greenhouse gas
GHGE	Greenhouse gas emissions
JI	Joint Implementation
LRTAP	Long Range Transboundary Air Pollution
MEP	Member of the European Parliament
Mt	Million ton
NAP	National Allocation Plan
NGO	Non-governmental organization
OECD	Organization for Economic Co-operation and Development
QMV	Qualified majority voting

SEA	Single European Act
TFEU	Treaty on the functioning of the European Union
UK	United Kingdom
UN	United Nations
UNCED	United Nations Conference on Environment and Development
UNEP	United Nations Environmental Programme
UNFCCC	United Nations Framework Convention on Climate Change
WBCSD	World Business Council for Sustainable Development
WTO	World Trade Organization
WWF	World Wide Fund for Nature (formerly World Wildlife Fund)

Part I
Introduction

1 Introduction: European Union political leadership in international climate change politics

Rüdiger K. W. Wurzel and James Connelly[1]

Introduction

At the beginning of the twenty-first century, few still doubt that climate change poses one of the biggest challenges facing humankind. Certainly, the European Union (EU)[2] and most of its Member States have made climate change a major political priority. For Commission president José Manuel Barroso '[r]esponding to the challenge of climate change is the ultimate political test for our generation' (CEC 2008: 2).

Early scientific discoveries about anthropogenic climate change can be traced to the nineteenth century (Rowlands 1995). However, it was only in the late 1970s that the first international meetings on climate change took place. The 'traditional position has been that only states are recognised as having legal personality in international law and therefore only states are capable of maintaining rights and contracting responsibilities' (Macrory and Hession 1996: 133–34). It was therefore not a foregone conclusion that the EU would become an independent actor in international climate change politics. In the environmental policy field,[3] it was the negotiations for international treaties to protect the stratospheric ozone layer which allowed the EU to establish its international 'actorness' (Vogler 1999; Chapter 2 by Vogler). However, while the EU acted as an environmental laggard in relation to ozone layer depletion diplomacy (dragged along by the USA's determined leadership), in international climate change politics by contrast it early took on the role of an environmental leader (Compston and Bailey (2008); Damro and MacKenzie 2008; Grubb and Gupta 2000; Schreurs and Tiberghien 2007).

Broadly speaking the following four phases of EU climate change policy can be identified: (1) late 1980s to 1992: formation and formulation phase; (2) 1992–2001: Kyoto protocol negotiation phase; (3) 2001–5: Kyoto protocol rescue phase; and (4) since 2005: implementation phase and Kyoto protocol follow-up agreement negotiation phase. Importantly, as is explained in more detail in the following chapters, various EU institutional actors, Member States and societal actors reacted differently to the challenge of global climate change while making use of the changing opportunity structures when trying to influence EU climate change policy: from their perspective the phases might appear differently.

Table 1.1 Main phases and key dates/events in EU climate change politics

First phase (late 1980s–1992): formation and formulation phase
- 1986: EP resolution favours a common climate change policy
- 1988: Commission communication on EU
  climate change policy
- 1990:
  - ➢ June: Dublin European Council called for early adoption of targets
  - ➢ October: Political agreement by joint Environmental and Energy Council: stabilise the EU's CO_2 emissions by 2000 (at 1990 levels) if other leading countries undertake similar commitments
- 1991: Commission proposal for EU climate change policies

Second phase (1992–2001): Kyoto protocol negotiation phase
- 1992 UN Rio summit adoptsUN FCCC:
  - ➢ EU accepted commitment to stabilise CO_2 emissions by 2000 (compared to 1990)
- 1997: Kyoto Protocol negotiations:
  - ➢ EU proposed 15% reduction of three GHG by 2010 (compared to 1990)
  - ➢ EU settled for 8% reduction of six GHG by 2008–12 (compared to 1990/1995)
- 1998: European and Environmental Councils: agreement on burden sharing
- 2000:
  - ➢ Commission Communication 'Towards a European Climate Change Programme'
  - ➢ Environmental Council Resolution on EU climate change programme
  - ➢ EP Resolution on climate change programme demands more ambitious measures

Third phase (2001–2005): Kyoto protocol rescue phase
- 2001:
  - ➢ March 13: President Bush announced that the USA would not ratify the Kyoto Protocol
  - ➢ March 31: Environmental Council agreed to pursue ratification of the Kyoto protocol
  - ➢ June: European Council statement in favour of Kyoto protocol ratification
- 2002:
  - ➢ February 6: EP votes (540 to 4 votes) in favour of ratifying the Kyoto Protocol
  - ➢ March: Environmental Council in support of Kyoto Protocol ratification
  - ➢ May 31: Kyoto Protocol ratified by the EU (and its member states)
- 2003: Commission proposal for an EU ETS

Fourth phase (since 2005): Kyoto protocol implementation and follow-up agreement negotiations
- 2005:
  - ➢ Kyoto protocol enters into force
  - ➢ EU ETS becomes operational
- 2006: Stern report: makes economic case for tracking climate change
- 2007:
  - ➢ Commission climate and energy package proposal
  - ➢ Fourth IPCC report

➢ March: European Council agrees ('20–20 by 2020') climate and energy package:
  ○ EU unilateral 20% GHGE reductions by 2020 (compared to 1990)
  ○ EU conditional 30% GHGE reductions by 2020 if 'comparable efforts' by other developed and 'adequate efforts' by leading developing countries
  ○ Binding 20% renewable energy target by 2020
  ○ Non-binding 20% energy efficiency improvement commitment by 2020
  ○ Stabilise temperature rise at 2° Celsius (compared to preindustrial level)
• 2008:
  ➢ Commission impact assessment of the ('20–20 by 2020') climate and energy package
  ➢ December: Poznań (Poland) conference
  ➢ December: European Council, EP and Council: extension of ETS to aviation by 2010, legally binding CO_2 limits for cars, and revision of the EU ETS for 2013–2020.
• 2009:
  ➢ December: European Council agrees €7.2 'fast track' money to help developing countries to adapt to climate change.
  ➢ December: Copenhagen (Denmark) conference adopts Copenhagen Accord
• 2010
  ➢ January: Environmental Council meeting in Seville: review of the EU's climate change strategy
  ➢ November: Cancún (Mexico) conference to decide on Copenhagen Accord/Kyoto follow-up protocol

---

Formation and formulation phase: late 1980s–1992

The late 1980s saw the beginnings of the EU's climate change policy during the preparatory phase of the 1992 United Nations (UN) Rio summit (Pallemaerts and Williams 2006). In 1986, the EP became the first EU institution to request a common climate change policy (Haigh 1996; Wettestad 2005). In 1988, which was the year when the UN's Intergovernmental Panel on Climate Change (IPCC) was set up, the Commission issued a communication that reviewed the scientific findings and possible EU actions. In June 1990, the European Council in Dublin adopted a resolution which called for the early adoption of greenhouse gas emissions (GHGE) reduction targets on the UN level. A joint Environment and Energy Council in October 1990 adopted a political agreement that the EU would stabilise its carbon dioxide (CO_2) emissions by 2000 (compared to 1990) if highly developed countries would take similar actions. It was the resolution by the joint Environment and Energy Council which enabled the EU 'to take a strong and leading role, particularly in relation to the United States' (Haigh 1996: 162).

But the EU signed the UN Framework Convention on Climate Change (UNFCCC) at the 1992 UN Rio summit without having adopted adequate common policy measures to implement the agreement (Haigh 1996;

Pallemaerts and Williams 2006). In early 1992, at a time of unprecedented public environmental awareness and strong support for deeper European integration amongst much of Europe's political elite, the Commission proposed an EU-wide CO_2/energy tax which, however, was vetoed by Britain.[4] The Commission's other three proposals – a Framework Directive on energy efficiency measures by Member States (SAVE), a Decision on renewable energy (ALTENER) and a Decision to monitor CO_2 emissions – were adopted by the Council although they were insufficient for reaching the stabilisation target.

The 1991 British EU Presidency pressed for a 'burden sharing' agreement because Member States' contributions to the EU's collective CO_2 emission output varied greatly and so did their emission reduction capability (Haigh 1996: 163). Britain and Germany made up about 40 per cent of the GHGE of the EU's 15 Member States (EU-15) (Schreurs, 2002: 193). Germany, which is the EU's largest economy, is responsible for almost one third of the EU's collective CO_2 emissions. Germany benefited from 'wall fall' profits in the form of reduced CO_2 emissions from the industrial decline in the former East Germany.[5] Britain's dash for gas (which has a lower carbon content than coal) took place in the 1980s but was unrelated to environmental policy objectives.[6] The EU's cohesion countries (Greece, Ireland, Portugal and Spain), on the other hand, wanted to continue catching up industrially and thus were keen to increase their CO_2 emissions. The EU's insistence on unitary GHGE cuts globally, while pressing for a flexible internal burden sharing agreement, ran into opposition from other UNFCCC signatories (Grubb and Gupta 2000a; Schreurs 2002).

Kyoto protocol negotiation phase: 1992–2001

Because the EU ratified the UNFCCC 'without having yet a concrete internal policy' (Peeters and Deketelaere 2006: 7) it was left to Member States to adopt national GHGE reductions programmes. The EU regained its leadership position when it proposed, at the beginning of the Kyoto protocol negotiations, a 15 per cent reduction in GHGE by 2010 (compared to 1990 levels) on condition that its main economic competitors (i.e. the USA and Japan) would accept similar reduction rates. However, cuts of this magnitude were unacceptable to the USA, which eventually accepted a 7 per cent reduction target while insisting on the inclusion of emissions trading in the Kyoto protocol. The EU therefore settled for an 8 per cent reduction target in GHGE by 2008–12.

In order to keep the USA on board the international climate change negotiations, the 1997 Kyoto protocol endorsed emissions trading and the following two flexible mechanisms: (1) joint implementation (JI) which allows certain countries jointly to implement GHGE projects; and (2) clean development mechanism (CDM) under which developed countries can sponsor certified GHGE reduction projects in the developing world. The EU (and particularly Germany) had fought hard to prevent the inclusion of emissions trading in the Kyoto protocol and, having failed, insisted on limiting the use of flexible mechanisms to 50 per cent of the domestic GHGE reductions. The inclusion of emissions trading in the Kyoto protocol was seized as an opportunity by the Commission to recommend an EU-wide ETS in its 1998 Communication *Climate Change – Towards an EU Post-Kyoto Strategy* (CEC 1998).

The Environmental Council reached political agreement on the EU's burden sharing agreement in 1998. Perhaps surprisingly the '1998 political agreement on 8% was more difficult to reach than the March 1997 agreement on the sharing of the more ambitious (but conditional emissions reduction target' (Pallemaerts and Williams 2006: 44). Under the EU's internal burden sharing agreement Germany accepted 21 per cent and Britain 12.5 per cent as national GHGE reduction rates by 2012 while the cohesion countries were allowed to increase their GHGE significantly.[7] At the time of the signing of the Kyoto protocol, the British government announced a national 20 per cent CO_2 reduction target while the German government offered a domestic 25 per cent reduction target by 2010 (Wurzel 2008b). These more ambitious national targets are not, however, legally binding; rather, they serve to flag up the political intentions of governments which are keen to be seen as taking on leadership positions in international climate change (See Chapters 6 and 7).

In October 2000, the Environmental Council accepted most of what the Commission had proposed in its communication *Towards a European Climate Change Programme* (CEC 2000) which it had published a few months earlier. However, the EP demanded a considerably more ambitious programme.

Kyoto protocol rescue phase: 2001–5

In March 2001, President George W. Bush announced that the USA no longer intended to ratify the Kyoto protocol that had been signed by his predecessor Bill Clinton. The Kyoto protocol would have been doomed to failure without the EU's leadership (Peeters and Deketelaere 2006; Wurzel 2008b). The 2001 Swedish Presidency managed to get agreement from all Member States for a strongly worded statement which criticised the US government and insisted on the need to ratify the Kyoto protocol even without America. On 31 March 2001, the Environmental Council agreed to pursue the ratification process, a decision which was supported by an overwhelming majority (540 to 4 votes) in the EP on 6 February 2002.

The EU ratified the Kyoto protocol in May 2002. A legally binding decision on the national GHGE reduction rates under the burden sharing agreement was adopted in 2003. After much lobbying from the EU, Japan and Russia finally ratified the Kyoto protocol which meant that it could enter into force in early 2005.

Encouraged by the success of early American emissions trading schemes (ETSs) and frustrated by the veto on the CO_2/energy tax and slow progress with the minimum harmonisation of Member State fuel taxes, the Commission's Directorate General (DG) for Environment commissioned studies on emissions trading in the late 1990s. Following meetings with member governments and stakeholders (businesses and environmental non-governmental organisations (ENGOs)), the Commission published its proposal for a directive establishing an EU ETS in 2001 (CEC 2001). The European Parliament (EP) and the Environmental Council adopted the Commission's EU ETS proposal within a period of less than two years in 2003 (Wettestad 2005; Wurzel 2008b). The EU therefore not only gave up its initial opposition to this novel market-based policy instrument but became an emissions trading pioneer when it set up the world's first supranational ETS (Jordan *et al.* 2010; Skjærseth and Wettestad 2008; Wurzel 2008b).

Kyoto protocol implementation and follow-up agreement negotiation phase: since 2005

The EU ETS, which became operational in 2005, has developed into the EU's main climate change policy instrument (Damro and MacKenzie 2008; Wurzel 2008b). It has been accompanied by EU Directives on energy efficiency, the promotion of renewable energy, a voluntary agreement with the European, Japanese and Korean automobile manufacturers on the reduction of CO_2 and harmonisation measures on fuel excise duties (Peeters and Deketelaere 2006).

The European Council meeting in March 2007 reaffirmed the EU's leadership ambitions in international climate change policy when it adopted a unilateral 20 per cent reduction target for CO_2 emissions by 2020 (compared to 1990 levels) and a conditional 30 per cent reduction target if other developed countries undertook equivalent actions. The climate and energy package which was adopted by the March 2007 European Council has become known as the '20–20 by 2020' climate and energy package because it also set an EU-wide 20 per cent target for the use of renewable energy. However, arduous negotiations took place on the review of the EU ETS and the effort sharing agreement (formerly known as burden sharing agreement) at the European Council in December 2008 under the French EU Presidency (see Chapter 7). The EU offer of an unconditional 20 per cent reduction target and a conditional 30 per cent reduction target by 2020 (compared to 1990) as well as a 'fast track' financial package to support adaptation measures in developing countries nevertheless positioned the EU as a leader for the 2009 UN Copenhagen conference. However, the EU's offer had no influence on the final outcome of the Copenhagen conference which adopted the Copenhagen Accord that amounts to an extremely weak and vague agreement leaving the decision on a more substantive international climate change treaty to the conference in Cancún (Mexico) in late 2010 (Egenhofer and Georgiev 2009).

EU environmental policy-making actors and leadership

At first sight the EU seems ill equipped to offer political leadership because decision-making powers are dispersed amongst a wide range of political actors including EU institutional and Member State actors. In the 1950s, when the EU was founded, 'efforts were made in "taming" the "beast" . . . of leadership' (Blondel 1987: 3) in order to avoid a third world war. A 'leaderless Europe' (Hayward 2008) has been tremendously successful in this regard. The dispersal of the EU's decision-making powers has, however, led to the emergence of a wide range of 'veto actors' (Weale 1996) which have repeatedly led the EU into political stalemate and 'joint decision traps' (Scharpf 1988) from which it is able to escape, typically, only after lengthy periods of arduous negotiations and by adopting sub-optimal policy solutions.

However, the environmental policy field in general, and climate change politics in particular, have shown that decisional stalemate can be overcome, while shared decision-making powers amongst EU and Member States (as well as societal) actors do not preclude the adoption of progressive common policy measures. Otherwise the EU would not be widely perceived as a leader in international climate change politics (Deketelaere and Peeters 2006; Damro and MacKenzie 2008; Gupta and Grubb 2000; Jordan *et al.* 2010; Oberthür and Roche Kelly 2008; Oberthür and Pallemaerts 2010). Schreurs and Tiberghien (2007: 24) have tried to explain the EU's leadership role in international climate change politics by arguing that the EU decision-making arena is an 'open-ended and competitive governance structure . . . [which] has created multiple and mutually-reinforcing opportunities for leadership. This suggests a kind of logic that is the reverse of that of veto points or veto players'.

In the EU there is no shortage of would-be environmental leaders (Wurzel 2008a: 77). The EU institutions (primarily the Commission, European Council, Council of Ministers and the EP), as well as several Member States have all, though to varying degrees, tried to offer leadership in EU environmental policy and/or climate change politics. Moreover, societal actors (such as ENGOs and environmentally progressive businesses) have also demanded the adoption of ambitious climate change measures. Importantly, EU environmental policy in general and climate change policy in particular have received strong support from the Member States' general publics (Eurobarometer 2008).[8] The EU's climate change policy therefore 'offers a chance for European citizens to find out what Europe can do, and to show the wider world what Europe can offer' (Gupta and Grubb 2000: 6). An ambitious common climate change policy clearly increases the EU's legitimacy domestically.

The EU is keen to act as a soft or civilian power which favours multilateral agreements in dealing with global governance problems (such as climate change): this offers an opportunity to provide political leadership on the international level. However, at times a 'capability-expectations gap'

(Hill 1993) has opened up between public expectations fuelled by the EU's political rhetoric in favour of ambitious international climate change targets and lacklustre EU and/or Member States implementation measures that would be required to achieve those targets. If the EU's internal and international leadership ambitions were to fail then this could have serious negative repercussions for both international climate change politics and EU integration.

The Commission occupies a central node within the EU policy-making process. It shares executive powers with the Council of Ministers and acts as the guardian of the Treaties. The Commission is a policy entrepreneur because it holds the formal monopoly on initiating EU legislation (although. since the 1993 Maastricht Treaty, the EP can ask the Commission to become active). Particularly in the early years of European integration, the Commission was widely seen as the engine of European integration. Commission President Barroso's belated 'conversion' to climate change has helped the Commission to take on an important role in EU climate change politics (see Chapter 3 by Barnes).

Heads of State and Government of the EU Member States are represented in the European Council which agrees the EU's broad political goals and strategies. Until the 1990s, the European Council only occasionally dealt with environmental issues. However, as is explained in Chapter 5 (by Oberthür and Dupont), climate change moved to the top of the political agenda of the European Council in the early 2000s. The EU and most of its Member States started to take climate change seriously in the run up to the 1992 UN Rio conference which adopted the UNFCCC. The EU strongly supported the Kyoto climate change protocol despite the fact that it was abandoned by the USA under President G.W. Bush in 2001 (see Table 1.1 above and Chapter 14 by Bang and Schreurs). In March 2007 the European Council affirmed the EU's leadership ambitions when agreeing on a unilateral GHGE reduction target of 20 per cent by 2020 and a 30 per cent target which is conditional on other highly developed states making 'adequate efforts' (European Council 2007). And in 2009 the European Council agreed to fast-track financial support for developing countries' efforts to adapt to climate change.

It is the Council of Ministers which adopts EU laws (together with the EP) under the co-decision procedure that is now the rule for the adoption of EU environmental policy measures, most of which fall under qualified majority voting. However, unanimity is still required for EU environmental measures such as eco-taxes and the choice of energy supply (Damro and MacKenzie 2008). As there is no 'Climate Change' Council, it is usually the Environmental Council which takes the lead on EU climate change dossiers within the Council of Ministers (see Chapter 5 by Oberthür and Dupont). The sixth-monthly rotating EU Presidency provides an 'agenda shaping' (Talberg 2003) leadership opportunity. However, Member States which hold the EU Presidency must also act as honest brokers (Wurzel 2002, 2004). The Council's informal so-called 'troika' has for a long time represented the EU in the international arena, for example during the negotiations of the UNFCCC. The troika was initially made up of the previous, current and next Presidencies. Since the 1999 Amsterdam Treaty, the troika has consisted of the current and next Presidency and the Commission. Some Presidencies (e.g. the 1997 Dutch, 2001 Swedish, 2005 British, 2007 German and 2008 French) have played important roles during key stages in international climate change politics (see also Chapter 5 by Oberthür and Dupont).

There is widespread agreement that Denmark, Germany and the Netherlands made up a 'green trio' which was extended to a 'green sextet' when Austria, Finland and Sweden joined the EU in 1995 (Andersen and Liefferink 1997; Wurzel 2002, 2008a). However, semi-permanent coalitions of environmental leader states do not exist on the EU level (Rehbinder and Stewart 1985: 263). Instead 'they have to be formed on an issue-by-issue basis and remain liable to defection' (Liefferink and Andersen 1998: 262) because the EU's environmental leader states often have national preferences for different problem-solving approaches and policy instruments (Wurzel 2002, 2008a: 80). Moreover, states can alter their overall position over time. For example, post-unification Germany has lost some of its environmental credentials although it has remained a leader on climate change issues (see Chapter 8 by Jänicke). For much of the 1970s/80s, Britain was labelled the 'dirty man of Europe'; however, since the early 1990s, Britain has adopted a leadership position in EU (and international) climate politics (Chapter 6 by Rayner and Jordan; see also Lorenzoni, O'Riordan and Pidgeon 2008).

The environmental laggard status of Southern and Eastern European Member States also needs to be qualified. Southern European states have long perceived the bulk of EU environmental legislation as reflecting the priorities of Northern European Member states (Börzel 2002; Weale *et al.* 2000). Their laggard status is therefore at least partly the result of different national priorities. The Eastern European states are characterised by an even lower level of economic development which is reflected in their generous national targets under the 1997 Kyoto climate change protocol.

Duncan Liefferink and Mikael Skou Andersen (1998) have propounded an analytical distinction which subdivides environmental leader states into 'forerunners' and 'pushers'. Forerunner states may act either defensively by trying to maximise their freedom to develop ambitious national policies, or proactively by setting a 'good example' for others to follow. States can, however, also adopt a leadership position which is based merely on symbolic politics rather than real commitments which are implemented later on.

Because the environmental leader state concepts are state-centric, they exclude an important institutional actor in the EU climate policy-making process, namely the EP, which is widely seen as the 'greenest' of all EU institutions (Burns 2005). The EP set up an environmental committee in 1979 and a temporary climate change committee in 2007 although the latter has no legislative competences. The EP was initially forced to influence EU climate change policy from the sidelines. However, the adoption of the EU's '20–20 by 2020' climate and energy package in 2007/08 allowed the EP to become a central actor in EU climate change policy. Under the co-decision procedure, which is now the rule for EU environmental policy, the EP has decision-making powers which are equal to those of the Council. However, the EP's influence on international environmental negotiations has remained limited (see Chapter 4 by Burns and Carter).

Businesses and environmental NGOs are also important players in EU climate change policy (see Chapters 12 (by Grant) and 13 (by Wurzel and Connelly) respectively). BusinessEurope (formerly UNICE) is the umbrella group for European businesses. However, almost all big European companies now have their own offices in Brussels and, moreover, most industries have their own sector-wide EU umbrella organisation. There is a divide between those businesses which oppose environmental policy measures on the grounds that they will lead to increased cost and bureaucracy and those companies which favour ambitious measures because they will increase the demand for their products such as climate change abatement technologies (Weale 1992). Europe's environmental groups have had a presence in Brussels only since the European Environmental Bureau (EEB) was set up in 1974. From the late-1980s interest in EU environmental policy amongst the big ENGOs increased significantly. Friends of the Earth (FoE), Greenpeace, World Wide Fund for Nature (WWF) and Climate Action Network (CAN) all set up offices in Brussels in order to influence the formulation of EU environmental and climate change policy.

Overall analytical framework and main themes

This book adopts an actor-centred approach to the analysis of EU climate change politics. The chapters which follow all address, from the perspective of the main actor(s) on which they focus, the following four key themes: (1) leadership, (2) ecological modernisation, (3) policy instruments, and (4) multi-level governance. Of these, leadership is the overarching theme. Tackling climate change requires long-term political leadership and 'a sustained pattern of policy innovation' (Schreurs and Tiberghien 2007: 19). It will certainly take a high degree of 'creative leadership' (Verba 1961: 114) to deal successfully with the enormous political challenges which climate change poses to Europe and the rest of the world.

But what is leadership? Table 1.2 (see below) presents a summary of the main types and styles of leadership which will be used for analytical purposes throughout this book. We agree with Young (1991: 281) that it is 'a complex phenomenon, ill-defined, poorly understood, and subject to recurrent controversy'. As a starting point for a better understanding of leadership it is illuminating to contrast transformational with transactional leadership (Burns 1978: 169–200). Leaders can be 'called *transformational* in the sense of changing what would otherwise have been the course of history' although this is often a matter of degree (Nye 2008: 7). Hayward (2008: 6–7) has usefully

Table 1.2 Types and styles of leadership

Types of leadership	Styles of leadership
1) *Structural leadership:* • Relates to the actor's hard power and depends on its material resources (e.g. economic strength).	a) *Heroic v. humdrum leadership:* • *Heroic* leadership relies on long-term objectives, strong policy coordination and the ambitious assertion of political will.
2) *Entrepreneurial leadership:* • Relates to diplomatic, negotiating and bargaining skills in facilitating agreements.	• *Humdrum* leadership is incremental, short-term and without the assertion of the ambitious assertion of political will
3) *Cognitive leadership:* • Relates to the definition and/or redefinition of interests through ideas (e.g. the concept of ecological modernisation).	b) *Transformational leadership v. transactional leadership:* • *Transformational* leadership leads to history changing events. • *Transactional* leadership leads to incremental policy change

4) *Symbolic leadership*
Symbolic leadership involves the posturing by political actors which is not followed up with substantive policy measures action and/or the lack of implementation of the adopted policy measures.

Sources: The leadership types 1–3 draw heavily on Young (1991) while the different leadership styles are based on Burns (1978), Hayward (2008) and Nye (2008).

distinguished 'humdrum and heroic leadership'. Following Lindblom's (1959) concept of 'muddling through', Hayward defined a humdrum leadership style as one which 'does not have an explicit, overriding, long-term objective and action is incremental, departing only slightly from existing policies as circumstances require' (Hayward 2008: 6). In contrast, heroic decision-making 'sets explicit long-term objectives to be pursued by maximum coordination of public policies and by an ambitious assertion of political will' (Hayward 2008: 7).

Making the distinction between four types and four styles of leadership is a fruitful way to structure the analysis of leadership in the EU context within which leadership has remained an underdeveloped research issue (although see Hayward 2008). The value of different types of leadership should not be taken to imply that it is necessary to extol the virtues of one above all others: political success often requires the employment of more than one type (and style) of leadership.

It is difficult to explain leadership without reference to power (although there are even more competing definitions of what constitutes political power).[9] There is widespread agreement about the following two aspects: first, that although political leadership is not identical with power it usually requires power; second, that political leadership and power are relational and context-bound (Blondel 1987; Burns 1978). Nye (2008: 27) argues that '[y]ou cannot lead if you do not have power. . . . Those with more power in a relationship are better placed to make and resist change'. The fact that 'Europe has made a principle of powerlessness' (Jean-Francois Revel, cited in Hayward 2008: 1) could therefore be a serious hindrance to the EU's efforts in offering political leadership in climate change politics. However, political leadership in climate change politics does not consist solely in the use of 'hard power' (Nye 2008) which cajoles other states to agree to ambitious GHGE reduction targets. It also involves 'soft power', such as new innovative ideas including ecological modernisation, which is based on the assumption that stringent environmental policy measures can be beneficial for both the environment and the economy.

Ecological modernisation has received considerable support in Europe (Jänicke 1993; Weale 1992; CEC 2008). On this view, ambitious environmental policy measures can help to create 'lead markets' (Jänicke and Jacob 2004) for environmental technology, which can then be exported thus creating a 'double dividend' and/or 'win-win' situation in which economic growth and the protection of the environment takes place. From an ecological modernisation perspective, climate change does not merely pose a threat but also creates opportunities such as a competitive low carbon economy. Moreover, the rapid domestic uptake of renewable energy increases the EU's energy security by reducing its dependence on energy imports (e.g. gas from Russia and oil from the Middle East).

The EU has become a leader in climate change policy because climate change represents a serious threat; however, it has also sought to assert the economic benefits of the development of new forms of innovative technology required by the climate change policies it is promoting. Climate change is a threat, but also an opportunity. Important EU policy actors have long been advocates of ecological modernisation, an attitude neatly captured in the words of Environment Commissioner Dimas:

> Building on Europe's pioneering emissions trading system, the [20–20 by 2020] package demonstrates to our global partners that strong action to fight climate change is compatible with continued economic growth and prosperity. It gives Europe a head start in the race to create a low-carbon global economy that will unleash a wave of innovation and create jobs in clean technologies (CEC 2008: 2).

The EU has tried to make a virtue of its relative lack of 'hard power' by relying heavily on 'soft power'. The EU does, however, wield some 'hard power' because it encompasses the world's largest internal market. It is arguably the mix of 'hard market power' and 'soft cognitive power' which has facilitated the EU's leadership ambitions on the international level. The EU might therefore be able to offer transformational leadership which, according to Joseph Nye (2008: ix), can be achieved only with a mix of 'hard power' and 'soft power' that may lead to 'smart power'. What role, if any, ecological modernisation has played – despite the credit crunch and economic recession – as an action-guiding norm for policy actors involved in EU climate change policy is a question addressed throughout this book.

The transformation process towards a low carbon economy requires leadership also with regard to the choice of the most effective and efficient policy instruments. Broadly speaking policy instruments can be grouped into the following three main categories: (1) traditional ('command-and-control') regulation which sets specific targets and deadlines; (2) market-based instruments (e.g. eco-taxes and emission trading); and (3) voluntary agreements and informational devices (e.g. Jordan, Wurzel and Zito 2005). Until the late 1990s, EU environmental policy relied almost exclusively on traditional regulation. Attempts to adopt more cost-effective market-based instruments failed when the Commission's 1992 proposal for a common CO_2/energy tax was vetoed by Britain (see above and Chapter 6). America was the first to innovate with emissions trading but the EU has since showcased its ETS for CO_2, which became the world's first supranational scheme of its kind, as a model for others to follow. Voluntary agreements and informational policy tools have often been promoted by businesses (see Chapter 12 by Grant) although ENGOs have remained sceptical about self-regulatory tools (see Chapter 13 by Wurzel and Connelly). The authors of the chapters which follow all assess what policy instruments and/or instrument mixes have been the most widely used and/or preferred policy tool(s) for the main actor which is assessed in their chapters.

EU climate change policy is not conducted in isolation from the Member State level and/or the international level. For that reason multi-level governance is also an important main theme for the chapters in our book. The common climate change policy has been developed within a multi-level decision-making arena within which the EU has acted as a collective entity that was able to exert more influence vis-à-vis the international community than if the Member States had acted independently (see also Chapter 2 by Vogler). Perhaps the best example is the effort sharing (formerly burden sharing) agreements which have allowed Member States to adopt individually differentiated GHGE targets without threatening the EU's collective leadership position in international climate change politics. Importantly, multi-level governance extends beyond the boundaries of the EU. This explains why our book also offers an external perspective provided by the USA (Chapter 14 by Bang and Schreurs) and China (Chapter 15 by Dai and Diao).

In other words, the book aims to explain who exercises what kind of leadership, how and when? The 'what' refers to the different types (structural, entrepreneurial and cognitive as well as symbolic) and styles (heroic/humdrum and transformational/transactional) of leadership explained above; the 'how' tries to unearth the different mechanisms used by leaders (e.g. the adoption of a forerunner position and the introduction of new ideas such as ecological modernisation); and, all chapter authors take a longitudinal perspective in assessing 'when' the actor on which their chapter primarily focuses has offered what type and style of leadership.

Structure of the book

Chapter 2 (in Part I) by Vogler focuses on the EU's ability to act as a global player in international climate change politics while contextualising further our four main themes. Part II of our book assesses when and why supranational institutional actors pushed the EU to adopt a leadership position in international climate change politics. The following parts analyse to what degree such a leadership position has been supported by its Member States (Part III) and important societal actors (Part IV) while also offering an external perspective (Part V). Accordingly Part II of our book analyses the role which the Commission (Chapter 3 by Barnes), EP (Chapter 4 by Burns and Carter), European Council and Council of Ministers (Chapter 5 by Oberthür and Dupont) have played in EU and international climate change politics. Part III provides an assessment of the three largest EU member states, including France (Chapter 7 by Szarka) and the EU's two largest CO_2 emitters, namely the United Kingdom (Chapter 6 by Rayner and Jordan) and Germany (Chapter 8 by Jänicke). Part III also provides an assessment of one small member state which has traditionally been an environmental leader (i.e. the Netherlands in Chapter 9 by Liefferink and Birkel) as well as one Southern (i.e. Spain in Chapter 11 by Costa) and one Eastern European country (Poland in Chapter 10 by Jankowska) which, at times, have acted as laggards in EU climate change policy. Part IV analyses the role of important societal actors, namely businesses (Chapter 12 by Grant) and ENGOs (Chapter 13 by Wurzel and Connelly). Part V contextualises the EU's climate change policy efforts through an external perspective by examining the actions of the USA (Chapter 14 by Bang and Schreurs) and China (Chapter 15 by Dai and Diao). Finally, the concluding chapter (Chapter 16 by Wurzel and Connelly) re-assesses the main themes within the light of the new empirical findings and theoretical insights presented in the various chapters of this book.

The chapters which follow all address, from the perspective of the main actor(s) on which they focus, the four key themes outlined above: leadership, ecological modernisation, policy instruments and multi-level governance. Leadership, as we have seen, can be differentiated according to different types (structural, entrepreneurial and cognitive) and styles (heroic/humdrum and transformational/transactional) which have been explored in the relatively sparse leadership literature flagged up above.

Notes

1 The authors are grateful for the extremely useful comments on an earlier draft which they received from two anonymous referees and Tanja Börzel in particular. The usual disclaimer applies.

2　For reasons of simplicity the term EU will be used retrospectively even when, strictly speaking, the European Community (EC) or European Economic Community (EEC) are meant.

3　The EU had already become a signatory to the World Trade Organization (WTO) which, however, was also signed by its Member States, making it a mixed agreement (Bretherton and Vogler 2006).

4　Southern European countries were also afraid that the CO_2/energy tax might curb their economic development.

5　The 'wall fall' profits were not cheap because German unification, which took place in 1990, led to massive financial transfers from the former West to former East Germany.

6　In the 1980s, the Thatcher government closed many coal mines and built gas-fired power stations for cost reasons and to break the political influence of the left-wing miners' unions. Schreurs (2000: 193) estimates that Germany reduced its GHGE by about 18.7 per cent due to wall fall profits and Britain by about 14 per cent due to its dash for gas.

7　Greece (25%), Ireland (13%), Portugal (27%) and Spain (15%) will be allowed to increase their CO_2 emissions.

8　In a representative survey, 57% of EU citizens picked climate change as the issues about which they were most worried out of a list of 15 environmental issues (Eurobarometer, 2008: 8). However, there were also significant national differences, with Cyprus (79%), Sweden (71%) and Germany (69%) leading the list of the most concerned public while the populations in Estonia (38%), Latvia (38%) and Lithuania (38%) were least worried about climate change.

9　Joseph Nye (2008: x) quotes a recent count which collected 221 definitions of political power between the 1920s and 1990s.

Bibliography

Andersen, M. S. and Liefferink, D. (eds) (1997) *European Environmental Policy. The Pioneers*, Manchester: Manchester University Press.

Blondel, J. (1987) *Political Leadership. Towards a General Analysis*, London: Sage.

Börzel, T. (2002) 'Pace-Setting, Foot-Dragging and Fence-Sitting. Member State Responses to Europeanization', *Journal of Common Market Studies*, 40(2), 193–214.

Bretherton, C. and Vogler, J. (2006), *The European Union as a Global Actor*, 2nd edn, London: Routledge.

Burns, C. (2005) 'The European Parliament: The EU's Environmental Champion', in A. Jordan (ed.), *Environmental Policy in the European Union*, 2nd edn, London: Earthscan, 87–105.

Burns, J. M. (1978) *Leadership*, New York: Harper & Row.

CEC (1998) *Communication from the Commission to the Council and the European Parliament. Climate Change – Towards and EU Post-Kyoto Strategy. COM (1998) 353 final*, Brussels: Commission of the European Communities.

CEC (2000) *Towards a European Climate Change Programme*, Brussels: Commission of the European Communities.

CEC (2001) *Proposal for a Directive Establishing a Scheme for Greenhouse Gas Emission Allowance Trading. COM (2001)581*, Brussels: Commission of the European Communities.

CEC (2008) *Boosting Growth and Jobs by Meeting Our Climate Change Commitments, Press Release IP/08/80, 23.1.2008*, Brussels: Commission of the European Communities.

Compston, H, and Bailey, I (eds) (2000) *Turning Down the Heat. The Politics of Climate Policy in Affluent Democracies*, Basingstoke: Palgrave/Macmillan.

Damro, C. and Mendez, P. L. (2003) 'Emission Trading at Kyoto: From EU Resistance to Union Innovation', *Environmental Politics*, 12(2), 71–94.

Damro, C., and MacKenzie, D. (2008) 'The European Union and the Politics of Multi-Level Climate Governance', in H. Compston and I. Bailey (eds), *Turning Down the Heat. The Politics of Climate Policy in Affluent Democracies*, Basingstoke: Palgrave/Macmillan, 65–84.

Egenhofer, C. and Georgiev, A. (2009) *The Copenhagen Accord – A First Stab at Deciphering the Implications for the EU*, Brussels: Centre for European Policy Studies.

Eurobarometer (2008), *Attitudes of European Citizens Towards the Environment*, Brussels: European Commission, <http://ec.europa.eu/environment/barometer/pdf/report_ebenv_2005_04_22_en.pdf>

European Council (2007), *Presidency Conclusions. Brussels European Council 8/9 March 2007, Press release 7224/07*, Brussels: Council of the European Union.

Grubb, M. and Gupta, A. (2000a) 'Climate Change, Leadership and the EU', in J. Gupta and M. Grubb (eds), *Climate Change and European Leadership. A Sustainable Role for Europe?* Dordrecht: Kluwer Publishers, 3–14.

Grubb, M. and Gupta, J. (2000b) 'Leadership', in J. Gupta and M. Grubb (eds), *Climate Change and European Leadership. A Sustainable Role for Europe?* Dordrecht: Kluwer Publishers, 15–24.

Gupta, J. and Grubb, M. (eds) (2000) *Climate Change and European Leadership. A Sustainable Role for Europe?* Dordrecht: Kluwer Publishers.

Haigh, N. (1996) 'Climate Change Policies and Politics in the European Community', in T. O'Riordan and J. Jäger (eds), *Politics of Climate Change*, London: Routledge, 155–86.

Hayward, J. (2008) 'Introduction: Inhibited Consensual Leadership within an Interdependent Confederal Europe', in J. Hayward (ed.), *Leaderless Europe*, Oxford: Oxford University Press, 1–14.

Hill, C. (1993) 'The Capability-Expectations Gap, or Conceptualising Europe's International Role', *Journal of Common Market Studies*, 31(3), 305–28.

Jänicke, M. (1993) 'Über ökologische und politische Modernisierungen', *Zeitschrift für Umweltpolitik und Umweltrecht*, 16, 159–75.

Jänicke, M. and Jacob, K. (2004) 'Lead Markets for Environmental Innovations: A New Role for the Nation State', *Global Environmental Politics*, 4(1), 29–46.

Jordan, A., Wurzel, R. K. W. and Zito, A. (2005) 'The Rise of "New" Policy Instruments in Comparative Perspective: Has Governance Eclipsed Government?', *Political Studies*, 53, 477–96.

Jordan, A., Huitema, D., van Asselt, H., Rayner, T. and Berkhout, F. (2010) *Climate Change Policy in the European Union. Confronting Dilemmas of Mitigation and Adaptation?* Cambridge: Cambridge University Press.

Liefferink, D. and Andersen, M. S. (1998) 'Strategies of the 'Green' Member States in EU Environmental Policy-Making', *Journal of European Public Policy*, 5(2), 254–70.

Lindblom, Charles (1959) 'The Science of Muddling Through', *Public Administration Review*, XIX(2), 79–88.

Lorenzoni, I., O'Riordan, T. and Pidgeon, N. (2008) 'Hot Air and Cold Feet: The UK Response to Climate Change', in H. Compston and I. Bailey (eds), *Turning Down the Heat*, Basingstoke: Palgrave/Macmillan, 104–24.

Macrory, R. and Hession, M. (1996) 'The European Community and Climate Change. The Role of Law and Legal Competence', in T. O'Riordan and J. Jäger (eds), *Politics of Climate Change*, London: Routledge, 106–55.

Nye, J. (2008) *The Powers to Lead*, Oxford: Oxford University Press.

Oberthür, S. and Roche Kelly, C. (2008) 'EU Leadership in International Climate Policy: Achievements and Challenges', *The International Spectator*, 43(2), 35–50.

Oberthür, S. and Pallemaerts, M. with Roche Kelly, C. (eds) (2010) *The New Climate Policies of the European Union: Internal Legislation and Climate Diplomacy*, Brussels: Academic Scientific Publishers.

Pallemaerts, M. and Williams, R. (2006) 'Climate Change: The International and European Policy Framework', in M. Peeters and K. Deketelaere (eds), *EU Climate Change Policy. The Challenge of New Regulatory Initiatives*, Cheltenham: Edward Elgar, 22–50.

Peeters, M. and Deketelaere, K. (eds) (2006) *EU Climate Change Policy. The Challenge of New Regulatory Initiatives*, Cheltenham: Edward Elgar.

Rehbinder, E. and Stewart, R. (1985), *Integration Through Law. Europe and the American Federal Experience*, Berlin: Walter de Gruyter.

Rowlands, I. (1995) *The Politics of Global Atmospheric Change*, Manchester: Manchester University Press.

Scharpf, F. (1988) 'The Joint-Decision Trap: Lessons from German Federalism and European Integration', *Public Administration*, 66, 239–78.

Schreurs, M. (2002) *Environmental Politics in Japan, Germany, and the United States*, Cambridge: Cambridge University Press.

Schreurs, M. and Tiberghien, Y. (2007) 'Multi-level Reinforcement: Explaining European Union Leadership in Climate Change Mitigation', *Global Environmental Politics*, 7(4), 19–46.

Skjærseth, J. B and Wettestad, J. (2008) *EU Emissions Trading: Initiation, Decision-making and Implementation*, Aldershot: Ashgate.

Talberg, J. (2003) 'The Agenda-Shaping Powers of the EU Council Presidency', *Journal of European Public Policy*, 10(1), 1–19.

Verba, S. (1961) *Small Groups and Political Behavior. A Study of Leadership*, Princeton, NJ: Princeton University Press.

Vogler, J. (1999) 'The European Union as an Actor in International Environmental Politics', *Environmental Politics*, 8(3), 24–48.

Weale, A. (1992) *The New Politics of Pollution*, Manchester: Manchester University Press.

Weale, A. (1996) 'Environmental Rules and Rule-making in the European Union', *Journal of European Public Policy*, 3(4), 594–611.

Weale, A., Pridham, G., Cini, M., Konstadakopulos, D. and Flynn, B. (2000) *Environmental Governance in Europe*, Oxford: Oxford University Press.

Wettestad, J. (2005), 'The Making of the 2003 EU Emissions Trading Directive: Ultra-Quick Process Due To Entrepreneurial Proficiency?' *Global Environmental Politics*, 5(1), 1–24.

Wurzel, R. K. W. (2002) *Environmental Policy Making in Britain, Germany and the EU. Europeanisation of Air and Water Pollution Control*, Manchester: Manchester University Press.

Wurzel, R. K. W. (2004) *The EU Presidency: 'Honest Broker' or Driving Seat?* London: Anglo-German Foundation.

Wurzel, R. K. W, (2008a) 'Environmental Policy. EU Actors, Leader and Laggard States', in J. Hayward (ed.), *Leaderless Europe*, Oxford: Oxford University Press, 66–88.

Wurzel, R. K. W. (2008b) *The Politics of Emissions Trading in Britain and Germany*, London: Anglo-German Foundation.

Young, Oran (1991), 'Political Leadership and Regime Formation: On the Development of Institutions in International Society', *International Organization*, 45(3), 281–308.

2 The European Union as a global environmental policy actor

Climate change

John Vogler

It has become commonplace in discussions of environmental and other global issues to treat the EU as if it were a single purposive entity. The Union is urged to act, even to lead and has rather ostentatiously ascribed such a role to itself during the ratification and implementation of the Kyoto Protocol and the search for a post 2012 climate regime. Leadership is logically inseparable from the capacity to act which may, inelegantly, be described as 'actorness'. Normally this point would hardly be worth making, and in this volume leadership roles are examined for a range of actors, constituent institutions of the Union, states and non state actors. However, with the EU as an entity in world politics, there is a problem that requires consideration of the definition of a political actor, something that is normally taken for granted. It is quite simply expressed. The Union is neither an emergent federal state nor an overdeveloped international organisation. In an international system where the capacity to act has conventionally been confined to sovereign states (although with some modification for certain types of international organisation) the EU is unique, an entity which is, according to the international lawyers, *sui generis.*

This chapter, therefore, sets up some criteria to establish the extent to which the EU may be regarded as an international environmental actor in general and more specifically in the field of climate change policy. The analysis is based upon previous work (Bretherton and Vogler 2006; Vogler 1999) and posits four characteristics that one might expect an international actor to exhibit. They are: autonomy, volition, negotiating capability and the ability to deploy policy instruments. All of these relate to the leadership types and styles set out in Table 1.2 of the introductory chapter by Wurzel and Connelly. If there is no autonomy then it would make little sense to consider the EU (as opposed to its Member States) as a leader. Structural leadership requires the ability to mobilise resources and without negotiating capability there will be little chance of entrepreneurial leadership. An 'heroic' leadership style implies real and continuing volition. These outward and visible signs of actorness rely upon various capabilities possessed by the Union, but they are also dependent upon its broader 'presence' in the global political economy and upon the opportunity structure that confronted Union decision-makers at particular points in the history of the international climate regime. While this structure may have facilitated the development of EU actorness and its leadership ambitions during the 1990s and in the first decade of the twenty-first century, there are already indications of significantly reduced opportunity as the search for a post 2012 agreement proceeds.

The status of an actor and the exercise of leadership are not automatic consequences of capability, presence and opportunity. Just as in the social life of an individual, actorness is conditional upon the expectations and constructions of third parties that serve to establish identity, reputation and credibility. The EU as actor may capitalise on such constructions, but they may equally prove to be damaging, as appears to have been the case with the Common and Foreign and Security Policy (CFSP) and Chris Hill's (1993) 'capability-expectations gap'. Leadership is a reciprocal process that requires recognition and acceptance by the led. It may involve the willing adoption of concepts and principles enunciated by the Union but also a more fundamental recognition that the EU is capable of acting as a unit and delivering upon its commitments. Over the life of the climate change regime the Union has in many ways been able to exceed the expectations of outsiders but this can no longer be taken for granted.

Autonomy

This broaches the difficult question of the extent to which the Union is a policy actor distinguishable from its component Member States. It involves formal questions of competence in external policy and legal recognition alongside the more subtle constructions of those who interact with the EU. The paradigm case of the EU as a single actor with evident, although circumscribed, independence from the Member States is to be found in the area of trade – the Common Commercial Policy under Article 207.[1] Here there is a clear treaty basis for exclusive Union competence in trade negotiations. The Commission has the right of initiative, there is qualified majority voting (QMV) in the Council (significant in terms of discussions of autonomy because it moves some way from the consensus rules that prevail in international organisations), and only the Commission represents the Union (Member States representatives are present but silent).[2] The Union, which has legal personality bestowed upon it by the Treaty of Lisbon, has since the creation of the World Trade Organization (WTO) in 1995, been a full member in its own right alongside the Member States.[3] This is a comparatively rare status for the European Union in international organisations where it usually only enjoys observer status (the Food and Agricultural Organisation (FAO) and a number of fisheries organisations provide exceptions to this rule as well as the Regional Economic Integration Organisations (REIO) provisions outlined below). To outside observers the Commission at the WTO and in bilateral trade discussions does appear to enjoy significant autonomy embodied in the focus on the Trade Commissioner who is seen to be locked in battle with the trade ministers of other major states. However, the Commission still functions as an agent for its Member States principals but with a significant degree of autonomy (Delreux 2009).

The environment did not, of course, figure in the Treaty of Rome so there was no explicit treaty basis for the externalisation of the EC's developing internal competences. However, the 1971 European Road Transport Agreement (ERTA) ruling of the European Court of Justice provided that once internal rules had been legislated by the Community the latter's competence also extended to related external policy. Thus external Community (now Union) competence was acquired alongside the achievement of internal competence in critical areas such as air pollution and waste treatment. This allowed the Commission to insist that it should participate alongside the Member States in international environmental negotiations, but competence was not exclusive. In contrast to the trade or fisheries examples, competence is shared although the degree of Union competence varies across particular issues. As has often been remarked, climate change is a quintessentially multi-sectoral problem that does not align easily with Union competences and where key issues of taxation and energy policy remain within the exclusive competence of Member States. The legal basis for Union action concerning the Kyoto Protocol remains Arts. 191 and 192 of the Treaty on the Functioning of the European Union (TFEU).[4] These articles refer in general to environmental protection but do not include specific mention of climate change. Climate change does appear in the text of the Lisbon treaty (Art. 4(2)(e)), but as a strategic concern and in a way that does not change the existing distribution of competences (House of Lords 2008). Thus, for negotiations under the United Nations Framework Convention on Climate Change (UNFCCC), shared competence means presidency leadership where the Member State, that is the President in Office, represents the Union assisted by other Member States who are recognised as lead states for particular issues (on the details see Chapter 5 by Oberthür and Kelly). The Commission appears alongside the 27 Member States and it has been said that the EU now negotiates 'at 28'. Judged only in terms of competence, this would tend to suggest a limited role for the Union and perhaps, by analogy with trade or fisheries policy, diminished autonomy for the EU as an actor. In fact this does not appear to have been the case although there have been issues, arising from shared competence, that are considered further below. It is important, therefore, not to assess the international actorness of the EU solely in terms of the extent to which the Union enjoys exclusive competence.

Even if the Union has competence for an issue, this does not necessarily mean that it will be accepted as an actor by other parties to a negotiation. It confronted this problem of external recognition in the late 1970s when, on the basis of its newly acquired competences for air pollution, it attempted to participate, alongside the Member States, in the Long Range Transboundary Air Pollution (LRTAP) negotiations that emerged from the East–West détente process. The 1979 LRTAP established a formula that continues to be used to allow Union participation in the UNFCCC and various other global environmental regimes. Under this formula, Regional Economic Integration Organisations (REIOs) can participate and sign agreements alongside state parties on condition that they do not acquire separate voting rights. That is to say that if the Member States vote then the Union cannot, but the Union is also able to cast the votes of all 27 Member States. The EC is the only extant REIO and appears alongside the Member States in the climate change negotiations.[5] It is worth recalling that this provides a great advance on the observer status of the EU elsewhere in the UN system and at UN Environmental Programme (UNEP).

Volition

The ability to formulate distinct policy is the second attribute of an actor. It is a logical precursor to attempts to exercise structural or entrepreneurial leadership. Clearly there are some areas of EU external relations; the Iraq imbroglio of 2003 springs to mind as well as failures in respect of a collective energy policy towards Russia, where woeful inadequacies in terms of collective political will reflect major differences in political interests and orientation between the Member States. There is no denying that national divergence over climate change arises from the often marked economic, energy and development differences among Member States as well as the different perspectives on environmental policy to be found in North, South and Eastern Europe. During the initial discussion of post 2012 targets under the Finnish presidency of 2006, for example, it was reported that UK, Germany and Sweden supported by Commissioner Dimas favoured a 30 per cent reduction target by 2020 while Hungary, Slovakia, Poland and Spain opposed, arguing that the EU should wait for other Kyoto parties before 'making a hasty declaration of commitment' (ENDS *Daily* 2006). There may also be 'inconsistency' between Member States and the Community, where both pursue separate policies sometimes in opposition. A lack of 'coherence' between Community policies is also often evident. Although such a situation is, of course, frequently to be observed in the foreign-policy making of states, it may be more difficult to resolve such conflicts in the EU. Trade and environment questions will inevitably be a source of some incoherence, from which climate change policy is not immune, alongside conflicts within the Commission over the extent to which international climate change commitments imperil the achievement of the Lisbon Strategy.

A salient example is provided by the issue of carbon leakage. This involves the extent to which the competitiveness of European energy-intensive industries would be damaged by stringent application of the Emissions Trading Scheme. Rising energy costs within the EU would, it was argued, mean the migration of industries to countries without carbon restrictions. Greenhouse gas emissions (GHGE) would thus 'leak' from the EU without the intended reduction, while at the same time it would incur serious economic damage.

Policy to counter this concern had implications both for the WTO and for the climate negotiations in that border tax adjustments were proposed as one answer both by the Commission and some Member States, including France. Not only would they protect EU industrial competitiveness but their threat might persuade (non Annex I) developing countries to negotiate seriously about post 2012 emissions reduction commitments (*European Voice* 2008, 8 May). In the event, to the consternation of environmental groups, the final climate change and energy package negotiated at the European Council of December 2008 bowed to German and other pressure by providing that heavy industries under 'significant risk' from international competition could continue to receive free carbon dioxide (CO_2) emission rights (*Euractiv* 2008, 12 December).

In this case and in previous discussions, effective international climate action and consequent obligations continued to be portrayed as an economic burden. That is to say, the theme of ecological modernisation did not figure largely in discussion of external climate policy. The conjunction of the need for a fiscal stimulus to promote European economic recovery and the necessity to agree a climate and energy package of internal measures to underpin EU leadership in advance of the 2009 Copenhagen conference (Conference of the Parties of the UNFCCC (COP 15)) appears to have changed this situation. The intellectual stimulus provided by the UK's Stern Review (2007) of the economics of climate change was also of significance. Environment Commissioner Dimas (2009), for example, while asserting EU leadership in the context of Copenhagen and the 2008 energy and climate package, argued that: '[b]y preparing Europe for a low carbon future, we are strengthening it in the face of globalisation and further consolidate our position in world markets. This is a typically win-win-win case!'

The key point is that, despite many sources of inconsistency and incoherence, the Union has generally been able to resolve the many conflicts within the Council and Commission such that, in the end, policy towards international environmental negotiations has been established without being condemned to move at the speed of the 'slowest ship' or to resort to the 'lowest common denominator' (Bretherton and Vogler 2006: 99). It would be fair to say that Union positions (in contrast to other Annex I parties) stand out for the seriousness with which they take both the emerging scientific evidence on 'dangerous' climate change (acceptance of the need to limit mean temperature increases to 2° Celsius) and the extent of the cuts in emissions that are proposed.

The history of EU climate policy is an extended one which must take in early problems with the failure to agree a carbon tax and a number of subsequent disagreements. However, in terms of demonstrating to the rest of the world a consistent policy line amongst an expanding system of diverse national economies, the record is quite positive. The Europeans were prepared in 1992 to agree on binding targets for Article 4.2 of the original UNFCCC, against US opposition. After both internal dissension and external failure, involving a 'policy and measures' approach, the EU moved to set the pace on 'targets and timetables' for Kyoto with its offer of 15 per cent GHG reductions (against a 1990 baseline). The 2000 Hague COP was not a happy occasion for an EU beset by internal differences on how to deal with the US, but following rejection of the Kyoto Protocol by the Bush administration in 2001, the Gothenburg European Council moved decisively to shoulder the burden of ensuring ratification of the Protocol even in the absence of the US. This objective was pursued relentlessly and successfully both in terms of negotiating the complex detail of a Protocol, which in 2001 was not capable of implementation, and ensuring the necessary ratifications to achieve entry into force in 2005. Subsequent policy in respect of a post 2012 agreement was, for a time (until March 2007), not so clear cut. Having approached the 2005 Montreal COP in reactive mode with no fixed proposals on the shape of a post 2012 agreement, in 2007 the Council finally agreed that the EU would commit itself to a 30 per cent GHGE reduction against a 1990 baseline '. . . provided that other developed countries commit themselves to comparable emissions reductions and economically more advanced developing countries to contributing adequately according to their responsibilities and respective capabilities' (European Council 2007: 31). Otherwise until 'a global and comprehensive agreement for the period beyond 2012 was achieved and without prejudice to its position in international negotiations'; the EU's firm independent commitment was to achieve at least a 20 per cent reduction in GHGE. Developed countries should achieve a collective target of the order of 60–80 per cent by 2050 and the European Council prefaced its Conclusions, as ever, by stressing 'the leading role of the EU in international climate protection' (ibid.). The hope was that the exemplary 'pledge and extend' offer made by the Union would give a lead to the long-awaited Copenhagen climate conference (COP 15), held at the end of 2009. In the event there were no followers, the parties merely recited their existing offers in the Copenhagen Accord and the EU's offer of a conditional 30 per cent reduction was essentially ignored.[6]

The credibility of the Union's attempts at leadership have been critically dependent upon the burden sharing agreement, colloquially known as the 'EU bubble'. Originally devised to provide a means of delivering the collective commitment to a 15 per cent GHGE reduction in advance of Kyoto, it allowed both sharp increases and decreases in the emissions of individual Member States amounting to an aggregate reduction of 10 per cent against a 1990 baseline. The 10 per cent was agreed on the understanding that in the unlikely event there was international agreement on the EU negotiating target of 15 per cent there would be further negotiation to achieve the remaining 5 per cent (Ringius 1997).

In the event the Kyoto COP agreed an aggregate 5.2 per cent for Annex I countries and a collective 8 per cent cut for the EU. This enabled the production of a new burden sharing agreement in which the respective national targets were revised downwards. It was unpopular with other Parties, who tended to regard it as a somewhat underhand ruse to allow certain European countries to avoid taking on any burdens, but by the same token it enabled the EU to act as one. As was very evident, it relied upon a particularly fortuitous set of circumstances relating to the use of the 1990 baseline. Both Germany and the United Kingdom were, through the circumstances of, respectively, reunification and the closure of most of the British deep-mined coal industry, able to promise large, but essentially painless, cuts in their GHGE. Southern 'cohesion' Member States were also persuaded to accept emissions targets that were somewhat less than those projected to ensure economic development (Vogler 2009). While the 1998 burden sharing agreement targets have not yet been fully achieved through, amongst other things, the Emissions Trading System (ETS), discussion has turned to the creation of new arrangements for the delivery of post 2012 targets in the climate and energy package, involving a much more extensive and centralised ETS and, to cover other emissions, new 'effort' rather than 'burden' sharing arrangements for the Member States (CEC 2008a, 2008b).

Negotiating capability

An observer of the complexities of shared competence, in the context of a Union that enlarged from 12 to 27 Member States within the lifetime of the climate regime, could be forgiven for assuming that the EU, despite its ability to set objectives, would be absolutely incapable of effective negotiation or the exercise of entrepreneurial leadership. There are certainly a number of impediments that include: reliance on a rotating presidency, the need for coordination meetings within a negotiation, the need to accommodate new Member States and the tendency of some Members to defy presidency leadership and to attempt to cut deals with other Parties (The Hague COP of 2000 provides an example of such a UK attempt to circumvent the presidency and negotiate a deal on sinks with the US). There is ample evidence in the negotiating record of the climate regime of EU inertia and what has been described as 'Herculean problems of co-ordination' (Grubb and Yamin 2001). One consequence of the EU's policy system for international negotiations, with coordination and reference back to the Council is that it lacks the necessary flexibility. This has been evident at critical points in the development of the climate regime, for example in its inability to respond to the US introduction of the Kyoto mechanisms and subsequently in its rigidity towards the US at the 2000 Hague COP (ibid.). Partly as a consequence of its profile and the arrival of many heads of government for its high-level segment, the 2009 Copenhagen climate conference provided a sobering demonstration of EU disarray. Connie Hedegaard, who chaired the early part of the COP and was later to become EU Climate Commissioner, acknowledged that Europe 'spoke with many voices' and was virtually unable to negotiate. 'A lot of Europeans in the room is not a problem, but there is only an advantage if we sing from the same hymn sheet. We need to think about this and reflect on it very seriously, or we will lose our leadership role in the world' (Phillips 2010).

On the other hand, the EU, despite its difficulties, has been able to make strong long-term commitments to which, until 2009, other parties have responded. At Kyoto it managed to obtain two key objectives, crucial to its subsequent success: first, the retention of the 1990 baseline and second, the acceptance of the controversial EU 'bubble'. Its inflexibility and cumbersomeness can on occasion be virtues not normally recognised in discussions of entrepreneurial leadership. It is, as one Commission official said, a 'slow but weighty ship' but one which has been an indispensable component of the international climate negotiations. Commitment to the Kyoto Protocol and targets and timetables, which on occasion in Brussels seemed almost to have acquired the status of religious belief, was in many ways admirable, but hampered the development of feasible post 2012 regime, when the United States was equally strongly opposed (See Chapter 14 by Bang and Schreurs). The 2007 Bali 'Road Map', which created two negotiating tracks on the future of the Convention and on Kyoto, allowed the US to rejoin negotiations by participating only in the former. Even more than this, the arrival of the Obama administration and the new hope for possible transatlantic cooperation on carbon trading allowed the EU to finesse its previous insistence on the extension of the Protocol (see Chapter 15 by Bang and Schreurs; Egenhofer *et al.* 2009).

In other areas of external policy there has been great emphasis on the Lisbon Treaty reforms to improve the efficiency of the EU as an international actor. The rotating six-month presidency does create problems for climate change policy and different presidencies have been more or less effective (van Schaik and Egenhofer 2003).[7] Better coordination between presidencies has been addressed, by the sharing presidency tasks over an 18-month cycle, and the EU continues to allow 'lead states' to make the running on particular issues. However, the new President of the European Council (van Rompuy) is just that, with the rotating presidency continuing to operate in formations of the Council of Ministers. It remains to be seen whether these arrangements will affect the conduct of the Union's external environmental policy.

Policy instruments

Actors in the international political system, if they are not to indulge in purely symbolic leadership, have to possess some capability to affect the decisions of others. Influence may be exerted through the power of example or through the dissemination of knowledge – described as cognitive or intellectual leadership. The EU has claims to both, but frequently there will be a need to back up policy positions through coercion or inducement in the exercise of structural leadership. The Union lacks military muscle, other than in the European Security and Defence Policy (ESDP), which in any event would be irrelevant to the problem of arranging international cooperation for the mitigation of climate change. Armed force is, of course, far from irrelevant when it comes to adaptation to climate change and to the management of its consequences, something that is increasingly recognised in Brussels.

The instruments potentially available to the EU in pursuit of its international climate cooperation strategies are, nonetheless, significant. They include the diplomatic resources of 27 states, the very substantial structural inducements and penalties arising from the control of access to the Single Market and the Union's large aid budget. It is worth stressing that these assets are 'potential' for it has not always proved easy to deploy them. External climate change policy does not suffer from the 'inter-pillar' problems of the CFSP, but there will still be difficulties in subordinating the objectives of trade to environmental policy and coordinating inter-governmental diplomatic cooperation.

In pursuit of Kyoto ratification, the EU deployed economic instruments in support of its climate policy. During 2004, when Russian ratification was absolutely necessary if the Protocol was to enter into force, a deal was concocted whereby the *quid pro quo* for Russian agreement would be EU support for its WTO membership plus some adjustments to the terms on which Russian gas entered the Single Market (Bretherton and Vogler 2006: 109). This may not be a particularly strong example, because no great sacrifices were entailed for Russia, which enjoys substantial quantities of 'hot air' under the Kyoto arrangements. Elsewhere it is difficult to establish such a clear linkage, but it is probably significant that the EU now prioritises support for its climate change positions within the trade-dominated bilateral relations that it maintains with the majority of states in the international system. The EU–China relationship, which has been developed extensively in the last decade, is of critical importance here but it is unlikely that direct economic inducements figure here, the emphasis being placed rather more on technological collaboration (see Chapter 15 by Dai and Diao). A very important, yet internally disputed, part of the Union's strategy in advance of Copenhagen was to put 'money on the table' in the form of €7.2 billion of 'fast start' funding agreed at a European Council in December 2009. This funding forms part of the Copenhagen Accord, but it failed to have the intended effect of inducing G77 countries to support a new climate agreement.[8]

Diplomatic coordination, frequently at head-of-government level was certainly achieved in the campaign to recruit ratifications of Kyoto. Between COP 6 of 2000 and COP 6bis EU diplomatic missions were undertaken to Australia, Canada, Japan, the Russian Federation and Iran. The UK, France and Germany made high-level representations to various other governments and notably Japan (IISD 2001: 176). Similarly, there is evidence of coordinated EU diplomatic effort through the G8 under the British and German joint presidencies in 2005 and 2008 with a personal intervention by Prime Minister Blair with President Bush to obtain a modification of the US position at the 2005 Montreal COP (Interview evidence 2006). EU foreign policy coordination is not always achieved, given the dispersion of effort between Commission Delegations and Member State embassies, but it is arguable that the salience given to the Union's climate change agenda has resulted in a more consistent effort, particularly on Kyoto ratification, that gave the EU the appearance of a purposive actor. Under the Lisbon Treaty changes these problems will be addressed through the creation of a new External Action Service incorporating Commission, Council and national officials.

The conditions of actorness: presence and opportunity

One framework for understanding the conditions under which the EU became, and might indeed recede, as an international actor involves three linked factors: presence, opportunity and capability (Bretherton and Vogler 2006). Capabilities have been considered in the preceding discussion, so it remains to consider presence and opportunity.

The concept of presence has been variously used in discussions of EU external policy (Allen and Smith 1990) but is defined here as:

> . . . the ability of the EU, by virtue of its existence, to exert influence beyond its borders. An indication of the EU's structural power, presence combines understandings about the fundamental nature, or identity of the EU and the (often unintended) consequences of the Union's internal policies. (Bretherton and Vogler 2006: 24)

Presence is, thus, essentially a consequence of being rather than denoting purposive action. The most obvious aspect of the EU's presence in the international system is the enormous scale and attractiveness of the Single Market for outsiders coupled with the magnetic effects of the Union for states and populations within its immediate and expanding orbit. One might add to this its internal policies and standards which are often simply adopted by external actors because it makes good commercial sense to do so. Such presence often provides a necessary foundation for the development of international 'actorness' and structural leadership and will frequently give rise to expectations that they will be developed. Perhaps the most poignant example of this is the 'capability expectations' gap itself and the idea that such a manifest economic giant cannot for long remain a political pygmy.

In terms of climate change the starting point for a discussion of presence must also be the scale of economic activity in the Union, its historic, present and future contribution to climate change. This provides a basis upon which the EU has been called upon to undertake its responsibilities as a major developed world emitter. For a long period, covering the foundation of the climate regime, the EU was second only to the US as an emitter of GHG. In 2002 US emissions totalled 6.9 million metric tonnes of CO_2, the EU 25, 4.8,

Russia 1.9 and Japan 1.3 (UNFCCC 2004: 14). By 2008 the first place in the international league of emitters had been taken by a rapidly developing China (USEIA 2010) while the EU's share of global energy-related CO^2 emissions had declined to 10.8 per cent (EEA 2008). Another important aspect of EU presence is its corpus of internal climate policies, from the ill-fated attempt to devise a carbon tax in the early 1990s through the development of the European Climate Change programme (ECCP) and, of course the ETS. If the latter were to be adopted outside the Union, as is evidently the ambition of its designers, then EU presence would be extended in ways similar to those experienced with the introduction of the euro in the international monetary system – where the Union still cannot be considered to be a monetary actor. With the ETS there is also a clear dimension of cognitive leadership, 'the EU has "first mover" experience in setting up the EU ETS as the world's largest cap and trade system. Interest in this system is growing rapidly in a number of other developed countries' and the EU should 'promote the creation of a robust OECD wide carbon market by 2015' (CEC 2009: 11).

The conversion of presence into actorness, even where capabilities already exist, requires opportunity. Opportunity refers to the external environment of ideas and events that enable or constrain purposive action. In general terms the very creation of the EU occurred within the opportunity structure of the Cold War, involving the strategic protection of the US bloc and benefiting from fixed currency parities pegged to the dollar. These conditions also limited the extent to which the EU could become an actor. It was able to do so in trade, fisheries and development but only to a very limited degree in foreign policy. During the Cold War the development of European actorness was also constrained by the robust opposition of the Soviet Union to any dealings with the European entity. The first serious foray of the Community into global environmental diplomacy in 1979 was in fact enabled by the willingness of the Soviet Union (as part of the détente process) to treat with it on environmental issues, apparently in the expectation that Comecon would be granted similar REIO status.

The end of the Cold War also coincided with a marked rise in the salience of environmental issues in world politics, symbolised by the convening of the 1992 Rio Earth Summit. Both factors provided opportunities for the external projection of European environmental policies. However, perhaps the major opportunity seized by EU leaders to establish policy leadership was the abdication by the United States of its previously leading role. This occurred in a number of areas, but its attitude to the emergent climate regime from Rio onwards was as important as any. The US virtually invented modern environmental policy and had been a forerunner in, for example, the use of market-based instruments in contrast to the EU's reliance on 'command and control'. This lends a touch of irony to the EU's crusading stance on behalf of emissions trading, which it had opposed prior to Kyoto (Cass 2005). On a whole swathe of issues, US governments had led the way and the EC could often be portrayed as a laggard, for example in the 1985–87 Montreal

Protocol negotiations which the Europeans were badly divided and frequently acted in support of national chemical industries. By the time of the Rio conference there had clearly been a change with US resistance to binding commitments under Art 4.2 of the draft UNFCCC and the pattern has tended to continue through subsequent administrations, culminating in the 1997 Byrd-Hagel Resolution and George W. Bush's 2001 denunciation of the Kyoto Protocol. By the time of New Delhi COP the US was actively attempting to undermine both the Protocol and the EU (Ott 2002). All this provided opportunities to be exploited by Brussels in developing its actorness and burnishing its identity as a climate leader, with the US, often unfairly, characterised as the main obstacle to progress. The arrival of the Obama administration in 2009 instantly altered this situation although not in the direction of US adherence to the Kyoto Protocol. In retrospect the ratification of the latter may have represented the zenith of opportunity available to the EU. Since then climate politics has begun to reflect a shifting international structure in which the BASIC countries (Brazil, South Africa, India and China) have begun to play a role commensurate with their growing economic weight. Commentary on the outcome of the 2009 Copenhagen climate conference has been virtually unanimous in observing that the EU was absent from the critical diplomacy conducted between the US and China or the US and the BASIC countries (Egenhofer and Georgiev 2009; Curtin 2010).

Constructions of actorness

In the final analysis the links between presence, opportunity and capability are socially constructed by subtle processes whereby the Union is treated as an actor and followers are prepared to recognise its leadership. The identity of the Union, it may be argued, is subject to continuous redefinition through its interaction with outsiders. This is of some consequence for the EU as an actor, not only because conceptions of interest logically precede interests, but also because '. . . understandings about the external context of ideas and events, or the appropriateness or feasibility of alternative courses of action, are shaped by identity constructions that are themselves shifting and contested' (Bretherton and Vogler 2006: 37). In a mundane, but important, sense the EU is constructed as an actor in day-to-day accounts of international climate politics and this is more than convenient shorthand for the Community acting within its competences as a REIO and 27 Member States. On occasion the attribution of 'actorness' to the Union has gone well beyond the strict letter of international law.

A significant dimension of the EU's collective identity is both essentially civilian and normative (Manners 2002) and sometimes subject to pejorative comparison with the United States (Kagan 2002). Both the Commission and the European Council are at pains to reiterate the leading and normative role of the Union on climate change and, unlike other Union policies, it is one that enjoys consistently high levels of popular support and involves flattering comparisons with the inaction of the United States (Vogler and Bretherton 2006). As US commentators have observed, climate change policy is significantly involved here and ranks alongside the anti-death penalty campaign and support for the International Criminal Court in the formation of the EU's international moral identity. A 2008 construction by a US government analyst puts it like this. Support for the UNFCCC is one example of '..what Robert Kagan has described as the European predilection for establishing a Kantian world order, in which contentious issues are addressed, and potential conflicts resolved, through the establishment of suitably empowered global structures of governance' (Schmidt 2008: 94). This is in part a product of the EU's own history, but also, the author argues, a consequence of social democratic approaches to policy and a regulatory culture of precaution and risk aversion. In fact this means that the EU is much more of an actor in climate policy than it is in other areas, notably the CFSP, where individual national interests tend to prevail:

> . . . on issues like global warming, where the risks involved invite precaution and uniquely or readily lend themselves to institutional regulatory solutions, Europeans are more likely to act in an EU context, pursue global remedies and in so doing give expression to their social democratic roots. (ibid.)

It goes without saying that this view has not necessarily been shared in the past by India and many other countries that have been extremely critical of EU climate policy. In the view of many of the EU's protagonists the adoption of a high moral tone on the climate obligations of developed countries and on 'common but differentiated responsibilities' also includes an element of hypocrisy, given the rather favourable terms that the EU managed to negotiate for itself at Kyoto. However, this can hardly be said of the current policy post 2012.

Critical to the maintenance of the identity of the Union as an international climate actor and its exertion of cognitive or intellectual leadership is its ability to deliver on the commitments that it has made under the Kyoto Protocol. This is all the more so because the EU 'bubble' and the achievement of the 1990 baseline made such targets relatively easy to obtain, in sharp contrast to the sacrifices that would have been required of the United States had it acceded to Kyoto (estimated as a 20 per cent reduction in actual emissions as between 2001 and 2012). Even so, as European Environment Agency (EEA) submissions to the UNFCCC indicate, the Union has struggled to keep on track with its 8 per cent reduction commitment (EEA, 2007). A heavy burden has been placed upon the ETS introduced a month before Kyoto entry into force in 2005 and charged with ensuring over 40 per cent of the EU's reduction commitment. Phase I of the ETS was not auspicious, with an over-allocation of permits in National Allocation Plans and a spectacular collapse in the price of carbon. Phase II, which started in 2008, was designed to be a great deal more rigorous and has annoyed a number of Member States governments, especially amongst the 2004 entrants, by mandating real reductions.

Conclusion

The Westphalian model of statehood cannot serve as a template for an entity such as the EU. Instead this chapter has attempted to consider the attributes of an international actor beyond the framework of statehood in terms of autonomy, volition, negotiation and implementation capacity as well as the significant aspects of third party recognition and construction. In global environmental policy and more specifically in the international politics of climate change, the Union has clearly been an identifiable and purposive actor and possesses many of the associated capabilities. The EU as an environmental policy actor has clearly been a great deal more successful than the EU as a foreign policy actor under CFSP. Although expectations of climate change leadership have been raised, a process encouraged by the Commission and successive European Councils, there is far less of a 'capability expectations gap' than in other domains of external policy. This is not to say that the EU is always an effective actor, and some significant problems with its capabilities have been identified. Nevertheless, it would be difficult for any observer of the development of the international climate regime to deny the centrality of its role – a role distinct from that played by various leading Member States.

It has been argued that EU actorness (and by implication its climate leadership role) have come about because of favourable circumstances in terms of EU presence and the available opportunity structure. There is evidence that such circumstances will not persist. The EU's global presence is in relative decline in economic terms, but also in respect of its share of global GHGE. At the same time the very favourable conditions, enabling the EU 'bubble', will not recur. The Union has become larger, but inevitably poorer through enlargement to 27. Enlargement has had implications for internal policy-making reflected in the current attempts to construct an effective ETS and a new basis for 'effort sharing', where some new Member States are far from happy with what are seen as restrictions on their economic growth potential.

The international system has altered significantly since European negotiators were first involved in the climate regime in ways that have served to bring the political structure more into line with the pattern of actual and future emissions. The opportunities available to the Union in the years preceding Kyoto were extensive. However, in the post 2012 situation China and India have begun to play a role which goes well beyond that of interested bystanders. As significant is the position of the United States. There is no question that US abdication of global environmental policy leadership enabled the activities of the EU and the establishment of the Union's special identity in contradistinction to the United States. It was unlikely, indeed undesirable, that this should persist but the uncomfortable experience of Copenhagen suggests that European leadership on climate change has been much diminished.

Notes

1 Article 207 of the Treaty on the Functioning of the European Union (TFEU) replaces Article 133 of the Treaty Establishing the European Community.
2 Policy is ultimately subject to MS agreement in the Article 207 Committee that convenes at various levels to monitor and guide the Commission.
3 Up until 2009 only the *European* Community enjoyed legal personality, originally granted by the Treaty of Rome. Under the Lisbon Treaty the Union became the successor to the Community acquiring legal personality. Discussions of competence prior to this date will refer to the Community, while the Union will mean the broader structure established under the Treaty of Maastricht 1992
4 Previously Article 174(4) and 175 of the Treaty Establishing the European Communities.
5 The relevant provisions are to be found at Arts 6, 4 (2b), 18 and 22 of the UNFCCC.
6 The Copenhagen Accord was not even agreed by the Conference, simply noted (UNFCCC 2009). Although the EU's central ambitions for developed country emissions commitments were not achieved, the EU's 2°C limit was incorporated in the text along with an acknowledgement that developing countries would need $100 billion climate-related aid by 2020, also part of the EU's position. The unilateral pledges, including one for a 20 per cent emissions reduction by the EU, were submitted to the UNFCCC during January 2010. Whether or not to move to a 30 per cent reduction regardless of action by others continued to be a hotly debated issue within the EU and a source of disagreement between Member States (MS) at the December 2009 European Council (European Voice 2009, 17 December)
7 For example, the Danish presidency at CoP 8 in 2002 pressed for developing country commitments which proved highly counterproductive (Ott 2002).
8 The funding had been disputed over the previous year by East European MS and there was no agreement on EU contributions to the longer-term funding target for the climate regime of $100 billion per year by 2020 (European Voice 2009, 17 December).

Bibliography

Allen, D. and Smith, M. (1990) 'Western Europe's Presence in the Contemporary International Arena', *Review of International Studies*, 16 (1), 19–37.
Bretherton, C. and Vogler, J. (2006) *The European Union as a Global Actor*, London: Routledge (2nd edn).
Cass, L. (2005) 'Norm Entrapment and Preference Change: The Evolution of the European Union Position on International Emissions Trading', *Global Environmental Politics*, 5 (2), 1–23.
CEC (2008a) *Proposal for a Directive of the European Parliament and of the Council amending Directive 2003/87/EC so as to improve and extend the greenhouse gas emission allowance trading system of the Community, COM (2008) 16 final, 23.1.2008*, Brussels: Commission of the European Communities.
CEC (2008b) *Proposal for a Decision of the European Parliament and of the Council on the effort of Member States to reduce their greenhouse gas emissions to meet the Community's greenhouse gas emission reduction commitments up to 2020,*

COM (2008) 17 final, 23.1.2008, Brussels: Commission of the European Communities.

CEC (2009) *Towards a Comprehensive Climate Change Agreement in Copenhagen. COM(2009) 39 Final, 28.1.2009,* Brussels: Commission of the European Communities.

Curtin, J. (2010) *The Copenhagen Conference: How Should the EU Respond?,* Dublin: International Institute of International and European Affairs.

Delreux, T. (2009) 'Cooperation and Control in the European Union: The Case of the European Union as International Environmental Negotiator', *Cooperation & Conflict,* 44(2), 189–208.

Dimas, S. (2009) 'Copenhagen Must Build the Road to a Sustainable Energy Future', *Rapid Press Release,* Speech /09/43, Brussels: Commission of the European Communities.

EEA (2007) *Annual European Community Greenhouse Gas Inventory 1990–2005 and Inventory Report 2007, Submission to the UNFCCC Secretariat,* EEA technical Report No.7/2006, Copenhagen: European Environment Agency.

EEA (2008) *Greenhouse Gas Emissions: Trends and Projections in Europe,* EEA Report No.5/2008, Copenhagen: European Environment Agency.

Egenhofer,C. and Georgiev, A. (2009) *The Copenhagen Accord – A First Stab at Deciphering the Implications for the EU,* Brussels: Centre for European Policy Studies.

Egenhofer, C., Pumphries, D., Ladislaw, S. and Georgiev, A. (2009) *Next Steps for the Transatlantic Climate Change partnership. A Report of the Global Dialogue Between the European Union and the United States,* Brussels: Centre for Strategic and International Studies.

ENDS *Daily* (2006) 'Council debates post-2012 climate options' 18 December.

European Council (2005) *Presidency Conclusions –* Brussels 22/23 March.

European Council (2007) *Presidency Conclusions –* Brussels 8/9 March.

Grubb, M. and Yamin, F. (2001) 'Climate Collapse at the Hague. What Happened and Where Do We Go from Here?', *International Affairs,* 77(2), 261–76.

Hill, C. (1993) 'The Capability-Expectations Gap or Conceptualising Europe's Intenational Role', *Journal of Common Market Studies,* 31(3), 305–25.

House of Lords Select Committee on European Union (2008) *Tenth Report,* Chap.10.

IISD (2001) *Earth Negotiations Bulletin,* 12 (176): 1–15.

Kagan, R. (2002) 'Power and Weakness', *Policy Review,* June–July, 3–28.

Manners, I. (2002) 'Normative Power Europe: A Contradiction in Terms?', *Journal of Common Market Studies,* 40(2), 235–58.

Ott, H. E. (2002) *Warning Signs from Delhi: Troubled Waters Ahead for Global Climate Policy,* Wuppertal: Wuppertal Institute for Climate, Environment and Energy.

Phillips, L. (2010) 'Hedegaard: EU Must Speak with One Voice on Climate', *EU Observer.com*/880/29278, 15 January.

Ringius, L. (1997) *Differentiation, Leaders and Fairness: Negotiating Climate Commitments in the European Community,* Oslo: Cicero, Report 1997: 8.

Schmidt, J.R. (2008) 'Why Europe Leads on Climate Change', *Survival,* 50(4), 83–96.

Stern. N. (2007) *The Economics of Climate Change: The Stern Review,* Cambridge: Cambridge University Press.

UNFCCC (2004) Information on National Greenhouse Inventory Data from Parties

Included in Annex I to the Convention for the Period 1990–2002 Including the Status of Reporting, Bonn, October 14, FCCC/CP/2004/5.

UNFCCC (2009) *The Copenhagen Accord*, Draft Decision-/CP.15, FCCC/CP/2009 L.7, 18 December.

USEIA, United States Energy Information Administration, 2010, *International Energy Statistics*, <http://tonto.ei.doe.gov>

van Schaik, L. and Egenhofer, C. (2003) *Reform of EU Institutions: Implications for the EU's Performance in Climate Change Negotiations*, Brussels: CEPS Policy Brief No.40.

Vogler, J. (1999) 'The European Union as an Actor in International Environmental Politics' *Environmental Politics*, 8 (3), 24–48.

Vogler, J. (2009) 'Climate Change and EU Foreign Policy: The Negotiation of Burden Sharing', *International Politics*, 46(4), 469–90.

Vogler, J. and Bretherton, C. (2006) 'The European Union as a Protagonist to the United States on Climate Change', *International Studies Perspectives*, 7, 1–22.

Part II
EU institutions

3 The role of the Commission of the European Union

Creating external coherence from internal diversity

Pamela M. Barnes

Introduction

The EU is the only supranational institution to have implemented an internal climate change policy which has allowed it to adopt the role of a leader in international climate change politics. Internal climate change policy and the approach adopted by the EU in international climate change politics are inextricably linked. The Commission is the institution with the right of formal initiation of policy and responsibility for ensuring policy is implemented. It therefore plays a central role within the EU climate change policy-making process. Agreement within the EU on policy emanates from complex interactions between its formal institutional actors – the European Council, Council of Ministers (Council), Commission, and the European Parliament (EP) with input from formal/informal networks of other actors (see Figure 3.1). Although it is often the European Council and/or Council which provides leadership for the EU in global climate change politics, the role of the Commission is crucial in the development of the internal policy which then becomes the accepted policy of the EU 'exported' to the global level.

The role of the Commission, as outlined in the EU's founding Treaties of the 1950s, was to be that of a small supranational executive taking the lead in policy proposals to facilitate the integration agenda (Hayward, 2008). Its President was to be 'primus inter pares' with decisions emanating from the deliberations of the College of Commissioners. Amongst specific tasks assigned to the Commission was that of consensus builder between the Member States and with the other institutions and policy actors (see Box 3.1). It is argued in this chapter that as the EU has enlarged the importance of the diplomatic and negotiating skills of the Commission President and the Commissioners and the ability of the institution to facilitate agreement between the other institutions and the national governments has significantly increased. It is in the exercise of leadership to broker agreements (i.e. entrepreneurial leadership) that the Commission has made a significant contribution in international climate change politics. The Commission also takes on an active role in the international climate change negotiations where it represents the EU within the so-called 'Troika' which it forms together with the current EU Presidency and the incoming EU

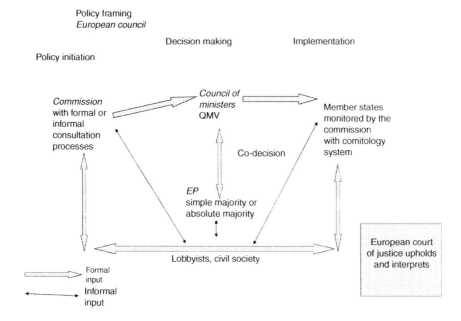

Figure 3.1 Making EU climate change policy.

Notes
1. Legal basis for climate action, Article 191 Treaty on the Functioning of the European Union (TFEU) ex Article 174 TEC.
2. Under the terms of the TFEU co-decision becomes the ordinary legislative procedure.

Presidency (see Chapter 5 by Oberthür and Dupont). The Commission's cognitive powers should also not be underestimated because climate change policy often requires a high degree of technical expertise. The Commission's structural powers (within the internal EU climate change policy-making process) are largely limited to its formal roles as the initiator of EU legislation and guardian of the EU Treaties during the implementation phase.

Box 3.1 Powers of the Commission, after Coombes (1970)

- Agenda setting
- Formal right to initiate legislation
- Consensus-building between the national governments, the EP and other interested parties and stakeholders
- Management of Commission programmes
- Representation of the EU in external (economic) relations
- Provides oversight and enforcement of European law
- Representation of the general interest of the EU.

The Commission continues as a bureaucracy but it has become more politicised in order to build consensus amongst the EU's 27 Member States. The Commission President provides the political leadership and overall direction within the Commission. Effective and/or radical climate policy proposals cannot come from the Commission without some measure of commitment from the President. The principle of the Commission President as *primus inter pares* within the College of Commissioners remains, but the role of the President has been more powerful. The Commission President is a member of the European Council. The President has competence for the management of the Commission and distribution of portfolios to individual Commissioners (Treaty of Amsterdam 1999). The position of the Commission President was enhanced through the differentiation of the election of the President by qualified majority voting (QMV) by the European Council and formal election by a majority of the EP (Treaty of Lisbon 2009). Within the Commission the Commission President therefore holds considerable structural leadership, although the College of Commissioners remains the nominees of the national governments whose appointment is ratified following a hearing in the EP. As shown below, some Commission Presidents have also managed to provide a high degree of entrepreneurial and cognitive leadership.

No single style of leadership (see Chapter 1 by Wurzel and Connelly) by the Commission's Presidents has dominated the period since the late 1980s when climate change gained a place on the political agenda of the EU. All Commission Presidents have demonstrated aspects of differing leadership styles and leadership types. Amongst the most important of the factors which have shaped the leadership of the Commission Presidents is their ability to influence the other core institutions and actors in the EU decision-making process. Because of the constraints imposed by the competences conferred on it the Commission President is unlikely to be able to exercise structural leadership without support from the Council and/or EP. The contribution of the

---

Box 3.2 Factors shaping the leadership style of the Commission President

- Belief in ability to influence the other actors and stakeholders in the EU's multi-level decision making
- Formal competencies conferred in the Treaties,
- Ability to achieve cohesion within the College of Commissioners
- 'Capture' of the leadership role by the European Council/Council of Ministers,
- Impact of changes to the powers and role of the European Parliament,
- Response of the Commission to enlargement,
- Context of the proposals, including commitment to the concept of ecological modernisation

Commission to the EU's approach to international climate change politics is most effective when the Commission President is able to provide clear direction to the Commission (heroic leadership) and actively supports the brokering of agreements amongst the national governments (entrepreneurial leadership).

Formal competences for providing leadership

The legal basis for action by the EU on climate change was initially provided through the introduction of an environmental chapter to the 1987 Single European Act (SEA) which amended the European Community Treaty (TEC). Climate change was included as part of the portfolio of the Environment Commissioner, a structure unchanged between 1987 and the ratification of the Lisbon Treaty. When it came into force on December 1st 2009 the Lisbon Treaty introduced an explicit reference to climate change for the first time (Article 191 (1) ex 174 TEC) which now commits the EU to '. . . promoting measures at international level to deal with regional or worldwide environmental problems and in particular combating climate change . . .'. Shared competence for climate change action between the national and supranational levels remained unaltered by the terms of the Lisbon Treaty.

When international commitments are accepted as EU policy the responsibility of the Commission is to ensure that all associated measures are implemented by all the Member States. As a result, measures to meet external commitments are not separate from internal climate change policy, but become a pillar of that policy. The Commission may not be able to propose radical initiatives on behalf of the EU in international climate change negotiations without a relevant mandate from the national governments. But this does not prevent the Commission from proposing radical initiatives for internal climate change policy. Nor does it prevent the Commission President and individual Commissioners from playing an active entrepreneurial leadership role in international climate change negotiations. Within the 'Troika' the Commission had the advantage of continuously being involved in the international climate change negotiations unlike the representation from the national governments which changed every six months (see Chapter 5 by Oberthür and Dupont).

The Commission is a non-state actor but has competence to be a signatory of the United Nations Framework Convention on Climate Change (UNFCCC) (1992) and the Kyoto Protocol (1997) on the basis of Article 24 (2) UNFCCC (see also Chapter 2 by Vogler). The Commission and Member State governments are not entitled to exercise concurrent responsibilities during negotiation. The role of the Commission is to exercise its competences to provide support and complementary actions to the European Council and/or Council in international climate change negotiations. The Commission therefore does not exercise formal political leadership for the EU in global climate change politics. Some Commission Presidents, Commissioners and senior Commission officials have been able to play a significant role in the international climate change negotiations because of their negotiating skills (i.e. entrepreneurial leadership) and ability to provide scientific expertise (i.e. cognitive leadership). President Barroso, Dimas, Environment Commissioner and 250 Commission officials, including the head of the climate change unit Directorate General (DG) Environment, were present during the Copenhagen climate change conference in 2009.

Leadership by the Commission President

The Commission is the EU institution which is charged with the formal initiation of policy. Its Commissioners serve under its President for five-year terms of office. The Commission, which was for long regarded as the motor for European integration, occupies a central node in the EU decision-making process. Theoretically the Commission should be able to provide long-term political leadership and introduce the innovative policy developments which Wurzel and Connelly (Chapter 1) highlight as of importance to meet the challenges of international climate change. But the Commission's ability to provide (structural, entrepreneurial and cognitive) leadership is severely constrained by its limited formal competences and other factors which are beyond its control (Peterson 2005: 15). This does not mean that the Commission is not prepared to make radical policy proposals and to adopt a heroic leadership style. But the credibility of the institution would be undermined if policy measures were repeatedly proposed which were not accepted by the Council and the EP. Those Commission proposals for internal climate change policy most likely to succeed are those which have support of at least some of the national governments. The Commission will then seek to build up the level of support until such time as the required level of national government and EP support is reached. Legislative instruments which are based on co-decision procedures and QMV in the Council allow the Commission a greater range of options when forming coalitions of support for measures.

Jacques Delors (1985–94) was seen as the exemplar of a president who often adopted a heroic leadership style during his successive presidencies. He sought to achieve long-term goals by ambitious assertion of his political will (Cini 2008; Drake 2000). He demonstrated cognitive leadership, gaining support from national leaders for innovative new ideas, through his mastery of the policy portfolios and the clear sense of direction he gave to the Commission. Delors also provided considerable entrepreneurial leadership by striking deals with national government after tireless negotiations with top national political leaders (Drake 2000). Delors did not only provide cognitive and entrepreneurial leadership for the Commission but he also exercised structural political leadership on behalf of the EU, while he gained an international reputation as the 'face' of the Union.

But leadership by Delors was less apparent in developing climate change policy. Delors found it more difficult to mobilise support from the national governments or achieve cohesion within the College of Commissioners in this policy arena. The Fourth Environmental Action Programme (EAP) introduced by the Commission in 1987 did not make reference to climate change. The EAP had contained reference to ensuring national implementation. Delors did not support the subsequent aggressive stance Ripa di Meana, Environment Commissioner, took towards national infringement of EU environmental legislation. Delors considered di Meana's actions to be contrary to the principle of subsidiarity as adopted in the SEA.

The Commission Communication on the Greenhouse Effect and the Community (COM (88) 656 final) did not outline policy options, but was a programme to evaluate policy options. However, by 1991 the Commission had produced a strategy to limit carbon dioxide (CO_2) emissions and improve energy efficiency:

1   Framework directive on energy efficiency (SAVE)
2   Decision on renewables (ALTENER)
3   Decision on a monitoring mechanism for CO_2 emissions
4   Directive to introduce a carbon/energy tax within the EU.

The most controversial element proposed by Ripa di Meana was the carbon/energy tax to target external environmental costs from energy usage and curb greenhouse gas emissions. Delors supported the proposal as part of the 'traditional' desire of the Commission to expand its competences. It was opposed by Scrivener, Taxation Commissioner, who was supported by a strong industrial lobby concerned that the proposal would undermine industrial competitiveness. Although the Commission amended the proposal to exempt the energy-intensive industries, it remained unsupported by the national governments. The UK and France considered it was an attempt by the unelected executive of the EU to undermine national sovereignty and it was eventually dropped in 1994. The SAVE and ALTENER initiatives retained a considerable level of discretion for the national governments with regard to their quantitative objectives and were adopted.

As the international community began preparations for the 1992 UN Rio 'Earth' Summit the disagreements between Ripa di Meana and Delors intensified. Di Meana resigned immediately prior to the Rio summit. Delors' disagreements with di Meana and Scrivener demonstrated his lack of political leadership and ability to develop cohesion within the Commission on climate measures. In contrast to his heroic leadership style on market integration, his leadership on the emerging climate change agenda was more prosaic and low key (consistent with the humdrum style of leadership). The disagreements within the Commission weakened proposals for common measures for the EU to reach the stabilisation targets agreed during the Rio summit. Instead the main element of the EU's policy remained the mechanism for monitoring and reporting on CO_2 emissions. However, Delors strongly supported the inclusion of a chapter in the Commission's White Paper on *Growth, Competi-*

tiveness, Employment (CEC 1993) which argues that stringent environmental measures may also be beneficial for the economy (CEC 1993).

Delors was succeeded in 1995 by Jacques Santer (1995–99) whose style of leadership of the Commission was humdrum. Santer began a process of devolution of powers to the Commissioners but was unable to provide the strategic focus and direction needed to ensure that devolved responsibilities were exercised effectively. Lack of leadership from the President did not prevent policy proposals but it undermined the potential of radical proposals. Santer's Presidency quickly became characterised by confrontation between himself, the members of his Commission, with the EP and latterly between Santer and the trade unions representing Commission officials. At the same time Santer could not rely on the support of the national governments for his proposed procedural reforms.

For Santer the first confrontation with the EP in the environmental arena came during the newly introduced procedures of Commission investiture hearings before the EP. When he outlined his programme on January 17th, 1995, Santer committed himself to 'do less but do it better' and he identified environmental policy as a priority for his Commission. His subsequent appointment of Ritt Bjerregaard to the Environment portfolio was controversial. The Chair of the EP Environment Committee, Ken Collins, commented that if she was representative of the whole Commission the EP would have to vote against its investiture (Europe Environment 1995a). But this criticism did not prevent Santer's Commission being accepted and it came into office on January 23rd, 1995. Almost immediately in October 1995 Bjerregaard caused further controversy leading to grave concerns about her ability to work with Santer and her colleagues.[1]

At the first Conference of the Parties (COP 1) meeting (Berlin 1995), the signatories of the UNFCCC had concluded that their 1992 commitments to greenhouse gas emission (GHGE) reduction were too vague and should be strengthened. Despite their differences of opinion, Bjerregaard was able to work with Monti (Internal Market and Taxation Commissioner), Cresson (Research) and Papoutsis (Energy) to prepare the EU's strategy for the Kyoto COP 3 negotiations (1997) but this was achieved without evident direction from Santer. The Commission's proposed strategy was a cut in emissions of the three most damaging GHGs by 15 per cent by 2015. DG Environment provided estimates that such a cut would impose a cost to the European economy of 0.2–0.4 per cent total GDP in 2010 if existing technology was used. The EU's national governments would agree to the 15 per cent reduction target only if it was matched by other major industrialised states. Reductions for the European states were to come from the Community as a whole. The national governments did not determine how this would be managed at the time of the Kyoto negotiations.

The international community decided to compromise during the Kyoto negotiations. The UNFCCC signatories agreed an overall 5.2 per cent reduction of emissions from six GHGs but with differing targets for different states. The EU appeared to enhance its position of global leadership by being prepared to adopt the more ambitious target of an overall 8 per cent reduction. Within the EU the loss of control by Santer, evident in the preparations for the Kyoto negotiations, was seen in other policy areas. Factionalism within the College of Commissioners increased, contributing to a lack of control of their individual portfolios by the Commissioners. At the beginning of 1998 a Committee of Independent Experts was established by the EP to investigate suspicions of Commission fraud and financial mismanagement. Its first report was published in March 1999 and the whole Commission, led by Santer, subsequently resigned.

The period following the adoption of the Kyoto Protocol was one of difficulty and loss of credibility for the Commission. Although the Commission retained its policy initiator role, the outcome of Delors' lack of leadership and Santer's ineptitude was that the EU's climate change policy by the end of the 1990s appeared little more than a '. . . collection of incentive, informative and co-ordinating measures without any real constraining effect . . .' (Peeters and Deketelaere 2006: 45). When the Americans refused to support the Kyoto Protocol the Council continued the EU's commitment to ratify it. The Commission was subsequently mandated to begin work to introduce appropriate instruments.

When Romano Prodi became President in 1999 he seemed to lack the charisma and ability to provide heroic leadership. Despite strong support within the EU to ratify the Kyoto Protocol, there was disagreement within the Commission between Environment Commissioner Wallström and Energy Commissioner de Palacio. De Palacio raised concerns about the economic costs of limiting GHGE in line with the Kyoto Protocol. She questioned the wisdom of implementing Kyoto if Russia failed to ratify the agreement. Prodi publicly rebuked de Palacio. He reinforced the importance of unity in the Commission to support the EU's leadership in international climate change politics. This signalled the Commission's return to a more proactive role in the preparation of a common climate change policy. The initiatives proposed by Wallström, supported by Prodi, focused on a mix of measures and approaches including market-based initiatives to replace the failed proposal for the carbon/energy tax.

The EU's Climate Change Programme (ECCP), introduced by the Commission in 2000, was criticised by the EP because it lacked ambition and contained few legislative proposals. The proposals were also weakened by the national governments. But the importance of the ECCP and its 2005 successor was that the national governments accepted Commission proposals for more flexible mechanisms and measures to target production and consumption of energy and transport use. It also represented a shift in focus to ensure that policy initiatives were more directed and targeting specific areas of the economy

The EU's Emissions Trading Scheme (ETS), which came into force from 2005, was the most far-reaching of the Commission's legislative proposals on climate change. It shows that the Commission can provide cognitive and entrepreneurial leadership even if some Member States (e.g. Germany) initially opposed its proposal for an EU-wide ETS (see also Chapter 8 by Jänicke). Commission President Prodi showed evidence of entrepreneurial leadership as he garnered support from the Commission where concerns about loss of competitiveness had been raised. He also had the support of the national governments for the ETS as the Danish and UK governments had introduced national schemes and the possibility of distortion of the European market had grown. For the Commission the proposal represented a change to the underlying paradigm which the Commission had supported as the most effective way of curbing CO_2 emissions. Unlike the carbon/energy tax which had required unanimous agreement from the national governments, the ETS was introduced using co-decision procedures including QMV in the Council. The Commission therefore had more opportunity to mobilise support for the initiative.

There were radical aspects to the proposed ETS, the most notable being the auctioning of all permitted allowances. The Commission was unable to gain support for the auctioning of allowances from the Member State governments who instead insisted on the free allocation of allowances during the first phase of the EU ETS (2005–8). This did not represent a failure of the Commission to provide cognitive and entrepreneurial leadership. Member State governments accepted the auctioning of parts of the emission allowances in the second phase of the EU ETS (2008–12). As the principle of emissions trading formed a crucial element of the agreements of the international community in the Kyoto Protocol, the introduction of the scheme in advance of the global trading scheme signalled the EU's global leadership ambitions.

The Barroso Commission I came into office in 2004 at the same time as an unprecedented wave of EU enlargement began. The Commission increased in size to 25 (2004) and then to 27 (2007) Commissioners, presenting challenges for cohesion within the College. Initially Barroso favoured incremental action, departing little from existing policies against the context of the political situation of the enlarged EU. He identified a number of priorities on which to work closely with the relevant Commissioners and Directorates-General, but this did not include action on climate change. Barroso was criticised by environmental organisations for giving economic development priority – a view which he appeared to reinforce in his 'three sick children speech' in 2005 when he emphasised jobs and growth, not environmental policy (Barroso 2005).

From 2007 a 'sea-change' in Barroso's approach came as heightened concern about energy security gained prominence on the EU's policy agenda. Barroso's belief in his ability to exert influence on the other EU policy actors and stakeholders increased. As Commission President his style of leadership became more heroic as he gave much clearer direction to the climate change policy agenda (Peterson and Birdsall 2008; Missiroli 2009). Within the Commission, close collaboration between Environment Commissioner

Diinas and Energy Commissioner Piebalgs was evident throughout the Barroso I Presidency, and a number of communications combining energy and climate change were adopted.

By the time of the European Council in March 2007, a political consensus on the importance of increased action on climate change mitigation had emerged within the EU and agreement on the 20 per cent by 2020 targets outlined by the Commission. These targets were based on Commission assessments that curbing the rise of global temperature by 2 degrees centigrade could be achieved at a cost remaining under 0.5 per cent of GDP a year by 2050 and that inaction would impose a cost of 5–20 per cent of global GDP (HM Treasury 2006). The EU states also agreed to the Commission proposal that commitment to a 30 per cent GHGE reduction should be made if other developed states agreed and the more advanced developing countries also made a contribution. Internally, despite the continued ambition of the EU to be a leader in the Copenhagen climate change conference negotiations of 2009, the targets proved controversial. Barroso's proposal that the EU adopt the overall target, but for the internal distribution of action to be decided during 2009, was accepted.

On 29–30th October 2009 the Heads of State and Government met to establish the EU's negotiating position for the Copenhagen summit. Barroso presented a number of estimates that the total costs of supporting mitigation and adaptation measures in the developing countries could amount to 100 billion euros by 2020 and that of this total between 22 and 50 billion euros of international public support would be needed. The Commission proposal was that between 2 billion and 15 billion euros per year of this public support should come from the EU. The Council endorsed the estimates from the Commission and proposed a comprehensive global distribution mechanism should be established based on emission levels and GDP reflecting the ability of a developing country to pay by the international community. But the national governments could not reach agreement on the specifics of the EU's contribution, instead indicating that the EU would contribute its fair share to the international efforts. The Council stressed the need for a legally binding agreement for the period following 1st January 2013 to follow the Kyoto Protocol and renewed the EU's commitments to cutting GHGEs by 20 per cent and 30 per cent if this was supported by the international community.

The Barroso I Commission ended its period in office on October 31st 2009. As a result of the delays to the ratification of the Lisbon Treaty the Barroso I Commission maintained a 'caretaker' role until the investiture of the Barroso II Commission was completed. Barroso presented an outline of political guidelines for his new Commission to the European Parliament in September 2009. In it he focused on the need to move to a low carbon economy, based on greater energy efficiency and wider use of renewable energy resources in order to stimulate economic growth, create jobs and curb climate change. Problems ensued during the investiture and appointment of the Barroso II

Commission in early 2010, which was delayed until the EP vote held in February. In turn this delayed the preparation of the EU strategy to respond to the failure to achieve a legally binding agreement at the Copenhagen COP summit and proposals for an EU energy efficiency strategy. Barroso appeared to remain committed to a more heroic leadership style, supportive of cognitive and entrepreneurial leadership from the Commission in the climate change policy arena. The Barroso II Commission created new administrative capacities (for providing entrepreneurial and cognitive leadership in particular) by establishing a new DG for Climate Action (DG CLIM) which is headed by Commissioner Connie Hedegaard (formerly Danish Environment Minister who had chaired sessions of the Copenhagen climate change conference in 2009).

Ecological modernisation and policy instruments

The Commission DG for Environment was not established until the late 1960s. Initially it was rather weak and ineffective, predominantly staffed by individuals recruited on the basis of their environmental credentials rather than from the mainstream of Commission officials. A number of factors coincided in the 1980s and the concept of ecological modernisation became an important aspect of policy discourse and the 'belief system' of the institution. The SEA also committed the EU to inclusion of environmental objectives in all sectoral policies. The appointment of di Meana as Environment Commissioner in 1989 marked a considerable step forward in bringing environmental concerns into the mainstream of economic integration policy. Climate change per se had not been a priority for the Delors I and II Commissions, but the introduction of the Fifth EAP in 1992 gave it prominence, identifying climate change as one of seven priority objectives.

As a result the Commission was provided with an opportunity to initiate a wider range of policy instruments, not relying solely on regulatory control, seen in the ECCPs. The Commission's first proposal for a market-based environmental policy instrument constituted its 1991 proposal for a carbon/energy tax which had been championed by the Environmental Commissioner Ripa di Meana at a time of high public environmental awareness (see above). However, the Commission's carbon/energy tax proposal was vetoed by Britain on sovereignty grounds (see Chapter 6 by Rayner and Jordan). Although providing less heroic leadership on climate change policy during his terms as Commission President, ecological modernisation was a dominant paradigm underpinning the *White Paper on Growth, Competitiveness and Employment* produced under direction of Delors in 1993. In it proposals were made to decouple economic prosperity from environmental deterioration through the creation of new clean technologies and the use of market-based policy instruments (such as eco-taxes) as a mechanism to overcome high levels of unemployment in the EU of the early 1990s (CEC 1993:146–48).

By 1995 support had grown in the international community for measures to strengthen the commitments of the UNFCCC. The Kyoto Protocol established GHGE trading as an instrument to combat global climate change. The Commission highlighted the problem of lack of EU progress on the commitments made in Rio and concluded that although there was considerable technical potential to limit GHGE, more ambitious measures were needed. In the early 1990s the Commission had been a reluctant supporter of emissions trading, preferring instead eco-taxes in the form of the above-mentioned carbon/energy tax. When it became apparent that some national governments did not support the adoption of EU eco-taxes, which required unanimous decision-making, the DG Environment began to focus on proposals for the EU ETS which could be adopted under qualified majority rules (see also Chapter 1 by Wurzel and Connelly and Chapter 5 by Oberthür and Dupont).

The EU ETS has become the cornerstone of internal policy demonstrating to the global community that transnational action is possible. It was based on a compulsory cap and trade scheme but did not stipulate national caps. Instead the national governments were asked to provide national allocation plans (NAPs) demonstrating how the allocations to the national companies would contribute to the overall objectives of the EU reduction targets under the Kyoto Protocol. During the first phase a number of innovations were introduced to enable the scheme to work, which included monitoring of NAPs by the Commission. In excess of 10,000 industrial installations (including power stations, oil refineries and steel mills) producing approaching 50 per cent of the total CO_2 emissions in the EU were targeted by the scheme (CEC 2008). But the first trading phase was undermined by national governments' overly generous allocation of allowances and the carbon market collapsed to almost zero in 2007. When the NAPs were presented to DG Environment for the second phase of the EU ETS, Environment Commissioner Dimas increased pressure on the national governments to reduce the number of allowances and the price of carbon was sustained at a higher level in 2008. The Commission clearly presented the scheme as a model for others to follow and is sympathetic to the idea that it might be linked with similar schemes elsewhere (e.g. America).

The concept of ecological modernisation became more important for the Commission's policy proposals towards the end of the Barroso I Commission. It was only in the proposed revisions of Lisbon Strategy for Growth and Jobs (initially devoid of explicit references to environmental protection) in 2005 that the Commission highlighted the link between job creation and support for the introduction of new technologies to mitigate climate change. Creating a positive ecological-economic relationship underpinned the package of climate and energy measures to achieve the targets of the '20% by 2020' agreement (CEC 2008). The proposal for a climate and energy package, the result of work by Piebalgs and Dimas, was presented to the Spring European Council by Barroso. The result of their collaboration was ambitious (House of Lords (HoL) 2008: 87). It included proposals to strengthen and extend the ETS, including full auctioning of emissions allowances to the power sector, with full auctioning introduced into other industrial sectors by 2020. Major transport sectors such as aviation and maritime transport were also targeted. Barroso confirmed the commitment to ecological modernisation in 2009 when he stated that the major public investment programmes being introduced to combat the global financial and economic recession of the late 2000s could stimulate innovation, foster growth and create jobs while reducing global GHG emissions and saving energy costs (CEC 2009: 1).

Multi-level governance and the response of the Commission

Although there may be a single formal source for a proposal, the Commission, there is no single source for the ideas upon which it is based. Successive Commissions have developed a number of formal and informal processes and structures to enable dialogue with various actors to take place. Delors convened a group of close advisors known as the 'cellule de perspective' who worked with him on the big projects of the SEA, the Single Market, the Maastricht Treaty and the *White Paper on Growth*. This suited his heroic style of leadership at a time when the Commission was small and national governments appeared willing to allow the Commission President to assume the identity of 'Mr Europe'. In contrast, Santer introduced a strategy of forming groups of Commissioners to deal with specific issues across portfolios. But the Santer groups acted as little more than a mechanism to improve communication between the Commissioners.

At the beginning of his term in office Prodi proposed an inner cabinet of ten vice-presidents for the Commission. This was rejected by most EU Member States and several of the Commissioners, e.g Kinnock and Patten (Peterson 2005). Enlargement in 2004/7 brought more coordination problems. Barroso returned to the strategy of forming groups or clusters of Commissioners to deal with specific issues with cross-sectoral dimensions. Initially five clusters were established, dealing with the Lisbon agenda, competitiveness, external relations, anti-discrimination and equal opportunities, and communication and programming. A cluster dealing with climate change, sustainable development and energy was added from 2007. This provided opportunities for Barroso to exercise heroic leadership and adopt a more hands-on approach through his chairing of the groups. The clusters were not intended to take decisions on behalf of the Commission, but to provide the policy input and guidance now needed in the larger Commission.

The hierarchical internal structuring of the Commission DGs developed on largely functional lines in accordance with the Monnet method of decision-making. The structure was maintained as a result of increased responsibilities for the Commission following phases of enlargement, increased numbers of policy issues, and incremental (often ad hoc) reforms responding to specific problems. It posed challenges in the development of initiatives to deal with climate action which require a cross-sectoral approach. Delors established a unit specifically focusing on climate change in DG Environment, but lack of communication between it and other DGs was of sufficient concern to be identified in the Fifth EAP as a target for action.

Within the Santer Commission an inter-service group from the DGs responsible for initiatives affected by climate change was established. However, this did not become a catalyst for serious integration of the different administrations of the Commission. The organisational structures of the DGs were the subject of reforms under the direction of Kinnock during the Prodi Commission. The focus of these reforms was to ensure that accountability was increased following the criticisms of the Santer Commission. Removing the hierarchical and vertically structured divisions between the DGs to enable more effective cross-sectoral climate change policy was not addressed.

Unlike the group of personal advisors Delors gathered around him, Barroso established a Bureau of Policy Advisors whose remit was to assist the President, the College of Commission and Commission services, in defining Commission annual policy and its Legislative and Work Programme. Within this Bureau an energy and climate change advisory working group, which included Sir Nicholas Stern, was convened from 2007. An inter-service coordination group of officials from a number of DGs began to convene in 2008 on an ad hoc basis but with meetings becoming monthly in 2009 as the preparations for the Copenhagen CoP intensified. The DGs represented in this inter-service group came predominantly from the DGs for Environment, Development, Transport and Energy, Research, Enterprise and Economic and Financial Affairs, although it was open to participation from all DGs. Criticisms may be made of the role and powers of these structures but they did enable more openness within the Commission and discussion between the relevant DGs.

Changes which Barroso made to the structure of the Commission for his second term included introducing a Commissioner for Climate Action and establishing DG CLIM. Creating a climate action portfolio was controversial as it involved moving units responsible for climate action from DG Environment, the activities related to international negotiations on climate change from DG External Relations and also units related to climate change from DG Enterprise and Industry. Concerns were raised that these changes would undermine the levels of expertise and competences in the arena of climate change action which the Commission had developed within DG Environment.

The Commission and societal actors

Proposals by the Commission emerge as a result of pressure from a number of directions – the stakeholders, the other institutions or from within the Commission itself, the necessity to respond to international commitments (e.g. re-negotiating the Kyoto Protocol post-2012), and/or wider public and media debate which has been very influential in helping to build the political momentum for action on climate change. Before initiating policy, one of the Commission's duties is to consult with a wide of interests, pressure groups, stakeholders to ensure that proposals are sound. In the early phases of policy preparation structures have been developed to bring the stakeholders together in open forum, seminars or conferences in addition to formal technical committees and working groups. None of these groups has formal competence as a scientific advisory body for the EU on the most effective instruments to introduce in internal climate change policy. That is the role of the European Environment Agency (EEA), established in the early 1990s. Other sources include input of information from the IPCC reports, the 2006 Stern Review and commissioned scientific reports.

The Commission, a small organisation compared with many national administrative bodies, is heavily reliant on the input of the pressure groups and lobbyists. Environmental interest groups (including those involved in climate change) are considered to be amongst the most effective and influential. The European Environment Bureau (EEB), a transnational grouping of ENGOs, has received support from the Commission since it was established in 1974 (see Chapter 13 by Wurzel and Connelly). More recent Commissions (particularly Barroso's) have not maintained as close a relationship with the EEB as the Delors Commissions of the early 1990s. Nevertheless it provides an important information resource for DG Environment. The interests of the business lobby have also dominated much discussion of policy instruments (see Chapter 12 by Grant). Many of the industrial sectors which are major producers of GHGEs oppose measures which they perceive will lead to a lack of competitiveness. This inevitably leads to tension with the Commission.

Conclusion

Policy in the EU is the result of complex negotiations and consensus building between large numbers of actors with differing interests to be taken into account. The argument of this chapter is that the Commission is the institution which is able to provide entrepreneurial leadership in the EU by facilitating and brokering agreements between these interests. The effectiveness of the contribution made by the Commission relies on the way in which the competences of the institution are exercised particularly the formal right of initiation of policy following agreement within the College of Commissioners (without a formal proposal there would be no legislation!). In order to perform an entrepreneurial leadership role the Commission requires someone as President to give the institution political leadership and direction. It has been argued that as successive Commission presidents have demonstrated heroic (Barroso) or humdrum (Santer) leadership style, the effectiveness of the Commission as an entrepreneurial leader has also varied. The Commission has also provided cognitive leadership, as can be seen from its proposal for an EU ETS which was adopted by the Council and EP within a period of less than two years. However, the Commission's ability to offer structural leadership has remained highly constrained by its competences under the EU Treaties.

The Delors Commissions were led by a charismatic leader who provided a heroic leadership style on issues such as the completion of the internal market and support for the introduction of the single currency, but climate change was not a priority amongst the big projects he initiated and supported. During the Delors Presidencies the provision of cognitive and entrepreneurial leadership on climate change was therefore largely left to the Environmental Commissioner and senior DG Environment officials. The Santer Commission was in office as global interest in climate change intensified and the Kyoto Protocol was negotiated. But Santer's lack of authority over the Commission led to a period of limited achievement in EU climate change measures. The Prodi Commission was led by an individual considered to lack charisma but who nonetheless ensured that disagreements within the Commission did not undermine the response of national governments to the Kyoto Protocol. As a result the Commission provided both entrepreneurial and cognitive leadership, resulting in the development of the ETS. On other issues such as the ECCP the Prodi Commission was not able to exercise the same level of entrepreneurial leadership because of the requirements to implement other long-term strategies, including the preparations for the 2004/7 enlargement.

The Barroso I Commission was initially constrained by the impact of enlargement on the size of the College of Commissioners and subsequently the difficulties associated with renewing the TEU. By linking climate change to job creation and energy security the Barroso I Commission acquired a new dynamism and ambition. The Lisbon Treaty (in force since 2009) introduced a commitment to climate change and also gave additional weight to the development of measures targeting energy usage. The roles formally conferred on the Commission were not altered by the Lisbon Treaty, but the balance between its competences has altered as more emphasis is given to ensuring that all commitments are implemented. This does not mean that that Commission will not make radical proposals in the future.

Prior to the 2009 Copenhagen climate conference Barroso had reminded EU leaders of the urgency and necessity of maintaining the ambition to take action on climate change irrespective of what the global community might decide (CEC 2009). Barroso demonstrated his commitment to entrepreneurial leadership on the issue of climate change through his appointment of a Commissioner for Climate Action. The new structure for DG CLIM, including the unit responsible for international policy developments, has raised the profile of the role played by the Commission during international climate change negotiations. The introduction of the position of High Representative of the Union for Foreign Affairs and Security, combined with the position of Vice-President of the Commission, increased the input of the Commission in the EU's international diplomacy. As the High Representative's portfolio of activities includes support for the developing world to respond to the problems of political instability resulting from climate change, it will arguably enhance the contribution of the Commission in international climate change politics. However, the ability of the Commission to use these new competences and arrangements remains dependent on the leadership given to the institution by its President and the ability of the Commission to facilitate and broker agreements amongst the various policy actors.

Note

1 In a book she had written (without consulting Santer), serialised in the Danish national press, she criticised Santer, other fellow Commissioners, and some heads of the EU governments.

Bibliography

Barroso, J. M. (2005) 'Working Together for Growth and Jobs: A New Start for the Lisbon Strategy', speech to Conference of Presidents, Brussels, European Parliament, 02.02.2005.

CEC (2008) *20 20 by 2020: Europe's Climate Change Opportunity*, COM (2008) 30 final, Brussels.

CEC (2009) *Towards a Comprehensive Climate Change Agreement in Copenhagen*, draft, 28.01.09, Brussels.

Cini, M. (2008) 'Political Leadership in the European Commission: The Santer and Prodi Commissions, 1995–2005', in J. Hayward (ed.), *Leaderless Europe*, Oxford: Oxford University Press 113–30.

Commission of the European Communities (CEC) (1993) *Growth, Competitiveness and Employment*, COM (93) 700 final, Brussels.

Drake, H. (2000), *Jacques Delors, Perspectives on a European Leader*, London: Routledge.

Europe Environment (1995b) *Climate Change: EU Commissioner Reports to MEPs on Berlin*, HighBeam Research, <http://www.highbeam.com> (accessed 12.0.2009).

Hayward, J. (2008) 'Strategic Innovation by Insider Influence: Monnet to Delors', in Hayward, J. (ed.), *Leaderless Europe*, Oxford: Oxford University Press, 15–27.

HM Treasury, (2006) *The Stern Review on the Economics of Climate Change*, available online at <http://www.hm-treasury.gov.uk/sternreview_index.htm>

House of Lords (HoL) (2008) *Initiation of EU Legislation*. London: The Stationery Office. EU Committee, 22nd Report Session 2007–8, 24th July.

Missiroli, A. (2009) *The next Commission President: Tips for the President-elect*, EPC Policy Brief, April available online at <http://www.epc.eu>

Peeters, M. and Deketelaere, K. eds. (2006) *EU Climate Change Policy*, Cheltenham: Edward Elgar.

Peterson, J. (2005) *The Enlarged European Commission*, Paris, Policy Paper number 11, Notre Europe, available online at <http://www.notre-europe.eu/en/>

Peterson, J. and Birdsall, A (2008) 'The European Commission; Enlargement as Re-invention?', in E. Best, *et al.* (eds), *The Governance of the Wider Europe: EU Enlargement and Institutional Change*, Cheltenham: Edward Elgar.

Spence, D. with Edwards, G. (2006) *The European Commission*, London: John Harper Publishing.

4 The European Parliament and climate change

From symbolism to heroism and back again[1]

Charlotte Burns and Neil Carter

Introduction

The European Parliament (EP) has historically had limited scope to shape the EU's climate change policy as the lead has traditionally been taken by the Commission and Council. The Parliament has a circumscribed *de jure* role in international environmental politics: under Article 218 of the Treaty on the Functioning of the European Union it has a right to be consulted by the Council and in some circumstances may offer its formal assent to international agreements to which the EU is party. But the EP has limited ability to shape negotiations. Consequently, although the EP has sent delegations to international events such as the regular Conference of Parties (COP) meetings on climate change and issued reports and resolutions for the attention of the other institutions,[2] its policy impact has been limited, a fact reflected in the literature on the EU and climate change where the EP is barely mentioned and then only in passing (e.g. Wettestad 2005; Schreurs and Tibergien 2007; Oberthür and Roche-Kelly 2008). Thus, while the EP is keen to present itself as a leader within EU environmental politics more generally, it has, until recently, been a bystander within the specific field of climate change. However, the concurrence of its increased powers in the form of codecision, together with the development of the EU's Emission Trading Scheme (ETS) and the parallel package of legislation, offered the Parliament a unique opportunity to shape the future direction and ambition of EU climate change policy.

The EP has typically sought to exercise cognitive and entrepreneurial leadership but its leadership style has typically been symbolic (Hayward 2008): it has sought to shape policy through its debates and non-legislative resolutions, which allow it to air ideas but do little to alter the substance of policy or to shape the structure of incentives faced by the key policy actors. However, the EP's increased institutional power opened a window of opportunity for it to shift from this rhetorical approach to a more heroic style as it sought to tighten and strengthen the climate change and energy package that was adopted by the EP and Council in late 2008. Yet, the Parliament found itself the victim of events beyond its control, and its ability to move the legislation towards its own preferences was circumscribed. The EP therefore fell back into its traditional role of offering symbolic leadership through the Temporary Committee on Climate Change, which provided it with a platform for making policy pronouncements but had no legislative force. Below, first we outline the EP's role as an environmental actor, before evaluating its attempts to exercise leadership over time through amending key legislative proposals and establishing the Temporary Committee on Climate Change. We then briefly discuss what this case study tells us about the EP's position on ecological modernisation and whether climate change has presented the Parliament with an opportunity to exercise leadership on the international stage.

The EP as an environmental actor

The EP has developed a reputation over the years of being the EU's 'environmental champion' (Weale *et al.* 2000; Burns 2005; Burns and Carter 2010); it 'often sees itself, and is seen by others, as the defender of environmental interests' (Weale *et al.* 2000: 91), and has performed an 'important leadership role' in relation to certain environment policies (Zito 2000: 4). The EP's scope to offer a traditional leadership role has been limited by its institutional location: it is essentially a reactive chamber that amends policy proposals put forward by the Commission, and must negotiate with the Council to see its preferences realised in the final legislative text (see Zito 2000; Judge and Earnshaw 2008). Nevertheless, the Parliament has consistently endeavoured to shape and strengthen EU environmental policy, deploying entrepreneurial leadership approaches to achieve its political ambitions (Zito 2000). Over the years the EP's Environment Committee has built close relations with officials in the Commission's DG Environment, in the Council and with the wider policy community of business and NGOs in order to shape the policy agenda (e.g. Judge 1992; Hubschmid and Moser 1997).

With the advent of codecision in 1993, the EP became better placed to shape legislation. Under codecision (or, as it is now known, the ordinary legislative procedure) the EP is able to act as a co-legislator with the Council – taking responsibility for negotiating joint texts with the Member State representatives and having ultimate power of veto if the negotiations do not produce an acceptable compromise (Shackleton and Raunio 2003) Between 1993 and 2006 the Environment Committee was the 'largest customer' of codecision legislation within the Parliament (EP 1999, 2004, 2006a).[3] As such the personnel on the Committee – which has the reputation of being more ambitious than the EP's plenary (EP 2006a: 4–5) – have been able to secure important compromises in relation to car emissions and consumer and health legislation (EP 1999; also see Friedrich *et al.* 2000). Indeed, the entrepreneurship of key individuals and the relative radicalism of the Environment Committee seem to have been critical in cementing the EP's reputation as an environmental leader.

The EP's evolving leadership in climate change politics

Yet, notwithstanding the EP's growing legislative stature and its skill in exploiting available resources, the Parliament's role in international negotiations is still limited by the Treaties, which allocate responsibility for negotiating international agreements to the Commission and Council. Hence, while the EP can play a significant role by amending legislation that has an impact on climate change, its ability to shape directly the position adopted by the EU in international negotiations is circumscribed. The EP's attempts to exercise leadership within the field of climate change therefore falls into two distinct phases: first, the1990s to 2001 when, despite the EP's attempts to offer cognitive leadership, its lack of structural power limited it to rhetoric only (the position adopted here is that leadership involves not only attempting to shape the agenda and policy but also being successful in that attempt); second, from 2001 to the present, when the EP's increased structural power under codecision opened a window of opportunity for the EP to offer cognitive leadership on core issues relating to the use of particular policy instruments to deliver climate change emission reduction targets and entrepreneurial leadership by establishing a new institutional forum (the Temporary Committee on Climate Change) to address the issue of climate change.

Phase 1: symbolic leadership

In the 1990s the structural constraints (lack of formal institutional power) that the EP faced in this field meant that its leadership was purely symbolic: it offered statements and resolutions in the run up to COP meetings, and statements afterwards delivering its verdict on the outcome of negotiations, but it was unable to influence international negotiations in any substantive way. Indeed, the EP, in its resolutions relating to international conferences, consistently complained about the EP delegation being excluded from key meetings and not being consulted (see, for example, EP 2000, 2002a, 2002b, 2006b). During this period the EP's approach was therefore based upon calling for the ratification of Kyoto, for the Commission and Council to offer leadership on the international stage, for the Commission to bring forward legislation to implement the Kyoto targets and chiding the United States for withdrawing from the Protocol (EP 1998a, 1998b, 2002a, 2002b). The EP also supported the Commission's attempts to promote the climate change agenda through the use of new instruments such as the carbon dioxide (CO_2)/energy tax, which the EP consistently supported (see, for example, EP 1998b), although the Parliament was much more sceptical about the use of voluntary agreements, such as that between the Commission and car manufacturers to reduce carbon emissions (ibid.). The EP has also consistently questioned the use of the Clean Development Mechanism (CDM) and Joint Implementation (JI) mechanism of the Kyoto Protocol in its resolutions on climate negotiations. Like several Member States, the EP's position was not based upon denying the potential utility of such instruments, but upon pointing out that these approaches should be used in addition to, rather than instead of, other more traditional means of cutting carbon emissions, such as regulation (e.g. see EP 2002b).

In addition to these statements of principle that, as Schreurs and Tiberghien (2007) point out, reinforced the Commission's attempts to offer leadership in the field, the EP also used its legislative powers under codecision consistently to tighten legislative proposals that limited emissions of greenhouse gas, such as the auto-oil programme which sought to combine regulation of emissions from cars with new rules on fuel quality standards. However, it should be noted that between 1993 and 1999 the EP could only offer opinions under codecision on proposals brought forward under the single market provisions of the Treaty, which limited its scope to shape proposals falling under the environmental provisions of the Treaty. The revisions of the Amsterdam Treaty in 1999 extended codecision to most environmental policy (excluding land use planning, water management and fiscal measures), thereby widening the scope of the EP's competence. Thus, once the Commission started bringing forward proposals to implement the EU's Kyoto targets, a window of leadership opportunity opened for the Parliament.

Phase 2: 2001 onwards – the window of leadership opportunity

Eight key pieces of legislation adopted since 2001 provided the foundation for the EU's putative leadership in international climate change negotiations: the initial ETS directive; the extension of ETS to aviation; and six pieces of legislation that comprised the climate change and energy package, encompassing five directives covering the extension of ETS, effort-sharing, Carbon Capture and Storage (CCS), renewable energy, and fuel quality, and a regulation on limiting CO_2 emissions from cars. As all these proposals were subject to codecision, the EP had the opportunity to amend their content and thereby help to strengthen standards within the EU as well as to consolidate the EU's wider leadership role on the international stage. On each proposal the EP adopted a consistent stance based upon strengthening standards and, where appropriate, introducing elements of auctioning into the ETS.

Emissions trading and aviation

The passage of the initial emissions trading directive was adopted quite quickly with little substantive change to the initial proposal (Wettestad 2005). One of the EP's main contributions to this proposal and subsequent amendments to the ETS was to introduce an auctioning requirement to ensure that some permits would have to be purchased. In this case the EP called for 15 per cent of the permits to be auctioned and after two readings managed to secure an agreement that up to 5 per cent could be auctioned in the first period of the scheme (2005–7), increasing to 10 per cent from 2008 to 2012.

When the ETS was extended to cover aviation the EP again sought to increase the number of permits to be auctioned by calling for a 50 per cent auctioning requirement compared to the Commission's original 10 per cent proposal. A final agreement was reached on 15 per cent. The EP also wanted the aviation emissions' cap to be set at 75 per cent of emission limits for 2004–6, compared to the Commission proposal of a 100 per cent cap. The final text contained a cap set at 97 per cent of 2004–6 levels from 2008 to 2012, reduced to 95 per cent from 2013 to 2020.

The most striking thing about the passage of these pieces of legislation is the extent to which the Commission, Council and EP were all committed to the ETS project and to establishing the EU as a climate change leader. As noted above, the Parliament had long been sceptical of the use of emissions trading as a policy instrument for achieving the EU's Kyoto targets, and had stated its preference for regulation and taxation as a means to bring down CO_2 emissions. However, the EP has also consistently called for the Commission and Council to take a leadership role at the international level. Once the US had withdrawn from the Kyoto process, and the rules on how to pursue emissions cuts had been tightened in the Marrakesh Accords, the Commission's proposal for an emissions trading scheme offered a genuine opportunity for the EU to be seen to be taking a transformational 'leadership by example' role (see Chapter 5 by Oberthür and Dupont). Thus, notwithstanding the Parliament's initial scepticism and in view of the shifting consensus that emissions trading was a viable option for delivering emissions cuts, the EP engaged in a strategy of constructive engagement. While it was supportive of the Commission's proposals, it still adopted amendments that tightened limits and introduced some auctioning requirements, thereby playing an important role in strengthening the overall package and reinforcing the EU's climate change leadership.

That said, the passage of the aviation extension was more controversial – it was the scene of heavy industry lobbying, which contributed to a split between the EP's environment and transport committees (*EURactiv*, 12/11/2007). The more febrile atmosphere surrounding the adoption of this directive reflected the changing economic and political context in which the actors were operating. This altered dynamic was to have a profound effect on the EP's ability to achieve its goals on the climate change and energy package.

The climate change and energy package

On the one hand, the run up to the launch of the climate change and energy package was auspicious in witnessing the emergence of a sense of public urgency about the need for a more radical response to climate change. In particular, the Stern Review published in the autumn of 2006 made a compelling economic case for radical action on climate change and the Intergovernmental Panel on Climate Change's (IPCC) fourth assessment report early in 2007 made clear that climate change is advancing faster than anticipated. In March

2007, in the wake of these events and in preparation for Copenhagen 2009, the European Council launched its 20/20 by 2020 strategy. It committed the EU by 2020 to a 20 per cent reduction of 1990 CO_2 emissions levels – increasing to a 30 per cent reduction if other leaders took the same approach in a new post-Kyoto international agreement – and to a 20 per cent share of energy supply from renewable sources. Six pieces of legislation, to be adopted under codecision, were brought forward to deliver these aims.

Yet the subsequent global economic and financial crisis pushed climate change down the policy agenda and strengthened the case against measures that might harm economic competitiveness. The industrial lobby – particularly the well-resourced car manufacturing and energy industries – was increasingly vocal and persuasive in resisting the adoption of stringent limits and many Member States, particularly new entrants, expressed their opposition to potentially costly legislation claiming that they had already made emissions cuts in the 1990s and that their contribution should now be recognised (*The Guardian*, 16/10/08; Chapter 12 by Grant). Indeed, Poland, Slovakia, Romania, Hungary and Bulgaria formed a coalition with Greece and threatened to block the package unless significant concessions were introduced (*The Telegraph*, 03/10/08). Furthermore, Italian Prime Minister Silvio Berlusconi told journalists it was 'absurd' to be talking about carbon emissions in the face of the financial crisis, stating 'It is like someone with pneumonia thinking about having a hairdo'.[4] Berlusconi was one of several new premiers who had not personally signed the March 2007 European Council agreement, while one of its prime movers, Tony Blair, had resigned and another, Angela Merkel, had become less supportive. Thus, the EP found itself constrained by events: what may have been possible before the crisis struck was no longer so and the risk of failure – the prospect of no legislation – loomed over all the institutions. Within the Parliament, the Environment Committee, which had argued in favour of a low carbon economy through ecological modernisation, now found it much more difficult to convince more sceptical EP committees (such as the Industry Committee) that ambitious EU climate change and energy policy measures would lead to a 'double dividend' that could deliver environmental protection and economic growth through the creation of new jobs in 'green' industries.

An important consequence of the changed economic context was that the key actors now advancing climate change leadership – namely the EP, the Commission and ENGOs – found themselves in a defensive position of simply trying to prevent the Commission's original climate change and energy proposals from being significantly weakened or vetoed, rather than pushing for a more radical agenda. As one ENGO representative put it, 'the Parliament was forced into trying to hold the line' (interview, March 2009). This situation was exacerbated by the complexity of the legislative package. The Council and Parliament decided, for reasons of efficiency and coherence, to link all six pieces of legislation into one package and dealt with them simultaneously in parallel negotiations. While this approach made sense, it created challenging coordination problems for the EP in particular, which does not have access to the same kind of expert scientific advice as the Council.

In addition, the co-legislators agreed that the entire package should be negotiated via a fast-track first-reading procedure under codecision. Under the fast-track approach the report adopted by the competent EP committee is taken as a mandate for opening negotiations with the Council. The EP's plenary then endorses by a simple majority a final text that has been negotiated between the two co-legislators (see Shackleton and Raunio 2003). The rapporteur and shadow rapporteur act on behalf of the EP along with other key personnel and support staff, while the Presidency staff take the lead for the Council.[5] The Presidency often plays a crucial role in determining the speed of the passage of legislation: if it is committed to completing a dossier within its six month term of office it will press for a swift resolution (ibid.). President Sarkozy was keen to conclude the dossiers during the French Presidency (July to December 2008) and in time for the Poznan COP meeting in December 2008, so he invested enormous political capital and energy into crafting an agreement that was acceptable to the EP and to the other Member States (interviews, January, March 2009) (see Chapter 7 by Szarka).

The majority of MEPs in the Environment Committee were also committed to that timetable because they feared that the next Presidency (Czech) would not be able to deliver the package and that the economic situation would further worsen the growing hostility to the dossiers emanating from some Member States. However, a core of MEPs, particularly German Christian Democrats, called for the ETS dossier to be delayed, which led to a division between the Christian Democrat rapporteur on the ETS proposal, Avril Doyle (Fine Gael, Ireland), and the rest of her group. However, the fact that other major political groups (the Socialists, Liberals and Greens) supported her approach and that only a simple majority was required for the proposal to be adopted meant that the fast-track approach remained a viable option.

All the dossiers were eventually adopted together in the EP's plenary in December 2008 but three of them (the ETS Extension, and the directives on effort-sharing and CCS) were controversial enough to be referred up to the European Council before a final compromise text could be agreed. Inevitably, the EP's ability to achieve its aims was more constrained on these dossiers as the European Council acts as a last court of appeal on legislative matters, and with states such as Italy threatening to veto the whole package, the EP's scope for negotiation was limited.

The EP adopted a consistent approach on all the dossiers based around trying to tighten or give legal force to reduction targets, to introduce sanctions for states that fail to meet the targets, to reduce the use of CDM credits and to make sustainability criteria transparent and meaningful. Unsurprisingly, the EP was more successful on amendments and legislation that addressed industry concerns and implied lower costs. For example, on the ETS proposal the EP supported several measures designed to reassure industrial interests concerned about the negative impact of inclusion in the ETS on their competitiveness. The EP therefore proposed that those sectors at significant risk of 'carbon leakage' would be entitled to receive up to 100 per cent of permits free of charge, although the qualifying sectors would not be named until an international agreement had been reached, and allocation would be at the level of the benchmark of the best available technology. The EP also raised the threshold for installations affected by the ETS from 10,000 to 25,000 tonnes of annual CO_2 emissions.

However, notwithstanding such sweeteners, where the EP tried to strengthen legislation it experienced mixed fortunes and the Council introduced some new provisions that considerably weakened several of the proposals. For example, again on ETS, the EP called for 'ring-fencing' of all auctioning revenues so that they could be used for climate-related purposes and tried to raise from 20 per cent to 50 per cent the share of the auctioning revenues that would have to be spent in less developed countries on a range of climate change mitigation and adaptation measures, including a new dedicated international fund and efforts to prevent deforestation. In addition, it wanted to require Member States to use the remaining auctioning revenues to address climate change issues within the EU. The final text reasserted the principle that Member States retain the autonomy to decide how they spend the auction revenues, but included a non-binding recommendation that they should spend at least 50 per cent on climate change measures. So the Member States paid only lip-service to the EP's ambition to impose binding hypothecation measures. Moreover, the Council diluted the original proposal for 100 per cent auctioning of allowances by 2020 to 70 per cent, with a view to reaching 100 per cent by 2027. These concessions will cut the overall auctioning revenues from the original forecast of €50 billion per year to nearer €30 billion, thereby reducing the money available for climate change mitigation and adaptation activities (ENDS *Report* 407, Dec 2008: 4–5).

On the effort-sharing directive one of the EP's key aims was to reduce the share of CDM credits available to Member States. However, rather than reduce it the final agreement included greater flexibility regarding the carry-over of CDM credits to subsequent years and 12 states were granted additional credits for projects in the least developed countries and small island states. It is estimated that up to 80 per cent of total national reductions may potentially be met through external offsetting – an outcome roundly condemned by the Green rapporteur, Satu Hassi.

On the renewable energy directive several of the EP's main amendments were not accepted, including the imposition of financial sanctions on Member States missing their targets. The EP also tried to strengthen the sustainability criteria governing the use of biofuels, by trying to include the impact of indirect land use in the formula to calculate a biofuel's overall CO_2 performance – i.e. calculating the impact of CO_2 emissions caused by deforestation and higher food prices arising from shifting land use to biofuel production (*EURactiv*, 05/12/09). Those criteria are included in the final text, but they are not legally binding; the Commission was simply asked to come forward with proposals to limit the indirect impact of land use caused by the switch to biofuels (*EURactiv*, 05/12/09). The EP also failed to resist the attempts of a group of states including the UK, Cyprus, Italy and Malta (*The Guardian*, 26/09/09) to exclude aviation from the 10 per cent biofuels targets.

Overall, despite the Parliament's best efforts, its ability to achieve its preferred outcome was limited. There are several reasons for the apparent failure of the EP to provide leadership and to achieve its goals: the changed economic context; the presence of hostile Member States in Council from both East and West; a vigorous industrial lobbying campaign; and the fact that this was a complicated, highly technical package of legislation that was negotiated at speed. Given these prevailing conditions it is unsurprising that the EP's ability to offer entrepreneurial and cognitive leadership was limited – ironically although the EP was in a better structural position to shape the package in terms of having more formal power – the other conditions that shape the EP's influence meant that its ability to offer leadership was constrained. However, the amendment of the climate change and energy package was not the only platform for leadership available: in April 2007 the EP established its Temporary Committee on Climate Change (CLIM) and while this body had limited legislative power it provided an alternative venue for the EP to express its preferences on climate change, thereby giving it a platform for cognitive leadership.

Institutional innovations in response to climate change

CLIM had a mandate for 20 months and was composed of 60 MEPs representing the political balance of the Parliament as a whole, drawn primarily from the Environment, Industry and Transport committees. The idea for the Committee emanated from the Socialist Group following the appointment of inexperienced Christian Democrat Czech, Miroslav Ouzký, as Chairman of the Environment Committee from 2006 to June 2009. Rumours abounded following Ouzký's appointment that he was a climate change denier (The Parliament, 2007), and the fact that he voted against the resolutions of the Temporary Committee on Climate Change twice, and was absent for the last vote in February 2009, did not enhance his reputation.[6] The Party of European Socialists (PES) secured the support of the EPP for CLIM by appointing former EPP Environment Committee chair Karl-Heinz Florenz as the rapporteur. The initial ambition of CLIM was to shape the Commission's climate change and energy package proposals, however, the legislation was brought forward faster than expected, and then pushed through rapidly via the fast-track first-reading procedure, thereby circumscribing CLIM's ability to feed into the proposal stage. As responsibility for the EP's reports on the climate change and energy package was shared between the Environment Committee and the Industry Committee, CLIM was left on the legislative sidelines. Nevertheless, it still performed several important functions: it provided a venue for the rapporteurs on the energy and climate change package to meet on a regular basis where the only issues on the agenda related to climate change; it facilitated discussion with key stakeholders in the policy field; and it kept climate change high on the agendas of the political groups, presenting opportunities for discussion of issues associated with the energy and climate change package via debates and reports on CLIM's activities (interview, January 2009). Thus, although the committee had limited structural power and therefore limited ability to offer entrepreneurial or structural leadership, it did still contribute to the articulation of the EP's position and was thereby able to offer some limited cognitive leadership within the Parliament. Its creation also bolstered the EP's external image as a serious political actor contributing to the climate change debate.

Moreover, because it had limited legislative power CLIM was liberated from the constraints facing the Environment and Industry Committees whose rapporteurs had to tailor their legislative proposals to attract cross-group support within the EP and sufficient support within the Council to stand a chance of being adopted. While the CLIM rapporteur, Karl-Heinz Florenz, also had to secure support from the different political groups within the EP, as CLIM's final report had no legislative force, the EP could use it as an opportunity to make stronger statements about the actions necessary to combat climate change. Thus the Florenz report called for a review of whether the EU's commitment to cut temperatures by 2°C will be sufficient to avoid 'dangerous climate change' (EP 2009a: 16) and demanded a 25–40 per cent reduction of greenhouse gas emissions (GHGE) by 2020 and 80 per cent by 2050. These positions were considerably more ambitious than anything Member States were prepared to see included in the legislative reports. The CLIM report (EP 2009a) also reminded parties to the Kyoto Protocol and Marrakesh Accords that they were expected to reduce domestic GHGE before taking advantage of external flexible mechanisms such as the CDM and stated 'that excessive CDM/JI use undermines the credibility of the European Union in the international UN negotiations and thus its leadership role in fighting climate change' (ibid.: 17). These statements were a clear indication of the Parliament's frustration at the Member States' desire to use the CDM to reach their targets rather than reducing domestic GHGE. Thus, when freed from the limitations imposed by the legislative process the EP returned to its usual position of offering clear cognitive leadership on the issue of climate change, but its efforts were symbolic rather than transformational.

New environmental policy instruments and ecological modernisation

The EP has long supported the use of new environmental policy instruments and the development of other principles of ecological modernisation as a way of getting business to support the environmental policy agenda. The institution's approach to the use of new policy instruments and of innovation within the field of climate change legislation has been characterised by remarkable consistency notwithstanding the fact that the EP's ideological balance of power has shifted to the right since the 1999 elections, and that it embraced new cohorts of MEPs from the accession states in 2004 and 2007. While the Parliament has always endorsed a mix of policy instruments, it has traditionally favoured those new environmental policy instruments that have as part of their repertoire an element of regulation or taxation. It has consistently called for limited use of offsetting via the CDM and JI mechanisms of the Kyoto Protocol. Its amendments to the climate change and energy package continued its long-held policy of tightening limits and introducing sanctions where appropriate. This continuity reflects the fact that the EP operates through coalition and consensus with voting behaviour dividing along ideological lines (Hix *et al.* 2007). Thus, while the emphasis on certain types of policy instruments may shift, for example the Parliament's willing endorsement of the ETS proposals was no doubt in part due to the shift to the right within the chamber, the need to keep at least the two major party groups on board has guaranteed a degree of stability and continuity over the years. Indeed, what is interesting about the passage of the climate change and energy package was the fact that the most contested divisions emerged within the European People's Party (EPP), rather than between the EPP and Party of European Socialists (PES). These splits reflect the controversial nature of the proposals under discussion and the strongly held national preferences that saw governments and industry fiercely lobbying their MEPs. The behaviour of those MEPs also reflects the unique nature of the European Parliament situated as it is at the interface between national and European levels of governance. MEPs may legislate at the European level but they are accountable to their national masters; consequently when matters of national interest are at stake, particularly close to an election, such splits on national line are unsurprising.

Climate change as threat or opportunity?

The EU's drive to play an international leadership role on climate change over the last decade has presented an opportunity for the EP to use its legislative powers under codecision in combination with its symbolic agenda-setting capacity though CLIM to advance EU leadership on the world stage. The EP achieved some success in strengthening the original ETS legislation, and its extension to aviation, notably by increasing the auctioning requirements. Significantly, this legislation was dealt with in a context when concern about climate change was steadily rising and all three institutions agreed on the need for action. However, the passage of the climate change and energy package took place in very different circumstances against the backdrop of a deepening international economic crisis, which had reduced the appetite for a radical energy and climate change package amongst the EU's Member States. In addition, there was a shift within the Council that saw previously committed Heads of Government leaving office or, in the case of Merkel, shifting position. The climate change and energy package also saw the emergence of a bloc of accession states prepared to threaten the overall package in order to gain concessions. This development reflects a new confidence amongst those states – since joining the EU the new states have kept a relatively low profile in Council (interview, January 2009), but the climate change and energy package suggests that where there are key economic interests at stake they will voice concerns. The fact that in most of those states the environment has low political salience (see, for example, Chapter 10 by Jankoswka) may not bode well for future EU environmental policy.

For the Parliament the passage of the climate change and energy package served to underline the limitations of its powers under codecision when the Council is intransigent. Rather than providing an opportunity for the EP to realise its long-held ambition to offer cognitive leadership, the climate change and energy package raised the spectre of failure if agreement between the co-legislators could not be reached. The 2009 Copenhagen climate change conference (the COP-15 meeting) further underlined the EP's limited power in this particular field of environmental policy. The resolution adopted by the Parliament prior to the meeting yet again called for the EP to be included in meetings of the EU negotiating team (EP 2009b), but yet again the Parliament's delegation was excluded. The reputation of the EP was also somewhat undermined by the inclusion of controversial UK MEP Nick Griffin, representing the far-right British National Party, and who has questioned the link between human activities and climate change. The failure of the Copenhagen meeting to deliver a concrete international agreement also calls into question the 30 per cent target agreed by the Council and EP. The EP's delegation was not the only one left out in the cold – reports from Copenhagen suggest that the EU delegation played a limited role and that the key decisions (or the lack thereof) took place in bilateral meetings between the US and key players such as China and India. The challenge therefore for all the institutional actors is to continue to provide international leadership in an economic climate that appears hostile to a sufficiently rigorous climate change agreement and in an international negotiating arena dominated once again by the US, and the increasingly confident Asian powers.

Conclusions

This analysis of the EP's role in climate change politics allows us to draw several conclusions relating to the core themes of this book: leadership, new environmental policy instruments, ecological modernisation and multi-level governance. First, the shifting fortunes of the EP in the field of climate change very clearly demonstrate that the EP's ability to exercise influence and therefore leadership is contingent upon a range of factors (Judge *et al.* 1994) – not least, the prevailing exogenous conditions such as the state of the international economy. The EP was forced to adopt a defensive position when dealing with the climate change and energy package to prevent the package being weakened or shelved altogether. Ironically, in this case the EP's scope to offer leadership was most limited where its formal power was greatest – as a co-legislator with the Council. Freed from the constraints of legislative partnership, the EP offered a much clearer leadership position in the report of its Temporary Committee on Climate Change. However, its leadership in this case was purely rhetorical. Thus the EP's attempts to be a heroic climate change leader failed and it fell back upon its traditional symbolic role.

The case also shows that the Parliament has adopted a fairly consistent position over the years towards the use of new environmental policy instruments associated with ecological modernisation. While sceptical about the use of some instruments, it has been prepared to engage in a policy of constructive engagement. However, the passage of the climate change and energy package demonstrates that despite the 'win-win' discourse of ecological modernisation it remains the case that there is a clear trade-off between economic growth and environmental protection. In uncertain and difficult economic times Heads of State and Government in the EU and elsewhere will shrink from offering leadership where leadership implies costs, and MEPs will be subject to pressure from national interests and governments. Their unique position at the interface of national and European levels of governance allows them, for much of the time, to be insulated from national pressures, but where the costs are high and key national interests are at stake they are as vulnerable as domestic politicians to pressure from their parties and governments.

Finally, the case demonstrates that the enlargement of the European Union has changed the dynamics of environmental decision-making in the EU; it has shifted the political centre of gravity of the Union and its institutions ideologically to the right and geographically to the East. With 27 members, many of which are poorly prepared to withstand a deep global downturn and view environmental policy-making as an expensive luxury, it will be difficult for the EU to develop and maintain a coherent leadership position in international environmental politics. Governance in this pluri-centric and diverse multi-level system of governance has become even more complex and this increased heterogeneity is having a clear impact upon preference formation within the institutions. These shifts have certainly constrained the EP's capacity to assume a leadership role because of both the changing intra- and inter-institutional balance of power. Enlargement resulted in the appointment of a chair of the Environment Committee from a new Member State who did not provide the leadership for which the Committee was renowned. The EP's committee reports contained amendments that carefully balanced the environmental and economic interests of its members, to assuage concerns of MEPs from both new and old Member States about the likely impact of legislation. However, the EP's rapporteurs frequently found themselves confronted by intransigent opposition to their greener amendments in the Council, where coalitions of new and old Member States resisted more stringent legislation. Under these circumstances, the EP and particularly its rapporteurs on the climate change and energy package, deserve recognition for preventing the Council from watering down those proposals even more than they did. While the future prospects for the EP as a Climate Change actor remain uncertain, the appointment of a new chair of the Environment Committee, from a German PES member (Jo Leinen, German, Social Democratic Party) may augur a new era of consistent leadership from the Committee. The appointment of a Climate Change Commissioner from Denmark (Connie Hedegaard), traditionally an environmental pioneer state, may offer a window of opportunity for the EP to engage in cognitive and entrepreneurial leadership via a partnership with this new actor within the Commission.

Notes

1 This chapter draws upon evidence from interviews with actors based in the EU's institutions and NGOs, conducted in January and March 2009. All interviewees wished to remain anonymous and emphasised that their views were personal and did not represent those of the institutions and organisations for which they work.
2 See European Parliament (2009a: 41) for a recent list of resolutions on Climate Change and Energy.
3 Between 1993 and 1999 the Environment Committee handled 36 per cent of all codecision dossiers and 29 per cent between 1999 and 2004 (European Parliament, 1999: 52; 2004: 55); 21 per cent between 2004 and 2006 (European Parliament 2006a: 9)
4 Evvidia News, 12/12/08. Online. Available HTTP: <http://www.evvidia.com/news/world.php?start_from = 80&ucat = &archive = &subaction = &id => (accessed 5 May 2009).
5 See the EP's Rules of Procedure, Rules 63–65; and the EP's Guidelines for First and Second-Reading Agreements (European Parliament 2006a, Annex B: 29–30)
6 OJC 138E, 05/06/08: 130–31; OJC 180E, 17/07/08: 185–87; OJC 74E, 28/03/09: 104.

Bibliography

Burns, C. (2005) 'The European Parliament: The EU's Environmental Champion?', in A. Jordan (ed.), *Environmental Policy in the European Union*, 2nd edn, London: Earthscan, 87–105.

Burns, C. and Carter, N. (2010) 'Is Codecision Good for the Environment?', *Political Studies*, 58 (1), 123–42.

ENDS Report (2008) 'Compromise EU Climate Package Hurried through Brussels Summit' ENDS *Report 407*, pp.4–5, URL <http://www.endsreport.com> (accessed 5 May 2010)

EP (European Parliament) (1998a) *Resolution on Environmental Policy and Climate Change Following the Kyoto Summit*, B4–0142, 0143, 0144, 0145, 0151, 0164 and 0165/98, OJC 80, 16/03/98, 227–31.

EP (European Parliament) (1998b) R*esolution on Climate Change in the Run-Up to Buenos Aires (November 1998)*, B4–0802/98, OJC 313, 12/10/98,169–72.

EP (European Parliament) (1999) *Activity Report 1 November 1993 – 30 April 1999 From Entry into Force of the Treaty of Maastricht to Entry into Force of the Treaty of Amsterdam of the Delegations to the Conciliation Committee*, PE 230.998.

EP (European Parliament) (2000) *Resolution on Climate Change: Preparing for the Implementation of the Kyoto Protocol*, B5–0118/1999, OJC 107, 13/04/00, 112–15.

EP (European Parliament) (2002a) *European Parliament Resolution on the Outcome of the Bonn Conference on Climate Change*, B5–0539, 0540, 0541, 0543, 0551 and 0552/2001, OJC 72E, 21/03/02, 321–23.

EP (European Parliament) (2002b) *European Parliament Resolution on the Follow-Up to Parliament's Opinion on the European Union's Strategy for the Marrakesh Conference on Climate Change*, B5–0686/2001 OJC 212E, 09/05/2002, 299–301.

EP (European Parliament) (2004) *Activity Report 1 May 1999 to 30 April 2004 (5th Parliamentary Term) of the Delegations to the Conciliation Committee*, PE 287.644.

EP (European Parliament) (2006a) *Conciliations and Codecision Activity Report: July 2004 to December 2006 (6th Parliamentary Term. First Half-Term)*.

EP (European Parliament) (2006b) *Resolution on the European Union Strategy for the Nairobi Conference on Climate Change*, B6–0543/2006, OJC313E, 20/12/2006, 439–42.

EP (European Parliament) (2009a) *2050: The Future Begins Today – Recommendations For the EU's Future Integrated Policy on Climate Change* ('CLIM report'), T6–0042/2009 (04/02/2009).

EP (European Parliament) (2009b) *European Parliament Resolution of 25th November 2009 on the EU Strategy for the Copenhagen Conference on Climate Change (COP15)*, B7–0141/2009, (25/11/09).

Euractiv (2009) 'Parliament Set to Vote for Tighter Emission Limits' (12/11/2007) URL:<http://www.euractiv.com/en/transport/parliament-set-vote-tighter-aircraft-emission-limits/article-168267> (accessed 5 May 2010).

Friedrich, A., Tappe, M. and Wurzel, R. K. W. (2000) 'A New Approach to EU Environmental Policy-Making? The Auto-Oil I Programme', *Journal of European Public Policy*, 7(4), 593–612.

Hayward, J. (2008) 'Introduction: Inhibited Consensual Leadership within an Interdependent Confederal Europe', in J. Hayward (ed.), *Leaderless Europe*, Oxford: Oxford University Press, 1–14.

Hix, S., Noury, A. G. and Roland, G. (2007) *Democratic Politics in the European Parliament*, Cambridge: Cambridge University Press.

Hubschmid, C. and Moser, P. (1997) 'The Co-operation Procedure in the EU: Why Was the European Parliament Influential in the Decision on Car Emission Standards?', *Journal of Common Market Studies*, 35(2), 225–42.

Judge, D. (1992) 'Predestined to Save the Earth: The Environment Committee of the European Parliament', *Environmental Politics*, 1(4), 186–212.

Judge, D. and Earnshaw, D. (2008) 'The European Parliament: Leadership and "Followership" ', in J. Hayward (ed.), *Leaderless Europe*, Oxford: Oxford University Press, 245–68.

Judge, D., Earnshaw, D. and Cowan, N (1994), 'Ripples or Waves: The European Parliament in the European Community Policy Process', *Journal of European Public Policy*, 1(1), 27–52.

Oberthür, S. and Roche-Kelly, C. (2008) 'EU Leadership in International Climate Policy: Achievements and Challenges', *The International Spectator*, 43(3), 35–50.

Parliament, The (2007) 'All Change on EU Parliament Committees', 1 February. Online. Available HTTP: <http://www.theparliament.com/latestnews/news-article/newsarticle/all-change-on-eu-parliament-committees/> (accessed 5 May 2009).

Shackleton, M. and Raunio, T. (2003) 'Codecision since Amsterdam: A Laboratory for Institutional Innovation and Change', *Journal of European Public Policy*, 10(2), 171–88.

Schreurs, M. A. and Tiberghien, Y. (2007) 'Multi-Level Reinforcement: Explaining European Union Leadership in Climate Change Mitigation', *Global Environmental Politics*, 7(4): 19–46.

Weale, A., Pridham, G. Cini, M., Konstadakopulos, D., Porter, M. and Flynn, B. (2000) *Environmental Governance in Europe*, Oxford: Oxford University Press.

Wettestad, J. (2005) 'The Making of the 2003 EU Emissions Trading Directive: An Ultra-Quick Process due to Entrepreneurial Proficiency?', *Global Environmental Politics*, 5(1), 1–23.

Zito, A. (2000) *Creating Environmental Policy in the European Union*, Basingstoke: Palgrave.

5 The Council, the European Council and international climate policy

From symbolic leadership to leadership by example

Sebastian Oberthür and Claire Dupont

Introduction

This chapter analyses the role of the Council of Environment Ministers (the Council) and the European Council in the evolution of EU leadership in international climate policy. It focuses on two dimensions of environmental leadership. First, we explore the role of the Council and European Council in the international climate negotiations since the early 1990s. Second, we review the role of the Council and European Council in the evolution of domestic EU climate policy because credible international leadership requires appropriate domestic measures ('leadership by example') (see also Gupta and Grubb 2000; Vogler 2005).

Overall, we argue that the Council and the European Council have been crucial in developing the international leadership record of the EU on climate change. Through them, the EU became a main pusher in international climate policy from the outset, but they have also been mainly responsible for the symbolic character of this leadership during the 1990s. In particular, insufficient internal climate policies during this period created the 'capability-expectations gap' well known in other policy areas (Hill 1993). In addition, problems of external policy coordination have continually plagued EU aspirations for international leadership on climate change. The Council and the European Council played crucial roles in improving the EU's leadership record on both fronts in the 2000s – although important challenges remain (see also Oberthür and Roche Kelly 2008).

The chapter proceeds in four main steps. First, the next section briefly examines the roles of the Council and the European Council in the making of internal and external climate policies of the EU. Second, we analyse the evolving contribution of both councils to the EU's international leadership record on climate change. Third, we analyse to what extent the Council and European Council have framed climate policy in terms of an opportunity for ecological modernisation over the years. Finally, we explore a number of internal and external factors that have contributed to the evolution of more credible EU international leadership in the 2000s. The final section provides the major conclusions of the chapter.

Council and European Council in internal and external EU policy-making on climate change

Council of Ministers

The Council of Environment Ministers has taken the lead in developing EU climate policy. Therefore, unless otherwise indicated, we refer to the Environment Council as 'the Council' in the following.

When it comes to determining *internal* EU environmental and climate policy, the Council shares its power with the European Parliament (EP) (see also Chapter 4 by Burns and Carter) and the European Commission (see also Chapter 3 by Barnes). In the applicable co-decision procedure for the adoption of EU legislation, the Council can block climate policy proposals, but it cannot easily move domestic EU climate policy forward on its own. The adoption of most climate policy proposals requires a qualified majority within the Council. However, the Council has to decide unanimously on measures of a 'fiscal nature' (e.g. environmental taxation), as well as 'measures significantly affecting a Member State's choice between different energy sources and the general structure of its energy supply' (Article 192.2 of the Treaty on the Functioning of the European Union, TFEU). Individual Member States thus possess veto power on significant parts of climate policy (Wettestad 2000).

In contrast, the Council is the single most important actor shaping EU *external* climate policy. Climate policy is an area of 'shared/mixed competence' between the EU and its Member States (see Chapter 1 by Wurzel and Connelly and Chapter 2 by Vogler). As a result, both the EU (represented by the European Commission) and its Member States are parties to the UN Framework Convention on Climate Change (UNFCCC) and its Kyoto Protocol and participate in the international climate negotiations. In practical terms, the Council determines the EU's international negotiation position, with active participation and input by the Commission. A working group of the Council develops the positions, which are then usually reflected in Council conclusions. These Council conclusions provide the basis for the Member States and the Commission to coordinate their strategy on a daily basis at the international negotiations. The EP only has a consultative role. However, with the entry into force of the Lisbon Treaty, the consent of the EP is required for the conclusion of international environmental agreements (while the Council decided, after consulting the Parliament, on the ratification of the UNFCCC and the Kyoto Protocol) (Article 218 TFEU; see also Groenleer and van Schaik 2007; Oberthür and Roche Kelly 2008; van Schaik 2010).

Rotating among the Member States every six months, the Presidency of the Council plays slightly different roles in internal and external EU climate policy-making. Internally, as the chair of Council meetings, it shapes the agenda and the conduct of meetings. It also plays a significant role in brokering compromise solutions and taking political initiatives. Externally, the Presidency acts as the main contact point and spokesperson for the EU. In the negotiations; the Presidency is flanked by the incoming Presidency and the European Commission, forming the so-called 'Troika' (Oberthür and Roche Kelly 2008; Schout 2008).

European Council

The European Council of Heads of State and Government (the European Council) can provide important guidance for both internal and external EU climate policy. Since it holds no formal competence in the legislative procedures of the EU, the European Council's impact derives from its political importance as the highest political gathering of the EU Member States. Relevant political statements on the direction of the Union's development are released after each European Council meeting as 'Presidency Conclusions'. Internally, the conclusions can provide the political impetus for the development of domestic climate policies. Externally, the conclusions of the European Council may give signals on the political commitment and leadership of the EU to international partners. The statements of the European Council have often come at crucial phases in the development of environmental and climate policy, helping to direct the Union's stance on these issues (McCormick 2001: 96; Oberthür and Pallemaerts 2010b).

Enhancing leadership: three phases

This section examines the roles of the Council and the European Council in the evolution of the EU's internal and external climate policies in three distinct phases and argues that both have played a crucial role in improving the EU's leadership record on climate change over time.

Creating the credibility gap: 1990s

During much of the 1990s, the leadership of the intergovernmental arm of the EU can be characterised as rhetorical, symbolic or humdrum. The actions of the Council and the European Council resulted in the establishment of a credibility gap that has characterised EU leadership on climate change ever since. On the one hand, they claimed and pursued an international leadership role pushing for far-reaching global agreements. On the other hand, Member State politics within the Council largely prevented the EU from making sufficient progress on the development of EU climate policy. Climate policy remained sharply limited in scope during this phase with activities focused on the Environment Council, while most other Council formations successfully avoided the topic. As a result, progress in reducing greenhouse gas emissions (GHGE) in the EU-15 in the 1990s was very limited (Figure 5.1) and due mainly to developments unrelated to climate change (the dash from coal to gas in the UK and German reunification) (See Chapters 6 by Rayner and Jordan and 7 by Jänicke). Emissions even increased slightly after 1994 and, at the turn of the century, were projected to increase further by 2010 without additional policies and measures (CEC 2001).

On the *international* plain, the EU aspired to become a leader on climate change during the negotiations on the UNFCCC in 1992 and its Kyoto Protocol in 1997. In June 1990, the European Council declared that the EU should 'play a leading role in promoting concerted and effective action at the global level' and urged all countries to adopt 'possible targets and strategies for limiting emissions of greenhouse gases'.[1] Other than that, the European Council was not involved in detail on matters of climate policy during this period (Figure 5.2). It was the Council that established the EU as a pusher in the negotiations on the UNFCCC in 1991 and 1992. After the UK relinquished its initial resistance, the Council of Energy and Environment ministers, meeting jointly in October 1990, committed to stabilising carbon dioxide (CO_2) emissions at 1990 levels by 2000 within the EU, and suggested this target for all industrialised countries (Wettestad 2000; Collier 1996).[2]

The Council further substantiated the EU's position as an international pusher on climate change during the negotiations on the Kyoto Protocol (concluded in 1997) and its implementing rules. First, in June 1996, the Council established the objective of limiting global temperature increase to two degrees Celsius above pre-industrial levels. Then, in March 1997, the Council proposed under the Dutch Presidency that industrialised countries should commit to cutting their emissions of three major GHGs (CO_2, methane (CH_4), nitrous oxide (N_2O)) by 15 per cent by 2010 (compared with 1990). In June 1997, it also suggested an interim reduction target of 7.5 per cent by 2005. This position was far ahead of other industrialised countries that proposed to stabilise emissions (US) or to reduce them by up to 5 per cent (Japan) by 2010 (Oberthür and Ott 1999: 54–58). In Kyoto, the EU took on the highest reduction target (minus 8 per cent) of all major industrialised countries for the first commitment period of the Kyoto Protocol (2008–12).

The coherence of the Council-led activities at the international level increased and EU external policy coordination intensified significantly during this phase. In the early 1990s, it was still common for individual Member States to take the floor in the actual negotiations on the UNFCCC and to submit specific proposals. The UK, for example, submitted a complete proposal for a framework convention on climate change. Towards the Kyoto negotiations, the EU increasingly spoke with one voice, namely the Council Presidency. In the aftermath of Kyoto, this trend continued and the Presidency increasingly became the exclusive voice of the EU in the international negotiations (Oberthür 2009). In parallel, the EU diversified and intensified its external policy coordination, including through the establishment of several groups of national experts under the responsible Council working group to assist it in developing EU positions.

While coherence and coordination generally enhanced the capabilities of the EU to exert structural, entrepreneurial and cognitive leadership, several related weaknesses hampered effective leadership. First, intensified internal coordination resulted in 'navel-gazing' and a 'bunker mentality' which left insufficient time and resources for outreach to other parties. Second, the enhanced role of the rotating Presidency aggravated the problem of a lack of institutional memory and continuity in policy development and representation (e.g. Oberthür and Ott 1999; van Schaik and Egenhofer 2005; Gupta and Grubb 2000; Lacasta *et al.* 2007). At the same time, the various Presidencies displayed different levels of effectiveness in fulfilling their enhanced role (with the Dutch presidency in 1997 considered relatively effective, in contrast to the Irish and Italian presidencies in 1996) (Schreurs and Tiberghien 2007; Schout 2008; Bretherton and Vogler 2006).

On the *domestic* side, the Council was in large measure responsible for a lack of progress of EU climate policies, which was at odds with the EU's international leadership ambitions (see also for the following Oberthür and Pallemaerts 2010b). In particular, the Commission's proposal for a combined European CO_2/energy tax, aiming to meet the EU's CO_2 emission stabilisation target, met with opposition from several Member States: the UK upheld the principle of subsidiarity; Ireland, Spain, Greece and Portugal requested additional structural funding; and nuclear-minded France called for a pure carbon tax. With environmental taxation requiring unanimity, the Council abandoned the idea of an EU-wide carbon/energy tax in 1994. Similarly, the Council substantially weakened ambitious proposals by the European Commission on promoting energy efficiency and renewable energies within the EU and cut back their budgets (Skjærseth 1994; Collier 1996; Wettestad 2000).

Limited progress was made on other fronts. The Council agreed to the establishment of a mechanism for monitoring GHG emissions in the EU Member States in 1993. It also, under the UK Presidency in early 1998, successfully adapted the initial internal 'burden-sharing agreement' of March 1997 (i.e. the differentiated contributions of Member States to the common EU emission reduction target) to the outcome of the Kyoto negotiations. In addition, voluntary agreements with European, Korean and Japanese car manufacturers regarding reduced CO_2 emissions from cars were concluded in 1998 and 1999, although this new policy instrument has proven ineffective in delivering the agreed emission cuts (ten Brink 2010). A few other measures with a positive effect on GHG emissions, including the Landfill Directive (Directive 1999/31/EC) requiring the recovery of methane from biodegradable waste in landfills, were motivated by other considerations (see overall Oberthür and Pallemaerts 2010b).

The 1995 enlargement of the EU to include Austria, Sweden and Finland did not favour the Council's ability to show 'leadership by example' in climate policy. Since Austria, Finland and Sweden had even higher domestic environmental standards than other 'green' Member States (Germany, Denmark, and the Netherlands) in 1995, they were expected to act as 'pushers' in EU environmental policy-making. However, the new Member States had limited capacity and political weight and could not undo the unanimity requirement applying to large parts of energy-related climate policies (Liefferink and Andersen 1998).

Improving the record: 2000–6

The beginning of the twenty-first century saw a substantial improvement of the Council's and the European Council's record. At the international level, both pushed the EU to maintain leadership on climate change and to upgrade its mechanisms for coordination and representation. At the same time, the Council played a constructive role in the elaboration of new domestic climate policies (while the European Council was hardly involved in domestic climate policy-making in this phase). As a result, the existing credibility gap was reduced but remained substantial, and the Council and the European Council increasingly moved to transformational 'leadership by example'.

Internationally, the Council and European Council led the EU after 2000 to become the champion of the Kyoto Protocol. First of all, in the negotiations on the implementing rules of the Kyoto Protocol that led to the adoption of the Marrakech Accords in 2001, the Council insisted on preserving the environmental integrity of the Protocol. Key planks in this strategy were the insistence on: domestic action by industrialised countries (instead of acquiring emission credits from elsewhere); a strong compliance system for ensuring that countries fulfil their commitments; the strict limitation of the possibility to offset emission mitigation action by carbon sinks (in particular, forest management); and rules on the use of the market mechanisms that ensure they deliver real, additional reductions (European Council, December 2000; June 2001; December 2001).

After the withdrawal of the US from the Kyoto Protocol in 2001, the Council and the European Council – in close cooperation with the European Commission – led the campaign to save the Protocol. The European Council tied itself to the Kyoto Protocol and pledged that the EU would reach its Kyoto target unilaterally (European Council, June 2001; Groenleer and van Schaik 2007). The Council also staged a concerted diplomatic effort by Member States to save the Protocol by sending missions to key countries (Bretherton and Vogler 2006: 108–9). Finally, the EU, led by the Council and European Council, successfully secured ratification by Russia and thus ensured the Kyoto Protocol's entry into force (Damro 2006).

The mechanisms for representation and coordination of external EU climate policy also made further substantial progress in the early 2000s. First of all, the new composition of the Troika that resulted from the Amsterdam Treaty enhanced continuity through the permanent involvement of the European Commission. Furthermore, a system of 'lead negotiators' and 'issue leaders' was introduced during the Irish Presidency in early 2004. Thereby, lead negotiators from various Member States and from the Commission represented the EU in various international negotiating groups over longer periods of time (on behalf of the EU Presidency). With more authority being transferred to the expert level, these negotiators also took the lead in developing the EU position in cooperation with selected 'issue leaders'.

In reality, the UK and the European Commission benefited in particular from this new arrangement (Oberthür 2009).

While these measures significantly enhanced the capacity of the Council to exert entrepreneurial and cognitive leadership, they also reinforced certain challenges. On the one hand, the new coordination system markedly increased the ability of the EU to develop specific positions and engage effectively and flexibly in the international negotiations on the growing number of international agenda items. On the other hand, the new system reinforced the independence and compartmentalisation of individual expert groups, which increased the challenge of their coordination. The resulting need for strong and continuous 'structural leadership' from the chair of the Council brought the weaknesses of the system of rotating Presidencies to the fore (Oberthür and Roche Kelly 2008: 38–39; van Schaik 2010).

At the domestic level, the performance of the Council with respect to advancing EU climate policy also substantially improved, while leaving room for further contributions (Oberthür and Pallemaerts 2010b). Both the Environment and the Energy Councils constructively participated in the adoption of an increasing number of legislative acts aimed at mitigating GHG emissions, which the European Commission initiated on the basis of its European Climate Change Programme (ECCP), launched in 2000. In what may be characterised as cognitive leadership, especially by the Commission, the ECCP marked a reframing of EU climate policy in environmental and market terms (as opposed to the earlier focus on fiscal measures). It also initiated an increasing integration of climate considerations in the activities of the Energy Council.

The 2003 EU Emissions Trading Directive (2003/87/EC), which sets limits for the CO_2 emissions of large installations that account for about 40 per cent of the EU's CO_2 emissions, formed the centrepiece of this new EU climate policy. While several EU Member States had a tradition of scepticism or even opposition to this policy instrument, it gained acceptance after the adoption of the Kyoto Protocol. An apparent over-allocation of emission allowances for the 2005–7 pilot phase led to more stringent review arrangements for national allocations under the EU system for 2008–12 (Delbeke 2006; Skjærseth and Wettestad 2008).

Further EU climate policies and measures adopted from 2001–6 especially by the Energy and Environment Councils (Oberthür and Pallemaerts 2010b) include:

- Directive 2001/77/EC on the promotion of electricity produced from renewable energy sources;
- Directive 2002/91/EC on the energy performance of buildings;
- Directive 2003/30/EC on the promotion of biofuels in transport;
- Directive 2004/8/EC on the promotion of cogeneration;
- Directive 2006/32/EC on energy end use efficiency and energy services, and
- Regulation EC 842/2006 and Directive 2006/40/EC on reducing the emission of fluorinated GHGs.

While the constructive engagement of the Council made this flurry of legislative activity possible, neither the Council nor the European Council became a major 'green' force for effective climate protection in the institutional triangle formed with the EP and the Commission. Most of the 'new' EU climate policy did not require unanimity for its adoption, which helped overcome marginal opposition among Member States. Nevertheless, Member States in the Council at times weakened climate policy initiatives. For example, one of the major weaknesses of the Emissions Trading Scheme (ETS), the free national allocation of emission allowances (instead of auctioning of emission rights), was the result of Member States' insistence (Skjærseth and Wettestad 2008). As a general rule (confirmed by exceptions), the EP and the Commission were 'greener' forces in the legislative processes than the Council (Liefferink and Andersen 1998; see also Chapter 3 by Barnes and Chapter 4 by Burns and Carter).

As with the 1995 enlargement, the 2004 enlargement of the EU with 10 Eastern and Southern European countries had no immediate substantial negative effect on the development of domestic EU climate policy. Some analysts had expected that the inclusion of states where environmental and climate policies had not been political priorities would negatively affect the development of the EU's internal climate policies. However, the enlargement did not significantly hamper the Council in following up on the legislative programme developed and proposed by the Commission under the ECCP in this period (Massai 2007; see also Skjærseth and Wettestad 2007).

The progress in the development of EU climate policies during this phase nevertheless remained insufficient. By 2005, the GHG emissions of the EU-15 were stagnating at 2 per cent below 1990 levels (Figure 5.1). Also, deficits in the implementation of existing measures left the emission reduction potential of EU policies and measures vastly under-exploited. The policies and measures enacted by the EU and the Member States were projected to

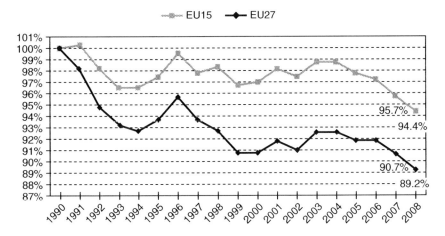

Figure 5.1 GHGE of the EU-15 and EU-27 1990–2008.

reduce GHG emissions to 4 per cent below base year levels by 2010. While this constituted a considerable improvement on the situation at the turn of the millennium, additional measures were required for the EU-15 to achieve their Kyoto target (EEA 2007).

Developments since 2007: enhanced credibility but less influence?

The year 2007 saw the beginning of a markedly enhanced involvement of the European Council in both internal and external EU climate policy (Figure 5.2), while the trend of a more proactive and progressive Council also continued. The European Council and, to a lesser extent, the Council have become major driving forces in EU internal climate policy, helping to reduce further the aforementioned credibility gap in support of international EU leadership on climate change, especially through the climate and energy package of 2008/2009. At the same time, the Copenhagen Climate Summit of 2009 raised questions about the viability of the EU's external climate policies for maintaining international leadership.

In March 2007, the European Council, building on important preparatory work of both the Environment Council and the European Commission, provided a major impetus to the development of EU climate policy. Reaffirming the two-degree target, the European Council (under the German Presidency) made an 'independent commitment' to reduce GHGE in the EU by 20 per cent from the 1990 level by 2020, and pledged to increase this target to 30 per cent if other industrialised countries make comparable commitments and if advanced developing countries agree to make adequate contributions. In

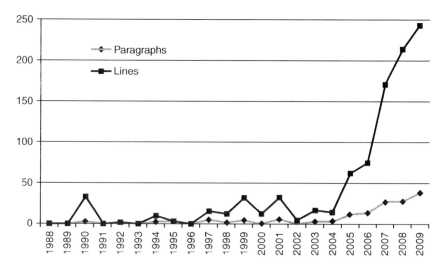

Figure 5.2 Climate change in the conclusions of the European Council 1988–2009.

Source: own counting.

addition, the European Council agreed to increase the share of renewable energy sources in the EU's energy supply to 20 per cent and the contribution of biofuels in transport to 10 per cent by 2020. It also approved the objective of saving 20 per cent on the EU's projected energy consumption for 2020. It mandated the European Commission to put forward appropriate proposals for implementing legislation (European Council, March 2007).

On the basis of Commission proposals presented in 2007 and 2008, the Council and European Council followed up on this agreement. They elaborated, in collaboration with the EP, a set of new domestic climate policies in 2008/2009 aimed at implementing the three 20-per cent targets for 2020 (see Oberthür and Pallemaerts 2010a), including:

- The inclusion of the aviation sector in the ETS by 2012 (Directive 2008/101/EC);
- Regulation (EC) 443/2009 on CO_2 emissions from new passenger cars;
- A revised Emissions Trading Directive covering the period 2013 to 2020 (Directive 2009/29/EC);
- A new decision on the effort-sharing among EU Member States of the 20 per cent reduction target by 2020 with respect to the sectors not covered by the EU ETS (Decision 406/2009/EC);
- A directive on the promotion of renewable energy, including binding national targets (Directive 2009/28/EC); and
- A directive on carbon capture and storage (Directive 2009/31/EC).

The Council and European Council played a leading, but ambiguous, role in the elaboration of the new climate policies of the EU. On the one hand, they clearly supported, and provided the main political impetus for, such strengthened measures. Unusually, the European Council even took the lead in hammering out a deal on the so-called climate and energy package (i.e. the last four of the measures listed above) in December 2008 – formally a deal between the Council and the EP (see also Chapter 4 by Burns and Carter). On the other hand, haggling among Member States was the main reason for a weakening of the legislative proposals during the last stages of the negotiations. German (cars, emissions trading) and Eastern European (emissions trading, effort sharing) insistence, in particular, resulted in significant derogations (auctioning/free allocation) and a weakened compliance schedule regarding car emissions (Oberthür and Pallemaerts 2010a).

The adoption of the new climate policies constituted a significant strengthening and communitarisation of the climate policy framework in the EU (Oberthür and Pallemaerts 2010a). The new policies, including a significant part of energy policy, together are expected to account for the lion's share of the EU's 20 per cent emission reduction commitment by 2020. Their implementation is far less dependent on EU Member States than the previous policy framework: the reformed EU ETS is based on European-level allocation and auctioning of emission allowances with a central sanctioning mechanism; CO_2

emissions from new cars are subject to a Regulation (with penalties applied directly to car manufacturers), and renewable energy targets are binding in supranational law. In line with the rulings of the European Court of Justice, this expansion of internal EU competence may well also affect external EU competence (van Schaik 2010). The revised ETS and the Effort-Sharing agreement may especially require re-visiting in case the EU decided to move to a 30-per cent reduction target in the context of an international agreement, as envisaged by the European Council in 2007.

The new EU climate policies nevertheless fail to close the credibility gap completely. In particular, they are still insufficient to meet the EU's objective of keeping the increase in global mean temperature below two degrees Celsius. This limit requires industrialised countries to reduce domestic GHGE by up to 40 per cent by 2020, and 80–95 per cent by 2050 (Environment Council, March 2009). Even a strengthened EU target of 30 per cent by 2020 could mean a reduction of emissions inside the EU of only about 10–15 per cent, while the remainder could be covered by emission credits acquired from developing countries and accounting of carbon sinks. Even without taking into account the possibility of implementation deficits, for example with respect to the Renewable Energy Directive, domestic emission reductions are thus likely to be too low to reach the two-degree target (Oberthür and Pallemaerts 2010b).

Nevertheless, the climate and energy package provided a sound basis for continued EU leadership in the negotiations leading up to the Copenhagen Climate Summit in December 2009. In the international negotiations, the EU again acted as the major pusher for a global, ambitious and comprehensive post-2012 agreement. The Council and the European Council, in October 2009, advocated, inter alia, that global GHGE should be reduced by at least 50 per cent as compared with 1990 levels by 2050. Developed countries should collectively reduce their emissions by 25–40 per cent by 2020 and by 80–95 per cent by 2050. Developing countries should achieve a substantial relative emission reduction in the order of 15–30 per cent from 'business-as-usual'. The European Council also declared its readiness to take on its fair share of total international public finance of 22–50 billion euro required per year for ambitious mitigation and adaptation strategies in developing countries, including 2.4 billion euro per year for 2010–12 (European Council, December 2009).

The EU's credibility was further supported by progress in reducing its domestic emissions. Since 2004, EU GHGE have followed a falling trend. According to provisional data for 2008, the EU-15 is on track to meeting its Kyoto target, which is also due to the economic crisis. The EU-27 has already achieved more than half its 2020 reduction goal of 20 per cent (Figure 5.1). Due to the deepening crisis in 2009, further reductions can be anticipated.

International EU leadership aspirations nevertheless had a rather hard landing in Copenhagen. The major outcome of the conference – the Copenhagen Accord – did not meet even more modest expectations. Also, the Union proved to have very limited influence, being sidelined in the final negotiations between the US and China, in particular. The Copenhagen Summit demonstrated the limits of EU power and the shifting geo-politics of climate change, in which other players may not see EU cooperation as vital anymore. While Copenhagen calls for a reassessment of the EU's international role and strategy, it is as yet unclear whether and in what form the EU may be able to maintain international leadership on climate change. Part of the considerations may well be a further development and reform of the EU's model of climate diplomacy (see Egenhofer and Georgiev 2009; also van Schaik 2010).

In addition, the financial and economic crisis of 2008 onwards looms large among the challenges for environmental and climate leadership by the intergovernmental arm of the EU. The crisis left its imprint on the new climate policies of the EU in the form of lowered ambitions during the last phase of negotiations in 2008. It also impedes further progress in the development of the domestic policy framework, for example on improving energy efficiency and enhancing policy coherence (including with regard to external policies, trade policies, the EU Common Agricultural Policy, and EU development assistance), and is unlikely to support EU unity and coherence, including bridging differences between old and new Member States.

Ecological modernisation and political opportunities

As the leadership record of the Council and the European Council improved in the 2000s, they increasingly highlighted the political and economic opportunities of effective climate policies. Both the Environment Council and the European Council have, to the extent that they addressed climate change, referred to the threats and political opportunities. The Environment Council was quicker than the European Council to pick up the economic opportunities presented by action on climate change in the 2000s, highlighting reasons of ecological modernisation. With the rise of climate change to high politics, the ecological modernisation theme is also increasingly found in the conclusions of the European Council (Figure 5.3).

Throughout the 1990s, the Environment Council regarded climate change more as an environmental and economical threat than an opportunity. When the Council, in October 1990, supported a stabilisation of CO_2 emissions at 1990 levels by 2000, it highlighted the dangers of the effects of climate change. Even in June 1996, it merely acknowledged that reductions in greenhouse gas emissions were 'technically possible' and 'economically feasible'. However, the Council considered taking action on climate change a significant political opportunity for the EU to play a leading role on the international stage (see, for example, December 1995, March 1997, October 1998).

From 2000, the Council began to pay more attention to the economic benefits associated with combating climate change, while continuing to recognise the risks of the effects of climate change (Figure 5.3). For example, the Council noted the 'scope for low-cost and win-win action in all economies' (June 2001) and that climate change constituted an 'opportunity for modernising the

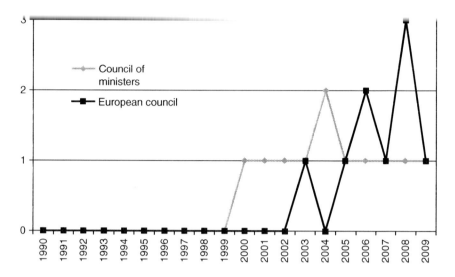

Figure 5.3 Climate change as an economic opportunity in conclusions of Environment
Council and European Council 1990–2009.

economy' (October 2002). In December 2004, the Council emphasised that
addressing climate change 'brings opportunities and incentives for innovation'. In February 2007, it recognised not only that 'the adverse impacts of
climate change would hamper economic and social development in all countries', but also that 'strategies to tackle climate change' could result in 'strengthened energy security, improved EU competitiveness and sustainability'.
In March 2008, the Council emphasised 'new opportunities to underpin
European competitiveness, growth and jobs across the EU'. In the context of
the financial and economic crisis, the Environment Council highlighted a 'need
to build on the synergies between action on climate change and economic
recovery actions' (March 2009). For most of 2009, the Council otherwise
focused much more on the political opportunity for the EU to show leadership in the international climate negotiations of the post-2012 period.

After a more sporadic treatment in the 1990s, the European Council
addressed climate change with growing intensity in the 2000s (see Figure 5.2)
and in so doing increasingly highlighted the economic opportunities arising
from effective climate policies (Figure 5.3). To the extent that the European
Council addressed climate change during the 1990s, it perceived it as a 'risk'
(June 1997) and as 'one of the most challenging environmental problems for
the next decades' (December 1998) as well as a *political* opportunity for the
EU to provide international leadership. It was only in October 2003 that the
European Council acknowledged that action on climate change could con-
tribute to 'boosting growth'. While the theme of ecological modernisation

gained prominence, the European Council continued to recognise the threats and political opportunities arising from climate change. As regards the political opportunities, for example, the European Council stated that the EU remains committed 'to maintaining international leadership on climate change' (June 2008) and 'to playing a leading role in bringing about a global and comprehensive climate agreement' (March 2009). In October 2009, the European Council reiterated that it was 'more than ever fully determined to play a leading role'.

Understanding the improved record

Several internal and external factors help explain the Council's and European Council's enhanced leadership record on climate change since the 1990s (see also van Schaik 2010). Since many of these factors go beyond environmental policy, they have had particular relevance and explanatory value with respect to the increasing engagement of the European Council with its broader perspective on strategic political issues and the integration of EU climate and energy policy.

First, the Council and European Council have increasingly realised that climate policy has the potential to enhance their legitimacy and reinvigorate European integration in general. After the failure of the Treaty Establishing a Constitution for Europe in 2005, the European institutions were looking for such opportunities. The urgency of acting on climate change increased with the release of the IPCC Fourth Assessment Report (IPCC 2007). In addition, public opinion polls showed strong support for European-level action regarding climate change. The Council and European Council, together with the other European institutions, grasped this window of opportunity by moving climate change into the centre of their agendas (Oberthür and Roche Kelly 2008).

Second, intensifying discussions on the security of future energy supplies to Europe have lent strong support to the enhanced leadership of the Council and the European Council on climate change in the 2000s. After 2005, especially, soaring oil and gas prices highlighted the EU's dependence on energy imports which, without targeted counter-measures, was projected to increase from 50 per cent in 2005 to about 70 per cent by 2030 (CEC 2006). At the same time as oil and gas prices increased, political developments in regions with major reserves, including the Middle East and Russia, fuelled concern about the security of Europe's energy supplies. The resulting energy security agenda raised the interest of EU governments in increasing energy efficiency, the use of alternative sources of energy, relevant energy market reforms and an agenda of ecological modernisation.

Third, the overarching goal to enhance the EU's role as a global actor and to support multilateralism has provided a strong rationale for the increasingly progressive role of the Council and the European Council on climate change. Strengthened efforts to become a world actor have been firmly

grounded in support for multilateralism and international law as the back-
bone of global governance (Telò 2009). Climate change was an area particu
larly well suited to the EU's pursuit of international leadership. First, the
withdrawal of the US administration of President Bush from the Kyoto
Protocol in 2001 left a void that the EU could fill. Furthermore, climate
change enjoyed an increasingly high international profile. Accordingly, the
timing of the legislative process of the new climate policies of the EU adopted
in 2008/2009 was clearly geared towards maximising the credibility of the EU
in the international process towards Copenhagen in late 2009.

Fourth, the Kyoto Protocol has helped push EU governments in the
Council to advance domestic EU climate policy and narrow down the credibility gap. The binding emission reduction commitments of the Kyoto Protocol
increased the pressure on the Council to implement effective measures. While
this pressure grew strongest after the entry into force of the Protocol in 2005,
it had already unfolded earlier due to the self-commitment of the EU to the
Kyoto Protocol (see, e.g., Skjærseth and Wettestad 2008).

Finally, a modified framing of climate policies has helped ensure progress
on domestic climate policy in the Council. For much of the 1990s, climate
policy was crafted either as requiring fiscal action (CO_2/energy tax proposal)
or as affecting Member States' choice of different energy sources and the
general structure of their energy supply. As a result, major legislative proposals required unanimity in the Council. In the 2000s, this balance shifted as a
result of what may be called 'cognitive leadership' by both the European
Commission and the Council. Climate policy has come to be considered
closely related to the EU internal market, serving general environmental
objectives and leaving sufficient choices for Member States as regards their
energy sources/supply. Consequently, legislative proposals can be adopted, in
principle, by qualified majority voting.

Conclusion

Both the Council and the European Council have gradually moved from
rhetorical, symbolic or humdrum leadership to transformational 'leadership
by example' on climate change. While they made the EU an international
environmental pusher from the early 1990s, this leadership remained symbolic during most of the 1990s, when the Council also framed climate change
more as a threat than as an opportunity. The gradual improvement of the
leadership record in the 2000s coincided with an increased emphasis on the
opportunities arising from progressive climate policy. When the European
Council increasingly grasped the issue after 2005 (see Figure 2), this eventually resulted in the adoption of a wave of new climate policies in 2008/2009,
which brought the intergovernmental arm of the EU close to the traditionally
greener European Institutions – the EP and the Commission. The new climate
policies also resulted in the communitarisation of this policy area – the full
significance of which is still to materialise.

The Council has also significantly enhanced the coherence, unity and effectiveness of the EU on the international stage. During the 1990s, the Presidency of the Council became the voice of the Union in the international climate negotiations. The differentiation of the mechanisms of coordination and representation of the EU has enhanced stability and coherence and has freed resources for outreach to negotiating partners. While they remain time-consuming and have not yet succeeded in ensuring complete EU unity and have also resulted in new challenges (e.g. a danger of a compartmentalisation of EU climate diplomacy), the less than central role played by the EU at the 2009 Copenhagen Climate Summit may well lead to a reassessment and reform of the EU's model of climate diplomacy by the Council.

Several internal and external factors have contributed to the advances of the Council and the European Council. The desire to upgrade the role of the EU as an international actor and to support multilateralism constitutes a long-established underlying motivation for pursuing international leadership on climate change. A reframing of climate policy in market and environmental terms (as opposed to fiscal and energy terms), which has gone along with an increasing emphasis on the economic and political opportunities arising from climate policy, has facilitated the adoption of legislative proposals (qualified majority). In the 2000s, the increasing political salience of climate change, the entry into force of the Kyoto Protocol, the search for legitimacy by all European institutions and the rise of the energy security agenda, all further improved the conditions for progress.

The future roles of the Council and the European Council nevertheless remain uncertain. On the one hand, the continued relevance of the aforementioned factors suggests that the intergovernmental arm of the EU will continue to push forward the climate policy agenda. On the other hand, both the experience of the 2009 Copenhagen Summit and the lasting impacts of the financial and economic crisis of 2008/2009 raise serious doubts in this respect. While the position of the EU as a vital player at the international level has been shaken, internal divergences and the crisis challenge the ability of the Union to advance its internal climate policies (including the further integration of climate concerns into other policy fields) and to reinvigorate its international role (including through advancing financial and technological cooperation with developing countries). Pending the EU's political response to these challenges, further advances towards effective EU international leadership on climate change cannot be taken for granted.

Notes

1 All Presidency Conclusions of the European Council of Heads of State or Government referred to in the following are available at: <http://ue.eu.int/showPage.aspx?id=432&lang=EN> (accessed January 2010).
2 All Conclusions of the Environment Council referred to in the following are available at: <http://ue.eu.int/App/newsroom/loadbook.aspx?BID=89&LANG=1&cmsid=356> (accessed January 2010).

Bibliography

Bretherton, C. and Vogler, J. (2006) *The European Union as a Global Actor*, 2nd edn, London: Routledge.

CEC (European Commission) (2001) *Third National Communication from the European Community under the UN Framework Convention on Climate Change*, Brussels: Commission of the European Communities.

CEC (2006) *Green Paper: A European Strategy for Sustainable, Competitive and Secure Energy*, 8 March, COM (2006) 105 final, Brussels: Commission of the European Communities.

Collier, U. (1996) 'The European Union's Climate Change Policy: Limiting Emissions or Limiting Powers?', *Journal of European Public Policy*, 3(1), 122–38.

Damro, C. (2006) 'EU-UN Environmental Relations: Shared Competence and Effective Multilateralism', in K. V. Laatikainen and K. E. Smith (eds), *The European Union at the United Nations: Intersecting Multilateralisms*, Basingstoke: Palgrave Macmillan, 175–92.

Delbeke, J. (ed.) (2006) *EU Energy Law, Volume IV*, Leuven: Claeys & Casteels.

EEA (2007) *Greenhouse Gas Emission Trends and Projections in Europe 2007. Tracking Progress towards Kyoto Targets*, EEA Report No. 5/2007, Copenhagen: European Environment Agency.

Egenhofer, C. and Georgiev, A. (2009) 'The Copenhagen Accord. A First Stab at Deciphering the Implications for the EU', *CEPS Commentary*, 25 December 2009, Brussels: Centre for European Policy Studies.

Groenleer, M. L. P. and van Schaik, L. G. (2007) 'United We Stand? The European Union's International Actorness in the Cases of the International Criminal Court and the Kyoto Protocol', *Journal of Common Market Studies*, 45(5), 969–98.

Gupta, J. and Grubb, M. (eds) (2000) *Climate Change and European Leadership: A Sustainable Role for Europe?* Dordrecht: Kluwer Academic Publishers.

Hill, C. (1993) 'The Capability-Expectations Gap, or Conceptualizing Europe's International Role', *Journal of Common Market Studies*, 31(3), 305–28.

IPCC (Intergovernmental Panel on Climate Change) (2007) *Climate Change 2007. Fourth Assessment Report: Synthesis Report*, available at www.ipcc.ch, Geneva: IPCC.

Lacasta, N. S., Desai, S., Kracht, E. and Vincent, K. (2007) 'Articulating a Consensus: The EU's Position on Climate Change', in P. G. Harris (ed.), *Europe and Global Climate Change. Politics, Foreign Policy and Regional Cooperation*, Edward Elgar Publishing Limited: Cheltenham, 211–31.

Liefferink, D. and Andersen, M. S. (1998) 'Strategies of the "Green" Member States in EU Environmental Policy-Making', *Journal of European Public Policy*, 5(2), 254–70.

Massai, L. (2007) 'Climate Change Policy and the Enlargement of the EU', in P. G. Harris (ed.), *Europe and Global Climate Change*, Cheltenham: Edward Elgar Publishing, 305–21.

McCormick, J. (2001) *Environmental Policy in the European Union*, Hampshire: Palgrave.

Oberthür, S. (2009) 'The Negotiating Capacity of the EU in International Institutions: the Case of Climate Change', Paper presented at 5th ECPR General Conference Potsdam, 10–12 September 2009.

Oberthür, S. and Ott, H. E. (1999) *The Kyoto Protocol. International Climate Policy for the 21st Century*, Berlin: Springer.

Oberthür, S. and Pallemaerts, M. (eds) (2010a) *The New Climate Policies of the European Union: Internal Legislation and Climate Diplomacy*, Brussels: VUB Press.

Oberthür, S. and Pallemaerts, M. (2010b). 'The EU's Internal and External Climate Policies: an Historical Overview', in S. Oberthür and M. Pallemaerts (eds.), *The New Climate Policies of the European Union: Internal Legislation and Climate Diplomacy*, Brussels: VUB Press, 27–63.

Oberthür, S. and Roche Kelly, C. (2008) 'EU Leadership in International Climate Policy: Achievements and Challenges', *The International Spectator*, 43(3), 35–50.

Schout, A. (2008) 'Beyond the Rotating Presidency', in J. Hayward (ed.), *Leaderless Europe*, Oxford: Oxford University Press, 269–87.

Schreurs, M. A. and Tiberghien, Y. (2007) 'Multi-Level Reinforcement: Explaining European Union Leadership in Climate Change Mitigation', *Global Environmental Politics*, 7(4), 19–46.

Skjærseth, J. B. (1994) 'The Climate Policy of the EU: Too Hot to Handle?', *Journal of Common Market Studies*, 32(1), 25–45.

Skjærseth, J. B. and Wettestad, J. (2007) 'Is EU Enlargement Bad for Environmental Policy? Confronting Gloomy Expectations with Evidence', *International Environmental Agreements: Politics, Law and Economics*, 7(3), 263–80.

Skjærseth, J. B. and Wettestad, J. (2008) *EU Emissions Trading: Initiation, Decision-Making and Implementation*, Aldershot: Ashgate.

Telò, M. (ed.) (2009) *The European Union and Global Governance*, Abingdon, Oxon: Routledge.

Ten Brink, P. (2010) 'Mitigating CO_2 Emissions from Cars in the EU (Regulation (EC) 443/2009)', in S. Oberthür and M. Pallemaerts (eds), *The New Climate Policies of the European Union: Internal Legislation and Climate Diplomacy*, Brussels: VUB Press, 179–210.

Van Schaik, L. G. (2010) 'The Sustainability of the EU's Model for Climate Diplomacy', in S. Oberthür and M. Pallemaerts (eds), *The New Climate Policies of the European Union: Internal Legislation and Climate Diplomacy*, Brussels: VUB Press, 251–80.

Van Schaik, L. G. and Egenhofer, C. (February 2005) *Improving the Climate – Will the New Constitution Strengthen the EU's Performance in International Climate Negotiations?* CEPS Policy Brief, No. 63. Brussels: CEPS.

Vogler, J. (2005) 'The European Contribution to Global Environmental Governance', *International Affairs*, 81(4), 835–49.

Wettestad, J. (2000) 'The Complicated Development of EU Climate Policy', in J. Gupta and M. Grubb (eds), *Climate Change and European Leadership: A Sustainable Role for Europe?* Dordrecht: Kluwer Academic Publishers, 25–45.

Part III

The EU and its Member States

6   The United Kingdom

A paradoxical leader?

Tim Rayner and Andrew Jordan

Introduction

The UK's engagement with the whole issue of climate change has been rather paradoxical. On the one hand it is widely regarded as a global leader, both in terms of its international diplomatic efforts to raise the profile of climate change and its domestic emission reduction performance (Darkin 2006; IEEP 2006). Domestically, it is one of only a handful of EU-15 Member States to have reduced emissions to below Kyoto target levels already by 2009 (EEA 2009).[1] To help achieve this, it has deployed a new generation of policy instruments (Jordan *et al.* 2003), such as emissions trading. Internationally, the UK has shown entrepreneurial leadership, principally during the Rio and Kyoto climate summits and as chair of the G8 and President of the EU. The authoritative Stern review of the economics of climate change (Stern 2006) can be regarded as a prominent example of cognitive leadership, as can decades of pioneering research at centres including the Meteorological Office and the University of East Anglia (UEA). In 2008, the UK was widely acclaimed as the first country to enshrine in law carbon emission reduction targets – of up to 80 per cent by 2050 – with a view to removing climate change from the vagaries of the 'issue attention cycle' (Jordan and Lorenzoni 2007).

On the other hand, the UK's substantive record in terms of emission reductions is patchy at best. To a large extent, the reductions achieved during the 1990s were a fortuitous by-product of unrelated policy reforms in the energy sector (RCEP 2000; Kerr 2007). In the 2000s, carbon dioxide (CO_2) emissions started to rise again, and the unilateral 1997 commitment to reduce such emissions by 20 per cent by 2010 was quietly dropped (DEFRA 2008). Moreover, it is questionable whether any politician in the UK – outside, perhaps, the Green Party – has really grasped the sheer size of the challenge of decarbonising the national energy system in just over one generation, widely regarded as necessary to avoid the worst effects of climate change.

In this chapter we outline the history of the UK's response to climate change, investigating the origins of the UK's position and the tensions it has in turn created within government and between government and society. We note the waxing and waning of leadership in the face of key constraints such as opposition from key stakeholders, economic pressures and the vicissitudes of the 'issue attention cycle'. The overall story is one of repeated attempts by governments of both right and left to 'join-up' government to deliver deeper emission cuts and a rather piecemeal approach to the introduction of new policy instruments. At key moments, governments have caved in to pressure from interest groups or the wider public. In other words, the ability of governments to lead a low-carbon transition has been rather more fitful and halting than the UK's international reputation would suggest.

National attitudes to climate change

Although the UK public has a comparatively high level of understanding of the issue, there appears to be a significant 'disconnect' between growing awareness and behaviour at the ballot box. Between September 1997 and April 2006, monthly polls consistently found less than 10 per cent regarded the environment as the most important issue facing the country (Ipsos-MORI 2007). At the 2005 election, only 2 per cent of voters considered it the most important issue (Whiteley *et al.* 2005). The apparent breakthrough of the Green Party at the 1989 Euro-elections (winning 15 per cent of the vote), which caused mainstream parties to respond with new policies, proved to be very short-lived. Until the election on May 2010, there had not been a single Green MP in the UK, and the Liberal Democrats, the most environmental of the three main parties, had had no experience in government since the 1970s.

Between 1979 and 1997, the Conservatives' engagement with environmental issues was inconsistent, and Prime Minister Blair's ambivalence towards environmentalism after 1997 has been well documented (Jacobs 1999). After 2006, however, climate change rose up the party-political agenda. There are different interpretations of how this came about. While Khatri (2007: 575) suggests that the initiative was Blair's, who 'undoubtedly [stole] a march' on the other parties by elevating the issue during the UK's Presidencies of the EU and G8 and commissioning the Stern review, McLean (2008) argues that the other parties felt obliged to respond to the rejuvenated Conservative party's call for the country to 'Vote Blue, Go Green'. Whatever the accuracy of the slogan, there is evidence that Blair's successor, Gordon Brown, was forced to respond *inter alia* by committing to build more 'zero-carbon' homes and adopting a Climate Change Act enshrining the 80 per cent reduction target.

As we shall see below, governments of the right and the left have been spurred into action by pressure from a range of stakeholders. Significantly, these have included not only the 'usual suspects' in the environmental movement, but increasingly business groups that have come to adopt an 'eco-logically modern' approach. Even the Confederation of British Industry, long renowned for its opposition to new forms of environmental regulation, has noticeably shifted its stance (CBI 2007). Environmental NGOs have responded to calls (apparently from within government) to mobilise a mass movement for more ambitious policy (Carter and Ockwell 2007). Friends of the Earth's 'Big Ask' campaign and the associated 'Stop Climate Chaos' coalition brought together an unprecedented coalition of environment and development charities, trade unions, faith, community and women's groups, in support of the Climate Change Bill (see also Chapter 13 by Wurzel and Connelly). However, prominent environmentalists feel that in the absence of strong and sustained leadership from government, new coalitions and sources of societal pressure will be needed if the 80 per cent reduction target is to be delivered (Hale 2008). Thus far, the only politician to have risked 'leading' the electorate on environmental issues has been former London Mayor Ken Livingstone, whose campaign pledge to introduce congestion charging was successfully implemented after his election in 2000. In 2008, however, his plan to extend the scheme was scuppered when he lost the election to the Conservative Boris Johnson. The general absence of government leadership has encouraged dramatic direct action protests from groups such as Plane Stupid, and the rise of the civil society initiatives such as the *10 10* campaign. which encourages voluntary emission reductions of 10 per cent in 2010 by a range of individuals and organisations.[2]

Phases of domestic climate change policy

Pre-1988

Although the Royal Commission on Environmental Pollution briefly mentioned climate change in its very first report (RCEP 1971), the issue lay dormant for the rest of the decade and most of the next. Interest was confined to scientific circles, where UK universities developed reputations for pioneering climate change science.

The most significant environmental policy initiatives in this phase came via the EU or various international commitments. But for the most part, the government's priorities were largely domestic and mainly non-environmental.

1988–92

The UK was not, however, immune to the wave of global concern about environmental issues that swept around the world in 1988. The then Prime Minister Margaret Thatcher's high-profile speeches to the UK's Royal Society and the UN General Assembly offered leadership, albeit of a rather symbolic kind. The most concrete outcomes were the establishment, in 1990, of the Hadley Centre for Climate Prediction and Research at the Metrological Office and the publication of a White Paper on environmental matters. This paper expressed support for a stabilisation of emissions and highlighted the potential of market-based instruments to achieve it (HM Government 1990). This new-found concern, however, did not translate into support for the development of a strong EU response: as described in Chapter 1, UK opposition was instrumental in the failure to adopt the carbon-energy tax. This dealt a fatal blow to the EU's leadership ambitions, although on the other hand the UK's Environment Secretary at the time, Michael Howard, is credited with having facilitated the deal on the UN Framework Convention on Climate Change (UNFCCC) at Rio (Haigh 1996).

In terms of its effect on UK emissions, this period is more significant for the developments in 'non-climate' policy. The privatisations of the oil, gas, coal and electricity sectors, many pushed through in the teeth of concerted political opposition, and the ensuing 'dash' for gas had the completely unintended effect of lowering the UK's emissions throughout the 1990s.

1992–7

The Major government (1990–97) ratified the UNFCCC in December 1993 and then set about implementing it. It established a target of returning greenhouse gas emissions to their 1990 levels by 2000, and in 1994 produced the UK's first Climate Change Programme. This relied heavily on voluntary measures, in what was termed a 'partnership approach', although more interventionist measures included the fuel duty escalator (introduced in 1993 at a rate of 3 per cent per year above inflation) and the imposition of VAT on domestic fuel in 1994. However, these fiscal instruments were arguably motivated more by revenue raising concerns than environmental ones. Emissions continued to decline during this period (see Figure 6.1).

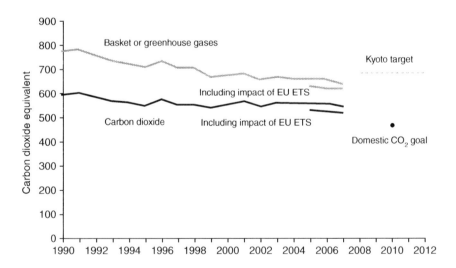

Figure 6.1 UK greenhouse gas emissions: progress towards targets and goals (2007 results are provisional).

Source: DEFRA (2008).

The election of the New Labour government in 1997 raised hopes among environmentalists. In opposition, Blair had made a manifesto commitment to reduce CO_2 emissions by 20 per cent by 2010; subsequently, the Treasury pledged to implement ecological tax reform, shifting the burden from 'goods' such as employment to 'bads' including waste and pollution (HM Treasury 1997). At Kyoto, Blair's deputy, John Prescott, helped to drive through an agreement based on the EU's favoured 'targets and timetables' approach. At home, he promised a more integrated and sustainable approach to national transport planning. The Climate Change Programme of 2000 set out a series of measures to implement these commitments. After a landmark Royal Commission report (RCEP 2000), the pace and urgency of climate policy making began to increase. The Climate Change Levy (CCL) on industry, linked to a system of domestic emissions trading, was a high-profile manifestation of Labour's new thinking on eco-tax reform. However, the so-called fuel-tax rebellion – a concerted public protest about the high price of transport fuels that threatened serious economic disruption – led to the suspension of the automatic fuel duty escalator in 2000.[3] By 2007, the proportion of all taxation made up by green taxes was markedly less than it had been in 1997 (EAC 2007).

2004–10

Although the 2006 revamp of the Climate Change Programme was widely condemned as a missed opportunity, by then the government had begun to see climate change as a business opportunity, a fact amply confirmed by Chancellor Brown's decision to convene the Stern review on climate change economics (Jordan and Lorenzoni 2007). In his final years in power, Blair became more committed to international climate diplomacy, partly to win over critics of his hugely unpopular policy in Iraq. In his premiership, Brown followed up by establishing the Department of Energy and Climate Change (DECC), adopting the landmark Climate Change Bill (see above), a broad-based Low Carbon Transition Plan (HM Government 2009), and elaborating a world-leading policy framework on adaptation to the effects of climate change. At EU level, the UK appeared relatively supportive of the key elements of the Commission's 2008 climate energy package. On the global stage, the UK campaigned actively for a deal at the December 2009 Copenhagen summit, including international financial aspects, and was among the Member States pressing for the EU to raise its unilateral emission reduction commitment from 20 per cent to 30 per cent (Taylor 2009).

Institutional responses, policy programmes and instruments

The overall story of the last two decades has therefore been one of repeated attempts by governments of both political colours to improve 'joined-up' government. However, these have been routinely compromised by the unwill-ingness of the most powerful departments to cooperate. Policy innovation has clearly been evident in the mix of policies deployed, but has mostly been of a rather piecemeal and incremental kind (Helm 2007a). More enduring has been the emergence of a comparatively sophisticated set of institutions for appraising and evaluating the UK's performance. In this section we highlight the role of the UK's rolling Climate Change Programme as a fairly constant presence, noting how the baton of achieving progress has passed from one department to another over time. We then outline the UK's main policy instruments and show how they have been deployed across key sectors.

Institutional responses

One way to tame the power of key departments such as finance, transport and trade, is to implement environmental policy integration (Jordan and Lenschow 2008). The UK has been willing (and able) to readjust the 'machinery of government' with a frequency that would be quite unthinkable in other Member States. In 1997, Labour attempted to 'tame' the powerful transport ministry by incorporating it within a 'super-ministry' that included the former Department of Environment and its planning functions. It was headed by no less a figure than the Deputy Prime Minister, John Prescott. However, ambitious pledges to integrate policy were gradually diluted and the department was eventually dismembered in 2001. Thereafter, the respon-sibility for climate issues was scattered across a number of departments – but *not* energy (the Conservatives abolished that in 1992 and vested its remaining functions in the trade ministry).

In 2006, the Government set up a new Office of Climate Change (OCC) as a shared resource across the main Departments with climate change-related responsibilities, which worked closely with Her Majesty's (HM) Treasury, the Cabinet Office and No. 10. In 2008, the trend towards greater concentra-tion went a step further, when Brown created DECC, as noted above. This was widely praised by both green NGOs and business groups, who had long called for greater coordination between the energy and climate change briefs. Arguably, the primary benefit of this new arrangement is that climate consid-erations will be given a stronger airing at the Cabinet table, from both DECC and the longer-standing Department of Environment, Food and Rural Affairs (DEFRA).

Beyond these machinery of government changes can be found a range of well-respected evaluation and scrutiny bodies. Since 1971, the Royal Commission on Environmental Pollution has regularly issued independent advice. In 2000 it famously called for a 60 per cent reduction in carbon dioxide emissions by 2050, based on the principle of contraction and convergence. In doing so it paved the way for the 80 per cent target now enshrined in legislation (RCEP 2000). In 2000, a Sustainable Development Commission, chaired by a prominent environmentalist, joined the scene. Since 1998, parliamentary committees have included the Environmental Audit Committee, which during Labour's second term in office explicitly made climate policy its main priority.

Policy programmes: the national climate change programmes

The first national climate change programme was launched in 1994 and was subsequently reviewed and updated by Labour in 2000 and 2006. The process of reviewing these programmes has helped to bring different actors together. However, the 2006 programme was criticised on a number of counts: it did not take sufficient steps to deliver the UK's domestic 2010 target; it neglected potentially effective measures that were deemed politically unacceptable (e.g. lowering speed limits) or could only deliver over a longer timeframe; and it did not devote enough attention to new fiscal measures (NAO 2007; EAC 2007).

The Climate Change Act noted above created new institutions for long-term climate governance. It put into statute national targets to reduce greenhouse emissions through domestic and international action by at least 60 per cent by 2050 and 26–32 per cent by 2020. It also required secondary legislation of binding limits known as carbon budgets on greenhouse gas emissions over five-year periods. To advise on these budgets and on the pathway to the 2050 target, a new independent body – the Committee on Climate Change – was created. A new system of annual Government reporting to Parliament in response to annual reports by the Committee on Climate Change on the UK's progress was designed to improve transparency and accountability.

Policy instruments

The UK's preference for market-oriented approaches is well illustrated by the case of renewable energy. Here, instruments have been designed to encourage the increased supply of electricity from renewable sources in the context of a liberalised market. The origins of the policy also highlight the extent to which UK climate policies have emerged as the fortuitous by-product of other interventions. For example, the Non Fossil Fuel Obligation (NFFO), introduced in 1990, was first and foremost a means to continue subsidising nuclear power. In its request to the European Commission for state aid clearance, the Government asked for 'non-fossil fuel' support to pay for specified renewable energy technologies. The justification behind the support of renewable energy was never clarified or widely agreed, an ambiguity which has 'dogged and constrained the design, success and cost of renewables energy policy . . . ever since' (Mitchell and Connor 2004, 1936). Since its introduction in 2002, the NFFO's successor – the Renewables Obligation – has required suppliers to purchase and supply a certain amount of generated electricity. However, the policy failed miserably to achieve the target of 10 per cent of electricity from renewable sources by 2010. In recent years, government has shown a greater willingness to adopt policy approaches – namely feed-in tariffs – that have proved successful in Member States with less liberalised energy sectors.

The introduction of the Climate Change Levy (CCL) in 1999 represented the most significant eco-taxation measure to date. It emerged from a report by a leading industrialist (Marshall 1998). The tax is levied on all non-household uses of coal, gas, electricity, and non-transport liquid petroleum gas. However, significant concessions to key industry sectors were deemed necessary, including an 80 per cent discount for energy-intensive users in return for the adoption of voluntary targets for improving energy efficiency through Climate Change Agreements (CCAs). As recommended by Marshall, eco-taxes (i.e. the CCL), voluntary agreements (i.e. the CCAs) and emissions trading (i.e. the UK ETS) became interlinked to form a mixed approach, but one which was criticised for being too responsive to industry pressure (Helm 2007a).

Compared to industry and energy, it has taken much longer for measures to be put in place in the domestic and transport sectors. One of the very first acts of the New Labour government was to cut the VAT levied on fuel used for home heating from 8 per cent to 5 per cent. Although this played well with Labour's core voters by reducing fuel poverty, it *increased* carbon emissions. It was not until 2002 that the main emission reduction policies for the household sector – the Energy Efficiency Commitment and reform of the Building Regulations – were introduced. Arguably government has mistakenly regarded energy efficiency as a no-cost option, whereas an effective approach requires significant up-front expenditure (EAC 2006).

In the transport sector, despite increasing rhetoric throughout the 1990s regarding the need to shift journeys from private cars to public transport, governments have been unwilling to address the long-term decline in the real costs of motoring since the 1970s. With the demise of the road fuel duty escalator (see above), road pricing has remained the only potential alternative. In 2006, a major policy review by another industrialist, Sir Rod Eddington, concluded that it had real potential, but despite repeated pledges to introduce a national scheme, the government has shied away, preferring a series of incremental supply-side initiatives instead.

Climate change: a threat or an opportunity?

During the 2000s, 'ecologically modern' storylines have been invoked as a form of cognitive leadership to win support for more ambitious climate change mitigation policies. Several policy documents (and speeches) could be cited, including the Treasury's Statement of Intent on Environmental Taxation (HM Treasury 1997) and New Labour's first climate change programme (DETR 2000). The UK emissions trading scheme introduced in 2002 was explicitly intended to deliver 'first mover advantages' to UK companies, by giving them experience prior to the launch (in 2005) of the EU's scheme. In 2004, Blair (2004) declared that 'the very act of solving [climate change] can unleash a new and benign commercial force . . . providing jobs, technology spin-offs and new business opportunities . . .'. The following year, during the UK's G8 Chairmanship, Chancellor Gordon Brown strongly endorsed this view (IEEP 2006).

The clearest and most authoritative expression of the ecologically modern framing of climate change – and act of cognitive leadership – came from the Stern review: 'Tackling climate change is the pro-growth strategy for the longer term, and it can be done in a way that does not cap the aspirations for growth of rich or poor countries. The earlier effective action is taken, the less costly it will be' (Stern 2006: ii). Although subsequently criticised for 'cherry picking' the most favourable evidence (Helm 2007b), it had the politically intended effect of demonstrating that Labour was taking the whole issue seriously (Jordan and Lorenzoni 2007) and galvanised support for stronger action at global level.

Interestingly, at times it has been industry – or at least sections of it – that have been the most emphatic exponents of ecological modernisation. In June 2006, the Corporate Leaders Group on Climate Change sent a public letter to the Prime Minister calling for government to provide a clearer and more ambitious framework for the 'transition to a low carbon economy' – even if that involved much more challenging targets and tougher regulations. Such lobbying doubtless contributed to the Government's decision to support the Climate Change Bill, with its proposal for national carbon budgets (Carter and Ockwell 2007). Even the CBI subsequently shifted its stance, noting that 'alongside the risks, the shift to a low carbon economy offers the UK a unique opportunity to develop innovative environmental technologies of the future and prosper in new, multi-billion-dollar world markets' – but only if research funding is better coordinated and prioritised (CBI 2007).

When the global financial crisis struck in 2008, an alliance of environmentalists pushed for a *New Green Deal*, stimulating economic recovery through investment in low-carbon technologies (Green New Deal Group 2008). The extent to which government has responded to its core message is discussed in the concluding section, but here we note that at EU level, unlike a number of other prominent leaders, Brown lent his support to the main components of the EU climate-energy package, stating that '[t]his is not the time to abandon a climate change agenda which is important for the future . . . [it] is part of the solution for many of the problems we face as a world economy'.[4]

Multi-level governance and leadership

In general, the relationship between UK national, EU and international policy should be seen against the backdrop of two underlying currents. The first is the UK's instinctive preference to exercise leadership at the international level (where its seat on the UN Security Council gives it a political weight disproportionate to its economic size) and in scientific fora (where arguably the UK also 'punches above its weight'). By contrast, it has been less comfortable exercising leadership in the EU (where voting rules are less favourable and domestic public opposition to deeper European integration is profound). That said, from the mid 1990s, Labour politicians did become much more willing to lead the EU towards deeper harmonisation in areas like energy and defence where national sovereignty has normally been jealously guarded. The second has been the steady flow of new environ mental policies from the EU, which have transformed national policy and politics (Bache and Jordan 2006). However, in the sphere of climate change policy, Europeanisation has been a less significant driver, not least because EU policy was slower to evolve; it only really took off in the period after *c*. 2000 (Jordan *et al*. 2010). In the remainder of this section we therefore mainly discuss the UK's leadership at the global level, and then its record of leadership in the EU.

Diplomatic leadership

As noted above, the UK played a much more active role than the European Commission in brokering the UNFCCC (Haigh 1996). The story goes that the UK Environment Secretary Michael Howard flew to Washington to broker a compromise that became enshrined in Article 4 (2) of the Convention (see also Chapter 1 by Wurzel and Connelly and Chapter 2 by Vogler). Whether this was a better outcome than a Convention without US participation is a moot point, but it was undeniably a case of skilful diplomacy – or entrepreneurial leadership – by a country that at the time did not hold the EU Presidency.[5] A similar point can be made about Prescott's role in negotiations at Kyoto, which contributed to (a brief) acceptance of targets and timetables by the US (see also Chapter 5 by Oberthür and Dupont). Subsequently, Prime Minister Blair has been credited with securing an unprecedented acknowledgement of the need to act on climate change from the George W. Bush administration.[6]

The UK has also achieved some notable international diplomatic successes acting in its capacity as the EU's Presidency. During the second half of 2005, its effort was focused on the UN climate change conference in Montreal. Faced with the real prospect of stalemate, the combined efforts of the EU and the Canadian hosts facilitated a decision to initiate talks on the future development of the global climate regime, ensuring that the momentum from the entry into force of the Kyoto Protocol was maintained (IEEP 2006). Failure to keep the process moving would have sent a negative signal to investors and been highly detrimental in particular to the further implementation of the Clean Development Mechanism (CDM).

Since 2006, the UK has also sought to link climate change to related challenges such as poverty alleviation and international security. These 'continued attempt[s]' aimed to 'shift climate change into the realms of high politics' (Khatri 2007: 591). In October 2006, the then Foreign Secretary, Margaret Beckett, delivered a speech in Berlin warning that the failure to tackle climate change could lead to mass migrations and overwhelm failed states. In April 2007, the UK pursued this agenda further by raising climate change for the first time at the UN Security Council, despite stiff opposition from the US, Russia and China.

EU leadership

The UK has shown itself willing to take on a relatively large share of total effort, under the EU's internal burden sharing agreements. In 1997 it offered to take on a 10 per cent reduction, but agreed to increase this to 12.5 per cent after the Kyoto Accord – the only state prepared to shoulder a greater burden (Jordan *et al.* 2010).

Having gradually adopted a more pro-European stance in the late 1990s (Jordan 2002), the UK was better placed to set the climate policy agenda in the EU through the development of domestic policy instruments (e.g. the UK emissions trading scheme) that could be 'uploaded' to the rest of Europe. These efforts were not entirely successful, however, and UK policy makers quickly learned the lesson that in a Union of 27 states, potential first mover advantages can be hard to translate into concrete policy outputs (Jordan *et al.* 2003). Nevertheless, the UK played a positive role during the preparations for the EU emissions trading scheme's (ETS) third trading phase beyond 2012, with British officials agreeing on the need for greater harmonisation, increased transparency and clearer allocation rules (Wurzel 2008). Although the Climate Change Act was not something that could be readily scaled up to the EU level, in 2009 an unprecedented partnership between government and NGOs toured European capitals promoting it as an example for other Member States to follow (Murray 2009).

The UK has also shown strong support for tackling climate emissions through strategic initiatives such as the Cardiff Process, which aimed to deliver greater environmental policy integration. Although it eventually ran out of steam, this process revealed a kind of cognitive leadership at work. In areas where EU policy had yet to substantially develop, such as aviation emissions, the UK has also shown leadership. In December 2005, the Environment Council gave the Commission a clear mandate to include it in the EU ETS (IEEP 2006).

While these examples tell a positive story about the UK's attitude to leadership in the EU, far less flattering cases are not hard to find. The UK's reaction – embarrassingly revealed in several leaked 'non-papers' – to key aspects of the Commission's climate and energy package, was far less enthusiastic about moves towards deeper European integration. Most notably, it pressed for a weakening of the revised emissions trading Directive by allowing greater use of external credits (ENDS Report 405: 46–47). And, faced with hugely demanding targets, the UK also sought to weaken the Commission's renewable energy proposal (Adam 2008). So overall, the pattern of leadership in the EU has been rather more variable than it has at the international level.

The domestic implementation of EU and international commitments

The UK has generally been in the somewhat fortunate position of being able to comfortably meet its legal emission reduction commitments. In 2006, emissions were 18 per cent lower than the 1990 base-year level, well below its burden-sharing target of minus 12.5 per cent. Initial estimates for 2007 showed UK greenhouse gas emissions at 639.4 million tonnes – 2 per cent below the figures for 2006 (DEFRA 2008). According to UK government projections, with existing policies and measures, emissions were due to further decrease to reach a level 16 per cent below base-year emissions by 2010. Carbon sink activities could further reduce emissions to a level 20 per cent below base-year emissions, (EEA 2008). Crucially, the UK's over-delivery of its commitment is expected to play a key part in allowing the EU to meet its overall 8 per cent reduction target.

The greatest reductions made by the UK are expected to occur in the waste and industrial processing sectors. Significant reductions are also expected in the agriculture, and the energy supply and use sectors (EEA 2008). More careful scrutiny of the figures, however, reveals that despite the downward trend in greenhouse gas emissions overall, CO_2 emissions have not been so easy to cut, with the period between the election of New Labour in 1997 and 2006 witnessing a cumulative total increase of around 5–6 per cent and the abandonment of the domestic 20 per cent by 2010 reduction target.

Despite the availability of gratis reductions, the costs of mitigation have still turned out to be far higher than anticipated. A core element of the climate change programme was the domestic renewables target of 10 per cent by 2010. Not only has this been impossible to achieve, but the cost per tonne of carbon saved has been between £280 and £510, making this an extraordinarily expensive policy (NAO/DTI 2005). An equally problematic issue is the emission profile of the transport sector. Given the background of steadily rising traffic levels, concessions on fuel duty and reliance on an ineffective EU-level voluntary agreement with car manufacturers to deliver more efficient vehicles, it is hardly surprising that road transport carbon emissions in 2007 were around 11 per cent above their 1990 levels (ENDS Report 409: 34–38).

As far as transposition is concerned, the UK has generally implemented its EU obligations. One prominent exception has been the UK's implementation of the EU ETS. In November 2004, the Government attempted to revise the National Allocation Plan (NAP) submitted in January, claiming it had simply been a draft. The new document increased the total number of allowances by 20 million.[8] Whether the British government's revised NAP was primarily driven by industry lobbying, or due to the publication of updated CO_2 emission projections, remains open to dispute (Wurzel 2008). The UK subsequently took the Commission to the European Court of Justice (ECJ), only to abandon proceedings to prevent uncertainty undermining investor confidence and the fledgling EU ETS, which the government strongly supported in principle (British official 2007, cited in Wurzel 2008).

It will be far harder, however, to maintain this compliance record in the future. The targets for 2020 are expected to provide a stronger test of the

UK's commitment to emission reduction than anything adopted thus far. Those for renewable energy will be particularly demanding for a country that has struggled to deploy new capacity, despite its excellent wind and wave potential.

Conclusion

In this concluding section, we reflect on the extent to which the UK has taken on a sustained leadership role in climate change politics, both in terms of achieving emission reduction domestically, and influencing political processes at EU level and beyond. Where it has been able to play this role, we suggest how this proved possible. We also reflect on the prospects for a more 'heroic' style of leadership, following the adoption of long-term targets in the Climate Change Act.

While the UK has not exercised the kind of structural leadership exhibited by Germany (which has a much larger economy, a larger population and greater emissions), it has been more able to demonstrate entrepreneurial and cognitive leadership, particularly on the international stage. This has to be seen against an underlying and ongoing trend away from defensive and introspective attitudes towards EU environmental policy since the UK's membership in 1973 (Jordan 2002).

In terms of leadership by example, the UK's record of emission reductions achieved appears fairly impressive. The EU as a whole – and in particular those Member States projected to miss their burden-sharing targets – do owe a debt of gratitude to the UK for the reductions it has made. Without its contribution (and that of Germany (see Chapter 8 by Jänicke)) the EU as a whole would now be facing an impossibly tough struggle to meet its 8 per cent reduction target. However, as we have noted, this has to a large extent been what Liefferink and Birkel (in Chapter 9 of this volume) refer to as 'cost-free' leadership. According to critics, emission reductions achieved serendipitously have allowed UK politicians to posture on the climate issue, rather than develop a coherent strategy for emission reductions more in line with the IPCC recommendations (Kerr 2007). On the occasions when real effort has been required, as when projections revealed a yawning gap between the UK's domestic emission reduction target and what was likely to be achieved, sustained leadership has been shown to be lacking. Specifically, the revamp of the Climate Change Programme in 2006 was widely perceived to have been a missed opportunity (IEEP 2006). The government's approach in critical areas such as eco-tax reform, renewable energy deployment and road pricing has fallen well short of environmentalists' expectations. All too often, the government has failed to make a coherent case to the public, arguably making future leadership in this area even more politically challenging.

In one important sense, the Climate Change Act has been a major demonstration of renewed leadership. In terms of the stringency and legal force of the 80 per cent target and the comprehensiveness of its associated evaluation machinery, the Act undeniably puts the UK in a world-leading position. However, it was only offered once key stakeholders had persistently lobbied the government to lead and, in effect, expressed *their willingness to be led.* The Committee on Climate Change subsequently set three 'intended' five-year carbon budgets up to 2022 which, if accepted, will see UK greenhouse gas emissions in 2020 cut by 42 per cent compared with 1990 levels.[9]

It is tempting to classify the Climate Change Act as a case of 'heroic' leadership, in that it 'sets explicit long-term objectives to be pursued by maximum coordination of public policies and by an ambitious assertion of political will' (Hayward 2008: 7). However, the extent to which the government will allow itself to be informed by the work of the new (and independent) Committee on Climate Change remains unclear. Policies that are seriously at odds with long-term decarbonisation did not take long to surface, most notably the 2009 decision to allow a third runway at Heathrow airport.[10] Uncertainty over proposed development of coal-fired power stations and timidity in relation to demand management in transport highlight continuing government ambivalence. Despite calls for a 'Green New Deal', to respond to the financial crisis of 2008, the UK's package of reflationary measures lacked the commitment to decarbonisation of its counterparts in the USA and elsewhere (ENDS Report 407: 45).

That said, the UK has demonstrated greater commitment, and offered a far greater degree of cognitive and entrepreneurial leadership, at international level. In terms of entrepreneurial leadership, Howard's intervention at Rio, Prescott's role at Kyoto and Blair's industrious elevation of the issue during the UK's chairmanship of the G8 in 2005 were especially notable (IEEP 2006).

In terms of cognitive leadership, the UK's sponsorship of major scientific events such as the symposium on avoiding dangerous climate change at Exeter in 2005, and its ongoing efforts to reframe climate change as an issue that extends well beyond the narrow environmental 'ghetto', deserve similar recognition. The Stern review was deliberately and very consciously targeted at a global audience (Jordan and Lorenzoni 2007), and represents an attempt by the UK to act as a global leader, by helping to break the logjam on commitments after the expiry of the Kyoto Protocol.

Our praise for successive Governments' international agenda-setting role is not unqualified, however. In particular, one of UK Prime Ministers' favourite messages – that climate change can be tackled adequately by the application of science and technology – underplays the scale of the economic and behavioural changes that will also be required to stand any chance of containing global temperature rise to 2°C above pre-industrial levels (Anderson and Bows 2008). Persuading electorates that a sufficient degree of emission abatement cannot be achieved without reductions in economic growth and material standards of living for some is a leadership challenge that remains to be confronted.

Notes

1 The other four are Germany, Greece, Sweden and France (EEA 2009).
2 See <http://www.1010uk.org/>
3 At the time of this writing, the escalator has still not been re-started; instead, decisions on duty level are taken on a yearly basis.
4 <http://www.number10.gov.uk/Page17192>
5 The UK took over the Presidency in the second half of 1992.
6 Although formally global legal deals can be struck at only UN level, the G8 can act as a forum in which new strategic directions for industrialised countries can be debated and agreed.
7 On the plus side, the UK successfully pressed for measures to finance carbon capture and storage (CCS) using allowances from the EU ETS. This was substantially more generous than the French Presidency proposal, but less than that requested by MEPs (ENDS Report 407: 4).
8 One 'allowance' corresponds to one tonne of carbon dioxide equivalent.
9 This figure would be conditional on the EU's 2020 commitment increasing to 30 per cent. The committee also recommended softer 'interim' budgets, with a cut of 34 per cent by 2020, in the absence of an international agreement at Copenhagen.
10 Even if aviation emissions are kept to 2005 levels (as announced by the Transport Secretary in making the announcement on Heathrow's third runway), by 2050 the sector is expected to consume all of the UK's permitted carbon budget (Bows and Anderson 2007).

Bibliography

Adam, D. (2008) 'Britain Tries to Block Green Energy Laws', *The Guardian*, 24 July.
Anderson, K. and Bows, A. (2008) 'Reframing the Climate Change Challenge in Light of Post-2000 Emission Trends', *Philosophical Transactions of the Royal Society A*, 3863–82.
Bache, I. and Jordan, A. J. (eds.) (2006) *The Europeanization of British Politics*, Basingstoke: Palgrave.
Blair, T. (2004) 'International Action Needed on Global Warming', speech at the Banqueting House, 14 September 2004; available online at: <http://www.number-10.gov.uk/output/page6333.asp>
Bows, A. and Anderson, K. (2007) 'Policy Clash: Can Projected Aviation Growth be Reconciled with the UK Government's 60% Carbon Reduction Target?', *Transport Policy*, 14(2), 103–10.
Carter, N. and Ockwell, D. (2007) *New Labour, New Environment?* London: Friends of the Earth.
CBI (2007) *Climate Change: Everyone's Business*, London: Confederation of British Industry.
Darkin, B. (2006) 'Pledges, Politics and Performance: An Assessment of UK Climate Policy', *Climate Policy*, 6, 257–74.
DEFRA (2008) *UK Climate Change Programme: Annual Report to Parliament*, July 2008, available online at <http://www.defra.gov.uk/ENVIRONMENT/climatechange/uk/ukccp/pdf/ukccp-ann-report-july08.pdf>
DETR (2000) *Climate Change – the UK Programme*, Norwich: HMSO.
EAC (Environmental Audit Committee) (2006) *Keeping the Lights On: Nuclear, Renewables and Climate Change*, Sixth Report, Session 2005–6, HC 584-I.

EAC (2007) *Pre-Budget 2006 and the Stern Review, Fourth Report of Session 2006–7*, HC 227, London: HMSO.

EEA (European Environment Agency) (2008) *Greenhouse Gas Emission Trends and Projections in Europe 2008*, Report No 5/2008, Copenhagen: European Environment Agency.

EEA (European Environment Agency) (2009) *Greenhouse Gas Emission Trends and Projections in Europe 2009*, Report No 9/2009, Copenhagen: European Environment Agency.

ENDS (Environmental Data Services) ENDS Report, various issues.

Green New Deal Group (2008) *A Green New Deal – Joined-up Policies to Solve the Triple Crunch of the Credit Crisis, Climate Change and High Oil Prices*, London: New Economics Foundation (NEF).

Haigh, N. (1996) 'Climate Change Policies and Politics in the European Community', in T. O'Riordan and J. Jäger (eds), *Politics of Climate Change*, London: Routledge, 155–83.

Hale, S. (2008) *The New Politics of Climate Change*, London: Green Alliance.

Hayward, J. (ed.) (2008) *Leaderless Europe*, Oxford: Oxford University Press.

Helm, D. (2007a) 'Climate Change Policy: Lessons from the UK', *Economists' Voice*, available online at <http://www.dieterhelm.co.uk/publications/Climate_change_policy_lessons_from_UK.pdf>

Helm, D. (2007b) 'Climate Change: Sustainable Growth, Markets, and Institutions', online at <http://www.dieterhelm.co.uk/publications/HDR_climate_change_apr_07.pdf>

HM Government (1990) *This Common Inheritance: Britain's Environmental Strategy*, Cm 1200. London: HMSO.

HM Government (2009) *The UK Low Carbon Transition Plan*, London: HMSO.

HM Treasury (1997) 'Statement of Intent on Environmental Taxation', <http://www.hm-treasury.gov.uk/topics/environment/topics_environment_policy.cfm>

IEEP (2006) *Climate Change Action. The UK: Leader or Laggard?* London: Institute for European Environmental Policy.

Ipsos-MORI (2007) *The Most Important Issues Facing Britain Today*, available online at: <http://www.ipsos-mori.com/content/the-most-important-issues-facing-britain-today.ashx>

Jacobs, M. (1999) *Environmental Modernisation: The New Labour Agenda*, London: Fabian Society.

Jordan, A. J. (2002) *The Europeanization of British Environmental Policy*, Basingstoke: Palgrave.

Jordan, A. J. and Huitema, D. *et al.* (eds) (2010) *Climate Change Policy in the European Union*, Cambridge: Cambridge University Press.

Jordan, A. J. and Lenschow, A. (eds.) (2008) *Innovation in Environmental Policy?* Cheltenham: Edward Elgar.

Jordan, A. J. and Lorenzoni, I. (2007) 'Is There Now a Political Climate for Policy Change? Policy and Politics after the Stern Review', *Political Quarterly*, 78(2), 310–19.

Jordan, A. J., Wurzel, R., Zito, A. and Brückner, L. (2003) 'Policy Innovation or "Muddling Through"? NEPIs in the United Kingdom', in A. J. Jordan, *et al.* (eds) *New Instruments of Environmental Governance*, London: Frank Cass, 179–98.

Khatri, K. (2007) 'Climate Change', in A. Seldon (ed.), *Blair's Britain, 1997–2007*, Cambridge: Cambridge University Press, 572–92.

Kerr, A. (2007) 'Serendipity is Not a Strategy: The Impact of National Climate Programmes on Greenhouse-Gas Emissions', *Area*, 39(4), 418–30.

Marshall, C. (1998) *Economic Instruments and the Business Use of Energy*, London: HM Treasury.

McLean, I (2008) 'Climate Change and UK Politics', *Political Quarterly*, 79 (2), 184–93.

Mitchell, C. and Connor, P. (2004) 'Renewable Energy Policy in the UK 1990–2003', *Energy Policy*, 32, 1935–47.

Murray, J. (2009) 'Britain Urges European Neighbours to Adopt UK-Style Climate Law', *BusinessGreen*, 16 Nov 2009 <http://www.businessgreen.com/business-green/news/2253190/britain-urges-european>

NAO (National Audit Office) (2007) *Cost-Effectiveness Analysis in the 2006 Climate Change Programme Review*, London: National Audit Office.

NAO/DTI (2005), *Renewable Energy*, *Report by the Comptroller and Auditor General*, *HC 210 Session 2004–5*, National Audit Office, Department of Trade and Industry, February 11th, London: TSO.

RCEP (Royal Commission on Environmental Pollution) (1971) *First Report*, Cmnd 4585, London, HMSO.

RCEP (2000) *Energy – The Changing Climate*, 22nd report, Cm 4794, London: HMSO.

Stern, N. (2006) *The Economics of Climate Change*, Cambridge: Cambridge University Press.

Taylor, S. (2009) 'Push for EU to Offer 30% Emissions Cut in Copenhagen', *European Voice* 10.12.2009, <http://www.europeanvoice.com/article/imported/push-for-eu-to-offer-30-emissions-cut-in-copenhagen-/66640.aspx>

Whiteley, P., Stewart, M., Sanders, D. and Clarke, H. (2005) 'The Issue Agenda and Voting in 2005', in P. Norris and C. Wleizen (eds), *Britain Votes*, Oxford: Oxford University Press, 146–61.

Wurzel, R. K. (2008) *The Politics of Emissions Trading in Britain and Germany*, London: Anglo-German Foundation for the Study of Industrial Society.

7 France's troubled bids to climate leadership

Joseph Szarka

Introduction

While numerous analyses have probed EU claims to climate leadership (Oberthür and Roche Kelly 2008; Schmidt 2008; Schreurs and Tiberghien 2007; Skodvin and Andresen 2006), less attention has been given to climate leadership bids by constituent members. France was historically a major power but, in the contemporary period, French aspirations to the 'politics of grandeur' (Cerny 1980) and to 'great nation' status have proved problematic (Cogan 2003; Maclean and Szarka 2008). Nevertheless, France not only maintains leadership ambitions in traditional arenas of international relations – as President Chirac's opposition in 2002 to the invasion of Iraq demonstrated – but advances claims in new arenas. The statement by Jean-Pierre Raffarin (2004) – made while Prime Minister – that France is moving from 'an era of pioneer initiatives to an era of national ambition' is representative of the received opinion among domestic policy elites that France is capable of climate and energy leadership.

France is one of few nations to have reduced its greenhouse gas emissions (GHGE). On the basis of this achievement, France has made three types of leadership bid: (1) as a pioneer in domestic emission reductions; (2) as an innovator in relation to policy norms; and (3) as a prime mover during international negotiations. The content and results of these bids will be investigated through the leadership typology provided by Young (1991), as adapted by Wurzel and Connelly in Chapter 1. The category of *structural leadership* refers to the exercise of material, economic and/or military power. *Entrepreneurial leadership* involves the deployment of negotiation skills to broker mutually acceptable and effective outcomes and a capacity for coalition building: both activities require understanding of the interests of key players. *Cognitive leadership* stresses the power of ideas in modifying the understanding, handling and resolution of policy dilemmas and in altering actor perception of their self-interest. These leadership types have proved particularly important in institutional bargaining processes and the emergence of a global climate protection regime – through the United Nations Framework Convention on Climate Change (UNFCCC) and subsequent Conference of the Parties (COP) negotiations. However, climate protection also involves policy norms implemented at national and regional levels. Hence for present purposes a fourth leadership type is taken from the literature, namely *directional leadership* by which Grubb and Gupta (2000) and Gupta and Ringius (2001) understood demonstration by example through taking concrete measures. This leadership typology provides a theoretical lens to investigate French climate leadership claims. The aims of this chapter are to explain and assess the bases on which these claims have arisen, and to report on their reception in international society. The interpretation offered is that France has consistently adopted a front-runner stance on climate policy, but has largely failed to persuade major partners of the credibility of its climate leadership bids.

National attitudes to climate change

Although favourable stances towards climate policy have increasingly characterised French public opinion, climate leadership ambitions have not emerged from bottom-up. In a Eurobarometer survey (2005: 82), respondents were asked which five environmental issues they were most worried about: in EU-15, climate change topped the list at 47 per cent but stood at 42 per cent in France, where larger proportions of respondents were 'most concerned' with man-made disasters (55 per cent), air pollution (49 per cent) and water pollution (48 per cent). In a 2008 survey, 84 per cent of French respondents considered that climate change was 'a very serious problem', rather more than the average of 75 per cent across EU-27. Yet the same survey found that 49 per cent of French respondents (as compared to 42 per cent in EU-27) thought that 'it is governments, companies and industries that have to change their behaviour, not citizens' (Eurobarometer 2008: 77). It is unclear whether these variations in responses across surveys reflect meaningful shifts in opinion or are artefacts arising from differences in question wording. At face value, however, these findings indicate a public opinion which is favourable to climate protection measures, but believes responsibility lies with government and business rather than the citizenry. This stance reflects the framing of climate mitigation by French policy elites, which has been characterised by its state-led and technology-focused orientation.

Phases of domestic climate policy: programmes and policy instruments

To understand French claims to *directional leadership* in climate policy, we next investigate performance and outcomes. French GHGE per capita and per unit of GDP have been on a falling curve for some two decades. Emissions per capita stood at 10 tonnes of CO_2 equivalent in 1990, falling to 9.1 by 2005; for the same years, EU-15 average emissions per capita were 11.7 and 10.9 tonnes of CO_2 equivalent (EEA 2007: 22). When emissions intensity – the relationship between emissions and GDP – is indexed at 100 for EU-27, the least emissions-intense nations are Sweden at 59 and France at 74

(EEA 2007: 22). Whereas French GDP grew by 19 per cent between 1990 and 2000, industrial emissions of CO_2 fell by 2 per cent, achieving considerable 'decoupling' in terms of carbon intensity (Baulinet 2002: 40). Moreover, France reduced GHGE from 563.3 million tonnes in 1990 to 541.3 million tonnes in 2006, a cut of 4 per cent (EEA 2008: 11). This makes France one of the few nations on the planet to achieve both emissions reduction and the decoupling of GHGE from economic growth. These achievements form the basis of French claims that they have led by example.

France achieved significant GHGE reductions *before* other nations. Energy-related emissions fell by 23 per cent between 1980 and 1990 (IEA 1996: 73–76). Subsequent to oil price shocks in the 1970s, energy policy measures included strict regulations to improve energy efficiency, high taxes on fuels and diversification of fuel sourcing within the power sector (French Government 1995: 82). Restructuring in electricity generation had its roots in the 1960s when first hydro and then nuclear power sources were strongly developed. In 1974, when the decision to accelerate the nuclear power programme was taken by the Messmer government, oil and coal still accounted for some 60 per cent of generation. By the late 1990s, two (largely) carbon-free sources accounted for around 90 per cent of French electricity sourcing: nuclear (*circa* 75 rising to 78 per cent depending on year) and hydro (*circa* 15 dropping to 12 per cent). By the 2000s, electricity generation was responsible for only 8 per cent of GHGE in France, as compared to 36 per cent in Germany and 40 per cent in the USA (MEDD 2004a: 42). On a variety of indicators, France can legitimately claim to be a front-runner in domestic emission reductions.

However, the initial credibility problem for French bids to climate leadership is that policy drivers had no connection with climate protection. The selection of the nuclear option was motivated by energy security and economic competitiveness. France became an 'inadvertent pioneer' (Szarka 2006) in that GHGE cuts were an unplanned and felicitous by-product of the economic and political goal of energy independence. A similar process occurred in relation to emissions from industrial processes (falling in 2005 by 27 per cent from 1990 levels), in agriculture (falling by 9 per cent) and in waste (also falling by 9 per cent) (French Government 2006: 48). In these sectors, measures to improve operational efficiency and reduce other pollutants were accompanied by a fall in GHGE. Derived gains can be consolidated, of course, once their relevance for other policy objectives is understood. But the subsequent credibility problem was that France held out for a target of merely stabilising emissions at their 1990 levels under the 1997 Kyoto Protocol and its translation into the EU's 1998 burden-sharing agreement. From the perspective of aspirations to climate leadership, this was a fatal error. France sent out the message that it would stand still while others caught up. This was a wasted opportunity since even a modest proposed cut – say matching the EU overall target of 8 per cent – would have enhanced the credibility of the 'French model' and probably eased the way to *entrepreneurial leadership* in climate negotiations.

The error arose from a failure in national self-confidence. The achievement of significant emission cuts ahead of other industrialised nations created economic anxieties in France, once the need for deliberate climate policy manifested. Reporting within the context of the UNFCCC, the French Government (1995: 6) complained that 'the cost of new measures liable to be taken in France will often be higher than in the other countries of the European Union or the OECD'. In the run-up to the Kyoto Protocol, it became clear that competitor nations had greater scope for cheap cuts. For example, the UK and Germany benefited more from the arbitrary choice of the 1990 baseline due to the 'dash to gas' in the former and 'wall fall' emission reductions in the latter (see Chapter 6 by Rayner and Jordan and Chapter 8 by Jänicke respectively). On the other hand, these countries had committed to much tougher targets, with cuts of 12 per cent and 21 per cent respectively. Consequently in the late 1900s, France appeared to rest on its laurels, with little climate policy innovation (Giraud, Collier and Löfstedt 1997).

By the turn of the century, the limits of this approach became clear when official analyses projected that France would overshoot its stabilisation target by some 25 per cent, due to rapid economic growth (Gouvernement français 2000: 29).[1] In response, the 'plural left' Jospin government drew up the year 2000 Climate Plan, which proposed new environmental policy instruments, including carbon taxation and emissions trading (Deroubaix and Lévèque 2006; Szarka 2003). Feed-in tariffs for renewable energy sources were also introduced (Szarka 2007: 79–82). Environment Minister Voynet – a historic 'Green' – brought forward an ecotax, called the *TGAP-Energie*. However, the Constitutional Council struck it down, since it discriminated among different categories of energy consumer, leading to the inequitable outcome that a lower level of consumption could incur a higher level of tax. This ruling undermined the Jospin Climate Plan.

Subsequent to Jacques Chirac's re-election as President in 2002 and a right-wing landslide at the parliamentary elections, the Raffarin government sought to improve on its predecessor's performance. The 2004 Climate Plan took two years to finalise, since the choice of instruments proved problematic. The mood had swung against carbon taxation, partly for political reasons, due to its association with 'red-green' governments in France and Germany, and partly for economic reasons, because of worries over hampering competitiveness during an economic downturn. Also, increases on vehicle fuel duty had provoked a backlash in 2001. Hence policy concentrated on incremental improvements across a range of sectors, rather than experimenting with an ambitious new instrument. The 2004 plan listed some 60 proposals, whose more innovative measures – such as the *bonus-malus* on vehicles – indicated renewed *directional leadership*. On the other hand, France decided to have almost no recourse to the Kyoto 'flexibility mechanisms'. The plan aimed to achieve emissions 'savings' of 72 $MtCO_2$ equivalent (MEDD 2004a: 77), bringing France back on track to emissions stabilisation at the 1990 level.

In a bold move, President Chirac committed France to the 'factor four' target of a 75 per cent reduction in GHGE by 2050, a target pledged by Prime Minister Raffarin in 2003 at the 20th plenary session of the Intergovernmental Panel on Climate Change (IPPC) in Paris (Boissieu 2006: 13). At one level, the pledge bolstered French climate leadership. But at another, it pointed up the disconnect between the short- and the long-term goals of French climate policy. The problem was worsened by dichotomous developments in emission trends. Whereas heavy industry and the electricity sector showed major GHGE reductions, emissions in the road transport sector rose by 18.7 per cent between 1990 and 2003 (accounting for a quarter of CO_2 emissions) and by 6.4 per cent in the residential and tertiary sectors (French Government 2006: 49). France is far from unique in these aspects. However, precisely because the 'low hanging fruit' of emission cuts in the power and industrial sectors had been largely exhausted, France needed to provide new evidence of *directional leadership*. The target of a 75 per cent GHGE reduction for 2050 was incorporated into the 2005 Energy Bill, making France one of the first countries to legally commit to a drastic, long-term emissions ceiling. But climate policy continued to be oriented towards upstream, supply-side solutions, focusing on energy efficiency and technology standards. The French Government (2006: 58) stated emphatically that 'energy efficiency is the main objective of French energy policy', aiming for an improvement of 2 per cent per year in end-use energy intensity up to 2015 (rising to 2.5 per cent to 2030) to occur primarily in the residential, tertiary and transport sectors. The official scenario for future emissions control perpetuated France's traditional energy and environmental policies.

Climate change as a threat and opportunity?

Climate protection has provided new legitimising discourses and commercial opportunities for technologies capable of reducing emissions. France considers nuclear power to be one of those and sought to exercise *entrepreneurial leadership* by its promotion. During COP-6 talks at the Hague in 2000, the French argued for inclusion of nuclear power within the Clean Development Mechanism (CDM). The aims were to restore the lost prestige of the industry, recognise its roles in ensuring energy security and climate protection, and improve investment conditions for an industrial sector where France has world-leading firms. To these ends, France tried to build a pro-nuclear coalition. This strategy illustrated both 'forerunner' and 'pusher' activity: Wurzel (2008a: 78) defined the former as the attempt to maximise degrees of policy freedom at the national level, while the latter relates to the export of domestic preferences to the EU level. However, only Finland was in favour, with the remaining 13 states of EU-15 opposing (Lajoinie 2001: 102–3). The wish to 'upload' national preferences to the international level through the Kyoto Protocol failed, even though the USA and China were favourable to inclusion of nuclear power within the CDM (Mühlenhöver 2002: 175–76).

The French nuclear industry had to be restructured in an uncertain political, regulatory and commercial environment (Szarka 2009). Areva – the French nuclear reactor supplier – closed the first export sale of its new European Pressurised Reactor (EPR) to Finland in 2003. France restated its preference for nuclear power in the 2005 Energy Bill, and the first of a proposed series of EPRs went into construction. In 2007, the sale of two EPRs to China was finalised. Nations who purchase French nuclear technology can, to a degree, be considered as 'followers' of the French emissions reduction model. Nuclear diplomacy towards China and India – two developing nations responsible for major and accelerating GHGE – now constitutes an important component of French *entrepreneurial leadership*. During 2005–6, the US and UK authorities also grew more favourable to nuclear power. The oil and gas price spikes of 2007–8, together with political tensions in the Middle East and with Russia, reinforced concerns over energy security. These developments gave opportunities to France's nuclear lobby, with the personal involvement of President Sarkozy, to push nuclear-sourced generation as a means to climate protection and energy securitisation.

French thinking on nuclear power converges with 'ecological modernisation' concepts which, in stressing the essential compatibility of economic and environmental desiderata, are gradually altering construals of national self-interest. However, France has proved unable to exercise *cognitive leadership* in this domain. 'Ecological modernisation' theory has arisen outside of France and does not cite nuclear power as a reference technology, while within France the theory per se is little known. At the commercial level, the French nuclear exports drive has been instrumental in creating a 'lead market' – though not of the variety envisaged by Jänicke and Jacob (2004). However, significant obstacles to the expansion of nuclear power persist due to its operational risks, economic performance, social resistance and the danger of nuclear arms proliferation (Ansolabehere 2003; Elliott 2007). Expressions of French intentions during 2007–8 to sell nuclear technology to Middle Eastern and African states aroused international disquiet. Further, nuclear phase-outs in Germany and Sweden underscore France's inability to build a pro-nuclear coalition within the EU. Contestation of nuclear power reveals the limits to French *entrepreneurial leadership* in energy and climate policy.

Multi-level governance and leadership

In arguing for pioneering norms during international negotiations, France has aspired to *entrepreneurial* and *cognitive leadership*. The 1992 UNFCCC set out in article three the principle of 'common but differentiated responsibilities' in relation to climate protection (UN 1992). A policy question arose over the translation of 'differentiated responsibilities' into meaningful measures. The Kyoto outcome was to set emission ceilings for industrialised nations alone. Yet this is one policy solution among many. As one of the first signatories to the UNFCCC, France put forward an alternative norm for GHGE control by stressing emissions per capita in its 1993 programme for combating climate change. It has since promoted this norm in international discussions, arguing for 'a convergence of emission levels based on appropriate indicators' (French Government 1997: 18). This illustrates France's bid for *cognitive leadership* by promoting an argument for policy norms based on fairness.

The French approach bears similarities to the 'contraction and convergence' model promoted by Meyer (2000), which views the atmosphere as a global commons and distributes national responsibilities on the basis of international and intergenerational equity. It favours a transition to common levels of GHGE by large cuts on the part of industrialised nations, while accepting that developing countries need to grow their economies – and their emissions. The difference is that the 'contraction and convergence' school argues for global equity, whereas the French preference was grounded in domestic interest. As noted above, France has relatively low GHGE per capita and per unit of GDP. A negotiating strategy to reduce per capita emissions in industrial countries to common levels applies pressure on the USA, Germany and other industrial nations, while requiring little effort from France. Although not 'regulatory competition' in the sense used by Héritier, Knill and Mingers (1996) in terms of *form*, this strategy served comparable *purposes*. But France again encountered a credibility problem in that the message to industrialised nations was to converge downwards to French levels, but with no matching commitment from France to drop towards developing country levels. With the attempt to secure national comparative advantage being transparent, peer-group negotiators responded in kind by defending their perceived economic interests and ignoring the emissions per capita argument. While France proved unable to exercise *entrepreneurial leadership*, the argument will not go away given support from the planet's largest nation – and now largest GHG emitter – namely China.

France was also frustrated in advocacy of international carbon taxation. In the 1990s, the French attached particular conditions to a carbon tax, namely that (a) it be based solely on the carbon content of fuel (and not on energy content, which would have penalised nuclear power), (b) be implemented in all EU states, and (c) precautions be taken to safeguard competitiveness should other OECD states not implement equivalent measures (French Government 1995: 6–7, IEA 1996: 75). The preference for uniform application of climate measures to ensure economic competitiveness has become a consistent element of the pragmatic French approach. However, the early EU coalition supporting a carbon tax broke down (Zito 2000). In 2006, France tried a different tack by proposing a CO_2 border adjustment tax. Prime Minister Villepin proposed that carbon-intensive imports into the EU be taxed in order to reduce market distortions (given the implementation of emissions trading in Europe alone) and increase the incentives for third party nations to participate in GHGE management (Damian and Abbas 2007). Whereas previous carbon tax proposals entailed domestic payments, the new tax would be levied on foreigners, so side-stepping national opposition and potentially building a European coalition. In seeking to protect European firms, the proposal also accorded with the French philosophy that climate measures should not harm competitiveness. However, in December 2006, Trade Commissioner Mandelson argued vigorously against the proposal on the grounds of incompatibility with WTO rules. Further, the proposal risked alienating key international partners in the run-up to COP-15 negotiations in Copenhagen. Another French leadership bid floundered.

The Presidency of the European Council from July to December 2008 gave France a unique opportunity to exercise *entrepreneurial leadership*. The objective was to finalise agreement on the 'climate and energy package' and its suite of four directives: (1) a directive on GHGE targets for 2020; (2) a new renewables directive; (3) a directive to extend the EU Emissions Trading Scheme (EU ETS); and (4) a new directive on carbon capture and storage. The EU pledge for 2020 was to reduce GHGE by at least 20 per cent, increase energy sourcing from renewables to 20 per cent and achieve a 20 per cent improvement in energy efficiency (CEC 2008). President Sarkozy managed to broker agreement in the December 2008 European Council, though at the cost of buying off Polish resistance with a reduced commitment under EU ETS (see also Chapter 10 by Jankowska). Nevertheless, the successful outcome considerably enhanced his climate credentials.

During 2009, France developed a major international initiative entitled the 'Climate Justice Plan'. Its aims were to establish financial mechanisms to support the poorest and most vulnerable nations in their adaptation to climate change, and build up a coalition to bring the Copenhagen talks to a successful conclusion. To clarify responsibilities and entitlements, the plan outlined a four-part typology of nations. The first category comprised the poorest countries who would be eligible for major international aid, but have no GHGE reduction target. The second was formed by 'developing' countries, whose need for economic growth would be supported by access to low carbon energy sources and who would prepare national climate strategies to manage emissions, but without targets. The third included 'emerging' countries who would reduce the carbon intensity of their economy, with peak emissions assumed for 2030. Industrialised countries constituted the fourth: they would pursue emissions reductions of 80 per cent by 2050, and provide financial support for adaptation projects around the globe. The 'Climate Justice Plan' proposed some $500 billion of aid to 2020, mostly to Africa. It called for the establishment of a World Environment Organisation to supervise common verification rules, the development of ambitious forestry conservation, accelerated research in low carbon technologies and access to fast-track finance as of 2010. It argued for innovative financial mechanisms with the main suggestion being a 'Tobin tax', namely a 0.01 per cent levy on stock market transactions globally.

The 'Climate Justice Plan' appears to be the brainchild of Ecology Minister Jean-Louis Borloo (Quéméner 2009). During 2009, Borloo sought to build a supportive coalition by meetings with representatives of some 80 of the poorest countries on the planet. President Sarkozy personally supported the French diplomatic charm offensive. In November 2009, he met with President Lula da Silva of Brazil and came to a common position which included components of the French plan (French Government 2009a). Subsequently Sarkozy presented the plan at the summit in Manaus of the eight member countries of the Amazon Cooperation Treaty Organisation, and then to the 53 heads of state gathered at the Commonwealth summit in Trinidad – the first time a French president had addressed either organisation. Talks were also held with China and India. Borloo communicated his proposal document to Copenhagen delegates in mid-November (Borloo 2009). On the 15th December, France and Ethiopia (officially representing African nations) issued a joint appeal calling for an ambitious Copenhagen Accord, for full transparency of commitments to be supervised by a World Environment Organisation and the adoption of a fast-track adaptation fund of $10 billion p.a. over 2010–12, to be financed inter alia by the creation of a tax on international financial transactions (French Government 2009b). With the aim of breaking the deadlock in COP-15 climate negotiations, President Sarkozy (2009) made an impassioned speech on the 17th December in Copenhagen which reiterated key elements of the French plan.

The 'Climate Justice Plan' illustrates French leadership ambitions along three dimensions. *Cognitive leadership* is displayed in brokering global solidarity and equity, sponsored by innovative financial mechanisms. This strategy had the potential to alter actors' perception of their self-interest, especially as the 'Tobin tax' proposal was (at face value) pain-free and borne by the most wealthy. The four-part typology of nations modified the understanding, handling and resolution of policy dilemmas through abandonment of the dichotomous language that typically marks international relations discussions – namely, 'North-South' terminology which pits 'developed'/industrialised nations *against* 'developing'/non-industrialised countries. Translation of this simplistic dichotomy into the Kyoto Protocol's categorisation of Annex 1 versus non-Annex 1 countries had created counterproductive fears that a post-Kyoto settlement required the imposition of an emissions ceiling on less developed countries. This aroused sentiments of injustice and hostility. It also barred the route back into the climate regime for non-participant or inactive countries. In contrast, the four-part typology placed countries along a *continuum* covering current needs, future actions and their timing, bringing fresh meaning to the UNFCCC's principle of 'common but differentiated responsibilities'. *Cognitive leadership* was the foundation for *entrepreneurial leadership*, as evidenced by the will to build a coalition of rich and poor nations ahead of a major round of institutional bargaining. In contrast to earlier French leadership bids, greater understanding of the interests of key players was displayed, probably indicating that lessons had been drawn from earlier failures to broker mutually acceptable and effective outcomes. Thus a more integrative orientation is manifested in the plan's ambitions to promote large-scale emissions reductions while supporting the most vulnerable countries.

This in turn enabled an element of *structural leadership*, which France had not previously been capable of exercising. However, whereas Young (1991) conceptualised that resources were *controlled* by a state or organisation, France sought to *mobilise* resources it did not own. On the one hand, these were the material and financial resources that innovative financial engineering would pool in common. On the other, they were the diplomatic resources that organisations of international cooperation held in common, principally the EU, the Commonwealth and the Amazonian pact. Thus France's attempt to exercise *structural leadership* was based on non-hegemonic power, and provides a current example of the Gaullist aspiration to construct a multipolar world through interventions in the institutions of global governance.

But was France's diplomatic offensive a case of 'too much, too late'? Press criticisms of the French plan were that it was overambitious and the core document was made public only a month before Copenhagen, leaving too little time to cement the international coalition or integrate the plan into a common EU position. Moreover, it is hard to detect a direct impact of the plan on the Copenhagen outcome. Although French coalition building may have helped negotiators arrive at an accord (rather than break up in acrimony), it mostly exposed that fact that structural power lay with the USA and China. Meaningful progress on climate talks is impossible without firm commitments from the USA and China and agreements between them – because of their material resources and because they are the world's largest polluters (see also Chapter 14 by Bang and Schreurs and Chapter 15 by Dai and Diao). Arguably, the fatal flaw in President Sarkozy's climate leadership was not so much a stereotypical French drift to last-minute improvisation as the misguided belief that multipolar diplomacy provides a *counterweight* to the major powers.

Yet despite the severe limitations of the Copenhagen Accord (UN 2009), correction may prove possible in upcoming venues. The French strategy embraced this eventuality: the joint appeal by France and Ethiopia looked to the G20 summit in 2010 for a report by the working group on innovative financial support mechanisms, while the Franco-Brazilian statement called for the establishment of a World Environment Organisation at the Rio+20 summit in 2012 (French Government 2009a, 2009b). These goals require a very high level of international consensus. Key questions for the future are therefore how the EU is to develop greater capacity than was demonstrated at Copenhagen, how France can integrate its diplomatic initiatives within a European framework and whether Europe will be capable of brokering a common climate position with the USA and China.

The domestic implementation of EU and international commitments

In marked contrast to its international leadership bids, France has been content to play the role of follower as regards the development of EU climate policy instruments. Emissions trading was trialled actively in the UK but resisted in France and Germany (Godard 2001; Wurzel 2008b). Introduction of the EU's Emissions Trading Scheme (ETS) could therefore be expected to induce top-down adaptation pressure of the variety identified by Börzel and Risse (2003) and Jordan and Liefferink (2004). In France, an early 'misfit' arose at the level of political preferences with emissions trading being scathingly referred to as *droits de polluer* – stock market papers conferring the 'right' to pollute. This resistance evaporated as implementation proved less threatening than anticipated. In practice, the methodology of ETS fitted comfortably with existing institutional arrangements in environmental policy arenas (Szarka 2008). Adaptation pressure proved limited and European policy was simply 'accommodated'. Indeed, the practical impact of the scheme has remained relatively low, since the allocation of quotas across the EU reflects domestic industrial structures, in particular the fuel mix in the electricity sector. Whereas 50 per cent of quotas went to the power sector at the EU level, only 25 per cent did so in France (Arnaud 2005: 94). This is because only a residual 10 per cent of French electricity is sourced from fossil fuels, whereas the latter account for the lion's share of generation in neighbouring countries. In phase one (2005–7), Germany received 23 per cent of quotas, 11 per cent went to each of Italy, Poland and the UK, but France was a marginal player with only 7 per cent: only 26 per cent of domestic CO_2 emissions were covered (Arnaud 2005: 95). The reduction targets were low, standing at 2.43 per cent in phase one (MEDD 2004b) while during phase two (2008–12) only a 1 per cent cut is expected (MEDD 2006a: 7).

The EU has set great store by renewable energy in ensuring climate protection. Renewable energy directives have created obligations and opportunities to which Member States responded in 'path dependent' fashion. In volume terms, France is the largest user of renewable energy sources in Europe, producing 18.3 millions of tonnes of oil equivalent in 2004, with 51 per cent coming from wood for heating, 31 per cent from hydropower and 12 per cent from waste; in aggregate some 6.6 per cent of primary energy consumption was from renewable energy sources, which is close to the EU average (French Government 2006: 61). However, these are long-standing sources of renewable energy, with little diversification into new forms such as wind-generated electricity and biofuels. Moreover, EU targets for renewable energy sources are 12 per cent in 2010, and 20 per cent in 2020.

To encourage the generation of electricity from renewables, directive 2001/77/EC set indicative targets for each Member State, leading to expansion across Europe particularly in wind power (Szarka 2007: 62–109). The 2010 target for France was 21 per cent of domestic electricity consumption, as compared to an outcome of 15 per cent in 1997. Most of the increase was budgeted to come from wind power, since France has one of the best wind regimes in Europe. But to date, wind power has been mostly uncompetitive in relation to conventional sources and required subsidy. In France a 'feed-in tariff' was established in 2001, guaranteeing kilowatt hour prices which exceeded market rates. The policy was strengthened in 2006, with an increase in subsidy levels and the introduction of 'wind power development zones' to ease planning problems. The policy led to an acceleration in deployment, with capacity increasing to 4,243MW in late 2009. Yet the rate of capacity expansion is still inadequate. Part of the explanation resides in underestimation, at both national and European levels, of the time-scales required to implement major infrastructural change. Additionally, wind power goes against the grain of French electricity sourcing traditions. The largely state-owned nuclear sector has left little room for new entrants, especially as the impact of EU electricity market liberalisation has been late and limited in France (Bauby and Varone 2008). The consequence is that France cannot reach its 2010 target.

Energy crops hold promise in reducing emissions and improving energy security. An expansion in biomass production was outlined in the 1990s (French Government 1995: 18), and implemented through the 2000–2006 'Wood Energy Plan'. Tax breaks for the purchase of high-efficiency stoves contributed to France becoming the largest producer of energy from wood within the EU (Delannoy 2007: 138–39). On the other hand, expansion in biofuels has proved uneven due to a combination of domestic and international circumstances. Directive 2003/30/CE aimed to source 5.75 per cent of vehicle fuels from biofuels by 2010. France set more ambitious targets of 7 per cent for 2010 and 10 per cent for 2015 (MEDD 2006b: 8). In Diester Industrie, France has the largest producer of biodiesel in Europe, but overall growth in domestic biofuel sourcing has been limited. Meeting demanding targets has led to reliance on imports, raising serious questions over the distorting effect of subsidy regimes (notably in the USA), deforestation in developing countries and competition with food production. Progress depends on clarifying sustainability criteria, and is slow.

In summary, the impact of 'Europeanisation' on French climate policy has been little and late. EU ETS has been the most radical policy instrument, yet its implementation in France has proceeded fairly smoothly. However, progress in sourcing from renewable energy sources has been disappointing, given that France traditionally had major recourse to renewables, has significant new resources to tap and sound reasons for exploiting them more. While a measure of policy 'misfit' between Brussels and Paris arose in the liberalisation of electricity markets, the open-ended nature of EU climate-related directives – focusing on broadly defined ends with means left to national discretion – lessens incompatibility. The influence of the nuclear lobby undoubtedly slowed the uptake of renewables. Former Environment Minister Corinne Lepage (2006: 90) charged that France was complacent over energy and climate policy because of reliance on nuclear power. This highlights the cognitive gap between France and Germany, since French policy makers have single-mindedly construed nuclear technology as the key energy source of the future, whereas Germany concentrates on renewables (see Chapter 8 by Jänicke). The cognitive gap illustrates the problem of applying 'leader/laggard' concepts (Andresen and

Agrawala 2002; Wurzel 2008a), and allows France to continue with the self-perception of being a climate leader.

Conclusions

In a context of accelerating global emissions and the real prospect of dangerous climate change – understood as a mean global temperature rise greater than 2 degrees C. – the reduction of GHGE in France is an important achievement. Yet most of the reduction was inadvertent, occurring *before* climate policy was institutionalised. This limits French claims to *directional leadership*. Further, although France is bettering its Kyoto target of stabilisation for 2008–12, the 75 per cent target for 2050 is exponentially more demanding, with uncertainty persisting over the adequacy of current policy initiatives to the 2050 target. This is particularly the case with technology choice. Viewed in cross-national perspective, France's concentration on nuclear power has been unique. Yet this technology base has proved narrow and problematic. While there is no international consensus on either a nuclear phase-out or a revival, the recognition that nuclear power must – at the least – be extensively supplemented by new low-carbon technologies has gained prevalence. In France, significant supply-side improvements are required in the availability and quality of energy sourcing, the promotion of new energy conversion technologies (notably renewable energy sources), and the improvement of energy efficiency and services in buildings and transport. But demand-side measures are also required, namely governance frameworks capable of guiding individual, household and community behaviour. Domestic policy in the 2000s has taken tentative steps in this direction, but remains underdeveloped. Further, France has played the role of a follower as regards the development of EU climate policy instruments, with no major initiative undertaken whilst manifesting reluctant cooperation. These features explain why French bids to *directional leadership* have remained troubled.

At the international level, France has repeatedly attempted to exercise *cognitive* and *entrepreneurial leadership*. The examples given related to emissions per capita targets, international carbon taxation, EU CO_2 border tax adjustment and the 'Climate Justice Plan'. These leadership bids have achieved little success. At the cognitive level, France has not persuaded industrialised countries of the desirability of emissions per capita targets. France has been unable to shape the thinking of other parties, partly because of the inherent intractability of the emissions per capita issue for US, European or Middle Eastern negotiators, partly because French advocacy looks very convenient from a developing country perspective. In terms of coalition formation, French exceptionalism in relation to nuclear energy has narrowed the scope for consensus within the EU, while international coalition broking remains inconclusive. Thus two significant disjunctures persist within French bids to climate leadership. One is the large gap noted between short- and long-term GHGE targets. The other lies in the contradiction between

France's preference for climate *leadership* at the international level and climate *followership* within the EU. Both gaps need to be closed if France is to gain greater climate credibility.

French prospects for climate leadership are tightly linked to EU policy coordination. President Sarkozy's strenuous promotion of the 'climate and energy package' in 2008 indicates recognition that France has no alternative but to pursue an EU 'common climate policy'. Yet France can also hope to benefit if the USA, China or India were to exercise *structural leadership* in a post-Kyoto settlement. This is because all three have reasons to advance nuclear power as a low-carbon technology. In addition, China and the developing world have a normative preference for the 'contraction and convergence' model. The French attempt to influence this part of the cognitive environment of climate policy negotiations could assume greater relevance, provided that it is renewed through demonstration of greater generosity and leading by example. The 2009 'Climate Justice Plan' saw meaningful progress in this direction, albeit at the eleventh hour for the Copenhagen Accord. Consequently France's bids to climate leadership retain their currency in the troubled negotiating environment of the 2010s.

Note

1 French GHGE had risen to 577 million tonnes in 1998, but dropped back to 556 million tonnes in 2000 – below the 1990 level – which they have not exceeded since (EEA 2008: 14).

Bibliography

Andresen, S. and Agrawala, S. (2002) 'Leaders, Pushers and Laggards in the Making of the Climate Regime', *Global Environmental Change*, 12(1), 41–51.

Ansolabehere, S., *et al.* (2003) *The Future of Nuclear Power: An Interdisciplinary* MIT *Report*, Cambridge, Mass: MIT, <http://web.mit.edu/nuclearpower> (accessed 9 November 2007).

Arnaud, E. (2005) 'Plan national d'allocations des quotas et territoires', *Revue de l'Energie*, 564 (mars–avril), 92–99.

Bauby, P. and Varone, F. (2008) 'Europeanisation of French Electricity Policy: Four Paradoxes', in E. Grossman (ed.), *France and the European Union: After the Referendum on the European Constitution*, London: Routledge, 57–69.

Baulinet, C. (2002) 'La lutte contre le changement climatique: les instruments de l'action gouvernementale et l'engagement des entreprises', *Annales des mines* (février), 39–44.

Boissieu. C. de, *et al.* (2006) *Division par quatre des émissions de gaz à effet de serre de la France à l'horizon 2050*, Paris: La Documentation française.

Borloo, J.-L. (2009) 'Copenhague: un projet pour le monde', <http://planete.blogs. nouvelobs.com/media/02/01/264458878.pdf> (accessed 4.1.2010).

Börzel, T. A. and Risse, T. (2003) 'Conceptualising the Domestic Impact of Europe', in K. Featherstone and C. Radaelli (eds), *The Politics of Europeanisation*, Oxford: Oxford University Press, 57–80.

CEC (2008) '20 20 by 2020: Europe's Climate Change Opportunity', COM(2008) 30 final <http://ec.europa.eu/energy/climate_actions/doc/com_2008_030_en.pdf> (accessed 13 February 2008).

Cerny, P. G. (1980) *The Politics of Grandeur: Ideological Aspects of De Gaulle's Foreign Policy*, Cambridge: Cambridge University Press.

Cogan, C. (2003) *French Negotiating Behavior: Dealing with La Grande Nation*, Washington, DC: United States Institute of Peace Press.

Damian, M. and Abbas, M. (2007) 'Politique climatique et politique commerciale: le projet français de taxe CO_2 aux frontières de l'Europe', *Revue de l'énergie*, 578 (juillet–août), 221–30.

Delannoy, I. (2007) *Environnement: les candidats au banc d'essai*, Paris: Editions de la Martinière.

Deroubaix, J.-F. and Lévêque, F. (2006) 'The Rise and Fall of French Ecological Tax Reform: Social Acceptability Versus Political Feasibility in the Energy Tax Implementation Process', *Energy Policy*, 34(8), 940–9.

EEA (European Environment Agency) (2008) *Annual European Community Greenhouse Gas Inventory 1990–2006 and Inventory Report 2008 Executive summary*, EEA Technical report No 6/2008, <http://reports.eea.europa.eu/technical_report_2008_6/en/Summary_Annual_EC_GHG_inventory_19902006_and_inventory_report_2008> (accessed 20 August 2008).

EEA (2007) 'Greenhouse Gas Emission Trends and Projections in Europe 2007', Copenhagen: EEA report no. 5, <http://reports.eea.europa.eu/eea_report_2007_5/en/Greenhouse_gas_emission_trends_and_projections_in_Europe_2007.pdf> (accessed 29 August 2008).

Elliott, D. (ed.) (2007) *Nuclear or Not? Does Nuclear Power Have a Place in a Sustainable Energy Future?* London: Palgrave Macmillan.

Eurobarometer (2005) 'The Attitudes of European Citizens towards the Environment', Special Eurobarometer 217, Wave 62.1, <http://ec.europa.eu/public_opinion/archives/ebs/ebs_217_en.pdf> (accessed 6 December 2007).

Eurobarometer (2008) 'Europeans' Attitudes towards Climate Change', <http://ec.europa.eu/public_opinion/archives/ebs/ebs_300_full_en.pdf> (accessed 27 January 2009).

French Government (1995) *First National Communication under the UN Framework Convention on Climate Change*, <http://unfccc.int/resource/docs/natc/france1.pdf> (accessed 15 October 2007).

French Government (1997) *Second National Communication under the UN Framework Convention on Climate Change*, <http://unfccc.int/resource/docs/natc/france2.pdf> (accessed 15 October 2007).

French Government (2006) *Fourth National Communication under the UN Framework Convention on Climate Change*, <http://www.effet-de-serre.gouv.fr/images/documents/4th per cent20National per cent20Communication.pdf> (accessed 15 October 2007).

French Government (2009a) 'Common Position of the Government of the Federative Republic of Brazil and the Government of the French Republic on Climate Change, Elysee Palace – Saturday November 14th 2009', <http://www.elysee.fr/documents/index.php?lang = fr&mode = view&cat_id = 8&press_id = 3097> (accessed 4.1.2010).

French Government (2009b) 'Joint Appeal of France and Ethiopia, Representing Africa, for an Ambitious Copenhagen Accord, Tuesday December 15, 2009',

<http://www.elysee.fr/documents/index.php?cat_id = 1&lang = fr&mode = view& press_id = 3195> (accessed 4.1.2010).

Giraud, P.-N., Collier, U. and Löfstedt, R. E. (1997) 'France: Relying on Past Reductions and Nuclear Power' in U. Collier and R. E. Löfstedt (eds), *Cases in Climate Change Policy. Political Reality in the European Union*, London: Earthscan, 165–83.

Godard, O. (2001) 'Les permis négociables, une option crédible en France?', in M. Boyer, *et al.* (eds), *L'Environnement, question sociale. Dix ans de recherches pour le Ministere de l'environnement*, Paris: Odile Jacob, 263–72.

Gouvernement français (2000) *Programme national de lutte contre le changement climatique*, Paris: République française.

Grubb, M. and Gupta, J. (2000) 'Leadership: Theory and Methodology', in J. Gupta and M. Grubb (eds.), (2000) *Climate Change and European Leadership: A Sustainable Role for Europe?* Dordrecht: Kluwer, 15–24.

Gupta, J. and Ringius, L. (2001) 'Climate Leadership: Reconciling Ambition and Reality', *International Environmental Agreements*, 1(2), 281–99.

Héritier, A., Knill, C. and Mingers, S. (1996) *Ringing the Changes in Europe. Regulatory Competition and Redefinition of the State: Britain, France, Germany*, Berlin: Walter de Gruyter.

IEA (International Energy Agency) (1996) *Climate Change Policy Initiatives*, Paris: OECD / IEA.

Jänicke, M. and Jacob, K. (2004) 'Lead Markets for Environmental Innovations: A New Role for the Nation State', *Global Environmental Politics*, 4(1) (February), 29–46.

Jordan, A. and Liefferink, D. (2004) 'The Europeanization of National Environmental Policy', in A. Jordan and D. Liefferink (eds) *Environmental Policy in Europe. The Europeanization of National Environmental Policy*, London: Routledge, 1–14.

Lajoinie, A. (2001) *L'Energie: repères pour demain*, Paris: Assemblée nationale, rapport no. 2907.

Lepage, C. (2006) 'Climat et action politique', *Ecologie et politique*, 33, 87–93.

Maclean, M. and Szarka, J. (2008) 'Globalisation and the Nation State: Conceptual Lenses on French Ambitions in a Changing World Order', in M. Maclean and J. Szarka (eds), *France on the World Stage: Nation State Strategies in the Global Era*, Basingstoke: Palgrave Macmillan, 1–19.

MEDD (Ministère de l'écologie et du développement durable) (2004a) 'Plan Climat 2004–12', <http://www.ecologie.gouv.fr> (accessed 1 December 2004).

MEDD (2004b) 'Plan national d'affectation des quotas – période de référence 2005–7', <http://www.ecologie.gouv.fr/article.php3?id_article = 2207> (accessed 28 February 2005).

MEDD (2006a) 'Projet de plan national d'affectation des quotas d'émissions de gaz à effet de serre (PNAQ II). Période: 2008 à 2010', <http://www.consultationpub-liquepnaq.com/download/PNAQII_v19ter.pdf> (accessed 8 March 2007).

MEDD (2006b) 'Actualisation 2006 du Plan Climat 2004–12', <http://www.ecologie. gouv.fr/IMG/pdf/1er_doc_INTRO_PLAN_CLIMAT_final.pdf> (accessed 16 November 2006).

Meyer, A. (2000) *Contraction and Convergence. The Global Solution to Climate Change*, Totnes: Green Books.

Mühlenhöver, E. (2002) *L'Environnement en politique étrangère: raisons et illusions. Une analyse de l'argument environnemental dans les diplomaties électronucléaires française et américaine*, Paris: L'Harmattan.

Oberthür, S. and Roche Kelly, C. (2008) 'EU Leadership in International Climate Policy: Achievements and Challenges', *The International Spectator*, 43(2), 35–50.

Quéméner, S. (2009) 'Borloo: un plan justice climat pour les plus vulnérables', *Le Journal du dimanche*, 31 octobre, <http://www.lejdd.fr/Ecologie/Climat/Actualite/Borloo-Un-plan-justice-climat-pour-les-plus-vulnerables-146604/> (accessed 4.1.2010).

Raffarin, J.-P. (2004) 'Biocarburants: discours du premier ministre à Venette', <http://www.premier-ministre.gouv.fr/acteurs/discours_9/biocarbura> (accessed 28 February 2005).

Sarkozy, N. (2009) 'Intervention de M. le Président de la République devant l'Assemblée plénière de la Convention climat des Nations Unies à Copenhague', <http://www.elysee.fr/documents/index.php?mode=list&cat_id=7&lang=fr> (accessed 4.1.2010).

Schmidt, J. (2008) 'Why Europe Leads on Climate Change', *Survival*, 50(4), 83–96.

Schreurs, M. and Tiberghien, Y. (2007) 'Multi-level Reinforcement: Explaining European Union Leadership in Climate Change Mitigation', *Global Environmental Politics*, 7(4), 19–46.

Skodvin, T. and Andresen, S. (2006) 'Leadership Revisited', *Global Environmental Politics*, 6(3), 13–27.

Szarka, J. (2003) 'The Politics of Bounded Innovation: "New" Environmental Policy Instruments in France', in Jordan, A.; Wurzel, R. K. W. and Zito, A. R. (eds), *'New' Instruments of Environmental Governance? National Experiences and Prospects*, London: Frank Cass, 92–114.

Szarka, J. (2006) 'From Inadvertent to Reluctant Pioneer? Climate Strategies and Policy Style in France', *Climate Policy*, 5(6), 627–38.

Szarka, J. (2007) *Wind Power in Europe: Politics, Business and Society*, Basingstoke: Palgrave Macmillan.

Szarka, J. (2008) 'France: the search for an alternative climate policy template', in Bailey, I. and Compston, H. (eds), *Turning Down the Heat: The Politics of Climate Policy in Affluent Democracies*, Basingstoke: Palgrave Macmillan, 125–43.

Szarka, J. (2009) 'Environmental Foreign Policy in France: National Interests, Nuclear Power and Climate', in Harris, P. (ed.), *Environmental Change and Foreign Policy: Theory and Practice*, London: Routledge, 117–33.

UN (1992) 'United Nations Framework Convention on Climate Change', <http://unfccc.int/resource/docs/convkp/conveng.pdf> (accessed 20 August 2005. – (2009) 'Copenhagen Accord', <http://unfccc.int/files/meetings/cop_15/application/pdf/cop15_cph_auv.pdf> (accessed 4 January 2010).

Wurzel, R. K. W. (2008a) 'Environmental Policy: EU Actors, Leader and Laggard States', in J. Hayward (ed.), *Leaderless Europe*, Oxford: Oxford University Press, 66–88.

Wurzel, R. K. W. (2008b) *The Politics of Emission Trading in Britain and Germany*, London: Anglo-German Foundation for the Study of Industrial Society.

Young, O. R. (1991) 'Political Leadership and Regime Formation: On the Development of Institutions in International Society', *International Organisation*, 45(3), 281–308.

Zito, A. R. (2000) *Creating Environmental Policy in the European Union*, Basingstoke: Macmillan.

8   German climate change policy

Political and economic leadership

Martin Jänicke

Introduction

The OECD has characterised Germany as 'a highly innovative country engaged in several initiatives to draw the maximum benefits and opportunities of globalisation to address environmental problems while boosting its environmental industry sector' (OECD 2007: 43). This seems a good characterisation especially for the climate policy since 1987.

Germany has played both a political and economic leadership role in climate change policy: these can be characterised as 'cognitive' and 'structural' (see Chapter 1 by Wurzel and Connelly). As early as 1990, Germany made major political contributions to the generation of a better *knowledge-base* for a far-reaching global strategy to combat climate change, thus acting as a cognitive leader. After 1998 the concept of ecological modernisation (*ökologische Modernisierung*) became central under a Social Democratic Party (SPD) and Green Party coalition government (the so-called Red-Green coalition). Ecological modernisation was developed into the concept of ecological industrial policy (*ökologische Industriepolitik*) by an SPD Environmental Minister (Sigmar Gabriel) under an SPD and Christian Democratic Union (CDU)/ Christian Social Union (CSU) coalition (the so-called grand coalition). More important is the role of German climate policy for international lesson-drawing, including the adoption of instruments like obligatory feed-in tariffs. Germany's leadership role in international climate change politics is to a high degree characterised by demonstration effects and *leadership by example*. The policy outcomes are therefore important for explaining Germany's leadership role within the European Union (EU) and on the international level. As early as 2007 Germany had surpassed its ambitious Kyoto target (-21 per cent), achieving a 21.3 per cent reduction of its greenhouse gas emissions (GHGE) compared to the 1990 base year. A broad range of economic co-benefits of this policy is part of this 'success story'.

Germany's economic strength, advanced innovation system and political visibility were necessary *structural* conditions for a leadership role as an international 'trend setter' (Jänicke 2008). The will and skill of central environmental policy actors including highly competent environmental ministers (Klaus Töpfer (CDU) 1987–94, Angela Merkel (CDU) 1994–98, Jürgen Trittin (Greens) 1998–2005 and Sigmar Gabriel (SPD) 2005–9) were also important. Germany's international leadership role would not have been possible without the support of Chancellors Helmut Kohl (CDU, 1982–98), Gerhard Schröder (SPD, 1998–2005) and Angela Merkel (CDU, since 2005). Of particular importance was the role that Chancellor Merkel played during the G8 summit in Heiligendamm (Germany) in 2007, where an expression of entrepreneurial leadership in international climate change politics could be observed.

Germany's climate policy exerts an even stronger international influence as a result of its *economic* success and the enormous boom in its domestic 'climate protection industry'. This effect has increased with the creation of lead markets and international activities such as the foundation of a renewable energy network (2002, 2004) and the lobby for the International Renewable Energy Agency (IRENA) which was launched in Bonn in 2009. All these initiatives helped to increase Germany's exports of climate-friendly energy technology, resulting in a competitive challenge for other countries. This is an important factor in German structural leadership in climate policy.

The national context of climate policies

Germany is a highly industrialised country with a population of 82.3 million, or 231 people per square kilometre (km^2). GDP per capita is €29,464 (2007). Total emissions of carbon dioxide (CO_2) and the five other major GHGs amounted to 945 Mt CO_2-equivalents (2008) most of which (832 Mt) was accounted for by CO_2 (*Statistisches Bundesamt* 2008). GHGE per capita in Germany are above the EU average. Emissions related to GDP are more in line with neighbouring countries (EEA 2007). In the early 1990s the largest part of the CO_2 emission reductions was achieved by the decline of energy-intensive heavy industry and the modernisation of the coal-based power companies in the former German Democratic Republic (GDR). Later GHGE reduction improvements were, however, caused by environmental policy interventions; this is particularly true for the time after 1998. According to the EU burden sharing agreement – later renamed 'effort sharing agreement' – (see Chapter 1 by Wurzel and Connelly), about 75 per cent (259 Mt) of the then EU-15 Member States' collective GHGE reduction target (342 Mt) have to be achieved by Germany alone.

Coal-based power and energy-intensive heavy industry are the main domestic causes of GHGE. Germany is phasing out its (highly subsidised) hard coal mining, although it still remains the most important producer worldwide of lignite coal: this is a highly problematic issue because of lignite's high carbon content. Even in 2008 the share of coal-based electricity was still 47.3 per cent. In 2008 the share of nuclear power amounted to 22.1 per cent, which constituted a clear reduction compared with 29.2 per cent in 2002, the year when the Red-Green coalition government adopted a law to phase out nuclear power. By 2009 the share of 'green' electricity had climbed to 16.1 per cent (BMU 2010).

In the early 1970s, under a Centre-Left SPD – Liberal coalition government led by Chancellor Willy Brandt (SPD), who showed a personal interest in environmental policy, Germany developed into one of the leading European countries in environmental policy. Germany has a strong environmental movement which has continued to rise to the present day (Markham 2008). With more than five to six million members, its membership is close to that of the trade unions. Nearly 9 per cent of the German population claim to be members of a green non-governmental organisation (NGO) (BMU, 2004: 71). In 1998 environmental organisations, such as BUND, the Association for Environment and Nature Protection Germany (Bund für Umwelt und Naturschutz Deutschland) and Greenpeace, ran a strong campaign for an ecological tax-reform shortly before the federal elections which brought to power a Red-Green coalition government. Environmental reporting by the media – especially the publicly funded media – has steadily increased in its quantity, range and importance. The Green Party has been represented in the German *Bundestag* (lower house) since 1983. Germany has several 'green' industrial organisations (such as BAUM, the Federal Working Group for Environmentally Aware Management (Bundesdeutscher Arbeitskreis für Umweltbewusstes Management), and Future) and the most highly developed environmental protection industry in Europe (Ernst & Young 2006). In addition, the adoption of voluntary agreements on climate protection by German industry in 1995 and 2000 shows a long-standing and generally positive attitude towards climate policy.

Phases of domestic climate change policy

German climate policy has developed under a number of very different coalition governments including a Centre-Right coalition made up of the CDU/ CSU and Liberals (1987–98), a Red-Green coalition consisting of the SPD and Greens (1998–2005), a Grand Coalition made up of the CDU/CSU and SPD (2005–9) and a renewed Centre-Right (CDU/CSU – Liberals) coalition government after 2009. Remarkably, the changes in party configurations within the various coalition governments did not appear to have made a great deal of difference to the overall direction of environmental policy. All three coalition governments played a leadership role in climate policy. Essentially climate change constitutes a cross-party consensus issue although the Liberals (more right) and Greens (more left) are furthest apart in climate change policy terms. The Red-Green coalition government focused more on developing a national pioneer or forerunner role (*Vorreiterrolle*) and the demonstration effect of ecological modernisation, while the Centre-Right coalition governments under Chancellor Kohl made stronger use of European institutions and the potential of multi-level games, thereby taking on the role of an environmental pusher prepared to accept more ambitious domestic environmental standards on the condition that economic competitors take on similar commitments (see also Michaelowa 2008; Oberthür and Pallemaerts 2010).

The Bundestag Enquete Commission 'Prevention to Protect the Earth's Atmosphere' (1987)

In August 1986 the influential weekly investigative magazine *Der Spiegel* published an article entitled 'The Climate Disaster' ('*Die Umweltkatastrophe*') (*Der Spiegel* 11.8.1986). In the same year the Bavarian state (*Land*) government launched an initiative in the *Bundesrat* (upper house) for the creation of an advisory body for climate policy (Grassl 1999: 100). The new issue of 'climate protection' was put on the political agenda in 1987 when the newly elected lower house (*Bundestag*) set up an enquiry commission called 'Enquete Commission "Preventive Measures to Protect the Earth's Atmosphere" '. The *Bundestag*'s Enquete Commission proved to be highly influential in the years to follow. Two discourses were relevant in this regard: first, the nuclear debate following the Chernobyl accident, in which the climate issue was used as an argument by the pro-nuclear parties, especially the Bavarian CSU; second, the environmental discourse which was intensified by the Greens, whose share of votes rose in the 1987 Bundestag elections and who cooperated with the other opposition party (the SPD) thus creating the foundations for a future Red-Green coalition government.

The Climate Enquete Commission became as influential as its predecessor, the Energy Enquete Commission (1980), which had discussed for the first time a domestic energy policy scenario (based on the assumption of slowly growing energy consumption) without further reliance on nuclear energy (*Deutscher Bundestag* 1980). The Climate Enquete Commission created the knowledge-base for understanding climate change and outlined possible policy solutions not only for the inner circle of the political elite but also for the interested wider public. Its 1990 report predicted a global temperature increase of 1.5–4.5° C in the event of a doubling of CO_2 concentrations in the atmosphere. The Climate Enquete Commission proposed a rather utopian German CO_2 emission reduction target of 30 per cent for the year 2005. It also proposed minimum targets for other industrialised countries (20 per cent) and the European Union (between 20 per cent and 25 per cent) (compared to the base year 1987). It envisaged reductions of 80 per cent by Germany, EU and other industrialised countries by 2050 (*Deutscher Bundestag* 1990: 42, 70ff).

The Enquete Commission therefore pushed Germany into a leadership role, though it argued that other economically 'strong' countries should also reduce their CO_2 emissions by 30 per cent by 2005. At the first Conference of the Parties (COP) of the United Nations Framework Convention on Climate Change (UNFCCC) in Berlin in 1995, Germany proclaimed a slightly reduced CO_2 reduction target of 25 per cent by 2005 (compared to 1990). This target was based on cross-party consensus in the German *Bundestag*.

Early activities of the Kohl government (1987–98)

The government's (subsequently adopted) climate change policy was strongly influenced by the Environment Minister Klaus Töpfer. A first step constituted the 'CO_2 Reduction Programme' of the federal government in 1990 and the setting up of the 'Interministerial Committee on CO_2 Reduction' which constituted a significant break with the tradition of strong independence of Ministries in the German government. The CO_2 Reduction Programme contained, amongst others, new regulations for energy efficiency and heating. However, the most important step was the Act on the Sale of Electricity to the Grid in 1990 which introduced obligatory feed-in tariffs for power from renewable energy. In 1991 the second *Bundestag* Enquete Commission 'Protection of the Earth's Atmosphere' was installed.

Germany ratified the UNFCCC in 1993. The first COP took place in Berlin in 1995. It adopted the so-called Berlin mandate which was strongly influenced by the German government in which Angela Merkel, who later became German Chancellor, was the minister for the environment. Germany's 21 per cent reduction target for GHGE under the 1997 Kyoto climate change protocol was again an expression of the ambitious leadership role which the German government had adopted in international climate change politics (Schreurs 2002 178ff).

The Red-Green government 1998–2005

German unification, which took place in 1990, resulted in challenging economic problems which changed the government's priorities: domestic climate policy subsequently became less impressive. The newly elected Red-Green coalition government (1998–2005) gave a strongly renewed impetus to climate policy. The year 1998 became the starting point for a more ambitious climate policy which later continued under the Grand coalition headed by Chancellor Merkel. The main general heading for environmental and climate change policy in the Red-Green governments' coalition treaties (adopted in 1998 and 2002) was 'Ecological Modernisation' (SPD/ Bündnis 90 – Die Grünen 1998). This gave an additional push to the innovation-oriented approach which had already characterised German environmental policy under the Kohl governments and its Minister for Environment, Klaus Töpfer.

The new 'Renewable Energy Act' of 1999 was an important first step by the Red-Green government in increasing the obligatory tariffs to a level high enough to cause a rapid growth of 'green' power (see Figure 8.1). The Red-Green coalition government also introduced an ecological tax reform in 1999. Most of the revenue (about €18bn) from this tax reform was used to reduce social security contributions. A smaller part was to support investment in renewable energy (*Marktanreizprogramm*). The Climate Protection Programme in 2000 introduced several new regulations and sectoral emission reduction objectives up to 2005 (energy/industry: 20–25 Mt, households: 18–25 Mt, transport: 15–20 Mt – all compared to the base year 1990) (see Federal Ministry for the Environment, Nature Protection and Nuclear Safety *Umwelt,*

11/2000). A 20 Mt CO_2 emission reduction by 2010 was planned through the adoption of a regulation preventing final deposition of solid waste without pre-treatment (a measure which also stimulated a high recycling quota).

The Red-Green coalition government's climate programme did not achieve the national 25 per cent CO_2 emission reduction target by 2005 because of a significant increase of emissions in the power industry after 1999. CO_2 emission reductions amounted to only 15.2 per cent (compared to 12.1 per cent in 1998). The climate programme was, however, the necessary basis for a more far-reaching climate policy that was announced in 2007.

Climate change was an essential factor in the re-election of the Red-Green government in the autumn of 2002, following heavy flooding of the Elbe in the former East Germany a few months before the *Bundestag* elections. Chancellor Schröder used the UN summit on sustainable development in Johannesburg in the summer of 2002 as a forum to make a strong plea for the expansion of renewable energies. In 2004, a major conference on renewable energy was held in Bonn. It illustrated German leadership for renewable energy sector and provided an important basis for further subsequent international actions in this policy subsector (REN21, 2008). The initiative to institutionalise efforts to boost renewable energy by setting up an International Renewable Energy Agency – IRENA – was a more visible result. In setting up IRENA Germany cooperated closely with Denmark and Spain in particular.

The Grand coalition government (2005 – 09)

The Grand coalition led by Chancellor Merkel generally followed the same path as the Red-Green coalition government in climate change policy (Jänicke 2010a). The Red-Green coalition government's concept of 'ecological modernisation' was now further developed into 'ecological industrial policy' (*ökologische Industriepolitik*) by the new Minister of Environment Sigmar Gabriel. This was primarily a semantic change, although ecological industrial policy closely resembles Social Democratic traditions of industrial policy (*Industriepolitik*). However, the new formula became connected with ambitious slogans and concepts such as 'Green New Deal' and 'Third Industrial Revolution' at the core of which was a new energy policy philosophy that was in competition with the conservative thinking of the Economics Ministry (Gabriel 2006; BMU 2008).

The EU emissions trading scheme became an essential policy instrument for German climate policy at this time. It was a policy instrument that had initially been opposed by Germany, which had acted as an emissions trading laggard (Wurzel 2008). The first German national allocation plan (NAP) for the years 2005–7 was very weak. It produced a significant over-allocation of emission allowances and showed a clear bias in favour of coal interests. Importantly, the coal industry and its unions had close links with the SPD. The NAP for the years 2008–12 was formulated by the Grand coalition government and Sigmar Gabriel as Environment Minister. This second NAP was again no pioneering proposal. It echoed the strong opposition of the main industrial organisations which had published harsh protests both against the Kyoto protocol and Germany's leadership role in international climate policy before the federal election of 2005 (DIHK 2005). However, interestingly enough, the EU Commission now forced the German government to stick to its self-proclaimed pioneer role. The Commission refused to accept the original second German NAP while demanding an additional reduction of 17 Mt CO_2. The government saw no alternative and accepted the Commission's demands for a significant reduction in the second German NAP. One reason was that Germany held the EU presidency in the first half of 2007 and the G8 presidency during 2007. Holding both these presidencies stimulated a new political leadership ambition in international climate change politics within the Grand coalition government. Germany's international leadership role was fully re-established within the context of the steeply rising energy prices and worrying news from the Intergovernmental Panel for Climate Change (IPCC) which published its fourth assessment report in 2007. The G8 summit in Heiligendamm in 2007 became a kind of celebration of Germany's leadership role international climate change politics.

The Integrated Energy and Climate Programme (Integriertes Energie und Klimaprogramm – IEKP) which the government conceived in Meseberg (August 2007) was the main domestic result of Germany's leadership ambitions in international climate change. The 40 per cent GHGE reduction target for 2020 was officially adopted at the cabinet meeting in Meseberg, which also adopted a broad range of implementation measures. However, the parliamentary process again showed the strength of some veto players: the car and the coal-based power industry. So far the expected effect of the 'Meseberg Programme' is a reduction of GHGE by 34 per cent in 2020 (compared to 1990). But there are good reasons to believe that additional measures will be adopted by the German government to achieve the 40 per cent reduction target. The recession of 2009, which contributed to a 27 per cent CO_2 emission reduction in the same year, has made it easier for Germany to achieve its reduction targets. The same is true for some forms of green investment. The activity of the state-owned Kreditanstalt für Wiederaufbau (banking group KfW) offers a good example: Credits for investment in renewable energy increased by 36 per cent to €5.7bn in 2009; credits for the modernising of buildings to improve energy efficiency increased by 41 per cent to €9bn (KfW, January 2010).

There was no significant immediate reorientation in German climate policy following the change in government coalition after the national elections in 2009. The possible exception constitutes phasing out of nuclear power which has been under review by the Centre-Right coalition government although it is likely that the several decades-long phasing-out process will be merely slowed down rather than reversed. The Centre-Right coalition government's Environmental Minister, Norbert Röttgen (CDU), underlined in his first speech in the *Bundestag* the path-dependency of environmental policy: through the use of 'ecological modernisation we want to be the most modern national economy' (Deutscher Bundestag, 17th legislature, 4th meeting, 11.11. 2009).

Policy instruments and policy outcomes

A broad range of policy instruments is used in German climate policy. It differs in each field of political intervention. A technology-based approach and a broad policy instrument mix have been the preferred options for German governments which have relied mainly on regulations and standards in domestic climate change policy. Three economic instruments, however, play a dominant role: the obligatory feed-in tariffs for green electricity; the ecological tax reform; and the EU emissions trading scheme. The ecological tax reform has contributed to a steady reduction of CO_2 emissions from road traffic since 1999. Together with standards and subsidies it also brought about improvements in the heating sector. The success of the obligatory feed-in tariffs for green electricity (Figure 8.1) stimulated a rapid rate of international diffusion. As mentioned above, emission trading had counterproductive results in the first allocation phase of the EU emissions trading scheme. Since then, however, emissions trading has become an important and strong instrument for German climate change policy. Voluntary agreements have played a minor role despite the above-mentioned climate change agreements put forward by German industry. The EU-wide voluntary agreement which the European automobile manufacturers (ACEA) put forward for the reduction of CO_2 emissions failed and has therefore been supplanted by EU regulation.

The emulation of pioneer countries' innovative policy *outputs* by other countries is a well-known mechanism of policy instrument diffusion (Busch and Joergens 2010). In the German case, however, policy *outcomes* have been the most important factor; a parallel case is Danish wind energy. Germany's

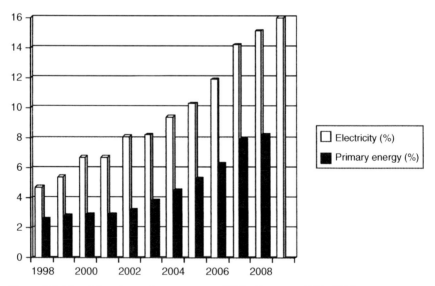

Figure 8.1 The rising share of green power (%) in Germany 1998–2009.

Source: BMU 2009, VDEW 2010

international leadership in climate policy was essentially the result of a demonstration effect: its ambitious policy turned out not only to be feasible but also to be surprisingly effective; and (above all) climate change policy has also become an economic success story. The German first-mover advantage has also caused a competitive challenge for other advanced industrial countries.

The most important result of the German climate policy so far is the achievement of the Kyoto target (21 per cent GHG reduction in 2012) already in 2007. The more ambitious 25 per cent target (1990–2005) has been missed. However, other unexpected successful developments include:

– The rapid increase of renewable electricity (Figure 8.1).
– the booming 'climate protection industry' increasing its share of the world market since 2000,
– the employment effect (Figure 8.2),
– the speeding up of the innovation process,
– the foreign capital inflow into the German lead market for renewables,
– and the probable net surplus of the climate programme.

The sections which follow explain the reasons for these successes.

The rapid increase of green power

The rapidly increased share of green power has led to a reduction of 115 Mt. CO_2 emissions in 2007 (compared to 85 Mt in 2005). The 2010 target for

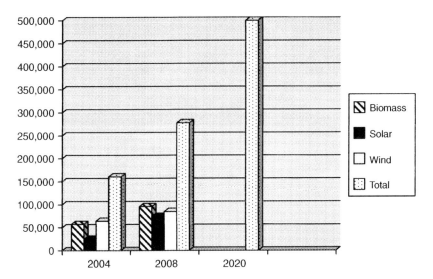

Figure 8.2 Employees in the renewable energy sector in Germany 1998–2008 and Forecast 2020.

Source: BMU 2009.

green power in the Renewable Energy Act, which was 12.5 per cent, had already been achieved by 2007. The 2020 target for green power therefore has been changed from at 'least 20 per cent' to at 'least 30 per cent', because of the unexpected rapid growth in renewable energy. A government study has shown that by 2030 it is possible for renewable energy to take a share of 50 per cent of electricity supply (*Umwelt*, 12/2008).

The main instrument constituted significantly increased obligatory feed-in tariffs for renewable energy, together with market incentives for investment in renewable energy. The higher price for electricity is being paid for collectively by customers (with a steady reduction over time to stimulate cost reductions). In 2009 the obligatory price for photovoltaic installations has been reduced more than planned. The reason for this is the rapid price decrease of photovoltaic installations.

The employment effect in the renewable energy sector (Figure 8.2) has been consistently pointed out by the Environmental Ministry. However, it constitutes only a small part of a total of 1.8 million employees in the 'environmental industry'. This so-called 'industry', which has no place in the traditional classification of different industrial sectors, is still underestimated in official statistics. There are two main reasons for the underreporting of the size of the 'environmental industry' sector. First, full data are not available on this newly emerging industry; secondly, mainstreaming of energy-efficient investment makes the 'environmental industry' almost 'invisible' (Jänicke and Zieschank 2008; DTI and DEFRA 2006).

A booming 'climate protection industry'

It was only in 2008 that a study found that not only had environmental policy created a new type of 'environmental industry', but that climate protection had also very quickly become a remarkable economic factor. Investment in climate-friendly products and processes made up nearly one fourth of the total investment in 2005 (BMU and UBA 2009).

Table 8.1 Climate-friendly investment (in € bn) in Germany 2005

Gross investment	Total investment	Climate-related investment	Additional investment IECP (2007)
Buildings	197	40	14
Machines	121	39	3
Power/Grid	12	5	10
Cars	50	10	2
Rest	20	1	1
Total	400	95	30
Share of GDP	20%	5%	1.5%

Sources: BMU and UBA 2009, 130; Data: DESTATIS (2008a), BEE (2006), BDEW

Table 8.2 Annual growth of climate-related technologies in Germany 2005–7

• Solar thermal heating:	110% (2006/8)
• PV:	50%
• Bio gas power:	37%
• Heat pumps:	28 % (2006/8)
• Wind energy:	19%
• Passive houses:	19%
• Green power:	18.2 %
• Contracting:	*ca.* 15% (2005/6)

Sources: Own compilation adapted from BEE, KfW and others.

This kind of 'climate-protection industry' had a 5 per cent share of the German GDP in 2005. If the effects of the new Integrated Energy and Climate Programme (2007) are included, the probable share could even reach 6.5 per cent of Germany's GDP (BMU and UBA 2009: 130).

Contrary to earlier calculations, the costs of the ambitious climate programme could be negative (depending on the assumed oil price). According to a government study a net surplus of €5bn could be achieved as a result of the climate change programme (*Umwelt*, 12/2007). Indeed, a McKinsey study for the Association of German Industries (*Bundesverband der deutschen Industrie* – BDI) concedes that the vast majority of climate change policy investments are profitable (McKinsey 2007).

Germany's new environmental industry is also highly competitive with a dominant position in the world market. Germany's world market share for environmentally friendly energy supply technologies is about 30 per cent; for energy-efficient technologies it amounts to 10 per cent (BMU 2007). The new industry is also characterised by high growth rates (Table 8.2).

Economic leadership: the fruits of ecological modernisation

German climate policy can also be described as an economic experiment, an experiment which started in 1998/9 with a strong policy input: the ambitious 40 per cent GHGE target by 2020 (compared to 1990) together with the mandatory phase-out of nuclear power. Although the experiment is still ongoing some remarkable economic results are already becoming visible.

The ambitious, broadly accepted and fairly reliable energy/climate targets have been an essential driving force for innovation – at least under the condition of the highly developed German national innovation system. Germany's climate change policy strongly supported the diffusion of renewable energy which stimulated the speeding up of the innovation cycle. The attractive feed-in tariffs for renewable energy caused a dramatic increase in new patents for this technology (OECD, 2005). Nuclear energy was not a necessary factor in achieving far-reaching climate protection targets. The decision to phase out nuclear power may even have increased the pressure for innovation and demands for renewable energy.

Within a few years a strong 'climate protection industry' came into being which is booming, innovative and highly successful in international markets. The new climate protection industry is comparable to the most important branches of traditional industry (e.g. the car industry). High energy prices have also been an important factor in leading the search for increased productivity.

The well-directed government support for green lead-markets has had several interesting results: the policy-driven markets for renewable energy attracted foreign investors; they also provided the conditions for successful export of climate-friendly technologies. Supporting the domestic markets is at the same time indispensable for paying the learning costs for better and cheaper technologies, which then could be diffused more generally, including to less developed countries.

The German climate policy has been successful as a technology-based innovation strategy; the concept of ecological modernisation (later 'ecological industrial policy') was a formula seeking consensus with the modernising part of the industry after 1998. The technological pioneer role of Germany – and the EU – caused a competitive push for other industrial countries. At the same time a *regulatory dominance* developed which other export countries were actually forced to adapt when entering the European market. Only Japan has had a similar influence on the innovation of energy-efficient products with its so-called 'top runner programme'. Climate policy as a technology-based policy has become a field of regulatory and economic competition. The impact of German (and European) leadership may therefore, to a certain degree, also result from the competitive dynamics which has increased the global convergence in climate protection policy.

The traditional neo-classic paradigm of environmental policy has proven to be essentially false because it overestimated the costs and underestimated the innovation effects of ambitious climate policies. This is also true as far as the innovative potential of policy regulation is concerned.

Conditions of political leadership

The most important factors which help to explain German leadership in international climate change politics will now be discussed. However, a situational condition (or *situative Bedingung*) should first be mentioned. German unification was accompanied by a general modernisation drive and the rapid decline of heavy industry and lignite-dependent power production in the former East Germany. This explains the early improvements in the 'new states' (*neue Bundesländer*) in the former East Germany. Germany's very ambitious CO_2 emission reduction targets therefore benefited at least partly from so-called 'wall fall profits'.

In general, however, government climate policy was the driving force behind the considerable GHGE reductions which Germany achieved. Its far-reaching targets may be explained by several factors. The first is a cross-party consensus based (paradoxically) on rather contradictory motives: both nuclear energy interests represented by the CSU and the environmental concerns of the Greens can be seen as driving forces. A second factor is the German political party system, which was strongly influenced by a Green Party that entered the *Bundestag* in 1983 and increased its share of votes in the 1987 election. The Green Party cooperated closely with the other opposition party, the Social Democrats, with 'ecological modernisation' becoming a common project in which they tried to offer cognitive leadership. The German Greens have not only become one of the strongest but also one of the most modern Green Parties in international comparison (after a 'fundamentalist' start in the early 1980s).

The 1997 *Bundestag* Enquete Commission on Climate Protection created the knowledge-base both for the core elite and the interested public. The Enquete Commission provided not only the necessary information about the possible long-term problems caused by climate change, but also pointed out available policy options to prevent or at least mitigate climate change. It also stipulated clear targets for the national, EU and international levels, while acknowledging the importance of multi-level governance structures in dealing with global climate change.

Institutional explanatory factors include support from Chancellors (Kohl, Schröder and Merkel) for a German leadership role in EU and international climate change politics and also from the capable Environmental Ministers Töpfer, Merkel, Trittin and Gabriel, who pushed for ambitious climate change policy measures on the national, EU and international levels. An important pre-condition for the adoption and successful implementation of ambitious climate change policy measures was the setting up of the 'Inter-ministerial working group CO_2 reduction' (*Interministerielle Arbeitsgruppe* (IMA) CO_2 reduction) in 1990. This constituted the first important step in the direction of integrating climate policy considerations into other policies within a domestic political system that is otherwise characterised by a high level of ministerial independence. Moreover, the IMA CO_2 reduction helped to reduce potential conflicts between Ministers from different political parties within the coalition government. The Integrated Energy and Climate Programme, which was adopted in 2007, was a programme in the formulation of which six different Ministries participated.

Public support — though sometimes critical — was essential in the 2002 *Bundestag* elections. The issue of climate change (together with public opposition to the Iraq war) was a major contributing factor in the re-election of the Red-Green coalition government in 2002; in addition, environmental NGOs, already historically strong in Germany, further increased their membership after 1998.

There was also a hidden alliance for ecological modernisation (Jänicke 2006). It included not only environmental NGOs and government institutions but also parts of industry. Industrial branch organisations like the German Engineering Federation (Verband Deutscher Maschinen und Anlagenbau –

VDMA) the German electronics industry association (BITCOM) and parts of the construction industry became winners (or potential winners) out of the implementation of climate policy and supported a more ambitious approach. This alliance proved especially strong when the renewable energy regulation had to be defended against opponents (Jänicke 2010a).

Multi-level governance

Germany has a long tradition of using both the EU and institutions at the global level for promoting domestic environmental policy innovation. Two motives are particularly salient. The international diffusion of German technology-based regulations (such as the Renewable Energy Act) can support domestic firms. A second possible motive for using the international level is to strengthen the domestic position for more ambitious climate change policies. Of course, it is also generally attractive for governments to play a pioneer role in the global policy arena. The applause which Chancellor Schröder received for his dramatic plea for climate protection and Germany's leadership position at the 2002 UN summit in Johannesburg was helpful for the federal elections which took place a few weeks later.

This approach to multi-level governance is especially important in the EU context (Knill and Liefferink 2007). The EU provided not only the policy arena for 'uploading' more ambitious German targets. It also prevented domestic backlashes against ambitious climate change policy measures. A kind of 'enforced leadership' can be observed in this context. The Commission's rejection of the second German NAP (under the EU emissions trading scheme) and the modification of German pro-industry positions in the EU's climate change and energy package in December 2008 are good examples to illustrate this point. In both cases the German pioneer role was secured only by the EU.

Contradictions

The German success story is not without contradictions and anomalies. The main restrictions on more wide-reaching achievement were the coal-based power companies and the car industry. Paradoxically it was under the climate change-conscious Red-Green coalition government that the energy sector steadily increased its CO_2 emissions, by more than 37 mt between 1999 and 2005 (*Umwelt*, 3/2010). Concessions to the power industry may have been (at least for the Social Democrats) the political price the government had to pay for tacit support for its anti-nuclear policies. The German car industry was very successful with the introduction of fuel-efficient diesel engines – creating a successful lead-market for this technology. However, at the same time the engine power of the car fleet increased by nearly 40 per cent between 1995 and 2007 which made it impossible to achieve the voluntary agreement (140 g CO_2 per km by 2008) that ACEA had put forward (SRU 2008). After 1998

Germany also remained the only country in Europe without speed-limits on highways. Here the 'automobile chancellor' (*Autokanzler*) Schröder was one of the main veto players. The Grand coalition too did not introduce speed-limits either, despite the fact that an oil price explosion had taken place which triggered a crisis particularly for the German automobile industry. The development in the power sector and car industry shows that potential GHGE reductions have been even higher than the ambitious policy has exploited.

Conclusion

The German pioneer role in climate policy is especially visible in the over-achievement of the ambitious Kyoto target for GHGE and the rapid domes-tic growth in renewable energy. Germany has exercised political *and* economic leadership, with each reinforcing each other. The 'demonstration effect' is most important for the German case. It amounts to 'leadership by example'. which proved that an ambitious climate policy is not only feasible but also effective. German climate change policy has also been a clear economic success which produced a large and rapidly growing 'climate protection industry'.

Germany's pioneer role in climate policy produced both structural and cognitive leadership (see Chapter 1 by Wurzel and Connelly). The high capa-city of the political and economic system to push for a stricter climate policy together with the competitive pressure that it caused in the global market amount to structural leadership. The conceptual and regulatory innovations which brought about political and economic success on the domestic level and stimulated international lesson-drawing can be characterised as cognitive and intellectual leadership. The German strategy was strongly innovation-oriented, with the concept of 'ecological modernisation' playing a central role after 1998, before it was supplanted by the concept of 'ecological industrial policy' in 2005. Particularly during the last decade, these concepts and Germany's cognitive leadership in climate change also had some influence on the EU. Germany also provided considerable entrepreneurial leadership during its EU and G8 presidencies in 2007.

The main national conditions of climate change policy success have been: (a) the early creation of a widely accepted knowledge-base for the political elite and the general public; (b) the cross-party consensus about the impor-tance of climate protection which was strongly influenced by (c) the Green party together with the (d) fast-growing new climate industry and a hidden alliance for ecological modernisation. Multi-level governance was an addi-tional supporting factor, as the EU occasionally forced Germany to live up to its self-adopted leadership ambitions in EU and international climate change politics.

The German case can be characterised as an experiment under extremely difficult conditions. The ambitious German objective of a 40 per cent GHGE reduction target by 2020 was accompanied by the decision to phase out nuclear energy This created extraordinary pressure for innovation of energy technology and policy. It resulted not only in high growth rates for the emerging climate change industry and lead-markets (especially for renewable energy) but also triggered the inflow of foreign investment and a high increase of patents. In times of high energy prices this has proven to be highly profitable. The acceleration of the innovation process may have been the most remarkable effect of this policy: It enlarged not only the technical potential for environmental improvement (lower costs and higher effectiveness, for example,of renewable energies) but also the political acceptance of an ambitious climate strategy. In 2009 nearly two-thirds of the German population agreed that a strict climate policy is an '*economic* advantage' (Jänicke 2010b).

There are, however, also contradictions in Germany's leadership role which were caused by veto players such as the coal-based power companies and the car industry. It is these industries which have been largely responsible for the non-achievement of the domestic 25 per cent CO_2 reduction target for 2005 and the failure of ACEA's voluntary agreement on CO_2 emissions from cars. In other words, even after the successful achievement of the 21 per cent GHGE reduction target for 2008/12, a high potential of climate protection remains unused so far. This is, nevertheless, no bad lesson to be drawn from the German experiment in climate protection.

Bibliography

BMU (2010) 'Erneuerbare Energien trotzen der Wirtschaftskrise', *Umwelt*, 4/2010.

BMU and UBA (2009) *Umweltwirtschaftsbericht 2009*, Berlin: BMU and UBA.

BMU and UBA (2008) *Die Dritte Industrielle Revolution – Aufbruch in ein ökologisches Jahrhundert*, Berlin: Bundesministerium für Umwelt, Naturschutz und Reaktorsicherheit.

BMU and UBA (2007) *GreenTech made in Germany – Umwelttechnologie-Atlas für Deutschland*, München: Verlag Franz Vahlen.

BMU and UBA (2004) *Umweltbewusstsein in Deutschland*, Berlin: Bundesministerium für Umwelt, Naturschutz und Reaktorsicherheit.

Busch, P.-O. and Joergens, H. (2010) 'Governance by Diffusion. International Environmental Policy Coordination in the Era of Globalization', Dissertation in the Fachbereich Politik- und Sozialwissenschaften, Berlin: Free University of Berlin Freie Universität Berlin (forthcoming).

Deutscher Bundestag (1980) *Zukünftige Kernenergie. Bericht der Enquete-Kommission des Deutschen Bundestages, Teil I, II. Zur Sache Nr. 1–80, 2–80*. Bonn: Deutscher Bundestag.

Deutscher Bundestag (1990) *Schutz der Erde. Eine Bestandsaufnahme mit Vorschlägen zu einer neuen Energiepolitik, Zur Sache Nr. 19/90*, Bonn: Deutscher Bundestag.

DIHK 2005) *Für einen Strategiewechsel in der Umweltpolitik – Erwartungen der deutschen Wirtschaft an die künftige Bundesregierung*, Berlin/Brüssel: Deutscher Industrie- und Handelskammertag.

DTI and DEFRA (2006) *Bridging the Gap between Environmental Necessity and Opportunity, First Report of the Environmental Innovation Advisory Group*, London:

Department for Trade and Industry/Department for Environment, Food and Rural Affairs.

EEA (2007) *Greenhouse Gas Emission Trends and Projections in Europe 2007*, Copenhagen: European Environment Agency.

Ernst & Young (2006) *Eco-industry, its Size, Employment, Perspectives and Barriers to Growth in an Enlarged EU*, Brussels: EU Commission DG Environment.

Federal Ministry for the Environment, Nature Protection and Nuclear Safety (various years) *Umwelt*, Berlin: Federal Ministry for the Environment, Nature Protection and Nuclear Safety.

Gabriel, S. (2006) *Ökologische Industriepolitik. Memorandum für einen „New Deal' von Wirtschaft, Umwelt und Beschäftigung*, Berlin: Bundesministerium für Umwelt, Naturschutz und Reaktorsicherheit.

Grassl, H. (1999) *Wetterwende – Vision: Globaler Klimaschutz*, Frankfurt and New York: Campus Verlag.

Jänicke, M. (2010a) 'Die Umweltpolitik der Großen Koalition', in Ch. Egle, F. Nullmeier and R. Zohlnhoefer (eds), *Bilanz der Großen Koalition*, Wiesbaden: VS Verlag (in press).

Jänicke, M. (2010b) 'Markt statt Kopenhagen', *Süddeutsche Zeitung*, 21. 1. 2010, p. 2.

Jänicke, M. (2008) *Megatrend Umweltinnovation. Zur ökologischen Modernisierung von Wirtschaft und Staat*, München: Oekom.

Jänicke, M. (2006) 'Trend Setters in Environmental Policy: The Character and Role of Pioneer Countries', *European Environment*, 15(2), 129–42.

Jänicke, M. and Zieschank, R. (2008) *Structure and Function of the Environmental Industry – The Hidden Contribution to Sustainable Growth in Europe, FFU-report 01–2008, Environmental Policy Research Centre* (Forschungsstelle für Umweltpolitik). Freie Universität Berlin.

KfW (2010), KfW erzielt Förderrekord in Deutschland, Pressemitteilung, <http://www.kfw.de/DE_Home/Presse/Pressearchiv/2010/20100128_34729.jsp> (accessed 2.2.2010).

Knill, C. and Liefferink, D. (2007) *Environmental Politics in the European Union. Policy-Making, Implementation and Patterns of Multi-level Governance*, Manchester: Manchester University Press.

Markham, W. T. (2008) *Environmental Organisations in Modern Germany – Hardy Survivors in the Twentieth Century and Beyond*, New York/Oxford: Berghahn Books.

McKinsey (2007) *Kosten und Potenziale der Vermeidung von Treibhausgasen in Deutschland*, McKinsey & Company, Inc.

Michaelowa, A. (2008) 'German Climate Policy between Global Leadership and Muddling Through', in H. Compston and I. Baily (eds), *Turning down the Heat. The Politics of Climate Policy in Affluent Democracies*, Basingstoke: Palgrave/Macmillan, 144–63.

Oberthür, S. and Pallemaerts, M. with Kelly, C. R. (eds) (2010) *The New Climate Policies of the European Union: Internal Legislation and Climate Diplomacy*, Brussels: Vrije Universiteit Brussel.

OECD (2005) *Environmental Policy, Technical Innovation and Patent Activity, OECD Environmental Policy Committee*, Paris: Organisation for Economic Co-operation and Development.

OECD (2007) *Environmental Innovation and Global Markets*, ENV/EPOC/GSP(2007)2/REVI, OECD: Organisation for Economic Co-operation and Development.

146 *Martin Jänicke*

REN21 (2008) *Renewables 2007 - Global Status Report*, <http://www.ren21.net>

Schreurs, M. A. (2002) *Environmental Politics in Japan, Germany and the United States*, Cambridge: Cambridge University Press.

SPD/BÜNDNIS 90 – DIE GRÜNEN (1998) *Aufbruch und Erneuerung – Deutschlands Weg ins 21. Jahrhundert. Koalitionsvereinbarung zwischen der SPD und Bündnis 90/Die Grünen, 20. Oktober 1998*.

SRU (2008) *Umweltgutachten 2008 – Umweltschutz im Zeichen des Klimawandels. Sachverständigenrat für Umweltfragen*, Berlin: Erich Schmidt Verlag.

Statistisches Bundesamt (2008) *Statistisches Jahrbuch 2008 für die Bundesrepublik Deutschland*, Wiesbaden: Statistisches Bundesamt.

Wurzel, R. K. W. (2008) *The Politics of Emission Trading in Britain and Germany*, London: Anglo-German Foundation for the Study of Industrial Society.

9 The Netherlands

A case of 'cost-free leadership'

Duncan Liefferink and Kathrin Birkel

Introduction

This chapter analyses the relationship between the development of domestic climate policy in the Netherlands on the one hand and the Dutch efforts in this field in the European and international arena on the other. To what extent has the Netherlands lived up to its reputation as an environmental 'pioneer' and in fact to its declared ambition to act as an international leader in this particular area? As the chapter will show, the implementation of domestic climate targets has been far from unproblematic. How could this be matched with the international ambitions of the Dutch? What consequences did the apparent gap between the two have, both for articulating the intended international role and for domestic policy practice?

In order to answer these questions, we will first sketch the national context of Dutch climate policy, followed by an analysis of the evolution of the policy field, paying attention both to domestic policies and to the Dutch role in European and global climate negotiations. A separate section focuses on the key policy instruments of Dutch climate policy. After that, the issue of Dutch leadership is addressed by linking the Dutch ambitions, efforts and achievements at the domestic and the European/international level. A few concluding observations serve to wind up the chapter.

National context of climate policies

The Netherlands is a small, highly industrialised country with a population of 16.3 million, or 481 people per km^2 (Centraal Bureau voor de Statistiek (CBS) 2008). In 2006, total emissions of carbon dioxide (CO_2) and the five other major greenhouse gases amounted to 209 Mt CO_2 equivalents.[1] Most of this, 173 Mt, was accounted for by CO_2 (Planbureau voor de Leefomgeving 2008: 193).

Emissions per capita in the Netherlands are at a level comparable to Belgium, Germany and also the Russian Federation, but above the EU average and considerably higher than in, for instance, the UK, Spain, France or Sweden. Emissions related to GDP are more in line with neighbouring countries but still significantly higher than in, for example, Denmark, Italy, France or Sweden (European Environment Agency (EEA) 2007; Milieu- en Natuurplanbureau 2008). Although the Dutch government boasts a decoupling of economic growth and CO_2 emissions over the years 1990–2003 (Ministerie van Volkshuisvesting 2005), it was not until 2005 that total greenhouse gas emissions (GHGE) reached a level below that of 1990 (Milieu- en Natuurplanbureau 2007: 61).

At first sight this is surprising, considering the large natural gas reserves in the northern part of the country and the Dutch parts of the Wadden Sea and North Sea. Natural gas has a lower CO_2 intensity than other fossil fuels and accounts for almost 50 per cent of domestic energy use, which is an unusually high share (The Netherlands Ministry of Housing 2005: 23). This natural advantage is partly outdone, however, by the presence of relatively energy-intensive industries in the Netherlands, notably a number of big refineries and chemical plants. These are predominantly located in Rotterdam, Europe's biggest port, but the presence of these polluting industries is – ironically – also related to the availability of natural gas, which is used as a basis for other products. Another sector benefiting from the Dutch 'gas bubble' is greenhouse horticulture. Dutch tomatoes could not be grown without cheap energy. A second factor contributing to relatively high CO_2 emissions in the Netherlands is the virtual absence of nuclear energy. Only a few per cent of Dutch electricity demand is covered by a single nuclear plant in the south-western part of the country. This is an important difference with neighbouring countries like Germany and, notably, Belgium and France. Renewables, finally, still play a modest role with a contribution to the total Dutch energy supply of no more than 2.7 per cent in 2006 (Milieu- en Natuurplanbureau 2007: 69f).

Historical development of Dutch climate change policy

When, in 1991, the Netherlands' finance minister of the time, Wim Kok, announced a rise on the levy on fuel to almost 25 cent/litre for unleaded gas, this measure was soon given the more succinct title of 'Kok's quarter'. Almost 20 years later, Kok's quarter enjoys a consistent unpopularity, but has so far defied all cries for abolition. In this respect, it is one of the few cornerstones in Dutch climate change policy that have been unharmed by the ravages of time – or rather, the ravages of changes in government coalitions since the advent of the topic in the late 1980s.

At that time, the issue of climate change hit a political agenda that was more than willing to embrace it. Environmental politics ranked high – high enough to make coalitions fall apart or to star in the Christmas speech of Queen Beatrix ('Slowly, the earth is dying'). Aiming at a stabilisation of CO_2 emissions in 2000, the 1989 National Environmental Policy Plan (NEPP) set the first nation-wide CO_2 target in the world (Nationaal Milieubeleidsplan (NMP) 1988–89; cf. Rowlands 1995: 77). During the campaign to the elections later that year, Ruud Lubbers, candidate of the Christian Democrats, used climate protection as one of his figureheads and promised annual CO_2 reductions of 2 per cent. Although this objective was not upheld, it merged into the later aim of a reduction of 3–5 per cent by 2000 (Nationaal Milieubeleidsplan Plus (NMP Plus) 1989–90), with an additional long-term goal of minus 60 per cent during the 100 years to come.

In order to fulfil this mission, the government opted for the introduction of an ecotax, which was then very much *en vogue* in both OECD and EU circles. In this respect, the government announced that it was in favour of an EU-wide solution, but also that the possibility of national action should be investigated (N.N. 1990).

Its national schemes place the Netherlands in the league of the most ambitious EU-countries at the time, and its international intentions surely did not lag behind. The Netherlands actively contributed to setting the agenda and building up political pressure in the run-up to the UNFCCC (United Nations Framework Convention on Climate Change), eventually signed in Rio de Janeiro in 1992. It saw no fault in going for a 'unilateral' EU-wide tax, rejecting a US equivalent as a precondition for its introduction (N.N. 1992).

By the time of the Second NEPP (Tweede Nationaal Milieubeleidsplan (NMP-2) 1993–94), which appeared at the end of 1993 and set out goals and measures for the period between 1995 and 1998, the main features of a distinctly Dutch climate change policy had emerged. Just like in other areas of environmental policy making, climate change policy had become the object of an effort to move responsibilities from government to private actors (Ministerie van Volkshuisvesting 1993: 42). Anticipating the turn-away from so-called command-and-control instruments which captured the rest of the EU in later years, the Dutch government was looking for alternative measures, based on either the market mechanism or negotiation and consensus, that would make use of the abilities of private actors without compromising too many of their liberties (Ministerie van Volkshuisvesting 1993: 128).

A prime example of this shift was the introduction of 'covenants', i.e. voluntary, not strictly legally binding agreements between the government and various industry sectors, aiming at improving the latter's energy efficiency (see below). In the same vein, the Netherlands proved to be very open-minded about the same flexible instruments that are now very much entrenched in the EU climate change agenda, but of which the effectiveness was still heavily debated at the time. For instance, the NEPP 2 mentions further investigation into the mechanism of emissions trading (Ministerie van Volkshuisvesting 1993: 183), an exploration of what is now called carbon capture and storage (CCS) and the intention to fulfil part of its reduction obligations by stimulating and financing projects abroad (Ministerie van Volkshuisvesting 1993: 74ff, 133, 220).

Compared to these measures in preparation, the envisaged CO_2/energy tax – despite its novel, market-based character – seemed to come closest to conventional 'hard' policy making. However, notwithstanding considerable efforts by the Netherlands and a number of other Member States, the EU-wide CO_2 tax never materialised, leaving not much but the option of the Netherlands 'going it alone'. Already in the early 1990s, however, serious doubts about a full-fledged national forerunner strategy and its allegedly disastrous consequences for the competitive position of Dutch industry had been expressed by the Ministry of Economic Affairs, the employers' organisations and the influential Wolfson advisory committee, among others. For this reason, the Dutch made a final attempt in 1995/1996 to revitalise the issue at the European level by convening a meeting of eight like-minded countries in The Hague, exploring the possibility of coordinating national CO_2 taxes outside the formal EU framework. This 'club', however, never took off either; eventually, a purely national tax scheme indeed was established, but only for small consumers and at a very low, in fact fairly symbolic, level.

In a way, this course of events reflects the overall development of climate change policy in the Netherlands in the post-NEPP 2 years. From being politicians' darling subject in 1989 elections, the environment and, more particularly, climate change had been moved to the dark cellars of politics by 1994, making space for the economy and employment to take their place. In the course of the year, the general energy reduction goal by 2000 was lowered from 20 per cent to 17 per cent and subsidies for energy reduction and renewable energy were being cut back (Vos and Herbergs 1995). At the end of the year, a newspaper stated that the Netherlands had been seized by an 'environment fatigue' (Westerman 1994).

The Netherlands also readjusted its vision on what its role could be within the EU and at the international level. Making an active contribution to international efforts and the intention to take, if needed, unilateral action for the sake of demonstration (Ministerie van Volkshuisvesting 1993: 15, 60) gave way to making multi-lateral commitment a precondition for national activities, i.e. a shift away from active, constructive pushing to something close to a wait-and-see approach. And while the spirit of ecological modernisation had imbued domestic environmental policy in the early 1990s (Ministerie van Volkshuisvesting 1993: 60), the Netherlands put renewed emphasis on 'the national interest' and 'the competitive position of Dutch industry' in the Third NEPP (Ministerie van Volkshuisvesting 1998) presented in February 1998. Environmental organisations, traditionally relatively powerful in the Dutch consensual system, were not able to counter this shift.

The tensions that this caused 'on the ground' can be seen when looking at the role played by the Netherlands in the context of the Kyoto conference. Being the EU president in the first half of 1997, the Netherlands ensured an EU-wide agreement on a common negotiating position for Kyoto by putting forward the 'triptych' approach. This approach provided a method for sharing the 'burden' of further emission reductions among the Member States in a 'scientific' or at least criteria-based manner.[2] On this basis, the EU delegation went to Kyoto with an opening offer of reducing GHGE by 15 per cent in 2008–12 (relative to 1990) for the EU as a whole, provided that other industrialised countries would go for comparable reductions. For the Netherlands, a target of minus 10 per cent was envisaged. This strategy came to no avail, however: the delegation returned home with a target of only minus 8 per cent for the EU, in the face of the low commitments of other parties. What happened back in Brussels, however, was less guided by the 'triptych' approach than by the basic principles of political horse-trading. The Netherlands joined the ranks of those countries that wanted to keep their national obligations as low as possible (Van den Biggelaar and Wams 1998) and eventually left the arena with a national target of minus 6 per cent. Moreover, the new coalition agreement of 1998 made the Dutch ratification of the Kyoto protocol dependent on that of countries such as the USA and Japan.

Despite the 'success' of being conceded the rather low target of minus 6 per cent GHG reduction in the end, the Netherlands was still struggling with how this could possibly be reached. It was true that the voluntary agreements with the industry had enhanced energy efficiency; however, the latter were more than outweighed by a surge in the overall use of energy (which was not taken into consideration in the agreements). For the transport sector, which accounted for an ever larger piece in the pie chart of emissions, there were hardly any policy measures in place which actually deserved the name – with 'Kok's quarter' having a more beneficial impact on treasury income than on driving behaviour.

The Netherlands consequently first turned towards other means to achieve its targets, e.g. reducing emissions abroad. Already before the Kyoto agreement, it entered joint implementation (JI) projects with East European countries such as Romania (Bennis 1997). After Kyoto the Netherlands wanted to follow the road taken by massively investing in projects under the new Clean Development Mechanism (CDM). Both the manner and the extent to which it was planning to do so, however, caused dismay in the Netherlands and in the rest of the EU. Nationally, the main bone of contention was the decision to finance CDM projects from money drawn from other official development assistance (ODA) projects in the field of the environment; EU-wide, it was the Netherlands' initial intention to reduce more than half of its emission reductions abroad (N.N. 1999).

With the organisation of the Sixth UNFCCC Conference of Parties (COP-6) in The Hague in November 2000 and the active role of the Dutch in COP-6bis in Bonn several months later, an environment seemed to have been created which allowed a reinvigoration of climate change policy. However, the 2001 Fourth NEPP still considered unilateral pressing ahead off-limits. Policies for industry kept relying heavily on voluntary agreements.

In 2002, Dutch climate change was for the first time evaluated for its integrity by the Dutch Court of Audit. The verdict was explicit: 'Today's policy is characterized by a lack of coherence and by shortcomings in the preparation of the policies. In addition, policy measures which are put in place are lacking concrete possibilities for enforcement or sanctions, with large-scale consumers being partly exempted' (Algemene Rekenkamer 2002: 6, own translation). The Court also criticised the lack of measurable targets and the virtual absence of monitoring of the actual impact of measures.

As a reaction, Jan Pronk, then Minister of the Environment, promised the introduction of reduction targets for different sectors. This promise was honoured by the subsequent, more right-wing government coalition, which, however, in other parts of environment and climate change policy opted for a 'new course'. The office of a Minister of the Environment was substituted by that of a State Secretary, or junior minister, carrying out a cut-down task with regard to climate-change policy making. With the introduction of target values for different sectors, the prime responsibility was shifted to the respective departments (i.e. agriculture, energy), the State Secretary executing merely a coordinating function (Ministerie van Volkshuisvesting 2005).

The principal focus now lay on 'less regulations, less money from the government' (cf. Ministerie van Volkshuisvesting 2002: 8). The first victim of 'less regulations' was road pricing, which was not introduced after all. Kok's quarter remained unharmed, but was now used to partly finance new road constructions (Ministerie van Volkshuisvesting 2006: 25). 'Less money from the government' resulted in cut-backs on, e.g., tax bonuses for energy-efficient cars. In its 2004 report, the Netherlands' Environmental Assessment Agency (Milieu en Natuur Planbureau, MNP) concluded that, from all cut-backs in the field of the environment, most were undertaken in the domain of climate change policy (Milieu- en Natuurplanbureau 2004: 31). In this respect, government attitudes seemed to resonate with those of the electorate; according to a survey, in 2005 70 per cent of the population were simply not interested in the issue of climate change (N.N. 2005).

However, just as the Stern/Gore wave swept over the rest of the EU, it swept over the Netherlands, even if it needed somewhat more persistence. The new Christian-democrat/social-democrat government, coming into office in early 2007, seemed determined to make use of this window of opportunity and announced nothing less than 'New energy for the climate'. This, at least, was the heading of its working programme on climate-change policy, *Schoon en zuinig*, presented in September 2007 (Ministerie van Volkshuisvesting 2007).

The 'show-pieces' of this programme were the new long-term targets: a 30 per cent reduction in GHGE by 2020 (base year: 1990), a 20 per cent share of renewable energy by the same year, and an annual energy saving rate of 2 per cent. These objectives are to be bolstered both by the provision of financial resources (an annual fixed budget of 1.3 billion, plus an additional annual amount that ranges from 140 million in 2008 to 500 million in 2011) and policy measures, including – once again – road pricing.

Although it has been doubted whether the proposed measures will be sufficient to meet the long-term goals (Platform Communication on Climate Change (PCCC) 2008: 20), the new climate programme promises to mark a new phase in both Dutch and EU climate-change policy. For the first time in years, the Netherlands has presented a programme which is not simply waiting on others to make the first step; rather, with a long-term goal that was decided upon even before the European Commission presented its proposals on future effort sharing, and the recognition that an active role within the EU can be played only if substantial steps are taken at home (Ministerie van Volkshuisvesting 2007: 53), the Netherlands appears to be back on the proactive constructive pushing track that it left in the years before. Unlike other EU Member States, it seems to be willing to follow this track 'in the good times as in the bad'. In various statements, Jacqueline Cramer, the Dutch Environment Minister, in the period 2007–2010 depicted the credit crunch as an opportunity to re-model the economic system in a sustainable fashion, rejecting demands for a less ambitious EU climate policy in times of crisis. Reflecting the delicacies of domestic climate policy and acknowledging the EU's key role on behalf of its Member States in the ongoing international climate negotiations, the Netherlands played a constructive rather than an ostentatiously activist part in the run-up to the Copenhagen conference (COP-13) held in December 2009.

Policy instruments

In the course of the 1980s, and in line with the country's neo-corporatist tradition, Dutch environmental policy shifted its focus from direct 'command-and-control' regulation to negotiation and consensus between the state and polluting sectors (Liefferink 1997, 1999; Liefferink and Mol 1998). This is also reflected in climate policy where voluntary agreements (or 'covenants') play a crucial part. Equally, the role of market-based instruments, notably emissions trading and CDM/JI, has been strengthened.

Voluntary agreements

From 1991 onwards, the Ministry of Economic Affairs concluded so-called Long-Term Agreements (LTAs) with 29 industrial branches, altogether covering 84 per cent of Dutch industrial energy use. For most sectors, the aim was to improve energy efficiency by 20 per cent between 1989 and 2000.

After the first round of LTAs, a more dynamic benchmarking approach replaced the LTA targets for the most heavy energy users (energy consumption per plant above 0.5 PJ per year). This select group comprises only a few hundred companies from sectors such as electricity generation, chemical industry, refinery and pulp and paper, but represents no less than 40 per cent of total Dutch energy consumption. Under the 1999 Covenant Benchmarking Energy Efficiency they commit themselves to belong to the 10 per cent best-performing companies in their branch worldwide as regards energy efficiency, ultimately by 2012. From 2005, some of these heavy energy consumers also take part in CO_2 emissions trading. The remaining, mainly medium-range industrial energy users started to conclude a second round of LTAs from 2000 (LTA2) and a third round from 2005 (LTA3), together aiming at a 45 per cent improvement in energy efficiency between 1998 and 2020 (SenterNovem 2008).

Throughout, both government authorities and business have been very pleased with the results of both conventional and benchmarking LTAs, with the industries in question usually attaining or even exceeding their targets. Environmental organisations, research institutes and other independent institutions, however, have been less satisfied. In 2000, the Central Planning Bureau argued that many of the LTAs did not go further in their targets than what would have been put into effect anyway. Accordingly, the Bureau claimed that LTAs accounted for only 30 per cent of the actual improvement on energy efficiency, with the rest being due to 'autonomous' causes (Centraal Planbureau 2000: 13, 90). In 2002, the Dutch Court of Audit took criticism to an even higher level, when it animadverted that LTAs made use of only (relative) energy efficiency targets instead of (absolute) targets in terms of CO_2 reduction (Algemene Rekenkamer 2002: 6). As a result, improvements in energy efficiency were outdone by the growth in production volume and a slight structural shift from low to heavy energy-consuming industries, notably chemicals (Enevoldsen 2005: 170–74). Since the introduction of the EU-wide emissions trading scheme (EU-ETS, see below), however, the LTAs have lost some of their central position in Dutch climate policy.

Energy taxation

Within the EU, the Netherlands was able to flaunt the unilateral introduction of an energy tax after fruitless efforts to raise a similar tax at the EU level or in accord with a group of like-minded countries. The 'Regulatory Energy Tax' (Regulerende Energie Belasting, REB) was imposed in January 1996. In view of competitiveness considerations, forcefully brought to bear by Dutch business, the tax was directed towards small consumers, with larger industries being practically exempted.

The Dutch energy tax has been subject to several hikes over the years. In total, its revenues have increased seven-fold between 1996 and 2006, with 2006 numbers lying at 4 billion euros (Planbureau voor de Leefomgeving 2010). The yield is, however, mainly used to lower other taxes, especially on employment, and therefore the tax can be said to be revenue neutral.

The actual effect of the Dutch Energy tax has been subject to discussion. Whereas consultant Ecofys reports a retained reaction by households (Joosen, Harmelink and Blok 2004: xiii), a report by SEO Economic Research insists that the latter have indeed been induced to reduce gas and electricity consumption in the period of investigation (1996 – 1999) (Energieonderzoek Centrum Nederland (ECN) 2001: 3f).

Flexible mechanisms: emissions trading, JI, and CDM

From very early on, the Netherlands had an affinity for so-called flexible mechanisms. First ideas about using the instrument of emissions trading in the Netherlands date back to the times of the Second NEPP. In early 2000, when the Commission proposed launching the EU-ETS, the Dutch government had already installed a special committee investigating the introduction of an ETS on a national basis. Nevertheless, actual plans had hardly crystallised and could not sufficiently be pushed in Brussels to be taken seriously as a potential model for the European scheme. Instead, 'first movers' UK and particularly Denmark largely determined the shape of the Commission's proposal and the later Directive (Knill and Liefferink 2007: 133–39; Veenman and Liefferink 2005).

The first phase of the EU-ETS, starting in 2005, included a few hundred of the Netherlands' large emitters, partly overlapping with the companies taking part in the Benchmarking Energy Efficiency Covenant. Due to a generous allocation of initial emission rights, the Dutch companies participating in the scheme easily kept their emissions well below the emission ceiling, resulting – with other Member States doing the same – in a plummeting of market prices. Allocation plans for the second phase were evaluated considerably more strictly by the European Commission, however, and the Netherlands was required to cut back its (intended) total allocation from 90.4 to 85.8 million tonnes CO_2, as well as to obligate approximately one hundred further companies to participate in the scheme.

With LTAs mainly focusing on the improvement of energy efficiency, the ETS has by now become the prime policy instrument stimulating actual CO_2 reductions in the Dutch industry and energy sector. The Netherlands was also an early bird with regard to JI and the CDM. As mentioned above, the Netherlands engaged in Joint Implementation even before Kyoto was ratified. Likewise it was the first country ever to make use of CDM in 2001.

Carbon capture and storage (CCS)

Longer than other EU Member States, Dutch governments have shown a special interest in the technique of carbon capture at the source, i.e. 'end-of-pipe' in large combustion plants, and subsequent underground storage. With the declared intention to become a 'frontrunner' in CCS development,[3] the Dutch government has decided to spend 80 million euros for further developing CCS and to instigate large emitters, particularly electricity plants, to invest in the technique.

Renewable energy

Compared to other EU countries, renewable energy (RE) has featured less prominently on the Dutch climate policy agenda. In 2006, the RE share in primary energy consumption was stagnating at 2.7 per cent – and thus far below the EU average of *c.* 6.5 per cent. The MNP assigns this to the fact that, in the Netherlands, room for growing biomass or installing wind generators is both scarce and expensive, and that the country simply is too flat to have potential for hydropower (Milieu- en Natuurplanbureau 2007:

70), Nevertheless, the 2007 climate work programme sets a target of no less than 20 per cent renewables for 2020 (Ministerie van Volkshuisvesting 2007).

So far, however, efforts by the authorities to foster the investment climate in this sector have been rather fickle. Unlike in Germany, there is no feed-in law; instead, subsidy schemes have been introduced, abrogated and reintroduced within only few years time. In 2008, a new subsidy scheme, the 'Stimuleringsregeling Duurzame Energieproductie' (SDE) has been set up to ensure investors more planning reliability, by promising subsidies rising from 10m euros in 2008 to 336m euros in 2015 (Ministerie van Economische Zaken 2008).

Multi-level governance and Dutch leadership

For most of the history of climate change politics, the Netherlands has striven to acquire a leadership role in global and European climate policy. In order to be convincing, an international pioneer role has to be backed up by a successful, or at least a forceful policy at the domestic level. Domestic climate policy in the Netherlands can hardly be described in these terms, however. Particularly noteworthy in this context are the instances in which the Dutch showed themselves ready to exploit the loopholes offered by weak international agreements in order to save their own face. This section will explore the sometimes ambiguous links between the Dutch ambitions and efforts in climate policy at the domestic, the European and the international level.

Even before climate change appeared on the political agendas worldwide, the Netherlands had built up a reputation as one of the environmentally progressive countries in the European Union (Liefferink 1997). The advent of climate change politics, however, not only offered the Netherlands a further possibility to strive for environmental protection. As it turned out, it was to become one of the fields where the Netherlands, as a geographically small state, was able to play in the premier league with the big ones – by compensating its lack of structural leadership with a seemingly fervent effort to score all the higher on the entrepreneurial and cognitive/intellectual level.

From the beginning, the Netherlands took every chance to make its presence felt and to be at the very start of new developments. Cases in point, discussed in more detail above, are the early nation-wide CO_2 target in the First NEPP, the active role of the Dutch in the run-up to the UNFCCC, the efforts to establish an EU-wide CO_2 tax, the introduction of the 'triptych' approach to secure agreement among the EU Member States about sharing the Kyoto 'burden', the significant Dutch contribution to the heavy logrolling at COP-6 in The Hague and COP-6bis in Bonn in 2000–2001, and the pioneering role in developing and mobilising the mechanisms of JI and CDM. The international efforts of the Dutch were based mainly on diplomatic skills, networking and coalition building (or 'entrepreneurial leadership') (Andersson and Mol 2002), with the Netherlands often trying to find the common ground between 'extreme' positions. Complementarily, however, it tried to persuade by expertise and good arguments. In this respect, the

Netherlands' reliance on science needs to be emphasised. Scientific experts were both engaged by the Netherlands itself and seconded to international institutions such as UNFCCC and IPCC (or cognitive or intellectual leadership). Rather than acting as a lonely forerunner and serving either as an example or as a laughing-stock for its neighbours, the Netherlands quite consistently tried to stimulate joint solutions by playing the role of a constructive pusher (Liefferink and Andersen 1998). As stressed by several interviewees from Environment ministries of other EU countries, moreover, this was recognised and generally positively appreciated abroad.

As has been emphasised time and again by the Dutch government since the Second NEPP, 'active environmental diplomacy' should be based on consistent and credible domestic policies (e.g. Ministerie van Volkshuisvesting 1993: 53; 2007: 57). In climate policy this adage proved very hard to fulfil. Instead of going down or even stabilising, Dutch GHGEs, particularly CO_2, have steadily been increasing until 2004. In the face of this, as described above, domestic targets were repeatedly tempered or shifted to a later point in time.

Arrears in the implementation of domestic climate policy were obscured not only by changing targets, but also by the formulation of some of the key instruments of the policy. Most conspicuously, both the LTAs on industrial energy efficiency and the 1999 Covenant Benchmarking Energy Efficiency deal with energy efficiency only in relative terms, making the effect on absolute emissions ultimately dependent on the development of the economy. In spite of the apparent effectiveness of the first round of LTAs, economic growth and a slight shift in the structure of Dutch industry resulted in an increase of *absolute* industrial energy consumption in the 1990s (Enevoldsen 2005: 170–74).

At the international level, Dutch ambitions did not easily materialise either. Considerable efforts by the Netherlands and a number of other EU Member States to introduce a common CO_2 tax – first within the framework, later with a smaller 'club' of countries – did not bear any fruit. A few years later, the EU's initial proposal to commit the industrialised world to a 15 per cent reduction target, bolstered by the Dutch 'triptych' approach, did not survive the tough give-and-take in Kyoto. Furthermore, attempts to include in the Kyoto Protocol explicit reference to common and coordinated policies and measures, championed particularly by the Netherlands, completely failed (Andersson and Mol 2002: 57ff).

Obviously, it would be futile to ascribe these European and international policy outcomes to 'failing' diplomatic efforts or a lack of credibility in the face of a domestic implementation gap on the part of the Dutch. These outcomes were the results of long and highly complex negotiation processes, in Brussels and elsewhere, involving a large spectrum of parties. As suggested by our interviews, the Dutch difficulties experienced in implementing effective policies at home were hardly even recognised by the international partners. In this context, it must be remembered that the Dutch were certainly not unique in this regard: severe implementation problems gradually came to the surface almost everywhere.

Much more interesting is what happened at home *after* these somewhat disappointing outcomes had been reached at the European/international level. As it turned out, the Dutch government was ready more than once to use these outcomes to close the gap between its high international ambitions and the tough reality at home. First, although a national CO_2 tax was established after it had become clear that an EU-wide tax was definitively doomed to fail, this unilateral tax had a highly symbolic character. Thus, notwithstanding the lost battle in Brussels, the Netherlands could boast of being one of the first countries in the world to have a CO_2 tax at all, while at the same time not doing any harm to its domestic industry. Second, one can hardly avoid the impression that the Dutch government was actually quite happy with the failure of the minus 15 per cent scenario in Kyoto. Why else did it make such efforts to reduce its share in the final EU bubble to a minimum? As Andersson and Mol remark, this behaviour of a reputed global climate policy 'leader' did not serve as a particularly positive example for other Member States, who perceived it as a licence to relax their ambitions too (Andersson and Mol 2002: 59). A more or less similar effect, finally, may be attributed to the Dutch intention of realising a considerable part of its Kyoto target through JI and CDM abroad. Many other Member States saw this as a cheap escape from the obligations to which the Netherlands had committed itself and – more importantly – to which it had tried to push other countries in the first place.

The examples of the CO_2 tax, the struggle for the lowest possible national burden share and the heavy reliance on JI and CDM, combined with the ambivalent performance of domestic climate policies almost inevitably convey the impression of symbolic, 'cost-free leadership' (Huber 1997). In addition to that, the readiness with which the Netherlands has tended to seize the opportunities offered by 'weak' international negotiation outcomes has strengthened the influence of those outcomes on domestic policy and thus contributed to a relatively high degree of Europeanisation of climate policy compared to other environmental areas (Liefferink and Van der Zouwen 2004). Several key aspects of the Dutch policy in this field have in fact been determined or at least strongly influenced by what happened at the EU level, including the overall reduction target and the package of instruments, notably the limited use of the tax instrument and the introduction of ETS. The latter has now started to interfere with what can be considered the most genuinely vernacular element of Dutch climate policy, the voluntary agreements. In line with this is the strong reliance on EU measures for achieving the Dutch domestic goals, as has been stated by Environment Minister Cramer and was confirmed once again in the run-up to the 2009 Copenhagen climate conference. Interestingly, this reliance does not limit itself to areas which are obviously within the EU's core competence, such as car emissions. With reference to the supposedly greater effectiveness of EU-wide measures, it also extends to fields where individual Member States could well play a significant role themselves too, such as energy-labelling and eco-design.[4] Conversely, the Dutch influence on EU policy has, after all, been limited. With the failure of the CO_2 tax, the emissions trading scheme being shaped mainly by other countries and the LTA approach being too strongly tied to the Dutch political culture of negotiation and consensus, the 'triptych' approach probably remains the most visible Dutch contribution to the area.

Conclusion

This chapter has examined if, how and why the Netherlands has acted as leader in climate policy. It has been argued that, generally speaking, domestic performance in this field did not live up to the European and international ambitions articulated by the Dutch. The question may be asked to what extent the observations at the domestic level and those at the European and international level are in fact connected.

Three points can be made in this regard. First, it appears that high ambitions and an active role at the international level are not necessarily based on outstanding policy performance at home. On the one hand, this may be related to the fact that the Dutch international pusher role was based primarily on expertise combined with diplomatic efforts – or 'intellectual' and 'entrepreneurial' leadership, respectively. A pusher role based on 'giving the good example' (cf. Liefferink and Andersen 1998) would quite obviously have required the availability of such examples. Consequently, this type of pusher role was never actually sought by the Netherlands, except perhaps on paper in the earliest years. On the other hand, it must be recognised that most of the Dutch international efforts were orchestrated by the Ministry of the Environment, whereas many operational competences in domestic climate policy resided with other government departments. As it appears, not all of these international efforts were fully coordinated among the departments involved and may in some cases also have been intended by the Environment Ministry as crowbars to push domestically – although not always with the desired effect.

Second, even if the Netherlands rarely referred to domestic 'examples' for convincing the European and international arena and even if poor domestic policy performance hardly caused any reputational damage abroad, the failure to achieve domestic reduction targets, the subsequent efforts to limit to a minimum the Dutch share in the European 'burden' after the Kyoto agreement and, on top of that, the heavy reliance on buying emission rights abroad for realising even that share, did not contribute to the Dutch credibility as a 'climate leader' and raised the suspicion that the Netherlands was cultivating a 'cost-free leadership'.

Finally, the chapter clearly shows that where domestic policies fail, European and international policies take over. Of course, this was so partly because European/international obligations simply filled the gap left by domestic policy failure. However, this appears not to be the whole story. In

160 Duncan Liefferink and Kathrin Birkel

this particular case, international policies generally also did not match the initial ambitions. The Dutch government was repeatedly eager to use these disappointing international policy outcomes as a basis for revising domestic policies in order to 'cover up' the shortcomings of earlier efforts. As an end effect, climate change ranks among the most Europeanised areas in Dutch environmental policy.

Notes

1 Total Dutch emissions of CO_2 (corrected for temperature effects), CH_4, N_2O, HFCs, PFCs and SF_6.
2 'The main characteristic of the 'triptych' approach was its sectoral approach; each Member State was divided into three sectors, namely the light domestic sector, the energy-intensive, export sector, and the electricity generation sector. An emission reduction target in each country was set by adding up the potential for emission reductions in each sector. The EU-wide target was set by totalling these figures' (Kanie 2003: 236).
3 Jacqueline Cramer at the opening of the EON carbon capture test facility near Rotterdam, 3 April 2008 (<http://www.vrom.nl/pagina.html?id=35749&term=ccs>, accessed 24 June 2008).
4 See also the statement of Jacqueline Cramer at the Public Debate of the 2856th Environment Council Meeting (Council of the European Union 2008: statement at approx. 1h 51min).

Bibliography

Algemene Rekenkamer (2002) *Bestrijding uitstoot broeikasgassen*, 's-Gravenhage: SDU.
Andersson, M. and Mol, A. (2002) 'The Netherlands in the UNFCCC Process – Leadership between Ambition and Reality', *International Environmental Agreements: Politics, Law and Economics*, 2(1), 49–68.
Bennis, M. (1997) 'Broeikas-effect veel goedkoper te bestrijden', *Algemeen Dagblad*, 22 March, 17.
Centraal Bureau voor de Statistiek (CBS) (2008) *StatLine – Regionale economische totalen 2001–2004*, viewed 28 May 2008, <http://statline.cbs.nl/StatWeb/publication/?VW=T&DM=SLNL&PA=37054reg&D1=0–1&D2=0,6–17&D3=a&HD=080528–947&HDR=T,G2&STB=G1>.
Central Bureau voor de Statistiek (CBS) (2000) *Naar een efficiënter milieubeleid. Een maatschappelijk-economische analyse van vier hardnekkige milieuproblemen*, Den Haag: Sdu Uitgevers.
Energieonderzoek Centrum Nederland (ECN) (2001) *Energie Verslag Nederland 2001*, viewed 18 June 2007, <http://www.energie.nl/dossier/ebesp2001.pdf>
Enevoldsen, M. (2005) *The Theory of Environmmental Agreements and Taxes. CO2 Policy Performance in Comparative Perspective*, Cheltenham: Edward Elgar.
European Environment Agency (EEA) (2007), *Europe's Environment. The Fourth Assessment*, Copenhagen: European Environment Agency.
Huber, M. (1997), 'Leadership in EU Climate Policy: Innovative Policy Making in Policy Networks', in D. Liefferink and M. Andersen (eds), *The Innovation of EU Environmental Policy*, Oslo and Copenhagen: Scandinavian University Press, pp. 133–55.

Joosen, S., Harmelink, M. and Blok, K. (2004) *Evaluatie van het Klimaatbeleid in de gebouwde omgeving 1995–2000*, Utrecht: Ecofys.

Kanie, N. (2003) 'Domestic Capacity, Regional Institution and Global Negotiations: Lessons from the Netherlands-EU Kyoto Protocol Negotiation', in M. G. Faure, J. Gupta and A. Nentjes (eds), *Climate Change and the Kyoto Protocol: The Role of Institutions and Instruments to Control Global Change*, Cheltenham: Edward Elgar, 230–47.

Knill, C. and Liefferink, D. (2007) *Environmental Politics in the European Union. Policy-Making, Implementation and Patterns of Multi-level Governance*, Manchester: Manchester University Press.

Liefferink, D. (1997) 'The Netherlands: A Net Exporter of Environmental Policy Concepts', in M. Andersen and D. Liefferink (eds), *European Environmental Policy: The Pioneers*, Manchester: Manchester University Press, 210–50.

Liefferink, D. and Andersen, M. S. (1998) 'Strategies of the "Green" Member States in EU Environmental Policy Making', *Journal of European Public Policy*, 5 (2) (June 1998): 254–70.

Liefferink, D. (1999) 'The Dutch National Plan for Sustainable Society', in N. Vig and R. Axelrod (eds), *The Global Environment: Institutions, Law and Policy*, Washington, DC: CQ Press, 256–78.

Liefferink, D. and Mol, A. (1998) 'Voluntary Agreements as a Form of Deregulation? The Dutch Experience', in U. Collier (ed.), *Deregulation in the European Union: Environmental Perspectives*, London: Routledge, 181–97.

Liefferink, D. and Van der Zouwen, M. (2004) 'The Netherlands: The Advantages of Being "Mr. Average" ', in A. Jordan and D. Liefferink (eds), *Environmental Policy in Europe. The Europeanization of National Environmental Policy*, London: Routledge, 136–53.

Milieu- en Natuurplanbureau (2004) *Milieubalans 2004*, Milieu- en Natuurplanbureau, Bilthoven.

Milieu- en Natuurplanbureau (2007) *Milieubalans 2007*, Uitgeverij RIVM, Bilthoven.

Milieu- en Natuurplanbureau (2008) *Milieu en Natuurcompendium – CO2-emissies in relatie tot bruto binnenlands product en bevolking, 2002*, viewed 27 May 2008, <http://www.milieuennatuurcompendium.nl/indicatoren/nl0171-Koolstofdioxide-emissies-in-relatie-tot-bruto-binnenlands-product-en-bevolking.html?i = 9–20>.

Ministerie van Economische Zaken (2008) *SDE*, viewed 25 June 2008, <http://www.ez.nl/Onderwerpen/Energie/Duurzame_energie/SDE>.

Ministerie van Volkshuisvesting, Ruimtelijke Ordening en Milieubeheer (VROM) (1993) *Tweede Nationaal Milieubeleidsplan*, 's-Gravenhage: SDU.

Ministerie van Volkshuisvesting, Ruimtelijke Ordening en Milieubeheer (1998) *Nationaal Milieubeleidsplan 3*, 's-Gravenhage: VROM.

Ministerie van Volkshuisvesting, Ruimtelijke Ordening en Milieubeheer (2002) *Vaste waarden, nieuwe vormen : milieubeleid 2002–2006*, Den Haag: VROM.

Ministerie van Volkshuisvesting, Ruimtelijke Ordening en Milieubeheer (2005) *Evaluatie klimaatbeleid 2005. Onderweg naar Kyoto*, Den Haag: VROM.

Ministerie van Volkshuisvesting, Ruimtelijke Ordening en Milieubeheer (2006) *Evaluatienota klimaatbeleid 2005: Onderweg naar Kyoto*, Den Haag: VROM.

Ministerie van Volkshuisvesting, Ruimtelijke Ordening en Milieubeheer (2007) *Nieuwe Energie voor het klimaat : werkprogramma schoon en zuinig*, Den Haag: VROM.

Nationaal Milieubeleidsplan (NMP), 1988–89, Kamerstukken II 21137, 1–2.

Nationaal Milieubeleidsplan Plus (NMP Plus), 1989–90, Kamerstukken II 21137, 20–21.

N.N. (1990) 'Nederland eens met EG-plan energieheffing', *NRC Handelsblad*, 24 December, p. 15.

N.N. (1992) 'Kabinet: ook energieheffing zonder de VS', *NRC Handelsblad*, 18 May, p. 3.

N.N. (1999) 'Nederland dwarsboomt klimaatbeleid', *Trouw*, 18 May, p. 16.

N.N. (2005) 'Wat kan het klimaat ons schelen?' *Het Parool*, 5 February, p. 27.

Planbureau voor de Leefomgeving (2008) *Milieubalans 2008*, Bilthoven: Planbureau voor de Leefomgeving.

Planbureau voor de Leefomgeving (2010) Compendium voor de Leefomgeving – Belastingen op een milieugrondslag 1990–2006, viewed 22 June 2010, <http://www.compendiumvoordeleefomgeving.nl/indicatoren/nl0359-Belastingen-op-een-milieugrondslag.html?i=10-72>.

Platform Communication on Climate Change (PCCC) (2008) *De Staat van het Klimaat 2007. Actueel onderzoek en beleid nader verklaard*, Wageningen: PCCC.

Rowlands, I. (1995) *The Politics of Global Atmospheric Change*, Manchester: Manchester University Press.

SenterNovem (2008) *MJA3: intensivering, verbreding en verlenging afspraken. Factsheet no. 2MJAF0803*, Den Haag: SenterNovem.

Council of the European Union (2008) *Public Debate: 2856th Environment Meeting Council*, viewed 30 June 2008.

The Netherlands Ministry of Housing, Spatial Planning and the Environment (VROM) (2005) *Fourth Netherlands' National Communication under the United Nations Framework Convention on Climate Change*, The Hague: VROM.

Tweede Nationaal Milieubeleidsplan (NMP-2), 1993–94, Kamerstukken II 23560, 1–2.

Van den Biggelaar, A. andWams, T. (1998) 'Streng milieubeleid is geen weggegooid geld', *Algemeen Dagblad*, 16 June, p. 11.

Veenman, S. and Liefferink, D. (2005) 'Different Countries, Different Strategies. "Green" Member States Influencing EU Climate Policy', in F. Wijen, K. Zoeteman and J. Pieters (eds), *A Handbook of Globalization and Environmental Policy. National Government Interventions in a Global Arena*, Cheltenham: Edward Elgar, 519–44.

Vos, M. and Herberigs, B. (1995) 'Heffing op energie is geheel uitgekleed', *De Volkskrant*, n.p..

Westerman, F. (1994) 'De grenzen van de offerbereidheid zijn bereikt; Moe van het milieu', *NRC Handelsblad*, 31 December, p. 6.

10 Poland's climate change policy struggle

Greening the East?

Karolina Jankowska

Introduction

Because Poland has failed to take on a climate change policy leadership role on any of the domestic, EU and international levels, this chapter will focus on Poland's attitude towards the adoption and implementation of EU and international climate change policy measures rather than on domestic climate change policies. The first domestic modern-day environmental regulations were adopted in Poland at the beginning of the 1990s. It is to be expected that the EU will play an important role in the formulation of domestic environmental policy because its formulation is taking place in parallel with European integration. However, since the announcement of the EU climate and energy package (see Chapter 1 by Wurzel and Connelly and Chapter 5 by Oberthür and Dupont) Poland is no longer simply a follower of EU policy. Instead it has started to play an active role at European level during the negotiations of the climate and energy package. Although many commentators have stated that Poland had actually been blocking the very ambitious original proposal of the EU climate and energy package, in this chapter it is argued that Poland's aim has rather been to try to reshape the EU policy in order to make it possible for Poland and other Central and Eastern European countries to attain the ambitious EU targets without suffering huge economic losses. According to Polish state officials such economic losses, would, for example, have resulted from the adoption and implementation of the Commission's proposal for the revision of the EU emission trading scheme (ETS).

National attitudes to climate change

According to a survey carried out for the Polish Department of European Integration (Gfk Polonia 2008), only 5 per cent of respondents are unaware of any evidence of climate change. Thirteen per cent of respondents stated their belief that climate change does not have anthropogenic causes. Almost half of the respondents (48 per cent) stated that the intensive development of Poland's economy justifies the increase of Poland's carbon dioxide (CO_2)

emission limit. According to research by *Eurobarometer* (2008: 295), Polish respondents are less worried about climate change than the general public in the EU (47 per cent in Poland, 57 per cent in the EU-27). According to Bokwa (2007: 121), the relatively low standard of living of the majority of the population, the increasing gap between rich and poor, and the high level of structural unemployment, are all severe obstacles to raising public awareness of environmental issues in Poland. This is because, according to Kocik (2000: 209), in such circumstances there is hardly any chance of persuading people to make sacrifices for the environment.

However, according to the principle of ecological modernisation, short-term 'sacrifice' for the environment can in fact significantly improve living conditions at least in the medium to long term (see Chapter 1 by Wurzel and Connelly). But there is an evident lack of social awareness in Poland of the link between quality of life and the state of the environment. Another important issue, according to Bokwa (2007), is that during the socialist period, Poland was isolated from Western-style goods. Therefore, the changes in Poland since 1989 have created very high consumer expectations in Polish society. Although sustainable development and the protection of the atmosphere are usually viewed as tasks demanding a certain reduction in consumption in rich Western European countries, the same demand would be regarded as absurd by most Poles because most of their families are barely able to satisfy their basic needs (ibid: 121–22). The issues of global climate change are therefore not yet widely recognised in Polish society, although there are some elite groups which promote strongly environmental issues (ibid: 122). Moreover, amongst political parties represented in the lower house of the Polish Parliament (*Sejm*), climate change also seems to be unimportant, and is hardly treated as a serious political matter. Apart from general statements about sustainable development, no suggestions about the need to combat climate change have been included in the manifestos of the main political parties.

Since 2004, a green party – *Zieloni* 2004 (Greens 2004) – has existed in Poland. This was set up by members of Polish NGOs, which realised that the environmental movement also needs to have political representation. It campaigns vigorously in favour of climate protection and proposes political instruments to match global environmental problems. They cooperate with the Greens/EFA Group in the EP. The party is not represented in the *Sejm* or the *Senat* (the upper house of the Polish Parliament).

In 2002 the Climate Coalition was established. This is an association of Polish environmental NGOs interested in activities dedicated to global climate protection, and it seems to both willing and likely to have a greater influence on Polish climate change policy. The long list of members of this coalition includes, for example, Greenpeace, the Institute for Sustainable Development (Instytut na rzecz Ekorozwoju) and the World Wide Fund for Nature (WWF).

Phases of domestic climate change politics

During the process of political transformation in Poland in the 1990s, the entire judicial and legal system was changed. Global warming issues were dealt with for the first time by the *Sejm* in the first *National Environmental Policy* report (Rada Ministrów). In Poland, domestic environmental policy is still formulated by the Ministry of Environment on its own, rather than by the government as a whole: environmental policies are put forward by the Environment Ministry and then have to be discussed and adopted by the national Parliament. The first *National Environmental Policy* was the first strategic environmental action programme in Poland (and in Central and Eastern Europe if not in the whole world) to treat environmental protection in an integrated manner (Bokwa 2007: 123).

The second *National Environmental Policy* report (Rada Ministrów [Council] 2000) is completely different to the first, mainly because it takes new conditions into consideration (e.g., the Rio Declaration and the new administrative division of the country). It mentions the need for the rational use of the environment in order to prevent or tackle climate change, but confines itself to merely indicating ways to decrease energy consumption and improve the use of renewable energy resources.

An important stage of development of climate change policy in Poland, especially in respect of renewable energy, was the adoption of the *Strategy for the Development of Renewable Energies* (Ministerstwo Środowiska). Since 2004 Poland has adopted the *mixed* system of support for renewable energy sources – it uses a quota mechanism combined with the tradable green certificates system. However, the facilitation of the growth of green electricity supply has been slow under the system. Also, the lack of social and political support for renewable energy is very restrictive for the development of renewable energies in Poland, as there is very little will to establish a domestic renewable energy market together with a more supportive mechanism to develop the use of renewable energy.

The most important Polish policy document to cope with climate change, which was adopted by the Polish government at the end of 2003, was the *Climate Policy of Poland* (Ministerstwo Ochrony Środowiska [Ministry of Environment] 2003). It was prepared as a requirement of Poland's participation in the UN Framework Convention on Climate Change (UNFCCC) which Poland had ratified in 1994. The aim of this strategy was to bring Poland's climate change policy in line with the climate change policy of the EU. This policy should have enabled Poland to fulfil its obligations under the UNFCCC which committed Poland to reduce its emissions by 6 per cent (in comparison to 1988 levels). However, at the time when the strategy was adopted, Poland had already reduced its greenhouse gas emissions (GHGE) by more than 30 per cent (in comparison to 1988 levels) (ibid: 4). This was because between 1988 and 2001 Poland's economy declined and many industrial enterprises were closed. The Kyoto Protocol's aim for Poland was therefore attainable without implementing any special climate change policy measures and/or tools. That is why a more ambitious aim was set under this strategy, namely, to reach a 40 per cent reduction by 2020. The domestic 40 per cent reduction target by 2020 was due to the greater pressure on Poland from the EU and from the wider international community. It was also motivated by the expected benefits from the emissions trading. However, this reduction target had only a declarative character and did not translate into action supported by new legislation which would have been needed for its realisation. Today Poland's economy is one of Europe's largest GHG emitters. Poland is also at the very top in Europe in terms of the ratio of CO_2 emissions per GDP, as can be seen from the report *Assessment of Greenhouse Gas Emissions Abatement Potential in Poland by 2030* (McKinsey & Company 2010: 8). Poland emits annually around 386 million tonnes of CO_2 (ibid.). To produce 1,000 dollars of GDP, about 760 kg of CO_2 has to be emitted (ibid.). In Europe only Estonia (820 kg) has a worse record than Poland. In France the corresponding figure is 290 kg, while in Germany – which also has a relatively high use of coal – it amounts to 400 kg (ibid.). Since 2002, CO_2 emissions in Poland have grown by an average of 1.4 per cent (ibid.: 7).

In March 2005, Poland's comfortable situation in terms of the need to reduce GHGE suddenly changed after the European Commission decided to reduce the approved limits of emissions previously set in the Polish *National Plan of Entitlements Distribution of CO_2 emissions for years 2005–2007* (i.e., Poland's National Allocation Plan (NAP)) (Ministerstwo Środowiska 2005). Under the EU emissions trading law the European Commission has the power to reject NAPs. The European Commission argued that a lowering of Poland's CO_2 emission allowances under its NAP would help the country to comply with its Kyoto commitments and the EU's burden sharing agreement (later renamed the effort sharing agreement). Granting Poland an excessively high number of CO_2 emission allowances would, on the other hand, lead to a massive sale of CO_2 allowances by Polish enterprises which in turn could lead to a significant reduction of the carbon price within the EU ETS, which in turn would discourage (medium- to long-term) ecological investment. Because of the European Commission's intervention, Poland had to prepare a new draft NAP for the years 2008–12 (*National Plan of Entitlements Distribution of CO_2 emissions for years 2008–2012*) which was approved on 1 July 2008.

Institutional responses, policy instruments and programmes

The document *Climate Policy of Poland* describes the preferred measures to tackle climate change (Ministerstwo Środowiska 2003). Its first recommendation states: 'For the realization of climate change policy, priority should be given to market-based instruments (emissions trading, green certificates) because they incur the lowest cost in achieving the policy goals' (ibid: 25). Another important group of policy instruments consists of so-called supporting measures, for instance information and educational campaigns or training programmes to provide the socio-economic background to enable the government to implement these kinds of instruments. These policy instruments are very important in a country which (unlike most Western European countries) does not have a long history of shaping its own environmental policy. Most Polish politicians as well as industry representatives do not yet have a high degree of environmental awareness. This is arguably one of the most important factors to bear in mind when considering the implementation of such policy instruments in Poland. In a rapidly transforming economy such as Poland, market-based instruments are also likely to be most effective because there is still a deep level of distrust of regulation stemming from the Communist past. Market-based policy instruments encourage industry to adopt a more proactive attitude towards environmental protection without incurring excessive costs and/or inflexibility. The adoption and/or implementation of market-based instruments in Polish climate change policy is strongly influenced if not imposed by the EU. The best examples include the renewable energy sources support system and the ETS.

At the end of 2000 the Ministry of Economy developed (on the base of the renewable energy sources targets which had been politically accepted in the *Strategy of the Development of Renewable Energies*) an ordinance with an obligation to purchase electric energy from renewable energy sources. The quantitative target which the ordinance set for the suppliers amounted to a 7.5 per cent share for green electricity by 2010. This was the least ambitious of targets that had been set out in the *Strategy of the Development of Renewable Energies*. In 2002/2003, following negotiations between the Polish government (represented by the Ministerstwo Gospodarki i Biuro Integracji Europejskiej (Ministry of Economy and European Integration Office)) and the European Commission (represented by DG TREN and DG Enlargement), the renewable energy sources targets for electricity production from the above mentioned ordinance were included in the EU Enlargement Treaty as Poland's national target; they were subsequently also incorporated into Directive 2001/77/EC. According to Wiśniewski (2008: 6), the national 7.5 per cent target of per cent gross electricity consumption from renewable sources by 2010 which became legally binding with the adoption of Directive 2001/77/EC, has become a key driving force for the development of further domestic legislation and for the increase in the amount of renewable electricity produced in Poland.

The Polish political discussion and institutional response to the Commission's proposal for a review of the EU ETS by 2013 will be assessed in the next section of this chapter. Because it explains the general perception in Poland of different types of policy instruments well, it is important first to assess briefly the mechanism of financial compensation as proposed under the EU's climate and energy package. The former Polish Prime Minister and current President of the EP, Jerzy Buzek, believes that the EU's climate and energy package stipulates that the revenue generated from the purchase of CO_2 emission allowances paid for by industry (and the power sector in particular) should flow into Member States' domestic budgets (Buzek 2008: 29). According to Buzek, it has become rather difficult to criticise the EU ETS, because EU finance ministers expect a sudden inflow of between five and seven billion euros. He is nevertheless highly critical, although his criticism is clearly coloured by his experience of Poland's Communist past: 'But we in Poland do not want a socialist-type budget any longer . . . We in Poland know very well what socialist-type redistribution was like 20 years ago. And we know how it all ended. We had artificial taxes, an artificial budget. We are trying to protect ourselves against that' (ibid). Under the Communist regimes price was, however, never perceived as an incentive for ecological modernisation. Moreover, the external costs of environmental pollution were not internalised as is the case under the EU ETS.

Climate change as a threat or opportunity?

During the Polish public debate of the EU climate and energy package, the Polish Green Party as well as members of the Climate Coalition, strongly emphasised the benefits of implementing climate change mitigation measures (as proposed by the European Commission) in terms of ecological modernisation for the entire Polish economy. On the other hand, Poland's political leaders and business representatives have tried to convince European officials and politicians that the proposed energy and climate change policy measures (and the EU ETS in particular) could severely affect the economies of the poorest European Member States. The European Commission's proposal for the climate and energy package had to be changed while taking into account some of Poland's demands before it was finally agreed in late 2008. Without the use of external EU pressure there would not have been an energy and climate policy in Poland even half as ambitious as it is now. Taking into account the main thesis of this chapter, which states that Poland's policy on climate change largely mirrors that of the EU (see also Bokwa 2007: 132), ecological modernisation in Poland seems to be driven largely through the process of domestic adaption to EU environmental policies and/or international commitments. This thesis also arguably applies to other Central and Eastern European countries, which worked together when trying to amend the European Commission's initial proposal for the EU climate and energy package.

In September 2007, after the European Council had announced the general targets of the EU energy and climate policy, a new government was elected in Poland and its Environment Minister, Maciej Nowicki,[1] was perceived as a supporter of the emission trading scheme on the grounds that it provided a great opportunity for ecological modernisation in Poland. However, the Ministry of Environment does not play a very important role in the Polish government where it has a much lower position in the ministerial hierarchy than the Economics Ministry. This is probably also why, at the time of the debate on the EU climate and energy package, strong opponents of ambitious measures to achieve the energy and climate goals played a dominant role within the Polish government. The review of the EU ETS has been criticised most, especially by the conventional (mainly coal-based) energy sector which found a good supporter of its interests in the Polish government.

To understand the position of the Polish government during the climate and energy package negotiations one has to look at Poland's energy mix. Hard coal and lignite are the most widely used energy sources in Poland – 86 per cent of primary energy and 93 per cent of electricity in 2008 was produced from hard coal and lignite (Główny Urząd Statystyczny 2009: 32 and 37). There is a big coal lobby in Poland, supported by trade unions, whose members fear mass unemployment following closure of unprofitable mines. Indeed, the restructuring and modernisation process of the Polish coal industry is likely to result in mass unemployment, because not every miner can be employed in the renewable energy sector, or at least not initially. Moreover, one of Poland's biggest concerns about the European Commission's proposal for a climate and energy package was, according to the Undersecretary at the State Ministry of Environment, Bernard Błaszczyk (*Polish Market* 2008: 27), the proposed full auctioning of emission allowances for the power generation sector under the revised EU ETS by 2013. (However, the energy sector will still get some allocations for free following the compromise which was adopted by the European Council in Brussels in December 2008). With the trading price of one tonne of CO_2 being forecast at about 40 euros in 2013, such a development would increase electricity prices in Poland by approximately 80 per cent for households and by approximately 70 per cent for industry. Such a price hike would be disastrous for Poland's industry and for the living standards of its population (ibid).

During the negotiations of the EU climate and energy package, the Polish authorities often declared that Poland was capable of meeting its obligations as laid down in European Council resolutions and EU laws. It was, however, unclear how the Polish government would achieve its political commitment and legal obligations. There is therefore no doubt that the EU climate and energy package gave rise to a domestic discussion about climate change policy which could bring about the ecological modernisation of the whole economy and thus enable Poland to fulfil its EU targets. Within a few months, the Polish government and its experts prepared an emission reduction scheme for Poland until 2020 (ibid). It consisted of many ambitious targets that had never previously been under serious consideration in Poland. This scheme has been incorporated into *Poland's Energy Policy until 2030* report which is the most important strategic document in the field of energy policy in Poland and which was adopted by the Council on 10 November 2009 (Ministerstwo Gospodarki [Ministry of Economy] 2009).The emission reduction scheme consists of the following five main points:

1   increase of energy efficiency in order to promote the development of the country without growth in energy consumption;
2   15 per cent share of renewable energy sources in gross energy consumption until 2020;
3   modernisation of at least 40 per cent of the generation capacity in coal-fired power stations;
4   construction of the first coal gasification and the first underground gasification installations as well as of two carbon capture and storage (CCS) units;
5   launch of the construction of a nuclear power station.

Moreover, during the negotiations of the EU climate and energy package, Poland took an active role in proposing amendments to the European Commission's proposal. The cooperative and agreement-oriented role of Poland in these discussions was underlined by many Polish politicians as an answer to allegations that Poland was against the package: 'That is incorrect. What we want is to amend the package to make it acceptable for all' – said Jerzy Buzek (*Polish Market* 2008: 29). The two most important points of Poland's amendments to the EU package were the following (ibid.: 28):

1   several years' derogation from entering the auctioning system for countries in which more than 50 per cent of electric and thermal energy is produced from coal;
2   treating the energy industry on a par with other industries by granting it free emissions rights in 2013 amounting to 80 per cent of real emissions, followed by a gradual reduction of that amount to 0 per cent in 2020.

The Polish political establishment has started to concern itself for the first time with the environment, particularly climate protection, as a way to bring about ecological modernisation on the domestic level. Nevertheless, the Polish position in the EU negotiations on the climate and energy package confirmed an existence of the conventional view of a trade-off between economic growth and environmental protection. The conventional view could be seen in the use of weakness of Polish (and other Central and Eastern European countries) economy in comparison to Western European countries as a justification for watering down the relatively ambitious EU climate change measures. The reduction of CO_2 emissions could have been undertaken, but only without raising the cost of electricity on the market. However, it should not be forgotten that the position of the Polish negotiators, politicians and industry lobbyists was based on the report by EnergSys, a Polish energy and environmental consulting firm (Karaczun et al. 2009: 45). In September 2008 Ernst & Young, a business consultancy, presented its own report, drawing on earlier research by EnergSys, which claimed that the EU's measures would damage growth, stoke inflation and undermine other important political goals such as the adoption of the euro in Poland (Kanter 2008).

During the negotiation of the EU climate and energy package, a coalition against ambitious EU climate change policy measures was formed which consisted of representatives from Polish business and industry. The biggest Polish GHG emitters organised within the Green Effort Group, which lobbied the Polish government as well as the European Commission and European governments. During the negotiations of the EU climate and energy package, the Polish government actually represented the position of this group as well as the position taken by the business consultancy Ernst & Young. When in November 2008, the Gdansk Institute of Market Economy published an analysis (Kanter, 2008) which stated that Poland 'will have enough time to develop economic, social and energy policies that would considerably minimize the potential negative impact of the European Union's measures', some members of the Polish political establishment strongly opposed this assertion. This illustrates the degree to which the Polish government supported Poland's business and energy industry during the EU negotiations. The environmental NGOs formed their own coalition which did not share the position of the Polish government (Polish Climate Coalition). Their position was supported by the Polish Green Party in its letter to the Prime Minister Donald Tusk (*Zieloni 2004* 2008).

At the European level Poland has initiated an interest coalition which consisted of the Visegrad four nations (Hungary, Slovakia, the Czech Republic and Poland) and the Baltic States (Lithuania, Latvia and Estonia). In November 2008, the prime ministers of these seven countries met in Warsaw to examine the climate and energy package and to discuss the formation of a possible coalition of states which would support Poland's position on the EU level. Although it was Poland which facilitated this coalition, in the end all of the seven participating countries took advantage of the fact that the EU climate and energy package had been watered down. In principle Poland managed to convince the other new Member States to come to a consensus and form a coalition for the protection of their common interests. The first bargaining success of this coalition was the final decision on the climate and energy package which had to be adopted unanimously by the European Council in December 2008. Changing the decision-making forum from the Environmental Council (which can adopt its decisions by qualified majority voting) to the European Council (which must adopt its agreements unanimously) could be described as the second success of the coalition of Central and Eastern European states initiated by Poland. Therefore, during the EU negotiations of the climate and energy package, the opportunity emerged for Poland to be seen as no longer a foot-dragger but as a country providing entrepreneurial skills in bringing about an EU compromise. This was a result of its success in devising mutually acceptable formulas and brokering the interests of key players in building support for these formulas. Poland did not block the EU climate and energy package but helped to find a compromise acceptable to all. This type of entrepreneurial skill was also offered by other Central and Eastern European countries, because their coalition (made up of states who were reluctant to accept ambitious EU climate change policy measures which would have had a significant impact on their economic development) was successful in representing the common interests of the Central and Eastern European states at the EU level. This coalition also relied on the power of the idea of 'European solidarity' and equity to shape the way in which officials and politicians from the 'old' Member States understood their position. The Polish government argued forcefully that the cost of meeting the targets of the ambitious EU energy and climate policy should be shared more fairly by taking into account the specific national conditions. At the European Council meeting in Brussels in mid-October 2008, Central and Eastern European states stressed in a joint declaration that it had been extremely important that the EU refrain from solutions which neglected the differences in the economic potential of the Member States. From their perspective this was seen as particularly important because the great majority of the EU's GHGE reductions had been achieved by the less affluent Member States which had incurred high social and economic costs (*Polish Market* 2008: 8). It could therefore be argued that Poland (together with the other Central and Eastern European countries) provided considerable entrepreneurial skills to form a coalition of Member States who were reluctant to accept what they preceived as overly ambitious EU climate change policy proposals.

The coalition of new Member States was influential also because Poland had threatened to use its veto in the European Council if no acceptable compromise could be found on the climate and energy change package. The compromise which was finally adopted will grant power plants in Poland (and other new Member States) up to 70 per cent of free allowances in 2013. This applies to energy companies which had been operating before the end of 2008. In subsequent years, the percentage of free allowances will be gradually reduced and in 2020 100 per cent of allowances should be auctioned (EUROPA-Press Release 2008). Two per cent of the whole amount of allowances will be divided between the states that have reached more than 20 per cent of emissions reduction in the first period of implementation of the Kyoto Protocol. Poland will receive 27 per cent of this allowance (European Union 2009, 87).

Another attempt to provide an active input into the EU climate change negotiations, although it relates only to the Visegrád Group Countries, could be observed during the climate negotiations before and at the Copenhagen climate conference (COP 15) in December 2009. At their 16th Meeting of the Environment Ministers which took place in Cracow (Poland) in July 2009, of the Visegrád Group countries,[2] they agreed for the first time on the importance of climate change policy measures and signed a joint statement which underlined the need to adopt a new global climate change agreement at the Copenhagen climate conference in December 2009. The joint statement illustrates the degree of cooperation on climate change issues which now takes place between the Visegrád Group countries and which has, at least partly, been facilitated by Polish leadership.

Multi-level governance: EU and international commitments

What has been achieved in terms of environmental policy and climate policy in Poland has mainly been the result of Poland's foreign policy: first the preparation for EU membership and more recently adjusting Poland's environmental policy to the EU's climate and energy package (Bokwa 2007: 134). Clearly the EU acts as the main driver for the adoption of ambitious climate change policy measures in Poland. However, the EU's influence on Polish climate change policy is supported by Poland's politicians and business only when it does not result in economic losses. According to Wurzel (2002: 9), the cost to a state's economy of a particular environmental policy measure is widely seen as an important variable which helps to explain a government's stance on environmental issues. In Poland, the CO_2 emissions limits imposed on Polish industry by the EU are seen as a cost burden for the economy. If there was an economic crisis then the Polish government would be less likely to favour stringent environmental regulation. The credit crunch and financial crisis has not had any significant impact on the Polish economy as there has not been a sustained period of economic growth in Poland for a long time. Polish politicians and industry representatives are opposed to changes which could endanger Poland's continued economic development. It could be described as a preferred mode of policy-making, which makes an economy in rapid transition less favourable to taking on the risk of external ecological costs. Another important variable is the non-existence of any public profile of green politics in Poland, as characterised by low public environmental awareness as well as a low level of environmental group activity and party political competition about green issues. There is also a lack of green party representation in the national Parliament, while little media attention has been paid to environmental issues in Poland. There is therefore no social power to balance the coal-energy lobby inherited from socialist times (Bokwa, 2007: 133).

The interest of the state – becoming an EU member was the main foreign policy of all governments in Poland from 1990 – was the only factor strong enough to counterbalance the political influence which the coal-mining and energy production sectors tried to exert in order to avoid any significant changes in GHGE. For the very same reason, Poland has supported European environmental standards, and in doing so it is in favour of the EU becoming an important actor in international climate change politics, although not necessarily a leader. Jerzy Buzek (2008: 29) argued: 'The European Union cannot do much by itself. We have to do it globally.' This statement is representative of the opinion of the Polish political establishment. The claim that the EU's multi-level governance arena has created multiple veto points rather than numerous leadership points where competitive leadership has been initiated is more accurate. In the past Poland has often made use of these veto points in EU climate change policy negotiations, although during the negotiations of the EU climate and energy package Poland tried to provide compromise proposals which salvaged the package by making it acceptable to all. As a result, Poland contributed to the formation of a coherent EU climate change policy (at the European level) and thereby also to international climate change politics. The EU agreed to reduce its CO_2 emissions unilaterally by at least 20 per cent (compared to 1990) and to the revision of the EU ETS, neither of which would have been possible without Poland's agreement.

Conclusion: political leadership in Poland

Considering the political, economic and cognitive obstacles mentioned above, it is clear that Poland is not yet able to provide political leadership in EU and/or international climate change politics in terms of pushing ambitious climate policy targets and measures. During its EU membership application negotiations Poland 'downloaded' EU environmental policy measures which it had not been able to influence. Once it was a full EU Member State, Poland initially tried to veto or at least water down what it considered as overly ambitious EU climate change policy measures because it perceived them as a threat to its domestic economic development. More recently Poland has shown considerable entrepreneurship in organising a coalition of Central and Eastern European states to defend its own economic and political interests (and the interests of Central and Eastern European states) while at the same time no longer simply blocking proposed EU policy. Poland therefore transformed from a 'policy taker' to a 'policy shaper' (Jordan and Liefferink 2004) in EU climate change policy. There are certainly signs of movement in Poland's attitudes as witnessed by its actions during the negotiations of the EU climate and energy package as well as during the 2008 Poznań climate conference (COP 14) and the 2009 Copenhagen climate conference (COP 15). The hosting of the COP 14 in Poland focused the attention of the Polish public and media as well as of Polish politicians on climate change. Moreover, the Polish Environment Minister, Maciej Nowicki, who acted as the main host of Poznań climate conference, put a lot of emphasis on improving the process of international climate change negotiations. The 2008 Poznań climate conference discussed the setting up of an adaptation fund to support the mitigation efforts which developing countries will have to undertake as a consequence of global warming. It should also have established a preliminary draft for a (Kyoto Protocol follow-up) climate agreement, the final adoption of which was initially scheduled for the Copenhagen climate conference in December 2009. However, no text for a preliminary agreement was agreed at the 2008 Poznań climate conference. Moreover, the arrangements concerning the adaptation fund were left vague, and assessment of the achievements of the Kyoto Protocol could only be described as a failure. The main success of the 2008 Poznań climate conference was arguably the agreement that the development of a global climate change policy depends on the sovereign decisions of the biggest GHG emitters, namely the USA, China, India, Brazil and EU. Their domestic climate change policy commitments are probably even more important for the future of the global climate than even the best international climate change agreement which the most important states do not want to ratify, and would probably not want to put it into effect even if they did. From that perspective the Polish insistence on watering down the EU climate and energy package might be regarded as reasonable. as Poland wanted to secure agree on commitments that can realistically be fulfilled. In any case Poland did not want to reject the package. Poland's 'leadership' style could be classified as transactional and humdrum in that it consisted in operating within what was possible in the political opportunity structure of the moment, as perceived by the majority of Central and Eastern European states. Poland's entrepreneurial organisational skills helped the Central and Eastern European states to identify and defend congruent interests and common objectives within the EU climate change negotiations.

At the 2009 Copenhagen climate conference, Poland supported the EU's unilateral 20 per cent emission reduction target until 2020. Poland was significantly more reluctant to announce its readiness to support the EU's more ambitious 30 per cent reduction target which is conditional on other industrialised countries making comparable efforts. Poland demanded that the actual financial capacity of individual Member States be taken into account. It also resisted making significant financial commitments towards supporting financially developing countries' efforts to adapt to global climate change (EurActiv.pl 2009). In the end Poland's demands, however, did not prevent the EU from adopting ambitious emission reduction targets. The EU could therefore enter the negotiations of the 2009 Copenhagen climate change conference as a leader in international climate change politics (although its leadership position failed to facilitate a legally binding climate change agreement in Copenhagen).

The Polish case therefore illustrates that the type (and style) of leadership which is offered by one particular country can be transformed over time. Poland initially acted only as an EU climate change policy laggard before it became more actively involved in EU climate change policy while also trying to facilitated compromises with a realistic chance of being implemented by all Member States – including the environmental laggards. This observation arguably also applies to some degree to other Central and Eastern European countries. This is not to argue that Poland has become a leader in EU climate change politics. However, Poland and the other Central and Eastern European countries have transformed from EU climate policy *takers*, which merely download EU policies to the domestic level, to EU climate policy *shapers*, which try to upload to the EU level at least some of their domestic goals and approaches (Börzel 2003) makes a similar argument for Southern European states) when the economic cost of meeting the EU's relatively ambitious climate change targets is perceived as too high by the political establishment in these countries. It has been entrepreneurial, but only in a narrow sense of using its diplomatic, negotiating and bargaining skills (and opportunities) to facilitate agreements which do not primarily promote the overall aspirations of EU climate change policy. In other words, in recent years Poland has developed considerable entrepreneurial skills while defending its structural powers (as the largest of the Central and Eastern European states that has joined the EU up to now) in the European Council which has to adopt its decision unanimously.

Notes

1 Nowicki resigned as Environment Minister after COP 15. He proposed Andrzej Kraszewski as his successor.
2 The V4 (Visegrád four countries) meetings serve as a forum to work out solutions to problems including environment protection as well as the occasion to exchange information and experiences. They have become more important especially after the V4 Member States' accession to the European Union; then, they play a basic role in creating regional common views.

Bibliography

Bokwa, A. (2007) 'Climatic Issues in Polish Foreign Policy', in P. G. Harris (ed.), *Europe and Global Climate Change. Politics, Foreign Policy and Regional Cooperation*, Cheltenham: Edward Elgar.

Börzel, T. (2003) *Environmental Leaders and Laggards in Europe. Why There is (Not) a 'Southern Problem'*, London: Ashgate.

Buzek, J. (2008) 'Global solutions are needed', *Polish Market*, 29–30.cop14.gov.pl (2009), 'First Climate Declaration of the Visegrad Group Countries', 7.10.2009. Online. Available HTTP: <http://www.cop14.gov.pl/index.php?mode=aktualnosci_extended&action=main&menu=1&id=129&lang=EN > (accessed 19 December 2009).

EurActiv.pl (2009) 'Dwanaście dni na uratowanie planety' ['Twelve days to save the planet'], 8.12.2009. Online. Available HTTP: <http://www.euractiv.pl/polityka-zagraniczna/artykul/dwanacie-dni-na-uratowanie-planety-001462 > (accessed 19 December 2009).

Eurobarometer (2008) 'Attitudes of European Citizens towards the Environment', *Special Eurobarometer 295*, prb. March 2008.

EUROPA- (2008) 'Climate Change: Commission Welcomes Final Adoption of Europe's Climate and Energy Package', Brussels, 17 December 2008. Online. Available HTTP: <http://europa.eu/rapid/pressReleasesAction.do?reference=IP/08/1998&format=HTML&aged=0&language=EN&guiLanguage=en> (accessed 20 December 2009).

European Union (2001) Directive on the Promotion of Electricity Produced from Renewable Energy Sources in the Internal Electricity Market of 27th January 2001 No. 2001/77/EC (O.J. L 283, p. 33 of 27th October 2000).

European Union (2009) *Directive of the European Parliament and of the Council amending Directive 2003/87/EC so as to improve and extend the greenhouse gas emission allowance trading scheme of the Community*, Brussels, 26 March 2009. Online. Available HTTP: <http://register.consilium.europa.eu/pdf/en/08/st03/st03737.en08.pdf> (accessed 20 December 2009).

Gfk Polonia (DA/UKIE) (2008) 'Społeczne poparcie dla członkostwa Polski w Unii Europejskiej. Pakiet Energetyczno – klimatyczny' [Gfk Polonia (for DA/UKIE – Polish Department of European Integration), 'Social Support for the Polish Membership of the European Union. Energy Climate Package'].

Główny Urząd Statystyczny (2009) 'Gospodarka paliwowo-energetyczna w latach 2007, 2008', Warszawa 2009 [Central Statistical Office, 'Fuel-energy economy in the years 2007, 2008', Warsaw 2009]. Online. Available HTTP: <http://www.stat. gov.pl/cps/rde/xbcr/gus/PUBL_PBIS_gospodarka_paliwowo_energetyczna_2007_ 2008r.pdf> (accessed 22 June 2010).

Jordan, A. and Liefferink, D. (eds) (2004) *Environmental Policy in Europe*, London: Routledge.

Jordan, A., Wurzel, R. K., and Zito, A. (ed.) (2003) *New Instruments of Environmental Governance*, London: Frank Cass.

Kanter, J. (2008) 'A Battle in Poland over the Cost of Climate Protection', *The New York Times Businnes 27.11.2008.* Online. Available HTTP: <http://greeninc.blogs. nytimes.com/2008/11/27/a-battle-in-poland-over-the-cost-of-climate-protection/> (accessed 18 December 2008).

Karaczun, Z. M., Kassenberg, A. and Sobolewski, M. (2009) *Polityka klimatyczna Polski – wyzwanie XXI wieku* [Polands climate change policy – challenge of the XXI century]. Warszawa. Polski Klub Ekologiczny Okręg Mazowiecki [Warsaw. Polish Ecological Club Mazowiecki Region].

Kocik, L. (2000) 'Między przyrodą, zagrodą i społeczeństwem' ['Among Nature, Farms and the Society'], Cracov: Jagiellonian University Publishing House, in Bokwa, A. (2007), pp. 121.

McKinsey & Company (2010) Assessment of Greenhouse Gas Emissions Abatement Potential in Poland by 2030. Online. Available HTTP: <http://www.mckinsey. com/locations/warsaw/files/pdf/Raport_Pelna_Wersja_PL.pdf> (accessed 28 June 2010).

Ministerstwo Gospodarki (2009) *RM przyjęła, Politykę energetyczną Polski do 2030 r.* [Ministry of Economy, 'Council adopted Poland's Energy Policy until 2030']. Online. Available HTTP: <http://www.mg.gov.pl/Wiadomosci/Strona+ glowna/RM+przyjela+Polityke+energetyczna+Polski+do+2030+r.htm> (accessed 2 December 2009).

Ministerstwo Ochrony Środowiska (2003) *Polityka klimatyczna Polski. Strategie redukcji gazów cieplarnianych w Polsce do roku 2020*, Warszawa [Ministry of Environment, 'Climate Policy of Poland. Strategies of Greenhouse Gases Emissions Reduction in Poland up to 2020', Warsaw], own translations from Polish.

Ministerstwo Środowiska, Zasobów Naturalnych i Leśnych (2005) *Narodowy Program Rozdziału Uprawnień do Emisji CO2 na lata 2005–2007* [Ministry of Environment, 'National Plan of Entitlements Distribution of CO2 emissions for years 2005–7']. Online. Available HTTP: <http://www.mos.gov.pl/kpau/uprawnienia. shtml> (accessed 3 August 2008).

Polish Market (2008) *Polish Market Special Edition 2008*, Warszawa: Oficyna Wydawnicza RYNEK POLSKI Sp. z o. o. [Warsaw: RYNEK POLSKI Publishers Co. Ltd.].

Rada Ministertwo (2000) *Strategia Rozwoju Energii Odnawialnych* [Council, 'Strategy of the Development of Renewable Energies'].

Rada Ministrów (1991) *Polityka Ekologiczna Państwa*, Warszawa, [Council, 'National Environmental Policy report', Warsaw].

Rada Ministrów (2000) *II Polityka Ekologiczna Państwa* [Council, 'Second National Environmental Policy report'].

Wiśniewski, Grzegorz (2008) 'Foreword' in Podrygała, I. (2008) *Erneuerbare Energien im polnischen Stromsektor. Analyse der Enstehung und Ausgestaltung der Instrumente zur Förderung der Stromerzeugung aus erneuerbaren Energien*, Stuttgart: ibidem-Verlag.

Wurzel, R. K. W. (2002) *Environmental Policy Making in Britain, Germany and the EU. Europeanisation and Water Pollution Control*, Manchester: Manchester University Press.

Zieloni 2004 (2008) 'Rządy przemijają, klimat zostaje', Komunikat prasowy partii Zieloni 2004, Poznań 7.12.2008 [Greens 2004, 'Governments Go By, Climate Remains', Press Announcement of the Greens 2004, Poznan 7.12.2008]. Online. Available HTTP: <http://zieloni2004.pl/news-2949.html> (accessed 19 December 2008).

11 Spanish, EU and international climate change policies

Download, catch up, and curb down

Oriol Costa

Introduction

Spain is a 'paradoxical case', when it comes to climate change. It is the industrialised country whose emissions have risen the most sharply since 1990 (just second to Turkey) (SBI 2007), and yet it is a Member State of the European Union (EU), allegedly the leader of international climate negotiations (Andresen and Agrawala 2002; Chapter 1 by Wurzel and Connelly). Moreover, despite the fact that for some time Spain dragged its feet regarding EU climate policies, it has subsequently acted as an 'improving laggard' in terms of policy outputs (Skjaerseth and Wettestad 2007: 165, 63). Further, Spain probably made the best deal out of the negotiation on the sharing of the EU's 2020 emissions reduction target, as it was permitted to take 2005 as its base year while *per capita* and *per production unit* are used as criteria to set the targets (CEC 2008).

This chapter addresses this state of affairs by examining Spanish policies on, and debates about, climate change. On a more analytical note, it will be argued that two key factors have shaped climate politics and policies in Spain. The first is the increase in emissions. Spain's greenhouse gas emissions (GHGE) have, over the last two decades, failed to meet Spain's international and European targets. The EU's 1998 effort-sharing agreement[1] allowed Spain to let its emissions rise by 15 per cent between the base year (approximately 1990) and the period 2008–12. However, in 2008 emissions had already increased by 42.7 per cent, despite a sharp drop in 2008 due to the economic crisis and a 31 per cent decrease in coal consumption (Santamarta and Serrano 2009: 2). Therefore, purchases of emissions rights under the Kyoto mechanisms will need to be around 60 million t CO_2-equivalent per year. This trend is the first factor shaping Spanish climate policies and politics. Some of these features can also be found in other southern European countries, but nowhere as intensely as in Spain (EEA 2008, 2009). The second factor is the interaction with EU climate discourses and policies, which has mostly taken place under the form of top-down Europeanisation, though since 2004 it has gradually given way to a two-way relationship. The rest of this chapter looks into this process and its influence on national attitudes and decisions.

National attitudes to climate change

Attitudes towards climate change are ambivalent in Spain, as shown in surveys, records of parliamentary debates, stances adopted by stakeholders, and available media analyses. Whatever sources one looks at, the preoccupation with climate change seems to be second only to the preoccupation with the consequences of climate policies.

Concerning public opinion, since 2005 the Barometer of the Real Instituto Elcano has shown that Spaniards perceive climate change as one of the three most important threats to Spain, normally just above or below international terrorism and (since 2008) the global economic crisis.[2] In addition, Spaniards are more focused on climate change than other Europeans, compared with other environmental problems (Eurobarometer 2008: 6). This probably has to do with the near absence of any widespread public debate on the environment prior to the raising of global warming as a popular issue. On the other hand, Spaniards shy away from concrete action when the discussion moves to specific measures. So, when asked about the priorities of the authorities to 'help people to reduce their consumption of energy', they prefer the provision of information more often than EU citizens and agree less with the rest of the options (Eurobarometer 2006: 8).

The political debate has also been ambivalent, and has focused largely on the adequacy of the 1998 effort-sharing agreement. At first, no political party thought the 15 per cent increase to be overly restrictive. The PP (People's Party/Partido Popular, conservative, in government from 1996 to 2004) considered it to be favourable for Spain, while the other parties (PSOE, Spanish Socialist Workers' Party/Partido Socialista Obrero Español, centre-left; IU, United Left/Izquierda Unida, left; and CiU, Convergence and Unity/Convergència i Unió, centre-right Catalan nationalist) regarded the Spanish target as excessively lax. There even emerged voices that complained about the weakness of Kyoto. The Environment Minister (PP) distanced herself from the Kyoto Protocol: 'you have never heard me saying that Kyoto was a success, because it wasn't'.[3] This consensus started to reverse in 2001, although the Spanish Presidency of the Council (first semester 2002) delayed the full expression of this shift until late 2002. Since then, it has become common currency to regard Spanish targets as unfair and excessive. Thus, the Secretary of State for the Economy under the Conservative Government stated that 'nobody will force us to comply [with Kyoto] over a cemetery of industries',[4] MP Rosa Maria Bonás (ERC, centre-left Catalan nationalist) called the effort-sharing agreement a 'trap' for Spain, and MP Josep Sánchez i Llibre (CiU) complained that Kyoto was a 'missile against the competitiveness of the Spanish industry'.[5]

Spanish business organisations have been hostile to European climate policies, especially during the debate on the EU ETS directive, to the point that Iberdrola, an electricity firm which maintained that compliance with Kyoto was possible, was considered to have broken the 'complicity between electric companies, business organizations and the government'.[6] The Spanish

Confederation of Employers' Organizations (CEOE) has rejected the central premise of ecological modernisation that climate policies can have a positive economic effect. In 2003 it published an 'influential report' that supported the renegotiation of the effort-sharing agreement (del Rio 2007: 206), and in October 2008 it released a report according to which the 2020 targets will cost the Spanish economy €2,764 million annually and 30,382 direct jobs.[7]

There are no systematic up-to-date studies on how the Spanish press has viewed climate change. A study covering the period 1990–2002 claims that there has been a fall in the number of articles on the effects and consequences of climate change, a constant number of stories on its causes, scientific uncertainty, and technical solutions, and an increase in the number of articles dealing with the political and social debate (Polo 2004: 9). In addition, the press has portrayed climate change mainly as an international problem and only rarely as a domestic issue (Saus 2007). The way newspapers addressed global warming changed in 2003, reflecting the change in how the political debate and industries were approaching climate change. All major newspapers grew critical of the Spanish targets and presented them as 'a bad deal' that forced Spain to choose between noncompliance and 'a major industrial crisis'. According to the centre-left leaning *El País*, the 'last hope' was that the EU would give up backing Kyoto, now portrayed as a 'time bomb'.[8]

Therefore, only generally weak environmental nongovernmental organisations (NGOs), some minor political parties, specialised MPs, and the Environment Ministry (from April 2008 the Ministry of the Environment and Rural and Marine Affairs) have openly and actively supported the EU's policies on climate change and have endorsed the discourse on ecological modernisation (see below).

Phases of domestic climate change policy

In Spain, it is almost impossible to distinguish between domestic and foreign climate policy. For a long time, Spanish climate policies consisted only in participation in international and European negotiations, while more recently the picture has been dominated by the downloading of EU-related measures and targets.

Up until 1997: the defence of the Spanish special context

Until 1997, Spain's climate policy basically consisted in defending, in European arenas, the view that Spain should receive special treatment. Though the EC/EU was to lead international negotiations and Spain was willing to defend European positions, Spain had to be allowed to increase her emissions, given her lower levels of economic development and per capita emissions (Costa 2006: 226). More specifically, Spain had three concerns. First, Spain opposed the proposal of an EU-wide tax on carbon dioxide and energy. So, Spain proposed that those countries whose emissions were below the European average should be exempt from the tax. Moreover, Spain favoured making the tax conditional on the adoption of equivalent measures by other industrialised countries. Second, Spain was reluctant to accept the stabilisation objective put forward by the EC/EU. She sought guarantees that the lesser-developed countries would be able to implement such commitments more flexibly. Third, Spain insisted on receiving a more favourable share of emissions within the overall reduction that was proposed by the EU in the negotiations that led to the Kyoto Protocol.

Moreover, under both socialist and conservative governments, Spanish negotiators paid scant attention to the rest of the debate. They even rejected attempts by other countries to reduce the scope of the targets and timetables or to make their implementation more flexible (Costa 2006: 228).

From 1997 to 2000: passive 'Kyotoism'

Once the debate on effort sharing was over, Spain felt comfortable with the Kyoto Protocol commitments. Thus, she was able to add her voice to the European consensus without reservation. Indeed, sometimes the political debate tended to praise the position held by the EU *before* Kyoto. Thus, criticism was levelled at flexibility mechanisms and sinks both by the government (Tocino 1998) and the rest of the factions in Parliament. Similarly, during the Conference of Parties (COP) in The Hague (November 2000), the Environment Minister (PP) called on the United States not to 'water down' the Kyoto Protocol, and perhaps more importantly pointed out that the EU had conceded 'prematurely'.[9] This was the logical consequence of the fact that EU stances were systematically regarded as more legitimate precisely because they *were* EU stances. Pre-negotiation positions were systematically regarded as better (more strictly European) than the agreements that emerged from compromises with other countries.

Nevertheless, the ambition displayed in international arenas was not matched by either the development of internal policies to limit GHGE or the building of institutional capacities able to bring about such policies (Tàbara 2003). The one outstanding exception was the adoption of Royal Decree RD 2818/1998 on the feed-in tariff scheme for renewable energy sources. Nevertheless, on the whole, until 2001 the Spanish government understood that, having achieved a favourable effort-sharing agreement, it was not necessary to develop any internal or external strategy on climate change, apart from defending EU positions. This approach reflected over-optimism regarding the evolution of Spanish emissions, but was also encouraged by the fact that the 2008–12 period was far in the future and by the perception that it was far from evident that the Kyoto Protocol would come into force.

From 2001 to 2004: initiation of the debate and reaction

After the stormy COP6, Spanish policy makers arrived at a number of conclusions. First, Spain was not ready to participate in the increasingly technical negotiations. Second, simply adhering to the EU position had inhibited Spain from formulating its own approach. Finally, all this was more compelling given the evolution of emissions, the adoption or discussion by the EU of important policies (i.e., the European Climate Change Programme, and the directive on emissions trading), and the Spanish Presidency of the EU Council during the first six months of 2002 (Costa 2006: 230).

To face these challenges, in January 2001, the Spanish Office on Climate Change (Oficina Española de Cambio Climático, OECC) was set up within the Ministry of the Environment. In addition, Spain developed a more pragmatic approach. Now it strongly supported flexibility mechanisms, it was against quantifying 'supplementarity,' and it endorsed a wide-ranging use of sinks (including under Clean Development Mechanism (CDM) projects). However, the fact that Spain held the Presidency of the EU Council constrained its ability to express its national interests. Spain needed to act as a mediator and broker in order to achieve its two main Presidency tasks within the Environmental Council; namely, the ratification of the Kyoto Protocol and the negotiation of the EU emissions trading directive. Consequently, Spain did not endorse the Danish initiative to renegotiate the effort-sharing agreement before the ratification of the Kyoto Protocol and was not among the seven states that in March 2002 put forward so-called scrutiny reservations on the EU emissions trading directive. Spain thus showed a modicum of entrepreneurial leadership during its Presidency.

However, climate change was no longer perceived as an issue only for the EU or international politics, but rather as a domestic issue that had relevant implications for the Spanish economy. This change in perception radically altered the debate. The Government Delegated Commission for Economic Affairs turned its attention towards the EU emission trading directive, pushing for the introduction of a *force majeur* clause in case CO_2 prices rose sharply (Article 29 is a watered down version of it). Similarly, the government hoped that the +15 per cent target would be renegotiated, or that the EU would understand Spain's noncompliance.[10] In addition, during the Environment Council of March 2004, Spain together with Italy proposed not to use the word 'targets' when talking about post-2012 reductions. Business organisations also became involved in the debate, demanding the postponement of emissions trading or the shouldering of its costs by the public sector.

In sum, this period was characterised by the construction of institutional capacities, the initiation of the debate on EU-internal climate policies, and a reaction against them.

From 2004: a two-way adjustment

The last period started after the March 2004 elections, which resulted in a socialist government. It has been characterised by Spanish efforts to catch up with the implementation of EU policies (Tàbara 2007: 162) while reducing the level of ambition for her GHGE targets.

First, Spain must adjust to her international and EU commitments. In 2004, the National Allocation Plan I (NAPI) for the EU emission trading scheme laid down a path for such an adjustment. Emissions had to stabilise around 2002 levels during the period 2005–7 so that they were no more than 24 per cent higher (compared to 1990) by 2008–12 (del Rio 2007).[11] In 2007 the NAPII revised this path and set the target for 2008–12 at an increase of no more than 37 per cent over 1990 levels. Nevertheless, Jon Birger Skjaerseth and Jorgen Wettestad have branded Spain as an 'improving laggard', at least with respect to emissions trading. Certainly, although by March 2004 the NAPI had still not been drawn up (although it was due by the end of the month), it proved to be 'comparatively acceptable' when it was finally published in June 2004 (Skjaerseth and Wettestad 2008: 63). In addition, the Spanish government has introduced programmes and passed legislation on energy efficiency and renewables (see the next section). In this regard, Spain has certainly outperformed other southern European states.

Second, while Spain no longer opposes EU policies, she still wants to reduce the ambition of her future commitments. The debate on the post-2012 targets illustrates this change. Initially, Spain opposed establishing quantified targets and agreeing on a maximum atmospheric concentration of CO_2. However, after November 2004 she changed her position, in exchange for the inclusion in the effort-sharing scheme of a reference to the principle of 'equity' (i.e., some sort of per capita or per production unit criteria) (Costa 2006: 234). In addition, some decisions on the part of Spain have been interpreted as a way of showing good will before negotiating the new commitments.[12] This strategy has worked rather well. According to the effort-sharing agreement for the 2020 target,[13] Spain must reduce its non-EU ETS emissions by 10 per cent relative to 2005, and by 21 per cent in the EU ETS sectors. These targets are softer than the ones for 2008–12, allowing Spanish emissions to be 30 per cent higher than the 1990 level. Reportedly, this was met with 'total satisfaction' in the Spanish Environment Ministry.[14] This has led Spain to maintain a conspicuously low profile during the pre-Copenhagen and Copenhagen negotiations in late 2009.

In sum, Spain has tried both to control its emissions and to curb the ambition of its EU and international commitments.

Institutional responses, policy instruments, and programmes

Spain did not start to respond to climate change at an institutional level until 2001, and the process only began to gather speed in 2004. Prior to that, Spain lacked the bureaucratic capacity to catch up with European decision-making processes and international negotiations, let alone adopt programmes or measures on climate change.

The National Commission on Climate was established on the 29 May 1992, just before the beginning of the UN Conference on Environment and Development (UNCED). It included representatives from government departments with climate-related competences, but it was less than effective. Despite the personal efforts of some officials, the institutional weakness was appalling. Thus, even though a first draft for a Strategy on Climate Change was ready in the mid-1990s, under a Socialist Government, it never made it through the Cabinet. Later on, the Conservative Government announced that the Strategy would be debated in Parliament in 1998, but it was not. Perhaps more revealingly, Spain (together with Greece and Portugal) was not even able to respond to the 2000 Green Paper on emissions trading (Skjaerseth and Wettestad 2008: 94). The only relevant measure of the late 1990s was the adoption of the Royal Decree on the feed-in tariff for renewables.

As was noted above, the OECC, which was the first bureaucratic unit dedicated to climate policy, was established in 2001. This illustrates a change in the perceptions about global warming. The harshness of the COP6 and the intra-EU divisions that surfaced there had a strong impact on Spanish policy makers. In addition, the EU was adopting or negotiating a number of intra-EU measures that had to be addressed. In sum, climate change was finally being regarded as a strongly political issue in Spain. The old National Commission on Climate was upgraded to a National Council on Climate, which included representatives from Autonomous Communities, the Spanish Federation of Municipalities and Provinces, researchers, trade unionists, industrial lobbies, and NGOs. The Council produced yet another draft of a Strategy on Climate Change, but it was completed only a few weeks before the 2004 elections, with the result that its adoption was delayed until late 2007. However, the drafting process helped to raise some interest among stakeholders and at other administrative levels. In addition, a Strategy on Energy Savings and Efficiency (also called E4) was adopted in late 2003.

Since 2004, there has been a remarkable reinforcement of both administrative capacities and policy measures. In May 2004, an Interministerial Group on Climate Change was created under the Government Delegated Commission for Economic Affairs. In March 2005, a Commission for the Coordination of Climate Policies was established that includes both central and regional governments, to streamline the implementation of the EU ETS and to give Autonomous Communities a voice regarding the functioning of the Designated National Authority (on flexibility mechanisms). In addition, the OECC has grown from having a staff of over 10 to a staff of over 40 and has been upgraded to a Directorate General. Further, from April 2008 there is a specific Secretariat General on Climate Change. The approval of laws and plans has also been more intense during this last phase. Naturally, some of the new legislation transposes EU directives or fulfils obligations under them. Outstanding in this group are Law 1/2005, which transposes the emissions trading directive (2003/87/CE), the two NAPs (2005–7 and 2008–12), and the Building Technical Code, which transposes the directive on energy efficiency in buildings (2002/91/CE). A number of other plans have also been approved. In 2007, the government finally approved the Climate Change and Clean Energy Strategy, which was joined shortly afterwards by a series of

Urgent Measures. To implement the E4, an Action Plan 2005–7 was passed in 2005, as well as another one for the 2008–12 period in 2007. Similarly, in 2005, the government adopted a Plan on Renewable Energy 2005–10, and in 2006, a National Plan for the Adaptation on Climate Change. The car registration tax has also been reformed to encourage the purchase of vehicles with low CO_2 emissions. Finally here, given the increase in emissions, the government has been rather active in promoting CDM projects, committing itself to investing up to €315m in carbon funds. In addition, Spain has signed Memorandums of Understanding with 20 countries, mostly in the Mediterranean region and in Latin America.

Climate change as a threat and opportunity?

In Spain, the perception of climate change as a threat or an opportunity has been different for each of the aforementioned four stages. Up until 2001, Spain regarded global warming primarily as an opportunity for the EU to act as a leader in international politics. This perception was particularly un-nuanced after 1997, when it became clear that Spain would apparently have easier targets to meet within the EU bubble. Given the difficulty of curbing emissions and the lack of a compelling reason to do so, climate negotiations were regarded by policy makers only as a matter of international politics. Furthermore, in view of the weakness of the *climate bureaucracy* (if any), officials in charge of the issue understood that the safe option was to take shelter beneath the umbrella of the EU (see Chapter 5 by Oberthür and Dupont), rather than adopting a uniquely Spanish approach to climate negotiations (Costa 2006: 229).

However, from 2001 on, the domestic implications of EU policies became clearer, and stakeholders and political actors started to portray climate policies as a threat for the Spanish economy. We have already referred to this shift in the domestic debate and to the fact that the effort-sharing agreement has been seen as imposing an unfair burden on the competitiveness of Spanish industry. It has become common wisdom to claim that German industry has been granted more allowances per production unit than Spanish industry (see Chapter 8 by Jänicke). The Economic and Social Council has declared that it is 'worried' by the effects that the 2008–12 targets may have in terms of production, investment and employment.[15] In 2004, the Minister for Industry, Trade, and Tourism (PSOE) sought to calm the fears of industry and said that its concerns would be taken into account by the government and that 'of course they would be conveyed wherever necessary; out of the limelight, perhaps, but with the objective of ensuring that they be heard'.[16] Perhaps more revealingly, as late as 2006, two MPs (representing PP and ERC) argued that the +15 per cent target needed to be renegotiated.[17]

Only the (socialist) Environment Ministry, together with a few minor parties and specialised socialist MPs, have endorsed the discourse on ecological modernisation and portrayed climate policies as an opportunity. More specifically, three claims have been made in this regard. First, the Kyoto Protocol has been portrayed as an opportunity 'to reduce the Spanish exposure to high energy costs', improve its energy efficiency, and strengthen its industrial competitiveness. Second, it has been claimed that CDMs are an opportunity for Spanish firms to internationalise their activity.[18] Finally, international policies on climate have been perceived as an opportunity for the fast-growing renewables industry to expand and develop their activity under a more favourable regulatory environment. The more recent endorsement of some of the rhetoric of ecological modernisation by Prime Minister José Luís Rodríguez Zapatero[19] promises a broader shift in public and political perceptions. The passing of a law on Sustainable Economy in November 2009 also points in this direction, although it has by and large been portrayed as a hollow law designed to get cheap headlines, or even as an outright unsustainable measure.[20] On the other hand, this coexists with the framing of public works oriented towards private transport or 'national coal' as a way to control unemployment under the economic crisis.[21]

In sum, while up until 2001 global warming was perceived as a global issue that enabled the EU to build up its international *actorness* (see also Chapter 2 by Vogler), from then on it has been regarded as a threat to the competitiveness of Spanish industry. Only a handful of admittedly well-placed actors have challenged this view, by pointing to the fact that the Spanish economy could use some incentives to promote efficiency and internationalisation, particularly after the housing bubble burst.

Multi-level governance and leadership

The relationship between Spain and supra- or intra-governmental levels of decision-making has predominantly been a top-down one, though since 2004 this pattern has given way to a two-way interaction. On the whole, Spanish climate policy has been strongly Europeanised. The EU has altered the distribution of resources among domestic groups, it has fostered the emergence of shared understandings of what constitutes proper behaviour, and it has encouraged processes of institutional adaptation (Börzel 2005: 52–58; Jordan and Liefferink 2004). In fact, this can be said of much of Spanish environmental policy in general (Font 2001; Borràs, Font and Gómez 1998). It is only recently that Spain has gained some influence in EU climate negotiations.

During the 1990s, Europeanisation delineated which discourses on climate change were legitimate or illegitimate. As argued, Spain faithfully reproduced EU positions. Even the defence of (perceived) national interests, which was more intensive before 1997 than after, was expressed in a way that did not question EU international stances. In addition, Spain's striking rejection of flexibility mechanisms for emissions trading (a view that did not begin to soften until 2001) shows her endorsing a policy stance that was regarded as legitimate simply because it had been adopted by the EU (Aguilar 2004: 183; Christiansen and Wettestad 2003).

From 2001 on, and in coincidence with the development of the bulk of EU internal policies, Europeanisation took two other forms. First, Spain built the institutional capacities to participate in the negotiation of EU internal policies and to implement them domestically. The setting up of the OECC, the reactivation of the National Council on Climate, and the creation of coordination bodies have very much to do with the need to participate in the formulation of EU policies and in international negotiations. Second, the existence of EU policies forced the more reluctant actors in Spain (industries, economic ministries, the PP and some minor parties) to address the issue. This modified the nature of the domestic debate, stressing the view that Spain has been treated unfairly and that EU climate policies threaten the Spanish economy.

Since 2004, Spain has offered the EU good will in exchange for targets that are easier to meet. Two points need to be made here. First, this strategy is largely shaped by Europeanisation, because it is the result of combining the evolution of Spanish emissions, the increasing stringency of EU policies, and the (strongly Europeanised) conditions of the domestic debate. Indeed, during 2004, the incoming minister Cristina Narbona succeeded in presenting climate policies as a matter of compliance with the EU, a claim that managed to overcome the nascent resistance of new economic ministers (Costa 2006: 232). Second, the strategy seems to be working well for Spain, as indicated by the agreement on the sharing of the 2020 targets. Interestingly, this time it is the whole EU scheme that favours Spain, and not any special treatment within the EU bubble. The distribution of emissions targets is based on the 2005 emission levels and includes both per capita and per production unit criteria, which were long sought after by Spanish officials.[22] However, this does not qualify as cognitive leadership, as Spain played no specific role in shaping the Commission proposal (CEC, 2008). Spain has limited itself to defending the scheme against the criticisms levelled by some Member States during the negotiations in the Council.

On occasions, Spain has seemed to be part of a group of southern European countries in the framework of EU negotiations. For example, Spain, Greece, Italy, and Portugal (together with Latvia, Lithuania, Poland, Slovakia, Finland, and Cyprus) presented similar amendments during the negotiation of the targets approved in the Environment Council of March 2005, according to which developed countries should reduce their GHGE in the order of 15–30 per cent by 2020 and 60–80 per cent by 2050, compared to 1990 levels. However, there has been no systematic coordination among these countries. To be sure, they all share lower per capita emissions relative to the EU15 average and suffer from important gaps between their 2010 GHGE projections (with existing measures) and Kyoto targets (EEA 2008: 13). It is thus only natural that they have shared negotiation positions. But there has been no joint strategy, let alone any sub-regional leadership role for Spain. Only during the negotiation of the effort-sharing agreement for the 2020 targets (2008) did the Spanish and Portuguese governments conduct regular consultations on this matter, under the impression that they had a shared interest in defending the Commission's proposal.

Finally, Spain has also developed mechanisms that might enable her to play a more active role in international negotiations, although this potential is yet to be realised. In September 2004, an agreement was reached to set up an Ibero-American Network of Climate Change Offices that includes 21 other countries. The most urgent objective of the Network has been to foster CDM projects. The Network has also adopted an Ibero-American Plan on Adaptation to Climate Change, which is claimed to be the first regional strategy on the issue. Spain initiated this process and is providing a good deal of cognitive leadership in it. In addition, the promise of CDM investments and the central role of Spain in the framework of the overarching Ibero-American Summits have also allowed Spain to display both structural and entrepreneurial leadership.

The domestic implementation of EU and international commitments

EU and international commitments regarding climate change are diverse, ranging from procedural to substantive. This has important implications when it comes to determining the extent of compliance. Assessing compliance with procedural commitments is fairly straightforward and illustrates the political will of governments. However, it says nothing about emissions. Assessing the implementation of substantive commitments is more difficult. Emissions targets are to be met during 2008–12, compliance depends on the purchase of emission rights abroad, and there is a well-known distance between the outputs and impacts of a policy. These difficulties notwithstanding, it is safe to say that Spain's compliance with both types of commitment has been poor, even though some progress has been made concerning procedural obligations. A similar trend can be found among other southern European countries, but with patchier records regarding procedural progress (EEA 2009; Skjaerseth and Wettestad 2008; Agostini 2007).

From 2001 to mid-2004, Spain failed to meet important deadlines. Examples abound. The Third National Communication under the United Nations Framework Convention on Climate Change (UNFCCC) was presented in April 2002, four months after its due date of 30 November 2001. Similarly, Spain was late in submitting data about the 2000 emissions to the Commission, which triggered the opening of an infraction procedure. Spain's adoption of the NAPI was also delayed considerably. However, a certain improvement can be observed since the second half of 2004, as illustrated by the fact that the NAPI was finally handed to the Commission on June 2004, 'considerably earlier than expected' (Skjaerseth and Wettestad 2008: 167).

When it comes to compliance with substantive provisions, the assessment is more worrisome. The European Environment Agency has claimed that Spain will not comply with its +15 per cent target (EEA 2008), or only by

purchasing large amounts of allowances (EEA 2009: 12). Spain is one of the
EU Member States furthest from its Kyoto target, even after including additional measures, sinks, and flexibility mechanisms in the analysis. As argued
above, the increase in Spanish emissions has been remarkable. While EU15
annual per capita emissions have decreased from 11.7 to 10.9t CO_2-equivalent,
the figures for Spain have risen from 7.4 to 10.2. This rise has to do with the
increase in transport- and energy-related emissions. In Spain, emissions from
passenger and freight transport rose by 86 per cent from 1990 to 2005, compared to only 26 per cent in the EU15. Furthermore, a 108 per cent increase
is expected for 2010. Regarding (non-transport) energy emissions, the Spanish
increase of 56 per cent between 1990 and 2005 contrasts sharply with the
EU15 decrease of 3 per cent during the same period (EEA 2007). These
increases are due to changes in the distribution of people and services within
Spain's territory, the use of transport, and the dependence of the economy on
relatively low energy prices (Santamarta and Rodrigo 2008: 19).

Furthermore, green NGOs and some minor parties have stressed that
some ministries are actually strengthening these trends. Thus, the Ministry of
Public Works has been criticised for the planning of some additional 6000 km
of highways under the Strategic Infrastructure and Transport Plan. Similarly,
Santamarta and Rodrigo (2008: 10) have pointed out that the Electricity and
Gas Sectors Planning for 2007–16, which was approved by the government in
March 2006, falls short of delivering the reductions foreseen in the NAPII.
In a similar vein, a green MP (Joan Herrera) has criticised the Industry
Ministry for vetoing a proposal by the Ministry for the Environment to
establish a yearly energy-saving target of 1 per cent.[23] Rather revealingly,
when the five major environmental NGOs reviewed the performance of the
government with respect to the environment, only the Ministry for the
Environment was assessed positively, while the Ministries of Industry and
Public Works were portrayed as the most problematic ones.[24]

To summarise, in spite of the improvement in procedural compliance,
Spain remains far from its substantive emissions targets. These shortcomings
with respect to compliance are rooted in deep-seated tendencies in the Spanish
economy, society, and government.

Conclusion: political leadership in Spain

Since the beginning of the 1990s, Spain has been downloading EU climate
discourses (up until 2000) and policies (since 2001). Even if Spain adopted
EU discourses uncritically during the negotiation of the UNFCCC, the
Kyoto Protocol, and the Bonn/Marrakech agreements, Spain has since been
much more reluctant to agree to EU policies. However, this reluctance has
nothing to do with defending a specific domestic policy style, as opposed to
an EU one. There is no such thing as a Spanish regulatory approach to
climate change. When studying the adoption of the EU emissions trading
scheme in Spain, Skjaerseth and Wettestad (2008: 106) found that there was

no mismatch because Spain had no domestic climate policy in place. Efforts by Spain have rather been focused on achieving more favourable emissions targets within the EU.

This has been done in two different ways. During the bargaining of the 1990–2000 stabilisation commitment and the negotiation of the 2008–12 targets, Spain demanded special treatment, on the grounds that cohesion countries could not be held to the same conditions as richer Member States. From 2002 onwards, the domestic opposition to the +15 per cent objective was consistent with this approach. However, Spain is dealing with the commitments for 2020 in a different way. Namely, Spain is trying to influence the whole effort-sharing scheme by pushing the principle of 'equity' and relating it to per capita and per production unit criteria. Paradoxically, despite the increase in her emissions, Spain will be granted an easier target to meet for 2020 than it was for the 2008–12 period. More importantly, the effort-sharing agreement is based on principles defended by Spain.

This is the first time that the relationship between the national and the EU levels is not a purely top-down one. Spain is not a mere (and reluctant) *taker* of EU climate policies and discourses anymore, but is finally having an influence on them. Yet again, Spain has taken on all the EU regulatory style and philosophy (Wurzel 2008: 69), because she lacks one of her own. Consequently, the influence that Spain exercises in Brussels does not entail her participation in any sort of regulatory competition. The focus is on percentages, not instruments. After having downloaded the EU approach to climate policies and having caught up with procedural and legal commitments, Spain is trying to curb its reduction targets.

Notes

1 The effort-sharing agreement was initially called the burden-sharing agreement.
2 The Real Instituto Elcano is a Madrid-based think tank on foreign policy. The Barometers of the Real Instituto Elcano (BRIE) are available at <http://www.realinstitutoelcano.org/wps/portal/rielcano/BarometroDelRIElcano>
3 Diario de Sesiones del Congreso de los Diputados, Comisión de Medio Ambiente. 18 February 1998, 11160.
4 'Las empresas advierten de que el Protocolo de Kioto costará hasta 4000 millones al año' *El País*, 3 November 2003.
5 Diario de Sesiones del Congreso de los Diputados, Comisión de Medio Ambiente. 27 June 2004, 11–13.
6 'Iberdrola rompe la baraja' *El País*, 23 November 2003.
7 *Estudio del impacto de la propuesta de modificación de la directiva de comercio de las emisiones*, Garrigues, CEOE, October 2008 (available at <http://www.ceoe.es/ceoe/contenidos.downloadatt.action?id = 5600430>) (accessed December 2008).
8 See 'Atrapados en los compromisos de Kioto' *El País*, 8 February 2004; and 'Una bomba de relojería' *El País*, 8 February 2004.
9 Diario de Sesiones del Congreso de los Diputados, Comisión de Medio Ambiente, 18 February 1998, 11149, 11151–53 and 11160. See also 'Matas teme que EE.UU. desnaturalice el acuerdo de Kioto contra la emisión de CO_2' *La Vanguardia*, 23 November 2000.

10 'Las empresas advierten de que el Protocolo de Kioto costará hasta 4000 millones al año' *El País*, 3 November 2003; 'Un fondo público y privado de 40 millones' *El País*, 3 November 2003.

11 This percentage is the sum of the 15 per cent increase allowed by the 1998 burden-sharing agreement, the 2 per cent to be absorbed by sinks, and the planned 7 per cent that will be bought on the international market of emission rights.

12 'El Gobierno aprueba un plan de ahorro para reducir un 20% la importación de petróleo' *La Vanguardia*, 9 July 2005.

13 European Parliament legislative resolution of 17 December 2008 on the proposal for a decision of the European Parliament and of the Council on the effort of Member States to reduce their greenhouse gas emissions to meet the Community's greenhouse gas emission reduction commitments up to 2020 (COM(2008) 0017-C6–0041/2008–2008/0014(COD))

14 'Europa asume el coste de ser verde' *El País*, 24 January, 2008.

15 The Economic and Social Council is a public institution that brings together trade unions, employers' organisations, and professional associations. See Diario de Sesiones del Congreso de los Diputados, Comisión de Medio Ambiente, 27 July 2004, 15.

16 Diario de Sesiones del Congreso de los Diputados, Comisión de Industria, Turismo y Comerio del Congreso de los Diputados, 30 September 2004, 19–20.

17 Diario de Sesiones del Congreso de los Diputados, Comisión de Medio Ambiente, 19 December 2006, 51

18 Diario de Sesiones del Congreso de los Diputados, Comisión de Medio Ambiente, 9 September 2004, 16; Diario de Sesiones del Congreso de los Diputados, Comisión de Medio Ambiente, 11 October 2006, 33.

19 *Press conference of the President of the Government after the meeting of the European Council*, 17 December 2008 (available at <http://www.la-moncloa.es/IDIOMAS/9/Presidente/Intervenciones/ConferenciasdePrensa/prrp17122008_ConsejoEuropeo.htm>) (accessed December 2008).

20 See 'La insostenible ley de Economía Sostenible', Ecologistas en Acción, 27 November 2009, available at <http://www.ecologistasenaccion.org/spip.php?article16006> (accessed December 2009).

21 'La Agencia de la Energía critica el plan español de ayudas al carbón' *El País*, 28 October 2009.

22 Diario de Sesiones del Congreso de los Diputados, Comisión de Medio Ambiente, 14 February 2006.

23 Diario de Sesiones del Congreso de los Diputados, Comisión de Medio Ambiente, 20 November 2007, 13.

24 See 'Un Programa por la Tierra. Análisis del cumplimiento de las propuestas ecologitas para la legislatura', prepared by the major Environmental NGOs (Amigos de la Tierra, Ecologistas en Acción, Greenpeace, SEO/BirdLife and WWF) on December 2005, available at <http://www.ecologistasenaccion.org/IMG/pdf/Analisis_programa_por_la_tierra.pdf> (accessed August 2008).

Bibliography

Agostini, D. (2007) 'Italy', in A. D. Ellerman, B. K. Buchner and C. Carraro (eds), *Allocation in the European Emissions Trading Scheme. Rights, Rents and Fairness*, Cambridge: Cambridge University Press, 213–46.

Aguilar, S. (2004) 'Spain. Old Habits Die Hard', in A. Jordan and D. Liefferink (eds), *Environmental Policy in Europe. The Europeanization of National Environmental Policy*, New York: Routledge, 172–88.

Andresen, S. and Agrawala, S. (2002) 'Leaders, Ushers and Laggards in the Making of the Climate Regime', *Global Environmental Change*, 12(1), 41–51.

Borràs, S., Font, N. and Gómez, N. (1998) 'The Europeanization of National Policies in Comparison: Spain as a Case Study', *South European Society and Politics*, 3(2), 23–44.

Börzel, T. (2005) 'Europeanization: How the European Union Interacts with its Member States', in S. Bulmer and C. Lesquene (eds), *The Member States of the European Union*, Oxford: Oxford University Press, 45–69.

Christiansen, A. C. and Wettestad, J. (2003) 'The EU as a Frontrunner on Greenhouse Gas Emission Trading: How did It Happen and will the EU Succeed?', *Climate Policy*, 3(1), 3–18.

Commission of the European Communities (2008), *Proposal for a Decision of the European Parliament and of the Council on the Effort of Member States to Reduce their Greenhouse Gas Emissions to Meet the Community's Greenhouse Gas Emission Reduction Commitments up to 2020*, Brussels, 23.1.2008, COM(2008)17 final.

Costa, O. (2006) 'Spain as an Actor in European and International Climate Policy: From a Passive to an Active Laggard?', *South European Society and Politics*, 11(2), 223–40.

del Rio, P. (2007) 'Spain', in A. D. Ellerman, B. K. Buchner and C. Carraro (eds), *Allocation in the European Emissions Trading Scheme. Rights, Rents and Fairness*, Cambridge: Cambridge University Press, 182–212.

EEA (2007), *Greenhouse Gas Emission Trends and Projects 2008. Tracking Progress towards Kyoto Targets*, EEA *Report No 5/2007*, Copenhagen: European Environmental Agency. Online. Available HTTP: <http://www.eea.eu.int> (accessed December 2008).

EEA (2008), *Greenhouse Gas Emission Trends and Projects 2008. Tracking Progress towards Kyoto Targets*, EEA *Report No 5/2008*, Copenhagen: European Environmental Agency. Online. Available HTTP: <http://www.eea.eu.int> (accessed December 2008).

EEA (2009), *Greenhouse Gas Emission Trends and Projects 2008. Tracking Progress towards Kyoto Targets*, EEA *Report No 9/2009*, Copenhagen: European Environmental Agency. Online. Available HTTP: <http://www.eea.eu.int> (accessed December 2009).

Eurobarometer (2006), *Energy Issues, November 2006*, Brussels: Commission of the European Communities.

Eurobarometer (2008), *Attitudes of European Citizens towards the Environment, March 2008*, Brussels: Commission of the European Communities.

Font, N. (2001) 'La europeización de la política ambiental: desafíos e inercias', in C. Closa (ed.), *La europeización del sistema político español*, Toledo: Istmo, 380–99.

Jordan, A. and Liefferink, D. (2004) 'The Europeanization of National Environmental Policy', in A. Jordan and D. Liefferink (eds), *Environmental Policy in Europe. The Europeanization of National Environmental Policy*, New York: Routledge, 1–14.

Polo, D. (2004) 'El cambio climático en la prensa española, 1990–2002', unpublished paper presented at the VIII Congreso Español de Sociología, September 2004, Alicante.

Santamarta, J. and Serrano, Ll. (2009) *Evolución de las emisiones de gases de efecto invernadero en España (1990–2008)*, Madrid: Comisiones Obreras. Online. Available HTTP: <http://www.fsc.ccoo.es/comunes/temp/recursos/22/194871.pdf> (accessed December 2009).

Guntamarta, J. and Rodrigo, F. (2008) *Evolución de las emisiones de gases de efecto invernadero en España (1990–2007)*, Madrid: Comisiones Obreras. Online. Available HTTP: <http://www.ccoo.es/comunes/temp/recursos/1/89724.pdf> (accessed August 2008).

Saus, L. (2007) 'El cambio climático en la prensa generalista española', unpublished Masters Dissertation, Institut Barcelona d'Estudis Internacionals.

SBI (2007), *National Greenhouse Gas Inventory Data for the Period 1990–2005, FCCC/SBI/2007/30*, December 2007, Bali: Subsidiary Body for Implementation.

Skjaerseth, J. B. and Wettestad, J. (2008) *EU Emissions Trading. Initiation, Decision-Making and Implementation*, Aldershot: Ashgate.

Tàbara, D. (2003) 'Spain: Words that Succeed and Climate Policies that Fail', *Climate Policy*, 3(1), 19–30.

Tàbara, D. (2007) 'A New Climate for Spain: Accommodating Environmental Foreign Policy in a Federal State', in P. G. Harris (ed.), *Europe and Global Climate Change. Politics, Foreign Policy and Regional Cooperation*, Cheltenham: Edward Elgar, 161–84.

Tocino, I. (1998) 'Kioto y el futuro del cambio climático', *Política Exterior*, 61(12), 49–58.

Wurzel, R.K (2008) 'Environmental Policy: EU Actors, Leader and Laggard States', in J. Hayward (ed.), *Leaderless Europe*, Oxford: Oxford University Press, 66–88.

Part IV

Civil society: business and environmental groups

12 Business

The elephant in the room?

Wyn Grant

The general line of argument pursued in this chapter is that it is difficult to devise and implement effective climate change policies and accompanying policy instruments without the active consent of business, yet securing that consent may risk diluting policy to such an extent that it is insufficiently effective. For example, business may favour market mimicking policy instruments such as emissions trading schemes which may have less impact than a carbon tax. The strong position of business in relation to climate change policies results in large part from its hard power capabilities exhibited in structural leadership, but also from cognitive leadership that seeks to shape the counters of the debate (entrepreneurial leadership is also exhibited, but is of less decisive importance in terms of policy outcomes). A secondary theme in the chapter is that business (which is not a homogenous category) has shifted its position over time from an initial denial of climate change by some interests to a more sophisticated strategy that attempts to influence the policy instruments deployed. It should be emphasised that this does not mean that business interests dominate the policy debate: indeed, at Copenhagen they felt somewhat excluded. As explained in Chapter 13 by Wurzel and Connelly, environmental non-governmental organisations (ENGOs) have a number of strategic and tactical advantages in relation to business that allow them to influence the debate and shape policy.

What is meant by 'business'? In simple terms, businesses are legally constituted entities that seek to make a profit by selling goods and services. However, when we talk about 'business', what is the level of aggregation at which analysis should take place? It is suggested that it is necessary to examine both the representative organisations of business and also individual firms. Large firms operate politically both on their own behalf and through associations.

As far as representative organisations of business are concerned, climate change is dealt with both as an important policy topic by existing business organisations and by new organisations that have a specific remit in relation to climate change such as the World Business Council for Sustainable Development (WBSCSD). Such organisations are of particular significance when the dimension of leadership is considered. It is here in these organisations that focus on climate change that one finds evidence of entrepreneurial leadership in terms of devising mutually acceptable formulas and brokering the interests of key players in building support for these formulas. This is then combined with elements of a transformational leadership style, at least in the sense of seeking to satisfy the higher needs of potential followers.

More typically, however, the leadership being exercised by business is structural in character. This reflects the fact that business enjoys hard power deriving from its economic strength (Coen, Grant and Wilson 2010). This exercise of structural power seeks to translate power resources into bargaining leverage in an effort to bring pressure to bear on others to support the stance being taken by business. Necessarily, this often produces a humdrum leadership style that is frequently reactive and incremental in character. There is, however, considerable variability in leadership styles within business in relation to climate change.

At the firm level it is necessary to consider the orientation of the particular firm. This will be influenced by, in part, the goods and services that the firm produces, but also by its particular history and culture. In Grant (1984) a distinction was made between 'tripartite' and 'capitalist aggressive' firms. One may reformulate this to replace the category 'tripartite', which reflected the policy priorities of the period, by 'environmentally friendly' and hence taking account of the debate on ecological modernisation. Thus, for example, within the airline industry, one firm may seek to claim that it is trying to do all that it can to moderate the climate change impact of flights by, for example, reducing fuel consumption or offering offsets. Another, Ryanair being a prime example, may simply deny the existence of the problem or its responsibility for it and take an aggressive stance on the issue in defence of its profits. Thus, 'a cleavage begins to open up not between business and environmentalists, but between progressive, environmentally aware business and short-term profit takers on the other' (Weale 1992: 31). Weale also suggest that the main dividing line no longer runs between business and environmental non-governmental organisations (NGOs) but between progressive/environmentally concerned businesses which often form (informal) alliances with reformist environmental NGOs and short-term profit takers. This chapter presents evidence of such collaborations.

Ecological modernisation theory would suggest that a positive response by firms to environmental challenges may be in their own interests. However, this may apply more clearly to pollution with a specific geographical impact than a global public bad like climate change. In the case of pollution, a firm may derive a number of benefits from taking action. It may avoid financial penalties for failing to act, but by making use of by- or waste products or increasing energy efficiency, its own capacity to make profits may increase. The relationship in the case of climate change between changes in practice and profits may be less clear. Actions taken by any one firm are not likely to have a major impact on the incidence of climate change, nor will that firm necessarily derive any specific benefits.

This suggests that what is needed is action by business as a whole or by significant segments of it, such as energy-intensive businesses. However, one then has a classic collective action problem with the likelihood of free riding. This does not necessarily imply, however, that only actions by governments or through international agreements are appropriate. The limitations of 'command and control' instruments in environmental policy in terms of transaction costs, enforcement problems, etc. are well known. In particular, it imposes 'uniform reduction targets and technologies which ignore the variable pollution abatement costs facing individual firms. In practice, marginal costs of pollution vary widely among industries'. Command and control 'is not only an expensive approach to pollution reduction, but one which, according to many analysts has also reached the limits of its environmental effectiveness' (Golub 1998: 3).

This led to a search for new instruments covering a range of environmental taxes and charges, tradeable pollution permit systems, government subsidies, ecolabels, ecoaudits, voluntary environmental agreements and 'altering liability and insurance rules in a manner which benefits the environment' (Golub 1998: 4). Government can, of course, initiate by itself the use of new policy instruments such as taxes and emissions trading. Nevertheless, that leaves plenty of scope for new policy instruments that take a partnership form in which government enters into either agreements with business or initiatives in which business constructs its own arrangements. In terms of the rational choice perspective on group activity developed by Olson (1971), such arrangements may work better where there is a limited number of actors and 'privileged' groups exist such that each firm's involvement makes a difference to the availability of the collective good and the absence of any one firm may undermine its provision. This is somewhat paradoxical in the sense that what competition policy seeks to avoid, oligopoly, may facilitate cooperation to produce public goods. Perhaps in such circumstances the term 'collusion' may be abandoned.

The fear of reputational damage

An important driver for businesses is the fear of reputational damage to their brand. A belief has become widespread 'that successful corporations must primarily produce brands, as opposed to products' (Klein 2000: 3). Corporations make substantial investments in the marketing and advertising of their brands, for example by paying considerable sums of money for them to be associated with major sporting events. Damage to the reputation of the brand means harm to the ability of the company to make profits and ultimately to survive. One way that a company can be damaged is if its actions, even if they are legal, are seen as harmful to the environment. The Brent Spar episode was not only damaging to Shell but 'perhaps signalled that all companies were vulnerable'. It 'was the pivot on which a more general business re-appraisal of the environment took place' (Jordan 2000: 8).

Business has to operate in a content in which it deals with the empowered consumer whose priorities go beyond the price and quality of the purchased good or service to embrace wider considerations. These more politically and environmentally aware consumers may exert substantial influence on the actions of business. Consumers who are dissatisfied with a company's actions may boycott its products, as happened with Brent Spar and Shell. The broader context here is the move towards 'reflexive consumption, whereby people think if themselves as active, discerning consumers whose choices contribute to their source of identity. Thus, 'Consumption choices take on considerable personal and social significance' (Lowe, Phillipson and Lee 2008: 228).

Business can and will attempt to structure consumer perceptions and it could be argued that the response of business to this enhanced consumer awareness amounts to little more than 'greenwash'. In other words, companies make a public relations response, perhaps based around a few token policies and activities, that seek to make them appear more environmentally friendly than they actually are. If you looked at some of the advertising for oil companies without any prior knowledge of their activities you might come to the conclusion that their principal activities were renewable energy. Exxon Mobil, which has the least favourable reputation of any oil company in relation to climate change, launched a new television advertising campaign in the summer of 2008 that referred to the challenge of developing energy in an environmentally friendly way. Exxon has shifted its position on climate change, having been an active funder of climate change sceptics in the pre-Kyoto period. Exxon stopped funding the Competitive Enterprise Institute, a Washington think tank that ran television adverts which said that carbon dioxide is helpful, along with five or six other groups active in the climate change debate. There are limits to this shift in position.

The changes in Exxon's words and actions are nuanced. The oil giant continues to note uncertainties in climate science. It continues to oppose the Kyoto protocol (Ball 2007). Nevertheless, a spokesperson for the Natural Resources Defense Council noted, 'They found that it was untenable to be in a position of casting doubt on whether global warming is happening and whether pollution is responsible for that' (Musson 2007). The terms of the debate were changing, leading Exxon to shift away from its former capitalist aggressive stance. It wanted to shape that debate so that any regulatory impacts on its own business were as limited as possible. Pragmatism driven by business considerations overcame ideology.

Leadership

By taking its own initiatives and exercising cognitive leadership, business hopes that it can avoid more onerous or intrusive forms of imposed regulation. Private systems of regulation may also be more attuned to the specific commercial needs of business, particularly in terms of protecting product reputation and the integrity of a brand. These considerations serve as the main drivers for political leadership in climate change policies in Europe. In response, business has evolved specialist organisations to serve as a rallying point for businesses that want to enhance their environmental reputation and which serves as venues in which entrepreneurial leadership can be exercised. The principal organisation, the WBCSD, operates at a global level but is characterised by strong European membership (see Table 12.1) and leadership. It was founded by a Swiss industrialist, is headquartered in Switzerland and has had a Swedish president since 1995.

The World Business Council for Sustainable Development (WBCSD) was founded on the eve of the 1992 Rio Earth Summit to encourage business to become involved in sustainability issues which are framed in terms of the three pillars of environmental, social and economic. It was thus well placed to engage in the debate leading up to Kyoto. Giving a rough equivalence to these different dimensions means, of course, that, for example, environmental needs have to be balanced against considerations of economic viability. In 1995 the Council merged with the World Industry Council for the Environment, a branch of the International Chamber of Commerce. It is a chief executive officer (CEO)-led, global association of some leading 200 companies with an exclusive membership which can be obtained only by invitation of the executive committee. The core teams in its 'focus areas' such as Energy and Climate include such well-known companies as British Petroleum (BP), General Electric, General Motors, KPMG, Sony, Toyota, Unilever and Vodafone. Its role is partly one of advocacy, to participate in policy development to ensure that the right framework conditions exist for business and that it can still operate, innovate and grow. It also seeks to demonstrate the business contribution to sustainable development. Internally, it

Table 12.1 WBCSD member countries by country/region 2007

Country/region	Number of companies
Europe	78
United States	39
Japan	28
Australasia	8
Other Asia	7
Canada	5
Korea	5
China	3
Russia	3
South Africa	2
Middle East	1

Source: Calculated from WBCSD data.

provides a forum within which business leaders can work with their peers to find business opportunities and solutions.

The World Economic Forum has also interested itself in climate change issues, making it a major theme of its 2007 Davos conference. In June 2008 it delivered a set of recommendations from company CEOs to G8 leaders intended to inform their discussions on a post-2012 framework for global climate policy. The document was put together in collaboration with the WBCSD.

The Business Environmental Leadership Council is also focused on climate change issues, but it is a US-based organisation and most of its member companies are American, although it includes European companies operating there such as BP and Royal Dutch Shell. One of its arguments is that companies that take early action on climate change policies will gain a competitive advantage over their peers.

The existing general EU business associations which treat climate change as one of the important issues they face is another arena in which leadership can be exercised, although there are significant differences between associations. A recurrent challenge for such associations, particularly when they are associations of associations, is reconciling the interests of 27 Member States and of industrial sectors with different interests, e.g., energy producers versus energy users, in such a way that they do not produce bland, lowest common denominator policies. As Chapter 13 by Wurzel and Connelly makes clear, ENGOs usually find it easier to focus on common goals.

This challenge has been one that has faced the Union des industries de la Communauté européenne (UNICE). It re-branded itself as BusinessEurope, the Confederation of European Business, in 2007 but it is questionable whether that has improved its capacity to exercise leadership other than of the humdrum kind. Its briefing on 'promoting a secure, competitive and climate-friendly energy system' written in 2007 seems somewhat bland and largely lacking in specific content. Although it calls for 'a new energy model inspired by a far-reaching vision', many of the statements are of a very general character. For example, it calls for support for energy efficiency in all sectors or strengthening the EU external energy policy, but no one presumably advocates opposing energy efficiency or weakening the EU's external energy policy (BusinessEurope 2008).

As an organisation made up of chief executives of leading European companies who have been invited to become members (like the WBCSD), the European Round Table (ERT) is far better placed to take a proactive stance on climate change issues. It is a lean organisation that is able to focus on selected high-priority issues and to take innovative stances that seek to move the debate forward rather than recycling tired old arguments. In other words, it meets the basic conditions for exercising political leadership.

The ERT is clear about the fact that it believes that climate change presents an opportunity to exercise leadership: 'ERT believes that there is a chance for the EU to assume a leadership role as countries of the world try to grapple with the effects of Climate Change' (European Round Table 2007: 1). ERT also considers that there is a marketing opportunity for European companies given their track record and experience in research and development (European Round Table 2007: 2). What is needed is a more active EU role in the coordination of research and development programmes to facilitate their integration. If it is to reach ambitious emission reduction targets, then business needs a stable decision-making environment which prevents excessive carbon cost fluctuations, but provides a reasonably predictable and stable price signal that indicates how much societies are prepared to pay for carbon dioxide reductions.

The ERT also seems to have picked up on the notion of an expectation-credibility gap, although it does not use those terms. It does not see this in terms of the balance between Member State sovereignty and the authority resources available to Brussels which, in any case, would be a difficult area for it to pronounce on. However, it does not consider that there is a need to fully integrate Europe's energy policy with its foreign policy. In the ERT's view, this requires some reorganisation of the EU's competences to provide a suitable institutional framework. In particular, there needs to be more systematic coordination among the responsible Commissioners with an 'Energy Standing Group' involving those with relevant responsibilities.

ERT is clear that business cannot exercise leadership in isolation, but only on the basis of networking and dialogue with a wide range of stakeholders including industry, academia and civil society. It is here that mechanisms such as the EU's High Level Group on Competitiveness, Energy and the Environment become potentially significant. As well as Commissioners, Member State representatives and environmentalists this body includes presidential level representation from WBCSD and BusinessEurope and executives from leading firms such as BP and Dow. The challenge it faces is, however, a considerable one in terms of the tension between competitiveness and environmental objectives, as is recognised in its Second Report:

> Scenario analysis suggests an energy future for the European Union unsustainable in terms of its competitiveness, its commitment to fight climate change in line with the Kyoto obligations and other unsustainable environmental trends, and the need to guarantee its security of supply (High Level Group 2006: 1).

Effective leadership is always contextual and business leadership has had to respond to the changing terms of the debate and heightened public awareness. Climate change denial, which in any case was always more popular in the United States than in Europe, went out of fashion for much of the first decade of the twenty-first century as the evidence of climate change mounted, was presented more systematically and more effectively publicised. However, in 2009–10 it enjoyed something of a resurgence as climate change became framed more as a typical left–right issue with suggestions that it was being used as a device by those on the left to increase regulation of business and society more generally. These suggestions, however, came from politicians on the right of the political spectrum, seeking to exercise a form of cognitive leadership, rather than from business leaders. Most business leaders felt impelled to engage proactively with the debate and bring forward their own novel solutions. Organisations with selective memberships of CEOs like ERT and WBCSD seem best fitted to perform this role because they can set priorities and respond quickly to changing events without being encumbered by the need to seek consent from elaborate committee structures.

Climate change as a threat and opportunity?

As indicated in the previous section, business perceptions of climate change have changed over time. Particularly in the United States, in the run up to Kyoto, the initial reaction was to see it as a threat to business. In part this was because the initial development of the climate change debate was being undertaken by environmentalists and their sympathisers. Given the weakening of the trade union movement in most countries, environmental groups had come to be seen as the main political threat to business interests. Climate change was seen as a challenge to the ethos of continuing economic growth, which in turn is seen as creating new and expanding markets, permitting company expansion and continued profitability. There is still a particular concern about business in developing countries being allowed to expand without check while constraints are placed on business in advanced countries, creating what is perceived to be an unbalanced competitive environment.

It might be objected that business managed to adjust to earlier developments in environmental policy which have imposed new regulatory requirements. However, regulation can sometimes be in the interests of business as it raises entry barriers in a market, making it more difficult for new firms to enter and squeezing out some existing ones. This reduces competition in a way that can facilitate profit maximisation. Measures to deal with climate change will be less differentiated and will affect all businesses to some extent, although some more than others. However, they are less likely to serve as entry barriers to markets.

New opportunities

Climate change does offer up new opportunities for firms producing technologies that reduce emissions or that produce energy in a renewable way. However, it has to be recognised that these industries, because they are younger and often quite fragmented, are often not as well organised as more mature industries and hence have less political displacement. Proponents of, for example, wind power, solar power or wave power want to promote their own particular technologies as solutions. Renewable energy firms are 'relative newcomers to the policy process' (Dunn 2002: 30), are generally smaller companies and lack the government relations divisions of big corporations or well-developed trade associations. In contrast, it is generally accepted that the chemical industry is one of the best organised industries in terms of influence on EU policy, as was evident in the discussion of the Registration, Evaluation, Authorisation and Restriction of Chemicals (REACH) proposals.

The comparable organisation for renewable energy is the European Business Council for Sustainable Energy (e5) which was founded in 1996. It is an umbrella organisation representing sectors such as wind, biomass, solar and natural gas industries, as well as power co-generation and energy efficiency businesses, and as well as energy users. Interestingly, it also embraces non-governmental organisations such as Germanwatch and World Wildlife Fund (WWF), alongside major companies such as Deutsche Telekom and Sony. However, the very range of interests represented must blunt its message and it is no where near as well resourced as the European Chemical Industry Council (CEFIC). It also has a strong German flavour, with headquarters near Frankfurt.

The case for renewable energy is by no means an uncontested policy space. For example, advocates of wind power have encountered opposition from powerful lobbies of bird lovers, as well as from those who object to the aesthetic impact of turbines on the landscape. Biofuels represent highly contested products in terms of whether they deliver a net environmental benefit, concerns that have been accentuated by rising food prices.

Differential impacts on business

Climate change is an arena in which the threats are differentially distributed among a range of business actors. 'The most important point of corporative relevance regarding the economics of climate change is that . . . the costs and benefits add up, they will be spread unevenly across different sectors of the economy, and even potentially within sectors' (Dunn 2002: 30). It is easier to identify losers than potential winners, including the energy-intensive manufacturing industries, such as steel, glass, aluminium, paper and ceramics as well as the power companies. As a general proposition, 'Since people are more sensitive to losses than gains, losers are more likely to mobilize politically than winners' (Daugbjerg and Svendsen 2001: 134). Threats are likely to be weighted above opportunities, particularly as a stimulus for political action.

However, the calculus of gains and losses can be more complex than it first appears. In many ways the energy production companies are in a more advantageous position than the intensive users:

> [Overall] we can talk about the power sector being differentiated from the industrial sector in three main ways: (i) it is more capable, at least in principle, of reducing carbon emissions fairly substantially in the short term (through fuel switching from coal to gas); (ii) it does not suffer from

the same exposure to international competition; and . . . (iii) it is generally more able to pass on the costs of the Scheme to its customers. (Environmental Audit Committee, 2007: 31)

The insurance industry: turning a threat into an opportunity

As far as companies that have an incentive to take action on climate change are concerned, 'Insurance and reinsurance companies are confronted with enormous liabilities from rising weather-related claims' (Dunn 2002: 31). The Association of British Insurers (ABI) states that 'An increase in the frequency or severity of extreme weather events could mean that insurers have to increase premiums to stay viable (Association of British Insurers 2008). In 2007 ABI launched the Climate Change Initiative to support climate change among the industry's customers and incorporate climate change into its investment strategies. The initiative was backed by 38 leading insurance companies, and although initially it was a UK initiative, it has been taken up on a global basis.

The industry considers that it is particularly well placed to influence consumer behaviour in both retail and commercial markets: 'Although consumers generally have limited trust in business on environmental issues, insurers are acknowledged as a major source of advice on risk. The industry can build on this authoritative role.' It considers that 'The market for climate-friendly and climate-proof insurance products and services should be significant' (Association of British Insurers, 2007: 2). Insurers with knowledge and skills related to special services such as insurance for domestic microrenewables or industrial green roofs would have a competitive advantage within existing markets. The industry also considers that as a major purchaser of goods and services it could use procurement policies to stimulate growth in climate-friendly measures. It considers that 'The reputational gains from providing insurance products that encourage and enable the adoption of climate-friendly and climate-proof technologies . . . would be substantial' (Association of British Insurers, 2007: 3).

The insurance industry believes that it faces some threats from climate change, but considers that if it responds to those challenges in the right way, it can turn a threat into a market opportunity which would also enhance the industry's reputation. It wants to be seen as part of the solution rather than a barrier to progress. It represents an interesting example of cognitive industry leadership, given that the insurance industry can have substantial influence on business through the way that it structures its policies.

The key role of large companies

Sectoral differences aside, leadership on climate change issues is really being exercised by a subgroup of the largest companies which like to see themselves as global citizens and regard mitigating climate change as a key element in a broader corporate social responsibility agenda. This is in part a response to the concern about damaging consumer perceptions of the brand, but it is also driven by a desire to develop adaptation strategies that will allow companies to stay ahead of their rivals. New market opportunities in terms of developing 'first mover' advantage through the deployment of new technologies have generally been a more important driver for smaller and emergent firms, but the case of the insurance industry illustrates the potential contribution of service sectors.

Although most firms generally accept the scientific consensus about climate change, there remains considerable uncertainty about the timing and extent of its effects. In that respect it is very different from, say, water pollution where the effects of effluent on a river and efforts to mitigate it can be quite precisely measured. Business in general abhors uncertainty and one way to cope initially was through simple denial. Now that the challenge has been accepted, an important driver for business is to reduce uncertainty so that appropriate investment strategies can be selected with a degree of confidence.

Policy instruments

'Policy instruments, often analyzed as peripheral in the understanding of public policy, are back in favor' (Lascoumes and Le Galès, 2007: 1). At one time they were viewed as largely technical choices between alternative mechanisms for achieving an agreed goal. However, there has been an increasing recognition of their substantive and symbolic political character and the way in which they mix technical and social components. It has become evident 'that instruments at work are not neutral devices: they produce specific effects, independently of the objective pursued . . . which structure public policy according to their own logic . . . [They] are bearers of values, fuelled by one interpretation of the social and by precise notions of the mode of regulation envisaged' (Lascoumes and Le Galès, 2007: 3–4).

In particular, the concept of efficiency, while it may have a specific meaning in economics, becomes contested in the political sphere. 'Among political actors, there are differing views on which instruments are economically efficient, meaning that in environmental politics, efficiency is a somewhat loose concept which can be defined in various ways to serve particular policy objectives.' The choice of instrument is influenced by its ability to mobilise political support and not a simple matter of whether it can fulfil policy objectives. 'This means that there is no direct link between an instrument's ability to achieve an optimal welfare economic situation and its political attractiveness' (Daugbjerg and Svendsen, 2001: 119).

As noted above, businesses want to reduce uncertainty as much as possible. This is particularly important in industries such as energy production where investments have to be planned within a very long time frame or insurance where the whole viability of the industry could be put at risk. Hence, a key demand of business is not only that policy instruments should be market based, but they should be as stable as possible over the long term. There is also a preference for, as far as possible, focusing on one central policy instrument rather than relying on a range of measures leading to double regulation and additional transaction costs.

It is important to remember that for all the excitement about New Environmental Policy Instruments, 'empirical research reveals that regulation is still the most widely used instrument of environmental policy' (Jordan, Wurzel and Zito 2005: 489). As far as taxation as a policy instrument is concerned, a minority of Member States 'has managed to block the EC's ability to innovate with environmental taxation that, unlike most aspects of EU environmental policy, still falls under the unanimity rule' (Jordan, Wurzel and Zito 2005: 492). This was a relevant consideration in the defeat of the carbon tax in the 1990s, which also faced intensive lobbying from a coalition of oil, motor and heavy industry interests. Zito (2000: 101) makes the point that 'Industrial groups have tended to support voluntary agreements and even command and control instruments over an environmental tax because industry can negotiate and consult with government during the policy implementation.'

EU emissions trading scheme

Business has been broadly supportive of the EU's flagship policy instrument of emissions trading. The greatest resistance has been engendered by the proposal to include civil aviation in the emissions trading scheme from 2011. The European Low Fares Airline Association (which was founded in only 2004) has been a particularly vociferous opponent, saying that it could not simply add the cost incurred by buying credits to fares. It argues that the aviation industry cannot replace oil with other fuels in the way that generation or energy-using industries can increase their use of renewable generation sources. Underlying this concern is no doubt a fear that its price-driven business model, already threatened by higher oil prices, would be hit hard by a further increase in fares.

The International Air Transport Association (IATA), representing airlines in general, joined the campaign with a press release and a full-page advert in the *Financial Times* at the end of June 2008. IATA called on the EU to put aside its 'single-minded focus on emissions trading', which was represented as tunnel vision. IATA claimed that the proposed measures would reduce mobility and put jobs at risk. It favoured a global solution brokered through the International Civil Aviation Organisation (ICAO) which, although it is a UN body, might well be better disposed to aviation interests and has not come forward with any specific proposals (International Air Transport Association 2008).

Not all airlines oppose emissions trading: Virgin Atlantic applauded the scheme and stated: 'emissions trading continues to present the best option for addressing climate change in the long-term'. Aviation should be included in the EU ETS as soon as practically possible. It believed 'that the EU ETS will be the best way to motivate meaningful behavioural changes in the aviation industry. Emissions trading encourages companies to invest in more fuel efficient and environmentally friendly technologies to reduce fuel consumption' (House of Commons 2008). These divisions of opinion are reminiscent of the distinction between environmentally friendly and capitalist aggressive companies outlined earlier. Within the aviation market, some companies may position themselves to cultivate a greener image.

The general business position is reflected by the Confederation of British Industry (CBI) when it stated, 'Over time, the CBI expect the ETS to become the central mechanism for incentivising investment in low carbon technologies and activities' (Environmental Audit Committee 2007: 128). Given that it allows companies scope to make decisions about how to respond, it is preferred to more interventionist instruments. Energy producers received their allocations 'largely free of charge . . . thereby realising significant windfall profits without environmental benefits' (European Chemical Industry Council 2008). There is no other game in town as far as business is concerned. It is by far the preferred policy instrument.

Multi-level governance

More than on possibly any other issues, business has organised itself effectively at a global level to deal with the issue of climate change, interacting with a wide range of international actors, including heads of government. Business has a comparative advantage in global representation as relatively few other interests are able to organise effectively at this level with the exception of a few environmental NGOs, but even they generally lack the access to top political leaders enjoyed by business. Regional solutions such as those adopted by the EU are seen as a second-best solution, giving their potential to create competitive disadvantages for European business. What business particularly does not want is the imposition of any tariffs on imported goods made in more carbon-intensive economies elsewhere. The UN mechanisms are seen as a somewhat cumbersome means of reaching agreement. The ETS is the only effective regional scheme available and business feels impelled to engage with it and with other schemes developed at a domestic level. One of the concerns of business is overlap and potential conflicts between schemes at the EU and Member State level, e.g., the Climate Change Levy (CCL).

European businesses have been in the vanguard of seeking an effective response to climate change, although American businesses are engaged in catch up. Business leaders do see the EU as exercising a leadership role: 'Europe can play a leading role if the EU and its Member States' actions are part of a formalised coherent long-term global plan covering all main emitting countries' (ERT 2007: 7). That claim was, however, somewhat undermined by the fact that the Copenhagen Accord was concluded by the United States with Brazil, China, India and South Africa, with the EU not in the room. However, business does not want the responsibility of leadership placed largely at its door. 'Business cannot fully capitalize on these new opportunities in an international policy vacuum: strong leadership from all governments, particularly those on the major economies, is essential' (World Economic Forum 2008: 9).

Although a definitive answer to this question would require more research, the general impression, confirmed by Chapter 13, is that agenda setting on climate change policy has not been done by business but by the Commission and by members and by influential NGOs, e.g., Climate Action Network (CAN) Europe. This is not to say that business has been a 'policy taker'. It has played a substantial role in vetoing some policy options (the carbon tax) and has been influential in steering policy in the direction of the market-based policy instruments that it favours. However, it has not really been able to upload its preferred policies and regulatory strategies at the EU or international level. Apart from anything else, business has been divided on how to handle this issue; often it is the policy entrepreneurs who consider that business has to engage constructively with the issues that have made the running, but they are not typical of business persons as a whole. Climate change deniers are not really a significant part of the policy debate in business circles and those pursuing very particular interests receive short shrift given the magnitude and importance of the problem.

The national chapters in this book provide evidence of the persistence of national regulatory styles and preferred policy instruments. However, the general trend would seem to be towards the Europeanisation and internationalisation of policy, given the nature and scope of the policy challenge being faced. Certainly, a recurrent theme of business is the need for the development of a globally harmonised approach, not just to overcome problems of a level playing field, but also because it is seen as the only effective long-term approach.

Conclusions

The general picture that emerges is that business, after a slow start, began to respond to the challenge of climate change, particularly after Kyoto, with CEOs in major companies taking a leading role and in some cases adopting a transformational leadership style. New organisations have been formed to respond to the challenge at a global level. The leadership offered by existing business associations, both general and sectoral, has been more variable in quality. However, some interesting examples of such leadership exist both at European and domestic level, e.g., the ERT and the ABI. The oil and coal, motor vehicle, heavy energy-using industries and civil aviation do remain a real obstacle, but climate change denial is no longer a respectable option, as shown by the case of Exxon Mobil. Fear of reputational damage has been a major driver of business responses, while some sectors and firms have discerned new market opportunities. In general, business favours stable, market-based policy instruments such as the EU ETS and does not want to see a proliferation of potentially contradictory instruments.

There is a risk of some backsliding against the background of the credit crunch and a turbulent economic environment. Just as with public attitudes, there is a risk that business could come to see environmental action as a luxury good. However, as Richard Lambert, the director-general of the CBI warned:

> Energy security and climate change are right at the top of the priority list for the CBI and will remain there over the long run. Stuff happens in politics to distract the focus of attention, but we know that the scale of the challenge must make it a business priority for the next 30 years.
>
> (Lambert 2008)

Business was, however, disappointed both with its role at Copenhagen and with the outcome which it felt failed to generate sufficient certainty about the likely direction of policy and policy instruments. This was seen as a particular challenge in terms of a clear signal on the carbon price and generating the 90 per cent of the $500bn a year investment required to be provided by the private sector (*Financial Times* 21 December 2009). Because Copenhagen was essentially an intergovernmental event, dozens of business executives who travelled there were denied entrance to the summit venue in the crucial final days of the negotiations. In particular the UN-backed Principles for Responsible Investment Group was critical of governments for excluding investors from negotiations (*Sunday Times* 20 December 2009).

The EU has made clear its continued commitment to a broad ecological modernisation strategy. Assistance provided to business in the context of the credit crunch has often been directed to climate change mitigation. For example, a major economic recovery package announced by Commission president Baroso in November 2008 focuses attention on energy efficiency and greener products, in particular giving financial aid to the automobile industry through a new 'green cars' initiative (ENDS *Europe Daily* 2008). In general, business is not reverting to a discourse that sees a trade-off between economic growth and environmental protection.

What is also clear from the analysis is that business does not think that it could or should act alone on this issue and an effective partnership with national governments, the EU and global organisations is essential to progress. The general preference of business is for the issue to be tackled at a global level, while acknowledging the importance of leadership by example offered by the EU. Business has also shown a capacity to exercise entrepreneurial leadership and develop a transformational leadership style.

The exclusion of the EU from the final decision-making phase at Copenhagen presents real challenges to those business interests who see it as a vehicle for developing a climate change strategy. The fact that the EU had signalled substantial emission cuts in advance, and was prepared to commit to more If the negotiations progressed, undermined its bargaining power. Business cannot provide EU with the input and output legitimacy that is required, a key area where ENGOs can offer more as is discussed in Chapter 13 by Wurzel and Connelly. Business remains the elephant in the room or perhaps just outside the door.

Bibliography

Association of British Insurers (2007) *Insuring Our Future Climate: Thinking for Tomorrow, Today*, London: Association of British Insurers.

Association of British Insurers (2008) Available HTTP: <http://www.abi.org.uk/Display> (accessed 26 June 2008).

Ball, J. (2007) 'Exxon Mobil Softens its Climate-Change Stance', *Wall Street Journal*, 11 January.

BusinessEurope (2008) Available HTTP: <http://www.businesseurope.eu> (accessed 24 June 2008).

Coen, D., Grant, W. and Wilson, G. (2010) 'Political Science: Perspectives on Business and Government' in D. Coen, W. Grant and G. Wilson (eds), *The Oxford Handbook of Business and Government*, Oxford: Oxford: Oxford University Press, 9–34.

Daugbjerg, C. and Svendsen, G. T. (2001) *Green Taxation in Question*, Basingstoke: Palgrave.

Dunn, S. (2002) 'Down to Business on Climate Change: An Overview of Corporate Strategies', *Greener Management International*, 39(3), 27–41.

ENDS Europe Daily (2008) '*EU* Economic Rescue Plan Puts Focus on Efficiency', 2666, 26 November.

Environmental Audit Committee (2007) *The EU Emissions Trading Scheme: Lessons for the Future*, House of Commons Environmental Audit Committee Second Report of Session 2006–7, London, HMSO.

European Chemical Industry Council (2008). Available HTTP: <http://www.cefic.be/Templates/shwStory.asp?NID = 537&HID = 538> (accessed 25 June 2008).

European Round Table (2007) *Achieving Secure, Competitive and Clean Sustainable Energy*, Brussels: ERT.

Golub, J. (1998) 'New Instruments for Environmental Policy in the EU: Introduction and Overview' in J. Golub (ed.), *New Instruments for Environmental Policy in the EU*, London: Routledge, 1–29.

Grant, W. (1984) 'Large Firms and Public Policy in Britain', *Journal of Public Policy*, 4(1), 1–17.

High Level Group (2006) *Second Report of the High Level Group on Competitiveness, Energy and the Environment*, Brussels, Commission of the European Communities.

House of Commons (2008) Available HTTP: <http://www.publications.parliament.uk/pa/cm0607/cmselect/cmenvaud> (accessed 25 June 2008).

International Air Transport Association (2008) Available HTTP: <http://www.iata.prg/pressroom/pr/2008-06-25-02.htm> (accessed 25 June 2008).

Jordan, A., Wurzel, R. K. and Zito, A. (2005) 'The Rise of "New" Policy Instruments in Comparative Perspective: Has Governance Eclipsed Government?' *Political Studies*, 53(3), 477–96.

Jordan, G. (2000) *Shell, Greenpeace and the Brent Spar*, Basingstoke: Palgrave.

Klein, N. (2000) *No Logo*, London: Flamingo.

Lambert, R. (2008) *Financial Times*, 24 June 2008.

Lascoumes, P. and Le Galès (2007) 'Introduction: Understanding Public Policy through Its Instruments – From the Nature of Instruments to the Sociology of Public Policy Instrumentation', *Governance*, 20(1), 1–21.

Lowe, P., Phillipson, J. and Lee, R. P. (2008) 'Socio-technical Innovation for Sustainable Food Chains: Roles for Social Science', *Trends in Food Science and Technology*, 19(5), 226–33.

Musson, S. (2007) 'Exxon Mobil Warms up to Global Climate Issue', *Washington Post*, 10 February 2007.

Olson, M. (1971) *The Logic of Collective Action*, 2nd edn, Cambridge, Mass: Harvard University Press.

Weale, A. (1992) *The New Politics of Pollution*, Manchester: Manchester University Press.

World Economic Forum (2008) 'CEO Climate Policy Recommendations to G8 Leaders', Cologny/Geneva: World Economic Forum, <http://www.weforum.org/documents/initiatives/CEOStatement.pdf>

Zito, A.R. (2000) *Creating Environmental Policy in the European Union*, Basingstoke: Macmillan.

13 Environmental NGOs

Taking a lead?

Rüdiger K. W. Wurzel and James Connelly[1]

Introduction

The European Environmental Bureau (EEB), which set up its office in Brussels in 1974, remained for more than a decade the only major environmental non-governmental organisation (ENGO) focusing primarily on European Union (EU) environmental policy. In 1974 the EEB had 25 member groups from 9 Member States; by 2010 its membership had risen to 143 groups from 31 European countries.[2] In the late-1980s there was an 'explosion of interest' in EU environmental issues amongst ENGOs (Long 1998:107); Friends of the Earth (FoE), Greenpeace, World Wide Fund for Nature (WWF) and Climate Action Network (CAN) all set up European offices in Brussels between 1986 and 1989. More specialised ENGOs (including the European Federation for Transport and Environment (T&E) and BirdLife International) moved to Brussels in the early 1990s. This mushrooming of ENGOs in Brussels allowed for 'an implicit division of labour' (Rucht 1993: 86) and fostered professionalisation (Hey and Brendle 1994; Long and Lörinczi 2009) and specialisation on issues such as EU climate change policy.

The European offices of the EEB, FoE, Greenpeace and WWF quickly cooperated closely within the 'Gang of Four' or 'G4' (a parody of the G7 meetings, the name given to the economic summits of the then 'great seven powers'). From the late 1980s onwards climate change became a major campaign issue for the Brussels-based ENGOs and the need to pool resources and coordinate strategies in order to influence EU climate change policy became acute in the run up to the 1992 United Nations (UN) Rio conference. The G4 gradually grew into the G10, comprising BirdLife International, CAN Europe, CEE Bankwatch Network, EEB, Health and Environment Alliance (HEAL),[3] Environment Network, FoE Europe, Greenpeace Europe, International Friends of Nature (INF), T&E, and WWF European Policy Office (Long and Lörinczi 2009). The EEB, FoE, Greenpeace and WWF have remained central players because they cover a wide range of EU environmental issues (including climate change) and represent a large number of members/supporters.

CAN Europe (initially Climate Network Europe, CNE) is the European branch of CAN International, which is an international network of ENGOs campaigning on climate issues. CAN Europe was not initially included in the G4 because it constituted 'an informal, under-staffed and loosely coordinated transnational group' (Rucht 1993: 91). However, CAN Europe quickly developed into an effective network for European ENGOs working on EU climate change issues and developed into a large network. By late 2009, 130 member organisations from more than 25 European countries had joined CAN Europe (Interview 2010).

CAN Europe's growing importance was partly at the expense of the EEB which has had only limited staff resources for climate change issues (although it ran a major campaign in favour of an EU-wide CO_2/energy tax in the early 1990s). In the late 2000s, the EEB had only one full-time member of staff working on climate change issues compared with CAN Europe's five. Coordination takes place between the Brussels-based ENGOs for four reasons. First, most European offices have meagre staff and financial resources, certainly by comparison with those of large companies (see Chapter 12 by Grant). Second, despite their heterogeneity, European ENGOs have similar goals and therefore find it relatively easy to form coalitions (Long and Lörinczi 2009). Third, competition between ENGOs for funding and sympathisers as well as for media and public attention is less marked at EU level compared with the national level (Rucht 1993: 90). The climate change activists within the Brussels-based ENGOs know each other well, often meet informally, and some have moved between groups over the years. Finally, alliances between ENGOs representing a large number of EU citizens enhance the chance of being taken seriously, in particular by those EU institutional actors keen to increase the EU's political legitimacy. Unlike businesses, ENGOs can help not only to increase 'output legitimacy' by providing technical expertise but also 'input legitimacy' by mobilising public support for EU policies and policy proposals (Beyers and Kerremans 2005: 114). The degree to which European ENGOs form part of an emerging EU civil society helping to reduce the EU's democratic deficit is contested (see CEC (2001), della Porta (2003) and Rucht (1993) for an optimistic view and Greenwood (2003) and Warleigh (2001) for a sceptical view); but it is undisputed that ENGOs not only try to influence EU policies but also attempt to change the wider political context by raising the public's awareness of climate change, thereby also possibly altering voters' preferences regarding the actions politicians should take to combat it. ENGOs also play an important role in framing (or reframing) the public debate about environmental issues. Although the Commission has, since the early 1990s, emphasised the need for more inclusion, openness and transparency. ENGOs' increased involvement has largely been limited to consultation despite the Commission's proposal to open up 'the policy making process to get more people and organizations involved in shaping and delivering EU policy' (CEC 2001:3).

Groups and alliances

As the G4 grew into the G10, ENGOs recognised that 'while different groups worked on different subjects, there was an advantage from being able to pool resources with one or more of the other environmental groups for certain campaigns' (Long 1998: 115). However, lobbying and campaign work is not undertaken solely by the G10. Over the years there was an emergence of ' "policy clusters" of individual NGOs drawn together for collective organization and action on specific topics that may not include all members of the G10. Non-G10 organizations are able to join these clusters and are encouraged to do so' (Long and Lörinczi 2009: 168). NGOs other than ENGOs have started to join networks campaigning for an EU leadership role in international climate change politics. Health groups (such as the European Public Health Alliance (EPHA)) have teamed up with ENGOs to form the Health and Environment Alliance (HEAL)[4] and development NGOs (such as Oxfam and Christian Aid) pooled resources with ENGOs in the run up to the UN climate change conference in Copenhagen in December 2009 (Interviews 2008–10). One of the most important clusters of European NGOs has formed around the EU's climate change and energy package, adopted by the Council and European Parliament (EP) in late 2008 (Long and Lörinczi 2009: 168). Building alliances, coalitions and networks amongst different NGOs (at times joining forces with environmentally progressive businesses such as the renewable energy industry) is an important part of the work of Brussels-based ENGOs and can improve the chances of success for 'bread and butter lobbying' activities (Long and Lörinczi 2009: 168–69).

The EU Commission encouraged the formation of European-wide interest groups by providing funding, information and privileged access for European umbrella organisations (Long 1998; Mazey and Richardson 1993). According to Greenwood (2003: 191) ENGOs received €32 million in EU funding in 2002–6. WWF's long-standing director, Tony Long (1998: 112), has pointed out that the opening of a Brussels office not only put WWF in a better position to influence EU policies, but also allowed the group 'to lever some of the considerable sums of EC aid money to be spent on conservation and development projects . . .'.

Although much interest group literature contrasts 'insider' with 'outsider' strategies (Grant 2000, 2003), most European ENGOs reject the view that these strategies are mutually exclusive (Interviews 2008–10; Richard and Heards 2005). One ENGO representative explained that 'most politicians realise that it takes pressure from outside which gives them more room for manoeuvre. An MEP or MP can then say: "I am under pressure from an NGO"' (Interview 2010). However, some European ENGOs have a stronger preference for adopting an insider strategy (requiring considerable technical expertise and staying power) than others, who show a greater disposition towards campaigns designed to attract media and public attention.

Greenpeace has become a widely recognised brand through the use of unconventional actions attracting media attention. However, Greenpeace's European office has often taken a less confrontational stand than its International office. Greenpeace does not accept funding from governments, EU institutions or the European Climate Foundation (ECF) for fear of compromising its independence. This is one of the main reasons why it has remained aloof from the EEB, which relies heavily on funding from the Commission and sympathetic governments. Although various national FoE groups have shown a considerable appetite for direct action, FoE's European office has taken a more pragmatic view on EU and government funding than Greenpeace. FoE is a strongly grassroots-centred umbrella organisation which grants considerable autonomy to its national, regional and local members (Rucht 1993).[5] Unsurprisingly FoE's European office therefore largely became a liaison office engaging in outreach and service functions (Greenwood 2003). The decision-making process within CAN Europe is consensual and principally takes places in a bottom-up fashion, although its most active member groups play a central role together with CAN Europe's Brussels offices staff.

Greenpeace and WWF are hierarchically structured organisations in which campaigns are carried out by professional staff, while grassroots involvement is negligible (Rucht 1993; Zito and Jacobs 2009). WWF is a strongly science-based organisation which has, nonetheless, occasionally conducted campaigns directed mainly at attracting media and public attention. Its European office developed from humble beginnings into the most well-staffed office of all Brussels-based ENGOs. Clearly the distinction, widely used in the ENGOs literature between moderate conservationist groups, largely adopting insider lobbying strategies, and more radical environmental groups, mainly adopting outsider strategies, has become blurred at EU level (Hey and Brendle 1994; Richards and Heard 2005). Radical so-called 'deep green' environmental groups, such as Earth First!, which endorse violence and exhibit a radical green ideology have little following in Europe (Carter 2007: 143–70); they play no role in EU climate change policy-making. Differences in strategy between the main European ENGOs can be explained by their different histories, organisational structures and the dominant worldviews of core activists.

As Rucht (1993: 90) has noted, 'despite their heterogeneity, environmental groups in Brussels do not have strong conflicts but tend to cooperate closely on the basis of an informal division of labour'. Working relationships are generally very good despite the occasional clash of personalities. Compared with businesses (see Chapter 12 by Grant), ENGOs usually find it easier to agree on common goals. According to one leading activist: 'environmental groups can work together on the basis of the *highest common factor principles* while some, although not all, of the interests which may be seeking to slow down environmental advance have to operate on the basis of *lowest common denominator positions*' (Long 1998: 117). Although differences exist about the best strategies, in many cases a 'creative tension' (Carter 2007: 161) encouraged a multitude of campaign activities on EU climate change policy.

Brussels-based think tanks which are active on climate change issues often also carry out policy advocacy. The Centre for European Policy Studies (CEPS) and The Centre have been involved on a range of EU issues including climate change issues. There are also smaller and more specialised groups which have taken on both think tank and NGO functions, such as Client Earth, which provides free legal expertise on climate change issues for ENGOs (and MEPs), and E3G which deals with sustainable development issues. Research institutes such as Ecologic, the Institute for European Environmental Policy (IEEP) and Öko Institut have produced research for ENGOs. Moreover, European ENGOs have participated in forums such as the Civil Society Platform (bringing together environmental, social, human rights and cultural NGOs) and the Agora forum, which is the EP's EU citizens' forum. CONCORD (the European NGO Confederation for Relief and Development) has started to take in interest in climate change issues. The increasing involvement of well-organised and -funded development NGOs in EU climate change politics has strengthened the voice of European ENGOs: so have alliances with consumer groups. Moreover, church groups which work on development issues (e.g. Christian Aid) have formed a network called Aprodev that has increasingly become interested in climate change issues.

Table 13.1 lists the most important European ENGOs, NGOs, think tanks and research institutes active on EU climate change issues. It also lists foundations which have funded climate change activities by European ENGOs. The European Climate Foundation (ECF) and Oak Foundation have provided significant funding for ENGOs active on climate change issues (interviews 2008–10). The ECF wants 'to promote climate and energy policies that greatly reduce Europe's greenhouse gas emissions and help Europe play an even stronger international leadership role in mitigating climate change'.[6] Bellona Europa (part of the Environmental Foundation Bellona), which is an anti-nuclear Norwegian ENGO that 'seeks to influence the making of EU legislation through alliances with other NGOs, industry, academics and progressive politicians, particularly members of the European Parliament',[7] has focused largely on advocating carbon capture and storage (CCS).

Leadership

As will be explained below, all Brussels-based ENGOs have consistently advocated a strong leadership role for the EU in international climate change politics. ENGOs themselves have also tried to provide leadership on climate change issues. In considering what types and styles of leadership ENGOs are able to offer we need to focus on a range of groups and networks. Although the G4 and G10 have provided structural, entrepreneurial and cognitive

Table 13.1 Brussels-based European NGOs, think tanks and research institutes active on EU climate change issues

---

ENGOs active on EU climate change policy issues:
G4:
EEB, FoE, Greenpeace and WWF

G10:
BirdLife International, CAN Europe, Central and Eastern Europe (CEE) Bankwatch Network, EEB, HEAL, FoE, Greenpeace, Friends of Nature International (NFI), T&E, and WWF

Four most active large ENGOs in EU climate change policy:
CAN, FoE, Greenpeace and WWF

Large European ENGO umbrella groups active on EU climate issues level:
CAN Europe
HEAL
T&E

Large European ENGO networks groups active on EU climate issues:
EEB
FoE
Greenpeace
WWF

Small ENGOs active on specific EU climate issues:
Belona
Client Earth
E3G

NGOs other than ENGOs active on EU climate change policy issues:
Aprodev
Christian Aid
Oxfam

Think tanks andlor research Institutes:
Centre for European Policy Studies (CEPS)
Ecologic
Institute for European Environmental Policy (IEEP)
Öko Institut
The Centre

Foundations which fund NGO lobbying activities on EU climate policy:
European Climate Foundation
Oak Foundation
Environmental Foundation Bellona

Wider civil society platforms:
Civil Society Platform
Agora
Concord

---

leadership (see Chapter 1), CAN Europe, FoE, Greenpeace and WWF have been the most important actors consistently taking the lead on a range of EU climate change issues (Interviews 2008–10). The EEB missed the opportunity to provide sustained leadership amongst European ENGOs when it failed to maintain its campaign for an EU-wide CO_2/energy tax (Hey and Brendle 1994: 503). Newer and publicly less well known groups like Bellona, Client Earth, E3G and The Centre have either specialised in specific climate change issues (e.g. Client Earth on legal issues and Belona on CCS) and/or facilitated network building amongst ENGOs, non-environmental NGOs and other EU policy actors. Internet-based communication has facilitated collaboration within the European NGO community and with NGOs from other parts of the world.

Prior to the 2008 European Council and Environmental Council meetings (see Chapter 4), which agreed the climate change and energy package in principle, CAN, FoE, Greenpeace and WWF ran a campaign 'Time to lead' urging the EU to adopt internally ambitious goals and measures to be able to offer leadership on the international level.[8] In the run up to the 2009 Copenhagen conference an even larger number of NGOs from different parts of the world drafted an alternative climate change treaty entitled A Copenhagen Climate Treaty. A Proposal for a Copenhagen Agreement by Members of the NGO Community (IndyACT *et al.* 2009). Furthermore, most of the large Brussels-based ENGOs and development NGOs pooled resources with other NGOs (such as Amnesty International) for a common campaign named 'Tcktcktck'[9] while more grassroots-oriented and/or radical groups teamed up for the 'Climate Justice Action'[10] campaign. The unprecedented level of NGO climate change activities both before and at the 2009 Copenhagen conference marked, for at least one ENGO representative, 'the beginning of a global civil society movement on climate change' (Interview 2010).

Leadership amongst the European groups campaigning on EU climate change issues is shared. The Brussels-based NGOs operate in formal and informal networks for strategy coordination, workload sharing and information gathering. For climate change issues CAN has become the main coordinator around which '[t]he NGO community is loosely federated' (Long, Slater and Singer 2002: 100). Within CAN, other European ENGOs share information, discuss joint strategies and agree on workload sharing. However, ENGOs such as WWF will often try to turn their own priorities into CAN positions (Long, Slater and Singer 2002: 100).

Cognitive leadership is provided by ENGOs (and other NGOs) which have been successful in influencing the wider political climate change discourse and/or framing the main issues at stake. ENGOs are credited with coining the term 'hot air' (Long and Lörinczi 2009: 172). Greenpeace (2008), which has been consistently engaged in promoting renewable energy, has demanded an energy (r)evolution in a document entitled *energy [r]evolution.* An important recent development has been the convergence of environmental and developmental NGOs on climate change issues. Oxfam and Christian Aid have brought new ideas and a 'different political discourse' to the climate change debate within the European NGO community (Interviews 2008–10). As one ENGO representative explained: 'it's very welcome that these groups are involved because they have much more experience with all kinds of governance issues – how to disburse money in developing countries. They have much more developed thinking on equity and fairness principles' (Interview 2009).

Additional cognitive leadership emerges when we consider the legitimacy that some (typically the larger) ENGOs have attained through their long-standing activities, especially as sources of information. This legitimacy, together with the concomitant veneer of professionalism they have acquired, works to their advantage – especially in contrast with businesses. As one ENGO representative stated: 'The advantage for NGOs is that people know where they come from. They know that we tell the truth. They know that I am not lobbying to keep my job' (Interview 2009). In the past NGOs were often perceived as non-professional and business was seen as professional. As a result it was easier for business to be heard; over the last decade the position has in many ways been reversed. ENGOs have become the most trusted source for environmental information for the general public in most EU Member States (Eurobarometer, 2008; Zito and Jacobs 2009: 109).

Entrepreneurial leadership is provided primarily by think tanks such as The Centre, which acts as a clearing house of ideas and contacts. It sees its role as bringing together key actors. It is committed to ecological modernisation and to the view that, pragmatically, climate change has to be presented also as an opportunity because otherwise resistance from key actors in business and government will be hard to overcome (Interview 2009).

ENGOs' abilities to provide *structural leadership* originates primarily from their large member base and ability to influence public opinion. However, ENGOs do not have the structural powers which business has in (financial and staff) resources and jobs (see Chapter 12 by Grant). ENGOs can nevertheless put public pressure on industrial laggards within business which fail to take climate change seriously while trying to form alliances with more progressive companies.

The ECF (established in April 2008), has developed into a major source of funding for ENGOs and other NGOs working on EU climate change issues. The Oak Foundation has also provided funding for NGOs' climate change campaigns. Client Earth was founded in 2007 to provide free legal advice for ENGOs (and MEPs) in recognition of the fact that industry can easily draw on specialist legal advice whereas most ENGOs cannot. Moreover, legal expertise is also required for drafting and/or interpreting international climate change treaties. Client Earth also guides ENGOs through the legal maze of the EU.

ENGOs which endorse unconventional direct action (such as FoE and Greenpeace) clearly try to offer 'heroic' leadership, although the EU's policy-making system tends to lead them to adopt a 'humdrum' leadership style with occasional heroic outbursts (see Chapter 1). This can be seen in the work of Greenpeace's European office, which has adopted largely a pragmatic strategy when dealing with EU policy actors. Greenpeace has shown a major interest in the energy sector and sees its role as influencing investment decisions into power plants by large power companies. From this starting point its European office worked in particular on the EU ETS, renewable energy and carbon capture and storage (CCS).

Most European ENGOs acknowledge that the EU is playing a leadership role in international climate change politics. However, they caution that the EU is very much 'the one-eyed amongst the blind' (Interview 2009) and that 'because the situation has been so dire and the progress so slow that anyone who comes up with a half decent idea or slogan or political commitment is automatically a champion' (Interview 2008). ENGOs have identified a gap between the EU's rhetoric and the poor implementation of its relatively ambitious goals.

Brussels-based ENGOs were disappointed with the EU's inability to provide leadership at the 2009 Copenhagen climate conference; they would have liked the EU to offer an unconditional 30 per cent (or even more ambitious) reduction target together with significant climate change mitigation funding for developing countries. Some ENGOs felt that the EU failed to use its structural powers as a negotiating lever (e.g. by threatening CO_2 import taxes), was unable to provide entrepreneurial leadership (because it was too soft on America), and lacked credibility (due to internal squabbling) when it came to convincing others of the environmental and economic merits (or 'double dividend') of a low carbon economy (Interviews 2009–10).

Threat and opportunity

Most European ENGOs perceive climate change both as threat and opportunity (Interviews 2008–10). However, their default starting point is to see it as a threat. This is inevitable, given their primary environmental concerns. However, ENGOs find it expedient to present the argument to business and government as both a threat and an opportunity. There is a clear view within ENGOs that people will benefit from a low carbon economy. This aligns ENGOs with ecological modernisation which assumes that ambitious environmental standards are (at least in the long term) beneficial for both the environment and economy. While this might not be the preferred approach for all European ENGOs, they take it to be the approach most likely to achieve results. The very fact that they lobby 'Brussels' indicates that they have adopted a belief in some form of ecological modernisation. Had European ENGOs not done so they would be operating elsewhere and in a different fashion.

Developmental organisations promote development, which, if climate change is to be mitigated, has to be sustainable. This requires commitment to ecological modernisation in which development and environmentalism are combined. For development NGOs climate change enters the equation as a direct threat to sustainable development in developing countries which are their primary concern. ENGOs and development NGOs have increasingly cooperated on climate change issues in the second half of the 2000s (Interviews 2008–10). Development NGOs are now acting within the environmental arena in a way in which until a few years ago they would not have done. This is because they no longer see climate change as a long-term issue by contrast with the immediate issues of hunger and poverty, but as an immediate threat. This is clearly expressed in a recent Oxfam campaign poster slogan: 'People in developing countries like Bangladesh aren't thinking about how climate change will affect them. They already know.'

The credit crunch in 2008 and subsequent worldwide economic recession have been identified by ENGOs as posing a serious danger to their ability to frame climate change as an opportunity for developing a low carbon economy and promoting ecological modernisation (Interviews 2008–10). ENGOs argue that '[i]ndustry has used [the economic recession] to water down the climate and energy package' while raising concerns that '[c]harity spending declines fast in credit crunch times. It might take ten years [to recover]' (Interview 2009).

Most ENGOs are convinced that the public disagreements between Member States – in particular between the more highly developed Northern member states and the less highly industrialised Southern and Eastern European Member States – about the merits of ecological modernisation (i.e. a low carbon economy's 'double dividend') have significantly weakened the EU's international negotiation position although 'it has not prevented countries like China and India [from making] major investments into renewable energy technologies' (Interview 2010).

Policy instruments

Policy instruments can be grouped into the following three main categories: (1) regulation (setting legally binding targets and deadlines); (2) market-based instruments (e.g. eco-taxes and emission trading); (3) voluntary agreements and informational devices (e.g. eco-labels) (e.g. Jordan, Wurzel and Zito 2006). Traditional regulation was long the favourite policy instrument for ENGOs, which were also early supporters of EU-wide eco-taxes Initially ENGOs were strongly opposed to emissions trading and rejected voluntary agreements while considering informational tools as supplementary instruments (see also Bomberg 2007).

All European ENGOs have campaigned for ambitious GHGE reduction targets and deadlines enshrined in legally binding EU/national regulations and international treaties. For ENGOs: '[r]egulation is not just a stick. It is an additional measure. The best way to handle climate change is regulation including energy efficiency standards' (Interview 2009).

The EEB and CAN initially took the lead on climate change and EU eco-taxes while Greenpeace started to work on this issue only belatedly (Hey and

Brendle 1994: 506). FoE and WWF tried to use CAN for lobbying in favour of an EU-wide CO_2/energy tax. In the early 1990s, the EEB organised a series of conferences on eco-taxes flagging up their 'double dividend'. However, the EEB found it difficult to keep up the momentum behind its campaign (Hey and Brendle 1994: 507). Greenpeace combined an insider with an outsider strategy when it first supported the Commission's CO_2/energy tax proposal but then started to collect signatures amongst MEPs for a vote of no-confidence in the Commission following the resignation of the Environmental Commissioner, Ripa di Meana, who had been the main champion of the proposal within the Commission (Hey and Brendle 1994: 503, 508).

European ENGOs were not able to counter the 'largely negative but highly targeted and effective lobbying by industry groups . . . [against] some form of carbon/energy tax' on the EU level (Long 1998: 116–17). The Commission's 1992 proposal for the CO_2/energy tax (see Chapter 3 by Barnes) was never adopted because it was vetoed by Britain, which has remained opposed to supranational taxes on sovereignty grounds (see Chapter 6 by Rayner and Jordan), while Southern European Member States raised concerns about the possible negative impact of such a tax on their economic development (see Chapter 11 by Costa). ENGOs in Denmark, Germany and the Netherlands in particular started to campaign for the adoption of national eco-taxes because the Commission's proposal for an EU-wide CO_2/energy tax remained deadlocked.

Frustrated by the veto to its CO_2/energy tax proposal and encouraged by the early American ETS experience, the Commission proposed a directive establishing an EU ETS in 2001. Within two years the EP and Environmental Council adopted the legislation for an EU ETS, which became operational in 2005. Up to the late 1990s, all European ENGOs strongly opposed emissions trading on ethical grounds. They compared the sale of GHGE allowances within ETSs with the sale of indulgences while arguing that 'no one should be allowed to profit from pollution' (Interview 2008; Wurzel 2008).

European ENGOs raised concerns about 'hot air' being traded by countries (such as Russia) which had been given overly generous GHGE targets under the Kyoto Protocol (Long, Slater and Singer 2002). However, European ENGOs gradually changed their positions on emissions trading once the EU had given in to American pressure to include it in the Kyoto Protocol. The USA also insisted on two other flexible mechanisms under the Kyoto Protocol, namely joint implementation (JI), which allows certain countries jointly to implement GHGE projects, and the clean development mechanism (CDM) under which developed countries can sponsor certified GHGE reduction projects in developing countries. European ENGOs were initially opposed to the flexible mechanisms.

Out of the Brussels-based ENGOs, CAN and WWF were relatively quick in accepting the inevitability of an EU ETS to reduce GHGE, although they demanded strict trading rules, close monitoring and heavy fines to prevent the trade in 'hot air' (Interviews 2008). FoE and Greenpeace remained ETS sceptics for longer. Once all Brussels-based ENGOs had accepted that the EU ETS was central to the EU's climate change policy instrument repertoire, they tried to tighten its rules. ENGOs opposed, for example, the free allocation of CO_2 allowances, which produced huge windfall profits for the power industry, demanding instead the auctioning of allowances in order to achieve a high price for carbon. Having initially opposed emissions trading, most European ENGOs are now campaigning for the inclusion of additional greenhouse gases and/or sectors under the EU ETS. For example, T&E, which is very active on CO_2 emissions from transport, has lobbied for the inclusion of the aviation sector under the EU ETS. T&E has run lobbying campaigns on CO_2 emissions from road transport together with FoE. T&E is aligned to CAN Europe but not a member, although many of its member groups are. However, the key players on the EU ETS were CAN Europe and WWF (Interviews 2008–10). By the time the Kyoto Protocol came into force in 2005, the main European ENGOs also endorsed CDM and JI projects for which they demanded the adoption of a stringent 'gold standard'. Since, then FoE has again started to oppose the CDM while the other Brussels-based ENGOs have been highly critical of many CDM and JI projects (Interviews 2009–10).

European ENGOs have remained highly sceptical about voluntary agreements. For example, the director of WWF's European office has stated:

> [E]uphemisms such as 'shared responsibility', 'partnership', and the 'voluntary approach' are gaining ground. They threaten in many cases to become poor substitutes for an explicit environmental policy with precise environmental targets backed up with legislative force where necessary and a range of fiscal incentives where these would be more appropriate.
>
> (Long 1998: 116)

In 1999, the European automobile industry and the Commission adopted an EU-wide voluntary agreement on the reduction of CO_2 emissions from passenger cars which set a reduction target of approximately 25 per cent (i.e. 140g/km) by 2008. It was initially hailed as a great success by the automobile industry and Commission. However, ENGOs demanded instead the adoption of binding EU legislation (EEB 2000). By 2005, the Commission expressed its dissatisfaction with the automobile manufacturers' lack of progress and threatened binding EU legislation. To the delight of ENGOs, the Commission put forward a proposal for mandatory regulation which was adopted by the Council and the EP in 2008.

Multi-level governance

The large international ENGOs (e.g. CAN, FoE, Greenpeace and WWF) are well adapted to influencing multi-level environmental governance structures. Venue shopping in order to maximise their chances of exerting influence has been widely practised by the large ENGOs (Mazey and Richardson 1993). Smaller ENGOs, however, often find it difficult to engage in a two-level game (on the national and EU levels) or multi-level game (which includes the international level) (Rucht 1993). However, even the climate change activists in the large Brussels-based ENGOs focus primarily on the EU level in their daily work (Interviews 2008–10). One explanation is that 'EU decision-making is a mix of intergovernmental and supranational bargaining . . . In such a differentiated institutional setting, the problem of interest groups is not a shortage but an over-supply of potential routes to influence between which they must allocate scarce resources' (Long and Lörinczi 2009: 163).

There is widespread agreement that ENGOs are most influential at the beginning and end of the policy-making cycle which, for heuristic purposes, can be divided into five phases: (1) agenda setting; (2) consultation; (3) negotiating; (4) decision-taking; (5) implementation. As explained below, ENGOs have managed to put issues onto the EU's agenda and acted as whistleblowers by pointing out implementation failures. The negotiating and decision-taking phases of the EU policy-making process are, however, dominated by EU institutional actors and member governments.

Most European ENGOs try to lobby all EU institutions directly involved in the EU climate change policy-making process, including the Commission, Council and EP, which propose, negotiate and adopt legally binding EU measures, as well as the European Council, which agrees the broader political goals. However, their contacts are closest with the EP and its Environment Committee and Temporary Climate Change Committee, although other committees (e.g. the Development Committee) have also been regularly lobbied (see Chapter 4 by Burns and Carter). In the past, ENGOs had the closest contacts within the Commission's Directorate-General (DG) for Environment (DG Environment), which has a dedicated desk official responsible for NGO contacts; they have also tried to gain allies within other DGs, including those for Energy, Industry and Development (see Chapter 3 by Barnes). The DG Climate Change, which was set up in 2010, forms for ENGOs an additional access point to the Commission. Brussels-based ENGOs will also approach Permanent Representation officials about the state of play of EU climate change dossiers within the Council (see Chapter 5 by Oberthür and Dupont). Lobbying of national governments is usually undertaken by national ENGOs, although European ENGOs often assist their national members with information and occasionally with resources, especially in Member States with weak civil society activism and/or under-resourced environmental movements. The large Brussels-based ENGOs have supported capacity building of ENGOs in Southern and Eastern European Member States. European ENGOs also lobby the holder of the EU Presidency, who often invites the EEB to attend parts of the informal Environmental Council meeting.

However, there are resource constraints even for the large Brussels-based ENGOs. One ENGO representative explained: 'I find it quite difficult to handle the multi-level governance structures. I must prioritise every day. I have more to do than what I can handle', while another ENGO activist stated: 'For the moment we are struggling with the international [level]. We believe that it is important to work at an international level, but for the moment we do not have the resources. For the moment we are focusing on the EU and key member states' (Interviews 2009).

CAN Europe and WWF's Brussels offices are best geared towards tracking the supranational and international levels as well as the Member State level, although their main task is to lobby the EU. Exchange of information between WWF's EU and international energy specialists is relatively easy because they share the same office in Brussels (Interview 2009). CAN Europe is taking advantage of the fact that it forms part of a much larger international network with seven regional offices in Africa, Central and Eastern Europe, Europe, Latin America, North America, South Asia, and Southeast Asia. It has tried 'very clearly to work on more than one level and also created very clear channels with groups that are working outside of CAN' (Interview 2008). However, integrating the different voices from different regions into a CAN International position is not always easy. In the run up to the 2009 Copenhagen conference, CAN International intensified its fundraising activities to strengthen capacity building on climate change issues in developing countries from where about one third of its members originate. CAN Europe's large influx of new members from development NGOs led to a change in language and priorities with issues such as funding for climate change mitigation measures in developing countries becoming new campaign issues. In 2009 CAN Europe imposed a temporary membership freeze in order to avoid uncontrolled growth having a detrimental impact on its effectiveness and identity.

FoE and Greenpeace have also run effective multi-level lobbying campaigns, although their international activities are usually separated out to their international offices. Greenpeace has a relatively large international office (in Amsterdam) but only a small EU office in Brussels.

ENGOs have benefited from the fact that some of its representatives have been allowed to join EU Member State delegations participating in international climate change negotiations. However, 'being part of the delegation is one thing. Actually having access to certain levels of meetings and information is a completely different thing' (Interview 2008). ENGO representatives on national delegations are normally excluded from EU coordination meetings because a distinction is made between national delegates and national observers. In a few cases ENGO representatives attended EU coordination meetings although, '[t]here are of course even closer circles of coordination within the EU. For example, only the heads of delegations and that is where they lose us' (Interview 2008).

Conclusion

Climate change has become an important issue for all European ENGOs. By the early 2000s, CAN Europe, FoE, Greenpeace and WWF had developed

Into the most active European ENGOs on EU climate change issues, with CAN Europe having assumed a coordination role. For major climate change campaigns ENGOs have joined forces with non-environmental NGOs (e.g. development and health NGOs) to form alliances and networks which are supported by think tanks (e.g. CEPS and The Centre) and funding bodies (e.g. ECF). However, much of the coordination of ENGOs' day-to-day work on EU climate change takes place informally between a handful of activists from, in particular, CAN Europe, FoE, Greenpeace and WWF. As one NGO representative explained: 'You don't have to coordinate with 20 people. You coordinate normally with three or four people. So it is a very small world out there' (Interview 2009).

ENGOs have made use of both insider and outsider strategies in seeking to offer leadership themselves and in urging the EU to provide leadership in international climate change politics. At the 2009 Copenhagen conference, Greenpeace was represented by activists who had been issued with yellow conference entry badges for NGOs and through paid up national delegation members with pink conference entry badges (Interview 2010). While Greenpeace activists scaled lamp posts outside the security cordon around the building in which the Danish Queen hosted a dinner for the Heads of State and Government, four of its activists, who had hired limousines and chauffeurs, managed to get into the building with banners which read: 'Politicians talk Leaders act' (*Spiegel Online*, 2009).

Brussels-based ENGOs have adopted few unconventional direct actions when campaigning on EU climate change issues. The reasons are, first, the EU exhibits complex multi-level governance structures in which different EU institutions and national governments share powers which, moreover, vary according to different phases of the EU environmental policy-making process. Singling out, for purposes of direct action, a particular EU policy actor as the environmental villain is often difficult. Second, there is neither a European-wide media nor a genuine European public (Eising and Kohler-Koch 2005: 35–36). Rather, national newspapers, TV and radio stations and internet news-sites cater for what essentially are still different national publics in the current 27 Member States. Finally, the EU's consensus-seeking decision-making style does not lend itself well to confrontational direct action (Eising and Kohler-Koch 2005: 36). These features of the EU decision-making process have not prevented Greenpeace in particular and FoE from staging some media and public attention-seeking actions, such as unfolding banners from the Council's building and bridges near the EP building in Brussels warning of the consequences of failing to tackle climate change (Interviews 2008–9). Despite these examples, unconventional direct action is significantly less common on the EU level compared to the national and/or international levels.

European ENGOs perceive climate change as both a threat, which will cause serious environmental damage if decisive action is not taken, and as an opportunity for developing a low-carbon economy through a process of ecological modernisation. In terms of policy instruments European ENGOs have a preference for regulation and eco-taxes while they oppose voluntary agreements and self-regulatory tools. European ENGOs were opposed to emissions trading being included in the Kyoto Protocol, primarily on ethical grounds. However, since the adoption of the EU ETS, they have campaigning for a tightening of its rules rather than its abolition.

Overall, the large European ENGOs are generally well adapted to multi-level climate change policy decision-making. Despite this, the complexity of the climate change issues and decision-making arenas stretches the activists in the Brussels-based ENGOs to the full, in respect of both the demands on their time and expertise required of them. For these reasons, they focus primarily on the EU level in their daily work while seeking to take full advantage of the alliances and networks that they have formed with other NGOs, think tanks and research institutes. Within the EU climate change policy network they have evolved coordinated collective responses which aim to maximise the impact of their campaigning on EU climate change policy.

Notes

1 Rüdiger Wurzel acknowledges British Academy funding (SG46048). Both authors would like to thank representatives from CAN Europe, Client Earth, EEB, FoE, Greenpeace, The Centre and WWF who gave up their precious time to be interviewed. Nine face-to-face and three telephone interviews were undertaken in November 2008, March 2009 and January 2010. All errors and normative judgements remain the responsibilityof the authors.
2 <http://www.eeb.org/how_the_EEB_works/Index.html> (accessed 12.1.2010).
3 Formerly EPHA – Environment Network.
4 See: <http://www.env-health.org/> (accessed 15.2.2009).
5 FoE's European organisational structure was initially called Coordination Européenne des Amis de la Terre (CEAT).
6 <http://www.europeanclimate.org/index.php?option = com_content&task = view&id = 14&Itemid = 28> (accessed 8.6.2009).
7 <http://www.bellona.org/subjects/1140449074.91/aboutussection_view> (accessed 1.6.2009).
8 <http://www.timetolead.eu/gallery/> (accessed 1.6.2009).
9 <http://www.timetolead.eu/> (accessed 11.1.2010).
10 <http://www.climate-justice-action.org/> (accessed 20.1.2010).

Bibliography

Beyers, J. and Kerremans, B. (2005) 'Bürokraten, Politiker und gesellschaftliche Interessen: Ist die Europäische Union entpolitisiert?', in R. Eising and B. Kohler-Koch (eds), *Interessenpolitik in Europa*, Baden-Baden: Nomos, 123–50.

Bomberg, E. (2007) 'Policy Learning in an Enlarged European Union: Environmental NGOs and New Policy Instruments', *Journal of European Public Policy*, 14(2), 248–68.

Carter, N. (2007) *The Politics of the Environment. Ideas, Activism, Policy*, 2nd edn, Cambridge: Cambridge University Press.

CEC (2001) *European Governance. A White Paper, COM(2001)428 final,25.07.2001*, Brussels: Commission of the European Communities.

Della Porta, D. (2003) *The Europeanisation of Protest: A Typology and Some Empirical Evidence*, EUI Working Paper 2003/18, Florence: European University Institute.

EEB (2000) *A Critical Analysis of the Voluntary Fuel Economy Agreement*, Brussels: European Environmental Bureau.

Eising, R. and Kohler-Koch, B. (2005) 'Interessenpolitik im europäischen Mehrebenensystem', in R. Eising and B. Kohler-Koch (eds), *Interessenpolitik in Europa*, Baden-Baden: Nomos, 11–78.

Eurobarometer (2008) *Attitudes of European Citizens towards the Environment*, Brussels: European Commission, <http://ec.europa.eu/environment/barometer/pdf/report_ebenv_2005_04_22_en.pdf> (accessed 2.2.2009).

Grant, W. (2000) *Pressure Groups and British Politics*, Basingstoke: Macmillan.

Grant W. (2003) 'Pressure Groups and the European Community: An Overview', in S. Mazey and J. Richardson (eds), *Lobbying in the European Community*, Oxford: Oxford University Press, 27–46.

Greenpeace (2008) *energy [r]evolution*, Amsterdam: Greenpeace International.

Greenwood, J. (2003) *Representing Interests in the European Union*, Basingstoke: Palgrave/Macmillan.

Hey, C. and Brendle, U. (1994) *Umweltverbände und EG*, Opladen: Westdeutscher Verlag.

IndyACT, *et al.* (2009) *A Copenhagen Climate Treaty*. Version 1.0, <http://assets.peggy.bluegecko.net/downloads/copenhagen_climate_treaty_060609_1.pdf> (accessed 8.6.2009).

Jordan, A., Wurzel, R. K. W. and Zito, A. P. (2007) 'New Modes of Environmental Governance. Are "New" Environmental Policy Instruments (NEPIs) Supplanting or Supplementing Traditional Tools of Government?', *Politische Vierteljahresschrift*, special issue, 283–98.

Long, T. (1998) 'The Environmental Lobby', in P. Lowe and S. Ward (eds), *British Environmental Policy and Europe*, London: Routledge, 105–18.

Long, T., Slater, L. and Singer, S. (2002) 'WWF: European and Global Climate Policy', in R. Pedler (ed.), *European Union Lobbying: Challenges in the Arena*, Basingstoke: Palgrave, 87–103.

Long, T. and Lörinczi, L. (2009) 'NGOs as Gatekeepers: A Green Vision', in D. Coen and J. Richardson (eds), *Lobbying the European Union*, Oxford: Oxford University Press, 162–79.

Mazey, S. and Richardson, J. (eds) (1993) *Lobbying in the European Community*, Oxford: Oxford University Press.

Richards, J. P. and Heard, J. (2005) 'European Environmental NGOs: Issues, Resources and Strategies in Marine Campaigns', *Environmental Politics*, 14(1), 23–41.

Rucht, D. (1993) 'Think Globally, Act Locally? Needs, Forms and Problems of Cross-National Cooperation among Environmental Groups', in J. Low, D. Liefferink and A. Mol (eds), *European Integration and Environmental Policy*, London: Belhaven, 75–96.

Spiegel Online (2009), *Greenpeace stört königliches Gala-Bankett*, Spiegel Online 17.12.2009, <http://www.spiegel.de/politik/ausland/0,1518,667793,00.html> (accessed 20.12.2009).

Warleigh, A. (2001) ' "Europeanizing" Civil Society: NGOs as Agents of Political Socialisation', *Journal of Common Market Studies*, 39(4), 619–39.

Wurzel, R. K. W. (2008) *The Politics of Emissions Trading in Britain and Germany*, London: Anglo-German Foundation.

Zito, A. and Jacobs, J. E. (2009) 'NGOs, the European Union and the Case of the Environment', in J. Joachim and B. Locher (eds), *Transnational Activism in the UN and the EU*, London: Routledge, 105–20.

Part V

Europe and the wider world

14 A Green New Deal

Framing US climate leadership

Guri Bang and Miranda A. Schreurs

Climate change politics in the United States clearly illustrates the importance of how an issue is framed. For many years under the George W. Bush administration, dominant actors in the federal government framed climate change as a problem that would result in major economic damage by requiring costly changes to U.S. ways of doing business. They argued that significant policy changes should only be made if developing countries – the major emitters of the future – also agreed to take substantial action. There was substantial questioning of climate change science and the seriousness of the climate change threat (McCright and Dunlap 2003; Jacques, Dunlap, and Freeman 2008; Jacques 2009). The end result was a climate policy that was based on a simple no regrets strategy. Basically only actions were taken that would make sense to take anyways, such as measures that would both control air pollution and reduce greenhouse gas (GHG) emissions or that would both cut costs and reduce carbon dioxide (CO_2) emissions – such as energy efficiency improvements. While funding for research and development in some new technologies was made available (e.g. for hydrogen fuel cars), there was little policy action to require major cuts in emissions. Unlike in the European Union (EU) where ecological modernisation is an accepted concept and the greening of the economy came to be seen by many political leaders as not only necessary for dealing with climate change but also as an economic opportunity, in the United States under President Bush, ecological modernisation had no traction. Linking climate change action to sustainable economic development was not accepted as an action guiding norm for climate policy. As a result, internationally, the EU took the lead on pushing for a global climate agreement (Schreurs and Tiberghien 2007; Oberthür and Kelly 2008; Schreurs, Selin, VanDeveer 2009b).

From its start, the Obama administration introduced a different set of policies and reframed how climate change was discussed (Romàn and Carson 2009). The top political leadership – the president, vice-president, and members of the Cabinet – have worked to redefine public perceptions of climate change, embracing the international scientific community's warnings about the implications of inaction. They are working to regain international cognitive and structural leadership on climate change for the United States.

Several questions are addressed in this chapter. Why has the framing of climate change started to change? Was it simply the election of a new president or is it an indication of a deeper change in U.S. politics? How are proponents of a more proactive U.S. role trying to reframe the debate? What are the ways in which the framing of climate change that held sway during the Bush administration is being discredited, altered, and replaced? How difficult will it be to realise the leadership necessary to bring about substantial policy change? The proponents of reframing climate policy as costly and as a threat to U.S. competitiveness were in positions of power for a substantial period of time. They were able to institutionalise many of their views in various policies, programmes, and organisations. How are proponents of a proactive climate policy trying to change and undo this institutionalised status quo in order for the United States to take on an international leadership role?

Actors, interests, institutions, and the framing of ideas

A critical element of democratic politics is the struggle to influence public policies and programmes among actors who hold different interests and beliefs. The stakes involved for different actors are high. For actors associated with carbon-emitting industries, such as the coal, oil, automobile, airline, agriculture, and manufacturing industries, policies designed to reduce CO_2 emissions present a significant challenge to traditional ways of doing business. Many fossil fuel-intensive industries have opposed the introduction of climate policies and programmes. For the community of non-governmental organisations (NGOs) and scientists concerned about the implications of an average warming of global temperatures for long-term human and environmental security, taking action to mitigate GHG emissions is basically a moral obligation (see also Chapter 13 by Wurzel and Connelly). For the insurance, renewable energy, and various hi-tech industries, pursuing policies to reduce GHG emissions is seen as important not only for the environment, but also for business reasons.

Each of these coalitions of actors works to shape or frame how the public and policy makers understand climate change – that is, their cognitive perceptions. To the extent that the public and policy makers can be convinced that climate change science is uncertain and action costly, the 'anti-climate' coalition can delay or prevent the introduction of regulatory policies. In contrast, to the extent that the proponents of 'climate change action' can persuade the public and policy makers of the seriousness of climate change, they are more likely to convince legislators to introduce policies and programmes to improve energy efficiency, promote renewables, and cut GHG emissions (Nisbet 2009).

The coalition of actors that is most successful in shaping policy makers and the public's views may have the ability to not only influence policy outcomes but also to shape political and economic institutions that structure activities in the long term in related fields (Baumgartner and Jones 1993). This includes federal research and development budgets, energy and transportation policies, the budgets and policy priorities of relevant agencies and departments (e.g. the Environmental Protection Agency (EPA), Department of Energy (DOE)), judicial and executive branch appointments, the size of block grants to the states for climate-related activities, among other areas. With a window of opportunity for policy change open after the election of Obama, climate-concerned politicians tried to exploit their agenda-setting privileges in the Congress to promote climate and energy policy change.

Phases of domestic climate change policy

The United States was for long unwilling to take the threat of climate change seriously. There were many factors contributing to this image. In the 1990s, the Global Climate Coalition was formed by industries with the goals of establishing a view of climate change science as uncertain, preventing passage of domestic climate legislation, and blocking the Kyoto Protocol. In many ways, this coalition – now defunct – was very successful. While they were not able to prevent the Clinton administration from signing the protocol, they could take heart that the agreement was never sent to the Senate for ratification. In 1997, the U.S. Senate signalled its unwillingness to support an international climate agreement that did not also require actions by developing countries when it passed the Byrd-Hagel Resolution with a 95–0 vote (Harris 2000). The climate sceptics further strengthened their position with the election of George W. Bush and Richard Cheney. In his first months in office, Bush back-peddled from his campaign pledge to regulate CO_2 as a pollutant and withdrew the United States from the Kyoto Protocol. He argued that participating in Kyoto would put U.S. firms at a competitive disadvantage and cost the economy jobs. In the ensuing years, Washington, D.C. did little to alter the country's heavy reliance on fossil fuels.

Climate policy was limited to voluntary emissions reductions schemes for large emitters, like industry, and subsidies for research, in particular for technology innovation. Neither eco-taxes nor emissions trading were accepted because the administration refused the idea of putting a price on carbon. Beyond this, Congress passed several resolutions and bills that severely limited the ability of agencies involved in climate policy to do their work. They cut funding and tried to prevent agencies like EPA and DOE from doing analysis of options that were being considered under the Kyoto Protocol. Furthermore, the development and application of climate expertise in the EPA was reduced and scientific views warning of climate threats were written out of policy documents. California's efforts to set the country on a new track were blocked. In other words, efforts were made to institutionalise the views held by climate sceptics (Bryner 2008).

International frustration with the United States was symbolised by the outburst of Kevin Conrad, Papua New Guinea's representative at the 2007 Bali Conference where a roadmap for a post-Kyoto agreement was being hammered out and the United States was blocking action. Conrad stated: 'I would ask the United States, we ask for your leadership. But if for some reason you're not willing to lead, leave it to the rest of us. Please get out of the way' (Revkin 2008).

The 2006 midterm election and a changing Congressional debate

The Democrats won the 2006 midterm elections, gaining a majority in both the House and the Senate, and leadership of all Congressional committees. Committee leadership generally means a lot for the ability to form and pursue a policy agenda. The Democratic leadership of the Environment and Public Works and the Energy and Natural Resources Committees in the Senate, and the Energy and Commerce Committee in the House led to a much intensified focus on clean energy and climate change. The Democrats put both climate change and energy security on the agenda in order to overcome resistance to policy change. House Speaker Nancy Pelosi formed a 'Select Committee on Energy Inde pendence and Global Warming' with the intention of focusing attention on the issues and to coordinate lawmaking among committees with relevant jurisdiction (Pelosi 2007). In the first six months after the election, a range of hearings on both climate change and energy security were held, and several bills were introduced, many with bipartisan sponsorship (U.S. Senate 2007).

One former government official said: 'the Congressional staff must be knowledgeable on the issue in order to prioritise it for politicians. There must be a bill in the works to make them focus on the issue, and we have seen more bills being introduced over the past year' (Interview with former Clinton Administration State Department official, 12 June 2007). As of July 2008, lawmakers had introduced more than 235 bills, resolutions, and amendments addressing global climate change and GHG emissions – compared with 106 bills during the previous Congress (2005–6) (Pew Center on Global Climate Change 2008a). The vast majority proposed putting a price on carbon and adopting an emissions trading scheme. In the process of hearings and debates in the Senate, a learning process occurred that positioned emissions trading as the preferred policy instrument.

The climate change discussion in the 110th Congress culminated with a floor debate in June 2008 on Senators Lieberman (I-CT) and Warner's (R-VA) Climate Security Act. This bill sought a bipartisan compromise on major climate and energy proposals. It was the first GHG cap-and-trade bill to come to the Senate floor through regular order. On 6 June, the Senate voted on whether to end debate on the bill by invoking cloture, but the motion was defeated 48–36, falling short of the 60 votes required, and the bill was withdrawn (Pew Center on Global Climate Change 2008b).

The election of Barack Obama: providing leadership from above

The election of Barack Obama as president was widely seen in the environmental community as a strong opportunity for climate and energy policy change in the United States. As a U.S. Senator, Obama was a co-sponsor of close to two dozen climate- and energy-related bills, including the Global Warming Pollution Reduction Act, the most ambitious bill in terms of targets for GHG emissions reductions discussed in the 110th Congress. During his campaign, Obama repeatedly signalled his intent to take the warnings of the Intergovernmental Panel on Climate Change (IPCC) seriously, re-engage in the international climate negotiations, and put the United States on a cleaner and more efficient energy path.

Whereas the Bush administration frequently focused attention on the costs of climate policy action, Obama highlighted the potential benefits action can bring. Shortly after being elected, in late November 2008, Obama began to discuss the idea of a 'Green New Deal'. In his 21 November weekly address as president-elect, Obama explained his Green New Deal:

> it will be a two-year, nationwide effort to jumpstart job creation in America and lay the foundation for a strong and growing economy. We'll put people back to work rebuilding our crumbling roads and bridges, modernizing schools that are failing our children, and building wind farms and solar panels, fuel-efficient cars and the alternative energy technologies that can free us from our dependence on foreign oil and keep our economy competitive in the years ahead.
>
> (Obama 2008)

The idea of a green new deal is similar to what in Europe is called ecological modernisation. It focuses on how economic opportunities can come from developing clean energy sources and shifting society towards a low-carbon economy. Obama was quick to embrace the need for major cuts in GHG emissions as had long been called for in Europe and some states in the United States, like California, Florida and New York. The Obama-Biden New Energy for America Plan, announced in late 2008, made clear that an 80 percent reduction in GHG emissions would be necessary by 2050 and that in order to achieve this, a cap and trading scheme should be introduced (Obama and Biden 2008).

The plan also advocated the need to reduce U.S. oil imports from the Middle East. Obama framed the question of U.S. dependence on Middle East oil as dangerous to U.S national security, bad for the economy, and a threat to the climate. Rather than emphasising policies to promote the exploration of domestic fossil fuel sources as the Bush administration did, he instead sketched out a programme for shifting the United States away from carbon-heavy fossil fuels. The plan called for investments of $150 billion over 10 years in clean energy, doubling energy research and development funding, developing and deploying clean coal technology, revisiting nuclear energy, and a major increase in fuel economy standards.

Once elected, Obama filled his staff with climate change and energy experts. His pick of Joseph Biden as vice-president came in stark contrast with Bush's pick of oil man, Richard Cheney. Biden is a long-term supporter of green initiatives, the only Senator to initially oppose the Byrd-Hagel Resolution when it came up for a vote in the Foreign Relations Committee in 1997 (although under party pressure he did later agree to support it), the sponsor of a 2007 Sense of the Senate Resolution calling on the U.S. to participate in the United Nations climate negotiations, and co-sponsor of several of the bills introduced in the U.S. Senate to initiate a carbon cap and trading system. Nobel-prize winning Steven Chu was appointed as Secretary of Energy, former EPA administrator Carol Browner as Assistant to the President for Climate and Energy, Heather Zikal as Deputy Assistant to the President for Climate and Energy, Lisa Jackson as EPA administrator, Todd Stern as the Administration's climate envoy and chief U.S climate negotiator, Jonathan Pershing as deputy climate envoy, and Nancy Sutley as Chair of the White House Council on Environmental Quality. With these appointments, Obama had picked a team with long-term administrative and political experience and a strong energy and climate expertise, to help develop an executive branch strategy. In doing this, he signalled a sharp shift in his administration's climate policy direction.

During his first week in office, Obama ordered the EPA to revisit a decision made during his predecessor's administration to reject California's request to introduce legislation (AB 1493, the Pavley bill) that would require automobile manufacturers to achieve the 'maximal feasible reduction' of CO_2 emissions from vehicles. He also ordered the Department of Transportation to draw up rules to implement a 2007 law requiring a 40 percent improvement in gas mileage for automobiles and light trucks by 2020. The Bush administration had failed to write up the rules necessary for the law to be implemented (Broder 2009). In April 2009, Obama announced national plans to back the development of high-speed rail corridors in several regions (Knowlton 2009), and in May 2009, plans for new fuel efficiency standards and the first ever federal greenhouse gas standards for automobiles. The plan set a 2016 deadline for meeting a fleet-wide fuel economy standard of 35.5 miles per gallon for models built starting in 2012 (White House Press Office 2009).

In February 2009, Obama pushed an economic stimulus package through Congress. The American Recovery and Reinvestment Act included a total of $787 billion in new spending and tax incentives. The new spending involved about $42 billion in energy-related investments, $21 billion in vehicles/transportation spending (transit assistance, energy-efficient fleets, etc.), $570 million in climate science research spending, and $21 billion in energy-related tax incentives, such as extending the renewable energy production tax credit, and an additional $1.6 billion in Clean Renewable Energy Bonds (Ling and Geman 2009).

Obama's efforts to break with the past and forge a new set of climate priorities can also be found in his 2010 and 2011 budget proposals. The 2010 budget blueprint called for cutting tax breaks for carbon-intensive industries and included objectives to reduce emissions from 2005 levels by 14 percent by

2020, and by 80 percent by 2050. It reaffirmed the campaign promise of a cap and trade programme with 100 percent auctioning of credits, and even daringly included expected revenue (approximately $650 billion between 2012 and 2019) from such a programme on the assumption Congress would pass a climate change bill. Obama proposed spending this fresh money for tax cuts for the middle class and the promotion of new, clean-energy technologies (Marshall 2009). The 2011 budget proposal was formulated at a time when the U.S. government was constrained by a massive deficit. The proposal called for billions in cuts across the government. Thus, for example, the Department of Agriculture budget was to be cut by $1 billion relative to the level enacted in 2010 by Congress. In contrast, the EPA budget was targeted for a smaller cut of $278 million. Meanwhile, the Department of Energy's budget was to be increased by $1.8 billion. Despite the projected cuts at the EPA, the agency requested that Congress increase funding for climate regulatory efforts by $43.5 million. Funding for measures to inventory GHG emissions, implement fuel efficiency standards, write regulations for airlines and other mobile sources of GHGs, and fund carbon capture and sequestration projects were included in the budget (Leber 2010), where the biggest changes to be seen were in the Department of Energy's budget request. Over $2.7 billion in tax subsidies for oil companies were to be slashed from the Department of Energy's budget and new funding was to be allocated for clean-energy projects. Perhaps the greatest controversy in the budget blueprint from an environmental perspective lies in the proposed increases in funding for nuclear energy (an increase to $54.5 billion from $18.5 billion) (Environment News Service 2010).

Facing up to the energy policy challenge is something that has been discussed in Washington, D.C. for 30 years. The Obama team's efforts in his first year in office were directed at framing climate change as a serious threat and linking policy action to the development of a cleaner, greener energy infrastructure that would make the U.S. more energy independent and sustainable. Green energy policy change was portrayed as an economic opportunity, and a possible way out of the financial crisis ailing the country in terms of creating new jobs and securing the states' economies. Still, Obama's efforts to win over sceptics has proven difficult, and conservative forces continue to challenge his new agenda.

Pressuring for change: demanding climate change leadership from below

Efforts to change U.S. climate policies and improve the country's international image became more focused towards the end of the Bush presidency. NGOs and climate experts that found themselves with little ability to influence the political debate in Washington expanded their efforts to educate the public and policy makers about climate change. They launched climate change campaigns and began efforts to win support from non-traditional cooperation partners in the business community. Partnerships formed among various NGOs, including the International Union for Conservation of Nature (IUCN), WWF International, Earth Watch Institute (Europe), and the World Business Council for Sustainable Development that was formed on the eve of the climate summit in Rio de Janiero in 1992. In 1998, the Pew Center on Global Climate Change formed the Business Environmental Leadership Council to highlight the growing number of businesses choosing to introduce measures to address climate change into their operations. A decade later, in January 2007, the Pew Center launched the U.S. Climate Action Partnership (USCAP), an alliance of business and environmental leaders committed to changing federal climate policies. USCAP states: 'In our view, the climate change challenge will create more economic opportunities than risks for the U.S. economy' (USCAP 2010). USCAP represents 26 major firms that have total revenues of close to $2 trillion, a collective workforce approaching $3 million, and operations in all 50 states (Environmental Defense Fund 2009). They presented a blueprint for federal legislation in 2009, and are working in favour of a cap-and-trade approach because 'swift legislative action based on the USCAP solutions-based proposal . . . would encourage innovation, enhance America's energy security, foster economic growth, improve our balance of trade and provide critically needed U.S. leadership on this vital global challenge' (USCAP 2010).

Large firms aware of and affected by regulatory developments in Europe, Japan, and elsewhere see it as an advantage to have a mandatory cap on GHG emissions to even the playing field internationally. They are also concerned about the patchwork of regulations and programmes emerging across the United States at the state and local levels and are increasingly eager to organise this domestic playing field. They want to ensure that they have an ability to influence the shape of pending regulation and that the U.S. remains a player that can shape international outcomes.

After largely disappearing from the political scene for a number of years, defeated presidential candidate Albert Gore, re-emerged as one of the most visible critics of the Bush administration's approach to climate change. His efforts culminated in the widely distributed documentary, *An Inconvenient Truth*, which was released in 2006. In 2007, Gore was awarded the Nobel Peace Prize for his efforts to inform the U.S. and international public about the climate change crisis. In this year he also teamed up with Kevin Wall, Chief Executive Office (CEO) of Control Room and founder of Live Earth Alliance to organise the first seven continent-wide simultaneous climate benefit concerts. They were backed by numerous international NGOs, including Climate Protection, Avaaz, The Climate Group (We're in this Together), and Stop Climate Chaos. Over 150 acts were performed in major cities around the world: New York, London, Sydney, Tokyo, Shanghai, Rio de Janeiro, Johannesburg, and Hamburg with special broadcast events in Antarctica, Kyoto, and Washington, D.C. (Live Earth Alliance). In this way, NGOs worked with film and music stars to bring greater visibility to the climate change problem.

Even in the military growing links are being recognised among energy security, climate change, and national security. For instance, in a recent report from a collaborative project between researchers and military servicemen, admirals and generals concluded that 'Climate change, national security, and energy dependence are a related set of global challenges. The national security consequences of climate change should be fully integrated into national security and national defence strategies' (CNA Corporation 2007).

By mustering support from these significant interest groups that for a variety of reasons are finding links between climate change and their priority areas of concern (e.g. business, national security, energy security) the promoters of an environmentally sustainable energy policy have been able to gain a stronger voice in the policymaking process.

Leadership in cities and the states: climate federalism

Supporters of climate change action also changed the venues where they tried to have influence. Originally their efforts were focused almost exclusively on the federal level. The more entrenched the anti-climate coalition became in Washington, however, the more pro-climate activists turned their attention to effecting change in urban and state governments (Klyza and Sousa 2008). Successes began to accumulate. Numerous mayors indicated that they were willing and interested in introducing their own Kyoto-like targets. In 2005, the mayor of the city of Seattle recognised the importance of what was happening and launched the US Mayors Climate Protection Agreement, giving a collective voice to dispersed activities. Close to 900 mayors had signed the agreement by the time Obama was elected (<http://www.seattle.gov/mayor/climate/>).

Also at the state level, numerous governors and state legislatures indicated their willingness to support renewable energy portfolio standards, green purchasing requirements, and climate change legislation (Rabe 2004, 2006; Schreurs, Selin, VanDeveer 2009a). Most important in this regard is California because of its economic size and unique political right under the Clean Air Act to introduce air pollution legislation that moves beyond federal policies. California attracted considerable attention and expressions of support from other states when it passed AB 1493 (the Pavley Bill), requiring automobile manufacturers to adopt strict CO_2 emission reduction requirements and AB 32, the Global Warming Solutions Act of 2006, setting a state-wide CO_2 emission target: stabilisation of emissions at 1990 levels by 2020 (which is equivalent to a 30 percent below business-as-usual projection given California's rapidly expanding population) (Mazmanian, Jurewitz, and Nelson 2008). In the meantime, New Jersey adopted legislation mandating a series of emission reduction targets: stabilisation at 1990 levels or lower by 2020 and 80 percent below 2006 levels by 2050. A large number of states have now introduced greenhouse gas emission targets (although not all of these have introduced enabling legislation) (Wheeler 2008). It is noteworthy that within his first days in office, Obama participated by video conference in the

Bi-partisan Governors Global Climate Summit organised by California Governor Arnold Schwarzenegger. In doing this he gave his nod of approval to these state-level activities and reached out to governors of both parties who have been active on climate change (Eilperin 2008).

In addition, a majority of states have indicated their intention to join regional GHG emission trading schemes. In late 2005, the Regional Greenhouse Gas Initiative (RGGI) was launched among ten northeastern states. The RGGI covers fossil fuel-fired power plants; trading of permits began in January 2009. The RGGI's target is to stabilise CO_2 emissions between 2009 and 2014, then cut annual emissions by 2.5 percent per year after this for a 10 percent reduction by 2018 in each state. The Western Climate Initiative, covering California, Oregon, Washington, Arizona, Montana, New Mexico, and Utah, and the Canadian provinces of British Columbia, Manitoba, Quebec, and Ontario has a goal of cutting emissions by 15 percent of 2005 levels by 2020 and between 50 percent and 85 percent by 2050. When trading begins in 2012, it will have a far broader coverage than the RGGI as it addresses emissions not only from the electricity sector, but also from transportation, residential, and commercial fuel use.

Other regional emission trading schemes are being developed as well, including the Midwestern Regional Greenhouse Gas Reduction Accord, the Energy Security and Climate Stewardship Platform for the Midwest, and the Western Governors' Association (WGA): Clean and Diversified Energy Initiative, and the Powering the Plains. This patchwork of emerging regional initiatives is an exciting development, but at the same time creates considerable confusion as each initiative has its own emissions goals, targets different industrial sectors, has a different starting period, and is based on a different emissions trading structure. The activities occurring at the local and state level create their own push for federal action that can create some degree of harmonisation among all of these various initiatives.

The pressure for climate policy change from new actor groups and from the sub-national level were central factors pushing for a reframing of climate change at the federal level. The several state and regional emission trading initiatives that developed in part in response to the European carbon emissions trading scheme (ETS) have reinforced tendencies to put emission trading at the centre of U.S. climate policy discussions. In this way, the EU's leadership role in international climate policy has impacted U.S. federal policy developments.

Barriers to US leadership in climate change policy

The emphasis on reframing the climate change issue is in part a recognition of the difficulties in achieving federal policy change. Basically since 1994, a majority of senators and representatives have opposed introducing federal climate policy requiring mandatory emission reductions. In general, more Republicans than Democrats are opposed to action. In addition there is also a regional divide that has become more cemented in U.S. climate politics over time. Politicians from states with a large coal, oil, manufacturing, and/or agricultural industry, regardless of party affiliation, have been inclined to vote against climate legislation because they see it as a threat to their state's economy and jobs. Obama must take the concerns of these lawmakers into account in order to be able to create a climate policy compromise that a majority across party lines in Congress can accept.

Democratic leaders in the 110th and 111th Congresses put climate change and energy security near the top of their agenda. The linkage of energy security with climate change opened up the possibility to argue for changing energy policies and reducing imports of foreign oil in a way that is also climate friendly (Bang 2010). All U.S. politicians agreed that there was an urgent need to reduce oil imports, but there was no agreement as to what the best policy alternatives were. Some argued that energy security concerns make urgent a new energy policy based on developing alternative and environmentally friendly energy sources and technologies. Others argued that the best route to addressing energy security is to enhance the development of domestic fossil fuel sources like coal and oil (Bang 2010). This disagreement was at the centre of Congressional debates, and reinforced the alternative framings of climate change.

Over time a network of moderate, centrist Democrats from the Midwest, Rustbelt and West has developed. This group of approximately 15 senators have a fence-sitting position on climate change, and represent states with a large share of energy-intensive industries and coal-fired utilities. Their support is pivotal if substantial policy change is to be achieved. They have a shared interest in preventing policy changes that will have negative impacts on their states' economies. This network has in the past been a veto player, and will in the future make or break a climate bill in terms of providing the necessary qualified majority on the Senate floor. Any climate bill proposal must be tailored to meet their concerns: to provide realistic alternatives to state economies and workforces that are dependent on fossil fuel energy. In 2008, the group became even more tightly knit as they came together and wrote a letter to the Democratic leadership expressing their concerns with some key issues in the Lieberman-Warner bill, especially regarding international competition, carbon leakage, technology, cost containment, and offsets.[1] Having been dubbed the 'Gang of 15', the Senators' staff met on a regular basis in the spring of 2009 to coordinate their positions for upcoming debates on climate legislation in the 111th Congress (Samuelsohn 2009b).

The standard bearing bill for the climate debate in the 111th Congress was introduced by Representatives Henry Waxman (D-CA) and Edward Markey (D-MA), and passed the House with a vote of 219 212 in June 2009. The bill included four titles. Title I contained provisions related to a federal renewable electricity standard, carbon capture and storage technology, performance standards for new coal-fuelled power plants, a low carbon fuel standard, and smart grid advancement. Title II addressed building, lighting, and appliance energy-efficiency programmes, as well as efficiency standards for the transport sector. Title III proposed a cap–and-trade programme with economy-wide coverage of emission sources over 25,000 tons per year, and emission caps that would reduce aggregate GHG emissions for all covered entities to 3 percent below their 2005 levels in 2012, 18 percent below 2005 levels in 2020, 42 percent below 2005 levels in 2030, and 83 percent below 2005 levels in 2050. Title IV included proposals designed to preserve domestic competitiveness and support workers, provide assistance to consumers, and support domestic and international adaptation initiatives (Pew Center on Global Climate Change 2009).

In the Senate, a similar bill passed the Environment and Public Works Committee in November 2009. Senators Kerry (D-MA), Graham (R-SC), and Lieberman (I-CT) took a lead role in consulting a broad range of senators to find enough common ground for the bill to pass in the Senate before the midterm elections in late 2010.

President Obama dealt with the opposition he faced from lawmakers in Congress to a climate bill by simultaneously pursuing a second route to implementing a federal climate policy. The EPA was directed by the Supreme Court in April 2007 to regulate GHG emissions under the provisions of the Clean Air Act. The Bush administration reacted to this ruling by simply stalling. It did not respond in any substantive way to the Court's ruling for the remainder of its period in office. On 17 April 2009 Environmental Protection Administrator, Lisa Jackson, announced that the EPA proposed an endangerment finding (i.e. that GHG emissions pose a danger to public health and welfare), hence opening up for the possibility of developing regulation under existing law. In December 2009, as the Copenhagen Climate Summit started, the White House finalised the endangerment finding and EPA presented rules for improving GHG standards for on-road vehicles and large stationary emission sources (above 25 000 tons/year). Jackson said:

> Business leaders, security experts, government officials, concerned citizens and the United States Supreme Court have called for enduring, pragmatic solutions to reduce the greenhouse gas pollution that is causing climate change. This continues our work towards clean energy reform that will cut GHGs and reduce the dependence on foreign oil that threatens our national security and our economy. (Statement by Jackson, 7 December 2009)

These new regulations are certain to meet a range of lawsuits before they can be implemented. The Obama administration's finding that GHGs endanger public health and welfare was a leverage for pushing reluctant lawmakers and industries towards support of climate legislation that would be more flexible – such as a cap-and-trade scheme – than regulations crafted by the EPA. Both Obama and Jackson repeatedly said that legislative action is much preferred to regulations developed under existing law. However, they also said that inaction was no longer an option, and if Congress failed to proceed on the issue the administration had no option but to start regulating emissions under the Clean Air Act. The very idea that the EPA will take charge of developing new regulations is unattractive to many lawmakers who either want to make their own mark on policy or prevent the administration from gaining so much power. The EPA endangerment finding therefore serves as an extra encouragement for Congress to take charge of the process, and develop an acceptable compromise before EPA gets too far in implementing policies that set the standard for the debate in a different place than many Congressmen and women would like.

Entrepreneurial leadership? Forging a post-Kyoto agreement

At the international scene the hopes went up among many foreign leaders, especially in Europe, that with Obama in the White House the United States could again take a leadership position in the difficult international negotiations about a post-Kyoto agreement. The capacities in the United States in terms of knowledge, wealth, and power are enormous. Traditionally, the United States uses its foreign policy to shape the policy of other countries in ways favourable to or in line with U.S. goals and interests. By re-entering the climate change negotiations in a more proactive manner, the Obama administration was eager not only to cooperate with other states willing to see policy action, but to try to frame the international climate change debate in directions that will align with the country's domestic priorities.

The Clinton administration's mistake at Kyoto was that they signed on to a treaty without securing the support of a sufficient number of members of the Senate for ratification. The Obama administration was acutely aware that a similar mistake must be avoided. As Todd Stern stated: 'I don't want to bring home a dead-on-arrival agreement. We tried that [in Kyoto]. It didn't do the world a lot of good.' (Samuelsohn 2009a). The U.S. Constitution grants Congress the right to advice and consent when it comes to treaty making. This means that 67 votes will be necessary to ratify a post-Kyoto treaty in the Senate. In addition, any treaty that is ratified requires passage of enabling legislation in both houses of Congress to specify exactly how the objectives and requirements of the treaty are to be fulfilled through domestic policy programmes.

It is important to realise, therefore, that the United States normally takes leadership in international negotiations and ratifies international agreements only when domestic policy is settled on the issue in question – most preferably through legislation enacted by Congress and implemented by governmental agencies (DeSombre 2000, Fisher 2004). This means that the Obama administration's first priority will have to be at the domestic level. Global partners acknowledge the importance of re-engaging the United States to improve the effectiveness of a post-Kyoto agreement. At the Copenhagen Climate Summit, this was reflected in the end result. Obama took leadership in brokering the Copenhagen Accord with the leaders of China, India, Brazil and South Africa. The deal broke through years of negotiating gridlock, and reflected three objectives that are critical priorities for the domestic U.S. policy debate. First, it includes (voluntary) GHG emissions reduction targets for all of the world's big emitters, a central objective since the adoption of the Byrd-Hagel resolution in the Senate in 1997. Second, it calls for the establishment of ways of measuring and verifying all countries' emissions cuts against their commitments and thereby safeguarding to at least some extent against carbon leakage. Finally, it opens avenues for investments and financing of mitigation and adaptation measures in developing countries that would help promote a business-smart transition to clean-energy technologies.

Two months after the Copenhagen Accord was negotiated, Obama announced that the US government would reduce its GHG emissions by 28 percent by 2020 (compared to 2008) (Sutley 2010). The White House has continued to take the initiative, keeping pressure on the Congress to act so that it can try to lead internationally.

Conclusion

With the election of Obama, the United States appears to be willing to engage more actively and constructively in international climate talks. Calls for a more active U.S. role in addressing climate change have not simply emanated from the global community, but also from within: from the grassroots level, from a Democratically controlled Congress, and from within the business community.

What is so fascinating is how the framing of an issue can be so radically changed. For more than a decade, opponents of major policy change had the upper hand. With a majority in Congress and a pro-oil presidency, climate change opponents shaped the climate change debate in ways that would limit the likelihood of major policy changes. The views of climate science sceptics were emphasised, the costs of climate change action highlighted, and the need to enhance energy security through the development of domestic fossil fuel sources pushed.

Over time, the proponents of action have altered how they talk about climate change. Climate change is no longer simply portrayed as an environmental threat, but also as an economic opportunity. In finding new framings and new ways of linking climate change to other policy priority areas, proponents of action have been able to widen their circle, bringing new supporters into their increasingly diverse coalition. Climate change is back on the agenda despite the strong efforts of conservative interests to undermine the Obama administration's initiatives.

Note

1 Letter to Senators Reid and Boxer from Sens. Rockefeller Jr., Stabenow, Levin, Lincoln, Pryor, Webb, Bayh, McCaskill, Nelson, and Brown. June 2008.

Bibliography

Bang, G. (2010) 'Energy Security and Climate Change: Triggers for Energy Policy Change in the United States?', *Energy Policy*, 38 (4): 1645–53.

Baumgartner, F. R. and Jones, B. D. (1993) *Agendas and Instability in American Politics*, Chicago: University of Chicago Press.

Broder, J. M. (2009) 'Obama Directs Regulators to Tighten Auto Rules', *New York Times*, January 26.

Bryner, G. (2008) 'Failure and Opportunity: Environmental Groups in US Climate Change Policy', *Environmental Politics*, 17(2): 319–36.

CNA Corporation (2007) *National Security and the Threat of Climate Change. Report*.

DeSombre, D. E. (2000) *Domestic Sources of International Environmental Policy. Industry, Environmentalists, and U.S. Power*, Cambridge, Mass.: MIT Press.

Eilperin, J. (2008) 'Obama Sends a Message on Climate Change to Governors', Washingtonpost.com, November 18. Available HTTP: <http://voices.washingtonpost.com/44/2008/11/18/obama_sends_a_message_to_gover.html>

Environmental Defense Fund (2009) 'Blueprint Lays Out Clear Path for Climate Action', April 20. Available HTTP: <http://www.edf.org/article.cfm?contentID = 5828>

Environment News Service (2010) 'Obama's 2011 Budget Trims Environment, Fattens Energy Spending', February 1. Available HTTP: <http://www.ens-newswire.com/ens/feb2010/2010-02-01-02.html>

Fisher, D. (2004) *National Governance and the Global Climate Change Regime*, Lanham, MD: Rowman and Littlefield Publishers.

Harris, P. G. (2000) *Climate Change and American Foreign Policy*, New York: St. Martin's Press.

Jacques, P. J. (2009) *Environmental Skepticism: Ecology, Power and Public Life*, Aldershot: Ashgate.

Jacques, P. J., Dunlap, R. E. and Freeman, M. (2008) 'The Organization of Denial: Conservative Think Tanks and Environmental Skepticism', *Environmental Politics*, 17: 349–85.

Klyza, C. M. and Sousa, D. (2008) *American Environmental Policy, 1996–2006: Beyond Gridlock*, Cambridge, Mass.: Massachusetts Institute of Technology Press.

Knowlton, B. (2009) 'Obama Seeks High Speed Rail System Across U.S', *New York Times*. April 16. Available HTTP: <http://www.nytimes.com/2009/04/17/us/politics/17train.html>

Leber, J. (2010) 'Obama Budget Pushes Climate Regulations Forward,' *Climate Wire, E&E News Service*, 2 February. Available HTTP: <http://www.eenews.net/public/climatewire/2010/02/02/2>

Ling, K. and Geman, B. (2009) 'Majority of Stimulus Provisions Protected from Hatchet', *E&E News Service*. February 13.

Live Earth Alliance Available HTTP: <http://liveearth.org/event.php>

Marshall, C. (2009) 'A Budget Plan that Stimulates a "Cap-and-Tax" Climate Debate', *E&E News Service*. February 27.

Mazmanian, D. A., Jurewitz, J. and Nelson, H. (2008) 'California's Climate Change Policy: The Case of a Subnational State Actor Tackling Climate Change', *The Journal of Environment and Development*, 17(4), 401–23.

McCright, A. M. and Dunlap, R. E. (2003) 'Defeating Kyoto: The Conservative Movement's Impact on US Climate Change Policy', *Social Problems*, 50(3), 348–73.

Nisbet, M. C. (2009) 'Communicating Climate Change: Why Frames Matter for Public Engagement', *Environment, Science and Policy for Sustainable Development.* March, April. Available HTTP: <http://www.environmentmagazine.org/Archives/ Back%20Issues/March-April%202009/Nisbet-full.html>

Obama, B. (2008) Available HTTP: <http://change.gov/newsroom/entry/2_5_million_ jobs/>

Obama, B. and Biden, J. (2008) Available HTTP: <http://change.gov/agenda/ energy_and_environment_agenda/>

Oberthür, S. and Kelly, C. R. (2008) 'EU Leadership in International Climate Policy: Achievements and Challenges', *The International Spectator*, 43(3): 35–50.

Pelosi, N. (2007) '100 Hours agenda and the Select Committee on Energy Independence and Global Warming', Memo.

Pew Center on Global Climate Change (2008a) 'Economy-wide Cap-and-Trade Proposals in the 110th Congress', Available HTTP: <http://www.pewclimate.org/ federal/analysis/congress/110/cap-trade-bills>

Pew Center on Global Climate Change (2008b) 'Analysis of the Lieberman-Warner Climate Security Act of 2008', Available HTTP: <http://www.pewclimate.org/ analysis/l-w>

Pew Center on Global Climate Change (2009) 'Analysis of the Waxman-Markey American Clean Energy and Security Act of 2009. March 31', Available HTTP: <http://www.pewclimate.org/acesa>

Rabe, B. (2004) *Statehouse and Greenhouse: The Emerging Politics of American Climate Change Policy*, Washington, DC: Brookings Institution Press.

Rabe, B. (2006) *Race to the Top: The Expanding Role of U.S. State Renewable Portfolio Standards*. Washington, DC: Pew Center on Global Climate Change.

Revkin, A. C. (2008) 'Issuing a Bold Challenge to the U.S. over Climate', *New York Times*, January 22.

Romàn, M. and Carson, M. (2009) *Sea Change: US Climate Policy Prospects Under the Obama Administration,* The Commission on Sustainable Development, Office of the Prime Minister (Regeringskansliet), Sweden.

Samuelsohn, D. (2009a) 'Obama Envoy Urges Congress to Act before Copenhagen Talks', *E&E News Service.* 3 March.

Samuelsohn, D. (2009b) 'Senate Cap-and-Trade Boosters Still Searching for Path to 60 Votes,' *E&E News Service.* February 10.

Schreurs, M. A., Selin, H. and VanDeveer, S. D. (eds) (2009a) *Trans-Atlantic Environment and Energy Politics: Comparative and International Perspectives*, Aldershot: Ashgate Press.

Schreurs, M. A., Selin, H. and VanDeveer, S. D. (2009b) 'Conflict and Cooperation in Transatlantic Climate Politics: Different Stories at Different Levels,' in M. A. Schreurs, H. Selin and S. D. VanDeveer (eds), *Trans-Atlantic Environment and Energy Politics: Comparative and International Perspectives*, Aldershot: Ashgate Press, 165–86.

Schreurs, M. A. and Tiberghien, Y. (2007) 'Multi-level Reinforcement: Explaining EU Leadership in Climate Change Mitigation', *Global Environmental Politics*, 7(4): 19–46.

Sutley, N. M. (2010) 'Leading by Example – Making the Federal Government More Sustainable', February 4, Available HTTP: <http://www.whitehouse.gov/ blog/2010/02/04/leading-example-making-federal-government-more-sustainable>

U.S. Climate Action Partnership (USCAP) (2010) 'A Call for Action: Consensus Principles and Recommendations from the U.S. Climate Action Partnership, A Business and NGO Partnership', *Report*, Washington, DC.

U.S. Climate Action Partnership (USCAP) (2010) http://www.us-cap.org/

U.S. Senate (2007) 'Overview of Active Legislation in the 110th Congress,' Available HTTP: <http://www.senate.gov/pagelayout/legislative/b_three_sections_with_teasers/active_leg_page.htm>

Wheeler, S. M. (2008) 'State and Municipal Climate Change Plans', *Journal of American Planning Association*, 74(4), 481–96.

White House Press Office (2009) 'Press Background Briefing on White House Announcement on Auto Emissions and Efficiency Standards,' May 18. Accessed from: <http://www.whitehouse.gov/the_press_office/Background-Briefing-on-Auto-Emissions-and-Efficiency-Standards>

15 Towards a new world order for climate change

China and the European Union's leadership ambition

Xiudian Dai and Zhiping Diao

Introduction

Traditional Chinese thinking holds that human development and nature are in 'one' (harmony, or 天人合一). The notion of harmony between nature and society suggests that the ancient Chinese were already aware of the importance of the ecological system to human life.

In order to boost agricultural production at all costs, Mao Zedong told his nation that human beings will eventually conquer nature (人定胜天). Contrary to this ambition, a much damaged environment fought back with numerous natural disasters. In a similar vein, Deng Xiaoping's economic reform and opening up policies turned China into a twenty-first century world factory, which is now warming up and waiting to be saved before it reaches 'burning' point. Will China succeed in pursuing economic development without destroying the long-perceived harmony between human beings and the environment? What impact does China have upon the international politics of climate change, and vice versa? Especially, what opportunities does China bring to the European Union (EU) for the latter to strengthen its global leadership in fighting climate change?

It is generally agreed that China's energy use will rapidly increase greenhouse gas emissions (GHGEs) at the global level (Konan and Zhang 2008) and that, therefore, the success of any global effort to address global climate change requires the active cooperation of all big GHGE emitters including China (Siddiqi 2008). On the other hand, international support is indispensable for China to achieve the dual goals of mitigating climate change and sustainable development, namely, a low-carbon economy (Ding, Dai, and Zhao 2008). In the view of the EU, China is not merely a contributor to global warming but also a contributor to global solutions to climate change problems. It is not inconceivable for EU–China relations in the field of climate change to develop into a win-win situation: the EU needs China on board to help achieve a post-Kyoto deal, while China recognises that the EU can offer China the latest clean-energy technologies thus reducing GHGE.

This chapter first looks into China's internal policy on climate change for the simple reason that the role of domestic policy in limiting the growth of

GHGE in developing countries is seen as crucial (Jotzo, 2008). This includes, beginning with the next section, a brief survey of the Chinese attitude towards the issue of climate change, before turning to the evolution of the Chinese climate change policy, institutional responses and the question of whether ecological modernisation constitutes a centrepiece of the Chinese policy. Secondly, this chapter analyses the interplay between China and the international community in climate change politics, with a focus on EU–China cooperation. This is followed by a discussion on China's implementation of its international climate change obligations, before concluding with an overall assessment of the extent to which cooperation between the EU and China has impacted upon the shaping of a new world order for climate change.

Chinese attitudes towards climate change

In international diplomacy, the Chinese view is that environmental degradation and climate change are by-products of industrialisation and economic growth. China is also convinced that without the ability to pollute it will forsake the right to grow in the way that developed countries have (McGregor 2007a).

The Chinese official attitude towards climate change is well summarised in a speech by President Hu Jintao, who highlights three key points: (a) China continues to be preoccupied with economic development and improving people's living standard before the completion of industrialisation and modernisation; (b) China's average emission level (and accumulated emissions), per capita is relatively low and much of its emissions are generated through meeting the basic needs of citizens' everyday life; (c) China today is responsible for an increasingly higher level of emissions deriving not from products manufactured for the domestic market, but from the international division of labour and international transfer of manufacturing into the country (Hu 2008). The notion of 'equal emission rights' at the international, national and individual levels is regarded as the most important principle to be advocated in dealing with climate change (Wang 2008).

Chinese views on the relationship between economic development and climate change are not entirely unfounded. Although China was estimated to have generated more GHGEs than the EU and USA in national total during the year 2005[1] (see Table 15.1) the per capita amount for China was significantly lower than that for the EU and the USA. Similarly, the level of China's electricity consumption per capital in 2005 was significantly lower than that of the EU and the US. The per capita share argument is also noted in many independent analyses (for instance, Brenton 1994; Dobson 2003; Grubb *et al* 1999).

China is increasingly coming under the spotlight, though. According to figures from the Netherlands Environmental Assessment Agency, China alone is currently responsible for nearly a quarter (24 per cent) of the total amount of CO_2 generated in the world, followed by the US (22 per cent) and the EU (12 per cent) (quoted in Watts 2009). In order to halt global warming,

Table 13.1 Selected statistics for China, EU and USA (2005)

	China	EU-27	USA
Population (millions)	1,305	491	297
GDP per capita (US$)	4,110	33,523	41,680
Electricity consumption per capita (kWh per capita)	1,718	5,616	13,698
Greenhouse gas emissions (metric tons CO_2e)	7,527	5,157	7,282
Greenhouse gas emissions per capita (metric tons per capita)	6	10.5	25

Sources: Figures for EU-27 are from CEC (2008), of which GDP figure was converted from euro at the rate of €1=$1.4265. Figures for China and the USA are from Leggett, Logan and Mackey (2008).

Note: 'CO_2e', or 'carbon dioxide equivalents', is the amount of greenhouse gases according to their estimated effects on global warming over a 100-year period.

'[d]eveloping countries, such as China and India, will also need to start limiting the growth in their emissions' (CEC 2007a: 5).

Regarding China's attitude towards a post-Kyoto deal, there are two leading views among Chinese commentators (Jacobson 2009). One school believes that China will accept a voluntary national target for emissions reduction in the event of the US adopting a binding target. The second view suggests that Beijing will not accept any emissions reduction target because of its primary concern with Party and national interests, which are both deeply embedded in a commitment to uninterrupted economic growth.

Phases of Chinese climate change policy

Chinese climate change policy can be divided into four main phases: (1) prior to the early 1990s: the absence of climate change from the official agenda; (2) early 1990s–2003: official recognition of climate change as an important issue; 3) 2003–7: a new vision on sustainable development; (4) since 2007: a proactive and comprehensive climate change policy.

The distinctive path of China's economic reform since the late 1970s has placed economic growth above environmental protection. It is therefore not surprising that in the first phase the Chinese climate change policy was characterised by the absence of the issue from China's official agenda.

It is during the second phase (early 1990s–2003) that climate change became recognised as an important issue in China's official agenda. This was due to two factors. Internally, a decade of exploitation of natural resources and growth in energy consumption to support economic development had brought many devastating natural disasters to China. In particular, China, along with India and other developing countries, 'became concerned about the possible disruption which changes in weather patterns could bring to intensive agriculture' (Brenton 1994: 180). Externally, this period coincided with the fact that climate change had become a hot topic for international politics, as highlighted by the 1992 UN Rio conference and the 1997 Kyoto Protocol. As the world's largest developing nation, China naturally became a new focus of international attention in the climate change debate. Key to this phase was the publication of the White Paper, *China's 21st Century Agenda: The Chinese Population, Environment and Development in the 21st Century*, in March 1994, as China's response to the UN Rio Declaration. Chapter 18 of the White Paper calls for the protection of the atmosphere with measures including: (a) preventing and controlling atmospheric pollution and acid rain; (b) preventing ozone loss; (c) controlling emissions of greenhouse gasses; and (d) developing systems for monitoring and forecasting climate change (State Council 1994).

The third phase, 2003–7, was a period when China embarked upon a new vision of sustainable development. In *China's Sustainable Development Action Plan for the Early 21st Century* of 2003, the Chinese government presented a new agenda on sustainable development, which was to be achieved through the strategic transition from an economy of high levels of energy consumption, high levels of pollution and low levels of efficiency to one that is supported by low levels of energy consumption, low levels of pollution and high levels of efficiency (State Council 2003). The title of this policy document suggests that sustainable development had replaced economic development as a priority.

More recently, into the latest phase of China's climate change policy (2007 and onward), the government came up with a comprehensive climate change policy, namely, *China's National Climate Change Programme*, published by the National Development and Reform Commission (NDRC) in 2007, followed by the release in 2008 of *China's Policy and Actions in Response to Climate Change* by the State Council. The role of new technologies was believed to be important as suggested by China's Scientific & Technological Actions on Climate Change (Ministry of Science and Technology, National Development and Reform Commission, Ministry of Foreign Affairs, *et al.* 2007) and a sense of urgency for tackling the challenges of energy shortage and heavy reliance upon fossil fuels was expressed by the government in China's Energy Conditions and Policies (State Council 2007).

In an attempt to raise its bargaining power in the run up to a possible post-Kyoto deal at the 2009 Copenhagen climate conference, the Chinese policy community proposed the idea of levying a climate change tariff on companies buying products made in China. More specifically, according to the Chinese proposal, 'importers of Chinese-made goods should be responsible for the carbon dioxide emitted during their manufacture' (BBC 2009). While being controversial, this idea has certainly placed China right in the centre of the international politics of post-Kyoto climate change. It is rather ironic that an opposing idea had been voiced by Nicolas Sarkozy during a speech in Beijing. Sarkozy warned his Chinese audience that the EU could penalize cheap imports from countries with a high level of GHGEs in order to protect EU companies in meeting strict environmental standards imposed upon them (Barber and Dickie 2007).

Institutional responses, policy instruments and programmes

Institutional responses

The importance attached to the climate change issue by the Chinese government is in part reflected in the process of institutional changes. This process has involved different 'homes' for the National Coordination Committee for Climate Change (NCCCC) within the central government hierarchy:

(1) The State Council sub-committee stage (1990–98). The NCCCC was initially attached to the Environmental Protection Committee of the State Council and chaired by then State Councillor Song Jian.
(2) The NDRC stage (1998–2007). During the central government reorganisations in March 1998, the NCCCC was given more power by the appointment of Mr Zeng Peiyan, Chairman of National Development and Planning Committee (NDPC, later re-named the NDRC). Due to its 're-housing' into the all-mighty NDRC, the NCCCC became better positioned to achieve coordination over a dozen government ministries/ bureaus.
(3) The State Council (or Cabinet) stage (2007–present). In June 2007, the State Council decided to establish the National Leading Group for Climate Change (NLGCC), chaired by the serving Premier. The NLGCC also functions as the National Leading Group for Energy and Emissions Reduction (NLGEER). The NDRC now serves as the secretariat for both the NLGCC and the NLGEER. Members of the NLGEER include State Councillors and about 30 heads of ministries/commissions and central government bureaus.

The mission of the Leading Group (in the capacity of both the NLGCC and the NLGEER) includes: (1) formulating China's national policy and strategy towards climate change, energy saving and emissions reduction; (2) coordinating national efforts in taking on the challenges posed by climate change; (3) scrutinising international cooperation and negotiations.

The establishment of the NLGCC brought national coordination over the climate change issue right to the top of the decision-making system – the cabinet level. This highlights both the importance and complexity of the climate change issue – it touches upon a wider array of policy areas, hence the need for the involvement of many government agencies. Cabinet-level coordination is especially necessary in view of 'continuous tug of war and turf fight battle' between the powerful NDRC, which plays a leading domestic role in climate change, and the Ministry of Foreign Affairs in charge of the country's international negotiations for climate change (Jacobson 2009: 7).

Policy instruments and programmes

China has primarily resorted to the use of traditional tools as environmental and climate change policy instruments, such as legislations/regulations, central government planning and government-sponsored programmes and projects.

Following the Environmental Protection Law a plethora of legislations and regulations have been passed by the Chinese legislature (the NPC or National People's Congress) and the Chinese cabinet (the State Council) with regards to various aspects of environmental protection and energy use (see Table 15.2).

In addition to policies and legislations, China has launched a wide range of programmes and projects to address environmental and climate change challenges.

New energy projects. Despite the wide protest and warnings of potential ecological risks, the State Council went ahead with the Three Gorges Dam Project to boost hydropower generation. This was complemented by another large-scale and multi-annual project, namely, the 'Southern Water to the North' project. On completion, this project will help solve the water shortage problem in northern China as well as provide new opportunities for generating hydropower. By 2007, China generated more hydroelectricity (483 billion kilowatts) than any other country. China also leads the world in the installation of solar power panels.

Table 15.2 Selected environmental laws and regulations of China

Title of law/regulation	Reference	Year of pass
The Recycling Economy Promotion Law	NPC Standing Committee	2008
Public Sector Energy Saving Regulation	State Council Degree, No.531	2008
Civilian Building Energy Saving Regulation	State Council Decree, No.530	2008
Renewable Energy Law	NPC Standing Committee	2005
The Prevention and Control of Atmospheric Pollution Law	NPC Standing Committee	2000
Cleaner Production Promotion Law	NPC Standing Committee	2002
Law on Energy Conservation	NPC Standing Committee	1997
Law on the Coal Industry	NPC Standing Committee	1996
Law on the Prevention and Control of Environmental Pollution by Solid State Waste	NPC Standing Committee	1995
Environmental Protection Law	NPC Standing Committee	1979; (revised 1989)

In addition, China has been promoting the development of nuclear power stations, which were to be constructed largely by foreign companies. In its *Medium and Long-term Development Planning for Nuclear Energy*, published in 2007, the Chinese government announced that a total of 40 million kilowatts of electricity by 2020, accounting for 4 per cent of total electricity, was to be generated through nuclear power stations. Given that over 20 provinces have already embarked upon nuclear power projects, it is believed that the total amount of nuclear energy to be generated by 2020 will exceed 70 million kilowatts (Yang 2009). A Chinese expert was quoted as saying that nuclear energy is the only possible solution to the problem of achieving GHGEs reduction and environmental protection (ibid.). China's thirst for nuclear energy showed no sign of abating during the global credit crunch.

Energy-saving projects. The Chinese government, through policy, regulatory and market measures, encouraged efficient use of energy by the public sector, private sector and individuals. Showing an interest in experimenting with new environmental policy instruments (NEPIs), China has used benchmarking to assist achieving government goals for efficient energy use. At the international level, China has a treaty obligation to provide the international community with national data on climate change. In part to fulfil this obligation, the NDRC and National Statistic Bureau published the *Communiqué on the Energy Consumption of Thousand Firms* in 2007. Through this Communiqué the Chinese government benchmarked domestic indicators of climate change against international counterparts thus to demonstrate the progress that the country had made and the gaps between China and the international community in meeting climate change targets.

Benchmarking, which is widely used in the EU as a tool for governance, has also been adopted by China to assist in helping to achieve its policy goals. For instance, the Chinese government has planned to roll out a national programme to promote low-carbon demonstration areas. In contrast with previous practices, this new programme focuses on the 'efficiency' levels, instead of the amount, of energy consumption thus offering those areas with energy-intensive firms a chance to become 'low-carbon demonstration areas', as long as they have an improved energy-efficiency level (compared with their own record).

Climate change as a threat and opportunity?

There is no doubt that China is becoming increasingly threatened by the consequences of climate change. Over the last 100 years, average annual temperature has increased by 0.5C to 0.8C in China, which was in part manifested in the fact that, during the period 1986 to 2005, China experienced 20 'warm winters' across the country (NDRC 2007: 4). Increasingly, people living in northern Chinese cities find their thick winter clothes redundant. On the other hand, radical weather change sometimes brought severe hazards. For instance, in December 2007, southern China was brought to a standstill by heavy snow, which had never happened in local residents' living memory. For the last half century, for example, glacial areas in the northwest of China have decreased by 21 per cent and the sea level along the coastal areas in China has been rising by an average of 2.5mm per year (ibid.: 5). Can China effectively address the challenges posed by global climate change, part of which is of its own making?

Testimony of the Beijing Olympics

Prior to and during the Beijing Olympic Games, the Chinese government implemented a number of measures including closing down or pausing production in many production plants (for instance, Capital Steel); encouraging the use of public transport (through reduction of bus and underground fares); completing a new underground link between the airport and the city centre; and launching a new express railway link between Beijing and Tianjin, two large and neighbouring municipalities (aimed at reducing car journeys).

In addition to symbolic politics, there exist many challenges to the Chinese climate change agenda. Central government policy and regulations stipulate that excessively energy-hungry enterprises would have to be dealt with, including closure as an ultimate solution. There are many instances of creativity in getting round regulations. For example, in a northwest city a large-scale brick making factory managed to stay operational by demonstrating that it had substantially reduced the level of energy use to become energy efficient. What actually happened was that the factory installed its in-house electricity generators, which produced electricity that did not get officially counted (Interview A).[2] Such cases of 'smart' performance are typical manifestations of what is described by some as a battle between Beijing and provincial/municipal authorities over implementing the central government's energy and pollution standards (McGregor 2007b). To the central government, a key indicator for judging the performance of local government officials is, undoubtedly, the level of economic growth in their respective areas. Until this is changed, local government officials will continue to place priority to economic growth, rather than mitigating climate change.

Green shoots of ecological modernisation?

The Municipal Government of Chengdu, capital city of southwestern province Sichuan, recently published new regulations on traffic control in the urban area. From the beginning of May 2009, motor vehicles failing to meet the local government's GHGE standard will not be permitted to enter areas within the third ring road. In addition, Chengdu has also decided to completely switch off coal burning within the urban areas (Interview C). These measures contribute in part to an emerging local agenda towards ecological modernisation.

Sichuan Province is endowed with rich tourism resources. The much-loved Chinese pandas live in Sichuan and some of the world's most spectacular attractions, such as the *Jiuzhaigou* scenery zone and the Emei Mountains as well as the numerous historical heritages can all be found there. As capital of China's most populous province, Chengdu is well positioned to gain from putting in place an active ecological modernisation agenda. Chengdu's commitment to moving away from old ways of economic growth is also indicated by the establishment of a large-scale hi-tech zone:

> With a focus on software development outside the city, the new hi-tech zone is merely 20 minutes of driving from the local airport thus substantially reducing road traffic to the city centre. In addition, software design rather than hardware manufacturing will fit better with our clean development strategy. (Interview D)

Chengdu is not alone in experimenting with ecological modernisation. For generations the local economy of Yangquan in Shanxi Province has been dominated by coal mining, iron and steel production and coal-fired electricity supply – industrial activities revolve around coal. For the local population of 1.3 million, Yangquan was becoming increasingly uninhabitable and ecological modernisation emerged to be a sensible choice. However, Yangquan and coal are almost synonymous – it would be impossible to even think about abandoning coal mining for the sake of climate change:

> No matter how the climate might change, coal mining will remain strategically necessary for at least the next 50 years. Virtually every village in the region has at least one small coal mine. Have a look at the brand new clusters of buildings in Mining District erected in recent years – they are evidence of Yangquan prospering from coal; hundreds of coal mine bosses [*mei laoban*, as widely known to the Chinese] have also bought expensive houses in places such as Beijing and Qingdao using the proceeds from coal – they like the money from coal but do not like to live in the place where coal is produced. (Interview B)

Faced with the challenges, Yangquan is beginning to embark upon a new course of industrial restructuring with ecological modernisation in mind. Yangquan Steel, for example, in the city centre was recently closed down and the factory site has been turned into a large communal park. After cooling down electricity generators, warm water is reused for growing fish and for boosting domestic central heating during the winter season. These are small measures but represent the beginning of an awareness of ecological modernisation in China's hinterland.

EU–China cooperation and the new world environmental order

China's evolving domestic agenda indicates a growing level of her willingness to become an active player in international climate change politics. To a certain extent, what China wishes to do, or not to do, will have significant implications: the establishment of 'a new world environmental order . . . will depend a lot on how China's environment market and innovative technologies are explored . . .' (Liu 2009: 9). In the meantime, this new world environmental order will also depend to a considerable extent on how China interacts with other leading players. The EU in particular was poised to demonstrate an international leadership role in the process of tense politicking related to a much anticipated post-Kyoto deal at the Copenhagen climate conference in December 2009. In reality, however, the EU failed to live up to the international expectation in terms of facilitating a new and legally binding climate framework. The EU's long-term cooperation with China in climate policy did not produce a close pact between the two parties with a view to influencing global agenda setting in December 2009.

EU–China cooperation on climate change

In June 2000 former President Jiang Zemin claimed that 'China's participation is a prerequisite for tackling critical issues such as global climate change, control of desertification and protection of biodiversity' (quoted in Xu 2004). This was echoed by the European Commission: 'As a major emitter of greenhouse gases, China's active participation in the debate on this subject [climate change] is vital' (CEC 2007b: 7).

In recent years, the EU has adopted a policy of engagement towards China. Through its dialogue and cooperation with China, the EU has effectively extended its global leadership position by actively pursuing a dialogue and cooperation programme with the Chinese. The European Commission was delighted to note that '[t]here is a genuine wish among policymakers in China to learn from EU experience . . .' (CEC 2007b: 7). The importance of the EU to the Chinese is explained by two main points. First, the EU is perceived to have the potential to act as a counterbalance to US hegemony in global issues (Barber 2009). Second, the EU has already become China's largest trading partner. In short, it is a type of structural leadership that China expects the EU to play. In climate change politics, the opting out by the US from international commitment has certainly reinforced the EU's global leadership position. It is not surprising that the new Obama administration is catching up with the EU by promoting a similar partnership deal with China on climate change (Goldenberg 2009).

Political and Institutional Structure. The annual EU–China Summit serves as the most important political structure to the development of bilateral relations. At the 8th EU–China Summit held in Beijing in September 2005, political leaders from the two sides agreed upon the Joint Declaration on Climate Change. This Joint Declaration heralded the official launch of the EU–China Partnership on Climate Change. Through this Partnership the EU and China have created a political framework for promoting bilateral activities in the field of climate change.

In successive EU–China summits, the issue of climate change has featured high on the political agenda. At the ninth EU–China Summit held in Helsinki in September 2006, political leaders from the EU and China agreed to further strengthen the dialogue and cooperation in tackling climate change. They also agreed that an integrated approach to climate change and energy is crucial, and particularly underlined the need to exploit the synergies between the promotion of energy security, and reduction of greenhouse gas emissions in order to ensure meeting the ultimate objectives of the UN Framework Convention on Climate Change (UNFCCC) without sacrificing energy policy goals (CEC 2008).

The issue of climate continued to dominate the agenda of the 10th annual EU–China Summit held in Beijing in November 2007. Among others, one of the major achievements of this Summit was the signing by the European Investment Bank (EIB) and Chinese Minister of Finance (MoF) of a loan at €500m to help combat climate change in China. In welcoming this deal, EU and Chinese leaders agreed on 'the significant potential economic opportunities of China–EU cooperation' in climate change (CEC 2007c).

Bilateral dialogue between the EU and China reached a height when the president of the European Commission led nine commissioners to visit Beijing in April 2008 to discuss about climate change. In January 2009, the two sides signed an agreement to establish a joint EU–China Clean Energy Centre in Beijing. A new €15m EU–China environmental governance programme was also expected to be a specific outcome of the much delayed 12th EU–China Summit (*ENDs Europe* 2008).

Cooperation Projects. Given the building up of political willingness to promote bilateral partnership, joint projects between EU and Chinese partners in the field of climate change have been launched. The near-zero emission coal (NZEC) technology project[3] and the Clean Development Mechanism (CDM) Facilitation Project are examples of this cooperation.

One of the biggest challenges to the Chinese climate change agenda is the country's heavy reliance on fossil fuels as an energy source. In 2005, coal accounted for 68.9 per cent of China's energy consumption, compared to 27.8 per cent for world energy consumption for the same year. EU–China cooperation in developing and utilizing clean coal technologies can contribute significantly to the reduction of China's CO_2 emission. In order to help China develop a low-carbon economy and improve energy efficiency, the EU and China have established a joint project to develop and promote the use of near-zero emission coal (NZEC) technology through carbon dioxide capture and storage (CCS), following the signing of a Memorandum of Understanding (MoU) between the Chinese Ministry of Science and Technology and the European Commission in Shanghai in February 2006.

The EU–China Clean Development Mechanism (CDM) Facilitation Project is also worth mentioning.[4] At an estimated cost of €2.8 million, the CDM Facilitation Project was launched in June 2007. The main objective of this project was to promote the development of the CDM market in China. European Commission President Barroso suggested that, by April 2009, EU involvement in Chinese CDM projects had already reached a total of €5bn (ENDS *Europe* 2008).

EU–China cooperation in environmental policy and climate change is further promoted at Member State level. For example, in January 2007, the former Finnish Ministry of Trade and Industry (now the Ministry of Employment and Economy) signed an MoU with the Chinese National Development and Reform Commission to promote export of Finnish environmental protection technologies to China. Following this MoU, the Finnish government established the Finnish Environmental Technology China Commission (FECC), which now has an office in Shanghai. The overall mission of the FECC is to promote Sino-Finnish cooperation in environmental protection and new energy industries.

As regards the CDM, a number of EU Member States including Denmark, France, Germany, Italy, the Netherlands and the UK have already launched bilateral cooperation projects with China. The mushrooming of Member State-level projects will certainly contribute to the development of the emerging Chinese CDM market through technologies and investments, thus demonstrating a leadership role for the EU *vis-à-vis* China as a follower. It is worth mentioning, however, that an over-enthusiastic response from the Member State-level could well cast a shadow over supranational-level coordination over the EU's climate policy on China.

Despite the various problems, the deepening of cooperation between the EU and China, and its impact upon climate change politics at the international level, is viewed as significant: 'If China and the EU aligned their standards for energy efficiency and carbon intensity they would *de facto* become global standards' (Preston and Findlay 2008: 5). Some even go further to emphasise the EU's structural leadership: 'Climate change and energy security have become the first issue in the EU-China relationship where the EU has been able to shift the fundamentals of Chinese policy' (Fox and Godeman 2009: 42).

EU–China partnership in an international context

During the period up until Kyoto, EU–China partnership on climate change represented an important step forward towards bridging the North–South divide. During the course of international negotiations on the Kyoto Protocol, China, hand in hand with India, managed to fight off attempts by industrialised countries to impose any concrete commitment to cutting GHGEs (see Brenton 1994). While the US remained non-committal to the Kyoto Protocol on the ground that major developing countries such as China and India were not included in quantitative targets, these two countries 'have ensured that the issues of development, sovereignty and equity have had a prominent place on the agenda' (Carter 2001: 237). China's leading position was further highlighted by the fact that 'China and the G77 maintained their basic opposition to joint implement' (Grubb *et al.* 1999: 89).

From Rio to Kyoto, developed and developing countries are generally clustered into two groups – a North–South divide in climate change politics. Being the fastest-growing and third-largest economy in the world, China has been able to provide its structural leadership within the South camp in bargaining with the North.[5] By sticking to the principle of shared but differentiated responsibilities, China has won herself many friends in the South while maintaining the moral high ground by contrast with the US under George W Bush.

Differing from the stand-off between the US and China, the EU was successful in establishing productive bilateral relations with China. This left the Obama administration with a catch-up exercise to undertake in seeking a similar partnership with China on climate change.

EU–China relations met with a new test at the Copenhagen climate summit, when China and the US became the new focus. While the US government insisted that developing countries' CO_2 emission reduction be subject to international monitoring and verification, China adamantly rejected any attempt by western industrialised countries to interfere with its domestic affairs. In a seemingly smart move to fend off western demand for making the CO_2 cut transparent,[6] China indicated that it would not ask for any amount of the newly proposed international climate change fund to be offered by developed countries to developing countries during the three years up until the end of the Kyoto Protocol. Faced with this contention between the two largest CO_2 emitters, the EU's ambition for achieving an international legal framework to succeed Kyoto has now been rendered a failed mission so far as Copenhagen is concerned.

The domestic implementation of international commitments

It would be foolhardy to suggest that China has taken important steps towards fulfilling its international obligations simply because of the influence of the EU. However, the EU has played an indispensable role in encouraging and helping China to become an important actor in international politics through various forms of bilateral interaction such as those discussed earlier.

As a developing country, China does not have specific quantitative targets as international obligations under the UNFCCC and the Kyoto Protocol. However, China does need to promote Clean Development Mechanism in cooperation with western industrialised countries. In this respect, China has set up a CDM Project Approval Board (CDMPAB), reporting directly to the National Leading Group for Climate Change. By January 2009, a total of 1,847 CDM projects had been approved by the CDMPAB, following the first project for a wind turbine farm set up by SenterNovem of an EU Member State (the Netherlands) with the Inner Mongolia Autonomous Region. As far as China's CDM market is concerned, the bilateral CDM Facilitation

Project between the EU and China represents a major development in an international context.

Despite the absence of quantitative emissions reduction target, China has set its own policy objectives for climate change. First, the new Climate Change Programme sets a specific target to be achieved by 2010, which required the reduction of energy consumption in unit GDP growth by 20 per cent of 2005 level. Second, actual utilisation of renewable energy will account for 10 per cent of total energy consumption by 2010. Third, afforestation will be increased to 20 per cent of the country's total land area by 2010. Finally, the development of a circular economy to achieve more efficient use of materials, and reducing GHGEs will be actively pursued. It is not surprising that references to most of these areas, such as the reduction of energy consumption, new and renewable energy and circular (or low-carbon) economy, are to be found in the EU–China Declaration on Climate Change.

Since the early 1990s, the Chinese government has sponsored a large number of research projects to help improve policy making on climate change at the national and international level. In 2007, China implemented the China Climate Change Science and Technology Special Programme, which targeted key issues related to climate change. During the 11th Five-year Plan (2006–10), government budget for climate change research was set at RMB7 bn (US$1 billion), compared to RMB2.5 bn for the previous Five-year Plan (2001–5). The 'Global Climate Change Forecast, Impact and Policy Reponses Study' and the 'Forecast of Trends of China's Future 20–50 Years of Living Environment Change' projects were among the key topics sponsored by government funding. By extending its Framework Programme to fund Chinese researchers, the EU has already been contributing to fostering China's research capacity in the field of climate change.[7] The EU's decision to set up a climate change research centre in Beijing will certainly add a new node linking the EU with China's national research policy.

Conclusion

This chapter has shown that policy makers in China have their desire to develop a benign development strategy in the twenty-first century: maintaining the momentum of economic growth as a developing country without further jeopardising the environment. This has led to the development of new policy programmes and institutional mechanisms for coordinating national actions in adapting to and mitigating climate change. Being the world's largest emitter of greenhouse gases, China, and the way it addresses climate change, has already become a focal point of political debate at the global level.

Instead of taking a confrontational approach, the EU sought to establish a bilateral partnership to engage China in an international effort to take on the challenges posed by climate change. Through this partnership, EU funding, technologies and expertise in good governance began to flow into China. The EU–China Partnership for Climate change was of course not a one-way street; rather, the EU has benefited as well. First, by encouraging and helping China to meet its international obligations, the EU has made a significant step forward in defining and realising its global agenda for mitigating climate change. No matter what shape the post-2012 deal takes, a higher level of commitment by developing countries, especially China, in a new global regime is expected. The EU's partnership with China is vital to this preparation. By helping others using its structural power, the EU has helped itself.

Second, having inserted a degree of influence on China through dialogue and cooperation projects, the EU has effectively improved its international standing *vis-á-vis* other actors, in particular the USA in climate change politics. By respecting the voice of developing countries and working together with them, the EU has, in dealing with the North–South divide, emerged as a very different sort of actor by comparison with the USA.

Third, by launching the CDM project, clean coal technology project and the climate change research centre with China, the EU has established a strong foothold in the world's largest developing country with the fastest-growing economy. These projects, and others, would help corporate Europe to take advantage of climate change related market opportunities that China can offer in the years to come.

In sum, the opting out by the US from adopting any quantitative emission reduction target has served as an opportunity for the EU to extend its leadership across the global North and the global South, as manifested in its relations with China in climate change. In the meanwhile, the growing challenge of climate change to economic development in the long term has prompted China to seek support from those willing industrialised countries, especially the EU. By deepening and widening their bilateral partnership and cooperation, the EU and China will undoubtedly have a significant influence over the shape of the post-Kyoto regime to come. The confrontational and hawkish attitude of the US towards China demonstrated at Copenhagen in particularly would likely push the latter towards seeking strengthened ties with the EU.

Notes

1 Although figures in Table 1 put China ahead of the USA, it is generally accepted that 2008 was the year when China overtook the US to become the biggest emitter.
2 This paper has benefited from four face-to-face interviews (Interviews A–D) conducted by the first author with a researcher based in Beijing and three local government officials from Chengdu (capital city of China's most populated province in the southwest) and Yangquan (one of China's major coal mining cities) during March–April 2009. The main purpose of these interviews was to identify local government responses to central environmental policies in areas that are subject to a growing level of climate change challenge. Anonymity was requested by all informants and quotes are based on interview notes.
3 Detailed information about this project is available at <http://www.ifp.com>.
4 The EU–China CDM Facilitation Project website is <http://www.euchina-cdm.org>.

5 For instance, according to Carter (2001), China, together with India, played an astute veto role in ensuring important concessions in the ozone negotiations (p. 238).
6 'Transparency' was dubbed 'one of the biggest stumbling blocks' to the Copenhagen summit. See ENDS *Europe*, 21 December 2009.
7 Note that China is now the largest recipient country outside the EU for research funding under the Framework Programme.

Bibliography

Barber, T. (2009) 'China Sees EU as Mere Pawn in Global Game', *The Financial Times*, 23 April.

Barber, T. and Dickie, M (2007) 'Sarkozy Warns China of Carbon Tariffs', *The Financial Times*, 27 November.

BBC (2009) 'China Seeks Export Carbon Relief', 17 March <http://news.bbc.co.uk/1/hi/sci/tech/7947438.stm> (accessed 17 March 2009).

Brenton, T. (1994) *The Greening of Machiavelli: The Evolution of International Environmental Politics*, London: Earthscan and RIIA.

Carter, N. (2001) *The Politics of the Environment: Ideas, Activism, Policy*, Cambridge: Cambridge University Press.

CEC (2008) *Energy, Transport and Environment Indicators*, Luxembourg: Office for Official Publications.

CEC (2007a) *Combating Climate Change*, Brussels: European Commission.

CEC (2007b) *China: Strategy Paper 2007–2013*, Brussels: European Commission.

CEC (2007c) *Joint Statement of the 10th China – EU Summit*, Beijing, 28 November. Brussels: European Commission.

CEC (2006) *Joint Statement of the Ninth EU–China Summit*, 9 September, Brussels: European Commission.

Ding, D., Dai, D. and Zhao, M. (2008) 'Development of a Low-Carbon Economy in China', *The International Journal of Sustainable Development and World Ecology*, 15(4): 331–6.

Dobson, A. (2003) *Citizenship and the Environment*, Oxford: Oxford University Press.

ENDS Europe (2008) 'EU Claims China Policy Movement on Climate', 25 April, available at <http://www.endseurope.com/15010> (accessed on 2 February 2008).

Fox, J. and Godeman, F. (2009) *A Power Audit of EU–China Relations*, London: European Council on Foreign Relations.

Goldenberg, S. (2009) 'Clinton Tries to Build China Climate Pact', *The Guardian*, 14 February.

Grubb, M., Vrolijk, C., Brack, D., *et al.* (1999) *The Kyoto Protocol: A Guide and Assessment*, London: RIIA and Earthscan.

Hu, Jintao (2008) 'Speech at the Big Economy Leaders Conference on Energy Security and Climate Change', available at <www.npc.gov.cn> (accessed 15 July 2008).

Interview A (2007) with scholar from the Chinese Academy of Social Sciences, Beijing. 25 March.

Interview B (2009) with local government official in Yangquan, Shanxi Province. 13 April.

Interview C (2009) with local government official in Chengdu, Sichuan Province. 15 April.

Interview D (2009) with local government official in Chengdu, Sichuan Province. 16 April.

Jacobson, L. (2009) 'China's Changing Climate', *The World Today*, May, London: Chatham House, 4–7.

Jotzo, F. (2008) 'Climate Change Economics and Policy in the Asia Pacific', *Asian-Pacific Economic Literature*, 22(2): 14–30.

Konan, D. and Zhang, J. (2008) 'China's Quest for Energy Resources on Global Markets', *Pacific Focus*, 23(3), 382–99.

Leggett, J. A, Logan, J. and Mackey, A. (2008) *China's Greenhouse Gas Emissions and Mitigation Policies*, CRS Report for Congress, RL34659, 10 September, Washington, DC: Congressional Research Service.

Liu, J. (2009) 'Asia-Pacific Has Vital Role in Climate Change', *China Daily*, 10 April.

McGregor, R. (2007a) 'Pressure Can Spur China into Climate Action', *Financial Times*, 10 May.

McGregor, R. (2007b) 'Wen Hits at Failure to Cut Pollution', *Financial Times*, 10 May.

Ministry of Science and Technology, National Development and Reform Commission, Ministry of Foreign Affairs, *et al.* (2007) *China's Scientific & Technological Actions on Climate Change*, Beijing: June.

National Development and Reform Commission (NDRC) (2007) *China's National Climate Change Programme*, Beijing: NDRC, June.

NCCCC (2005) *Measures for Operation and Management of Clean Development Mechanism Projects in China*, Beijing: NCCCC, 29 November.

Preston, F. and Findlay, M. (2008) *Low Carbon Zones: A Transformational Agenda for China and Europe*, London: Chatham House and E3G, October.

Siddiqi, T. A. (2008) 'Asia's Changing Role in Global Climate Change', *Annals of the New York Academy of Sciences*, 1140(1): 22–30.

State Council (2008) *China's Policy and Actions in Response to Climate Change*, Beijing: The Foreign Language Press, October.

State Council (2007) *China's Energy Conditions and Policies*, government white paper, Beijing: State Council, December.

State Council (2003) *China's Sustainable Development Action Plan for the Early 21st Century*, Beijing: State Council, 24 July.

State Council (1994) *China's 21st Century Agenda: The Chinese Population, Environment and Development in the 21st Century*, Beijing: State Council, 25 March.

Wang, Xiaowen (2008) 'How to View Equal Right Emission in Climate Change?', *The Science Time Newspaper*, 27 August 2008, available at China Climate Change Info-Net, <http://www.ccchina.gov.cn/cn/index.asp> (accessed 5 Sept 2008).

Watts, J. (2009) 'China Considers Setting Targets on Carbon Emissions', *The Guardian*, 20 April.

Xu, Huaqing (2004) 'Global Climate Change and China's Efforts', *People's Daily*, 2 Dec 2004, <http://www.people.com.cn/GB/huanbao/8220/41430/41433/3029121.html> (accessed 17 August 2008).

Yang, L. (2009) 'China's Nuclear Energy Dream', *China Aviation Journal*, 13 April, 4.

Part VI
Conclusion

16 Conclusion

The European Union's leadership role in international climate change politics reassessed

Rüdiger K. W. Wurzel and James Connelly[1]

Introduction

The preceding chapters assessed who exercised what type and style of leadership in climate change politics, how and when. In Chapter 1 we introduced different leadership types (structural, entrepreneurial and cognitive as well as symbolic) and leadership styles (heroic/humdrum and transformational/transactional as well as symbolic) (see Table 1.2). The 'how' concerns different strategies (e.g. 'leader by example'), ideas (e.g. the use of ecological modernisation as an action guiding norm) and policy instruments (e.g. market-based instruments) that were favoured by different EU climate change policy actors. The 'when' relates to the timing and sequencing of different leadership types and/or styles.

All chapters adopted an actor-centred approach to the analysis of EU climate change politics while focusing on the following four key themes: (1) leadership, (2) ecological modernisation, (3) policy instruments, and (4) multi-level governance. Because leadership has been the overarching analytical theme, the preceding chapters have shed light on the paradox that the EU developed into a leader in international climate change politics despite having been set up as a 'leaderless Europe' (Hayward 2008) in which power is shared amongst a wide range of EU institutional, Member State and societal actors thus increasing the potential number of veto actors. Schreurs and Tiberghien (2007: 24) argue that the EU's climate policy-making process follows 'a kind of logic that is the reverse of that of veto points or veto players' because it offers an 'open-ended and competitive governance structure . . . [which] has created multiple and mutually-reinforcing opportunities for leadership'. The empirical evidence and theoretical insights offered in the foregoing chapters suggest that resistance from (potential) veto actors to the EU's leadership role in international climate change politics can be overcome but only under certain conditions and with the help of certain types of leadership which we will now review. We will also briefly explain how the different types of leadership interact with the preferences of different EU institutional, Member State and societal actors for certain leadership styles.

Leadership

The preceding chapters provide relatively few empirical examples of *structural* leadership (which relates to an actor's hard power and depends on material resources such as economic strength) compared with the more widespread occurrence of *entrepreneurial* leadership (i.e. diplomatic, negotiating and bargaining skills in facilitating agreement) and *cognitive* leadership (i.e. the definition/redefinition of interests through ideas such as the concept of ecological modernisation). This could be interpreted as support for the claim that the EU is primarily a 'normative power' (e.g. Manners, 2002) which advocates 'an EU-topia for global governance' (Nicolaidis and Howse 2002: 782) based on a Kantian world order (Chapter 2; see also Schmidt 2008). It could, however, also be construed as evidence for claims (e.g. from neorealists/intergovernmentalists) that because the EU is not a state it lacks the kind of structural powers which powerful states exhibit.

Table 16.1 lists the key EU institutional, Member State and societal actors in EU climate change politics and identifies examples of different leadership types.

Structural leadership

The EU constitutes the world's largest internal market and hosts a population of almost 500 million people from currently 27 Member States. It therefore possesses considerable economic structural powers (although its military powers are less developed). But the EU often punches below its economic weight because it is either unable or unwilling to translate its putative economic structural powers into bargaining leverage in international climate change negotiations. Within the context of international climate change politics this became arguably most apparent at the 1992 UN Rio conference which adopted the relatively vague UN Framework Convention on Climate Change (UNFCCC) and in particular at the 2009 Copenhagen climate conference (constituting the 15th meeting of the Conference of the Parties (COP-15) of the UNFCCC) which agreed the even vaguer Copenhagen Accord. Neither the 1992 Rio conference (e.g. Brenton 1994; Gupta and Grubb 2000) nor the 2009 Copenhagen climate conference (e.g. Chapter 5; Egenhofer and Georgiev 2009) endorsed the EU's preference for relatively ambitious targets, clear timetables and monitoring requirements for the reduction of greenhouse gas emissions (GHGE). On the other hand, without the EU's determined leadership in the 1990s there would not have been a Kyoto Protocol (Chapters 2 and 5; Compston and Bailey 2008; Gupta and Grubb 2000; Harris, 2007; Oberthür and Roche Kelly 2008). And, although the 2009 Copenhagen climate conference dealt a serious blow to the EU's climate change leadership ambitions, it did not produce a knock-out blow for a legally binding post-Kyoto protocol within the UN framework which has remained the EU's preference even after Copenhagen (Chapter 5; Egenhofer and Georgiev 2009; Oberthür and Pallemaerts 2010a).

Table 16.1 Key actors and types of leadership

	Key EU institutional actor(s)	Key Member State(s)	Key societal actor(s) represented on the EU level
Structural leadership	• European Council since about 2005	• Large member states (and Germany in particular)	• Parts of business (e.g. renewable energy producers and insurance companies) • ENGOs with a large membership
Entrepreneurial leadership	• EU Presidency • Commission • Environmental Council	• Netherlands (e.g. triptych approach) • UK (e.g. UNFCCC and Kyoto protocol negotiations; 2005 EU and G8 Presidencies) • Germany (e.g. 2007 EU and G8 Presidencies) • France (e.g. alliances with African countries)	• Parts of business (e.g. World Business Council for Sustainable Development) • Some ENGOs (e.g. ENGO representatives in national delegations)
Cognitive leadership	• EP (Environment Committee and Temporary CLIM) • DG Environment • Environmental Council	• Germany (ecological modernisation/ecological industrial policy) • UK (e.g. policy instruments, Stern report 2006) • Netherlands (e.g. scientific expertise) • France (e.g. equity issues and CO_2 import tax)	• ENGOs (e.g. 'hot air' and ecological modernisation)

Realist/neorealist international relations theory and intergovernmentalist EU theories argue that only the most powerful states possess sufficient hard power to be able to influence 'high politics' decisions (e.g. Moravcsik 1999). At first sight, this analytical perspective seems to be confirmed by the empirical findings provided in the preceding chapters which show that large Member States exhibited greater structural powers than medium-sized or small Member States. In fact, only Germany's economic strength, advanced innovation system and political visibility seems to have enabled it to act as what Jänicke (Chapter 8) calls an international 'trend setter'. But its 'leader by example' strategy, which resulted in the creation of a large and rapidly growing 'climate protection industry', is not merely the result of 'hard powers' which Germany translated into structural leadership. Instead it also relied heavily on entrepreneurial and cognitive leadership (Chapter 8) which depends heavily on what Nye (2008) has called 'soft power'. An exclusive focus on Germany's 'hard power' capabilities could not adequately explain its leadership role in EU (and/or international) climate change politics. Likewise a narrow focus on the EU's structural powers cannot explain sufficiently its leadership role in international climate change politics.

Rayner and Jordan (Chapter 6) contend that although the UK has not displayed the degree of structural leadership exhibited by Germany, it has offered considerable entrepreneurial and cognitive leadership. France exhibited some structural leadership when it promoted significant GHGE reductions while supporting the positions of developing countries in an attempt to promote equity concerns (e.g. GHGE per capita) and to create new strategic alliances. For Szarka (Chapter 7) this constituted an example of 'the Gaullist aspiration to construct a multipolar world through interventions in the institutions of global governance'. Costa (Chapter 11) maintains that Spain has offered only tentative structural leadership (e.g. at Ibero-American summits) while Poland has, as Jankowska (Chapter 10) highlights, not (yet) been in a position to offer structural leadership. Importantly, the Netherlands tried to compensate for its lack of structural leadership capacity with ardent entrepreneurial and cognitive leadership efforts (Chapter 9).

EU climate change policy became a major agenda item for the European Council only from about 2005 (Chapter 5). In other words, Member States' Heads of State and Government have only belatedly tried to provide continuous structural leadership through the European Council, which has made EU climate change policy an essential part of the wider European integration project only in the twenty-first century.

Barnes (Chapter 3) attributes considerable structural powers to the Commission only in internal EU climate policy-making where it acts as 'initiator' and 'guardian' of EU laws. Vogler (Chapter 2) points out, however, that the EU now negotiates 'at 28' because the Commission appears alongside the 27 Member States in international climate change negotiations. A good example for the structural powers of the Commission (which derive from its role as the 'guardian' of EU laws) is provided by Jänicke (Chapter 8), who argues that the Commission's rejection of Germany's second national allocation plan (NAP) under the EU emissions trading scheme (ETS) amounted to 'enforced leadership'. This example also shows clearly that the EU's internal and external climate change policies are inextricably linked, because the Commission was able to reject the German second NAP on the grounds that it had failed to conform with Germany's relatively ambitious GHGE reductions targets under the EU burden-sharing (now 'effort-sharing') agreement, which was itself derived from the EU's collective GHGE targets under the Kyoto Protocol.

Under the co-decision procedure, which has been applicable for most internal EU climate policy measures (but not EU energy policy measures) since the late 1990s, the EP has formal legislative competences which equal those of the Council. As Burns and Carter explain (Chapter 4) the adoption of the EU emissions trading scheme (ETS) and the 2007/08 climate and energy package offered the EP a unique opportunity to influence EU climate change policy, although its structural leadership capacity remained contingent upon factors such as the wider economic context. The 2008 credit crunch and subsequent economic recession clearly constrained the EP's scope for tightening the Commission's climate change policy proposals.

Grant (Chapter 12) and Wurzel and Connelly (Chapter 13) argue that businesses and environmental NGOs (ENGOs) also possess some structural leadership capacities through their ability to create economic wealth and jobs (business) and their large supporter/member base (ENGOs). To argue that EU institutional and societal actors have *some* structural leadership capacity is not to say that they have the *same* structural leadership capacity as (large) Member States. But the climate change policy preferences of all Member States are at least partly influenced by important societal actors such as businesses and ENGOs. It is not by chance that Spain and Poland, where the activities and influence of environmental ENGOs are few and limited, have frequently opposed ambitious EU climate change policies, while Britain, France, Germany and the Netherlands, where ENGOs' activities are extensive, have often pushed for relatively ambitious EU environmental policy measures. That business can act as 'the elephant in the room' (Chapter 12), significantly influencing the behaviour of governments even in environmental leader states, is well illustrated by Chancellor Merkel's insistence (during the revision of the EU ETS) on favourable rules for carbon-intensive German coal-fired power stations, and her attempt to water down EU carbon dioxide (CO_2) standards for cars (Chapter 8). These examples demonstrate that the veto powers of business, and/or its 'negative leadership' capacity, can constrain 'positive' structural leadership by (Member) States.

Entrepreneurial leadership

In our characterisation of leadership we adopted Underdal's (1998: 101) view that 'a leader is supposed to exercise what might be called "positive" influence, guiding rather than vetoing or obstructing collective action'. Similarly Young (1991: 285) defines leadership as 'the actions of individuals who endeavor to solve or circumvent the collective action problems that plague the efforts of parties seeking to reap joint gains in processes of institutional bargaining'. Moreover, Young (1991: 293) identifies as crucial for entrepreneurial leaders the 'negotiating skills to frame issues in ways that foster integrative bargaining'. It follows, then, that the 'entrepreneurial' activities of Member States in wielding their veto powers under the unanimity rule, or organising coalitions of climate change laggards, with the aim of vetoing or watering down ambitious EU climate change policy measures, do not count as leadership.

Jankowska (Chapter 10) and Costa (Chapter 11) show that Poland and Spain initially tried to veto EU climate change policy proposals for fear that they might stifle their economic development. On those occasions where they had been unable to use their veto (e.g. because of qualified majority voting (QMV)) they had to 'download' to the domestic-level EU climate change policies. The top-down one-way Europeanisation of Polish and Spanish climate policies has given way to a two-way adjustment process in which Spain (since the early 2000s) and Poland (since around 2007) metamorphosed from 'policy takers' into 'policy shapers' taking on a more constructive role in EU climate change policy-making (Chapters 10 and 11; see also Börzel 2002; Jordan and Liefferink 2004).

Grubb and Gupta (2000: 19–20) have argued that 'the EU is clearly ill suited to a strictly entrepreneurial style of leadership . . . [because n]egotiators for the EU . . . have more limited scope for entrepreneurial action than representatives of equally weighty nation-states'. The six-monthly rotating Presidency however, provides, the office holder with considerable entrepreneurial leadership opportunities for bringing about integrative bargains in both internal and external EU climate change policies. The rotating Presidency acts as chair, mediator and initiator within the Council and (prior to the Lisbon Treaty coming into force in December 2009) also within the European Council (e.g. Wurzel 1996). Importantly, it also formally speaks on behalf of the EU in international climate change negotiations.[2] In order to achieve greater continuity, so-called team Presidencies have been formed between three Member States which adopt 18-month Presidency programmes. To accomplish greater continuity and better EU representation in the international climate change negotiations a system of 'lead negotiators' and 'issue leaders' was introduced under the 2004 Irish Presidency according to which Member States take the lead on particular issues for longer than merely six months (Chapter 5).

The Lisbon Treaty, which came into force shortly after the 2009 Copenhagen climate change conference, has left unchanged the rotating Council Presidency but introduced a President for the European Council who is elected for a two-and-a-half years' renewable term in office. Whether the creation of an elected President will facilitate a higher level of integrative bargaining *in* and more effective external representation *of* the EU's climate change policies remains to be seen.

Important entrepreneurial leadership examples by EU Presidencies include the 1997 Dutch Presidency's proposal for a 'triptych approach' (Chapter 9), the UK 2005 Presidency's determined efforts with regard to the implementation of the Clean Development Mechanism (CDM) (Chapter 6), the 2007 German Presidency's aiding of a political compromise on the EU's climate and energy package which was finally adopted under the 2008 French Presidency (Chapter 7) and the 2010 Spanish Presidency's efforts to get Member States to agree on a post-Copenhagen EU leadership strategy.

The Presidency is occasionally rivalled by the Commission, which, since the 1997 Amsterdam Treaty, has formed part of the troika (comprising the Commission and the existing and succeeding Presidencies). Individual member governments also launch diplomatic climate politics activities which are often not coordinated on the EU level. Vogler (Chapter 2) and Oberthür and Dupont (Chapter 5) emphasise that the EU's international leadership ambitions have been hampered by its frequent inability to present a unified EU position.

Rayner and Jordan (Chapter 6) highlight, however, the importance of repeated high-profile UK diplomatic efforts for progress achieved in international climate change negotiations. Many of these were aimed at the USA and took place within the context of a special relationship between the UK and America (see also Jordan and Rayner 2010: 60). On the other hand Szarka (Chapter 7) characterises the flurry of French diplomatic activities in the run up to the 2009 Copenhagen climate conference aimed at African countries in particular as 'too much, too late'.

Germany's active climate change diplomacy has also not been limited to the EU level. Against initial American resistance, Germany managed to get the goal of limiting the rise in global temperature to a maximum of two degrees Celsius above pre-industrial levels included in the G8 *communiqué* adopted in Heiligendamm (Germany) in 2007. When the UK (2005) and Germany (2007) held the Presidencies of the EU and G8 simultaneously they made climate change one of their main priorities within both the EU and G8 decision-making arenas. Of the existing 27 Member States, only France, Germany, Italy and the UK are represented at G8 (and G20) meetings at which the Commission participates only as a player of secondary political importance.

Spain is a driving force behind the Ibero-American Network of Climate Change Offices that includes 22 countries (Chapter 11), while Poland tried to form alliances with the Visegrad nations (Czech Republic, Hungary, Slovakia and Poland) and the Baltic States (Lithuania, Latvia and Estonia) around the time of the COP-14 which took place in Poznań (Poland) in 2008 (Chapter 10).

Cognitive leadership

A high level of scientific expertise is a necessary but not a sufficient condition for providing cognitive leadership in climate change politics. With the exception of the purely social science-based European University Institute in Florence, the EU does not have its own research institutes and/or universities although it provides considerable funding for climate change research. The EU's cognitive leadership in this area thus largely relies on the Commission's ability to draw together research and policy approaches and to weld them into innovative EU policy proposals which are then modified and adopted (or rejected) by the Council and EP.

The Commission has tried to recast climate policy from a purely environmental problem to one which encompasses energy security issues (i.e. the need to reduce the EU's dependence on oil from the Middle East and gas from Russia) and the modernisation of Europe's economy into a low-carbon economy. The Council (and belatedly) the European Council have accepted the new focus on energy efficiency and renewable energy gains to reduce the environmental threat of climate change and to increase the EU's energy security. The EP has continuously advocated ambitious EU climate change policy measures as producing a 'double dividend' in environmental protection and job creation (Chapter 4).

According to Liefferink and Birkel (Chapter 9) the Netherlands tried to compensate for its lack of structural powers by providing cognitive (and entrepreneurial) leadership: it sought to persuade through expertise and scientific knowledge. The wider Dutch strategy of setting a 'good example' could be perceived as cognitive leadership because it relies on persuasion rather than hard power. Liefferink and Birkel warn, however, that Dutch leadership efforts often amounted to little more than 'cost-free leadership' (or symbolic leadership) because it was not followed up with substantive domestic action.

For Rayner and Jordan (Chapter 6), the UK provided the clearest expression of cognitive leadership in the Stern report (Stern 2007) which framed the issue firmly within the bounds of ecological modernisation by presenting ambitious climate change policy measures as a pro-growth strategy. British scientists and scientific institutions have also made important contributions to EU climate change policies. Jänicke (Chapter 8) explains that Germany has offered cognitive leadership by also providing a better 'knowledge-base' and by advocating ecological modernisation.

The EU's 1998 'burden-sharing agreement' and 2008 'effort-sharing agreement', which stipulate differentiated GHGE reduction targets demanding more strenuous efforts from the highly developed richer Northern European Member States than from the less highly developed poorer Southern and Eastern European Member States, show that equity considerations are taken seriously within the EU's climate change policy.[3]

EU cognitive leadership in international climate change politics has continuously emphasised the importance of equity considerations for integrative bargains. The EU's insistence on developing countries' right to economic development and the developed countries' obligation to take the lead in cutting GHGE has, however, been challenged by the USA (Chapter 14). France's failed attempts to lobby for EU and international GHGE reduction targets on the basis of per capita emissions was justified by equity considerations by its government which, however, also hoped it would facilitate export opportunities for the French nuclear industry.

ENGOs have been highly active in providing cognitive leadership by framing (or at least influencing) the European public debate about climate change. ENGOs coined the widely used term 'hot air', which crystallised their objections to merely symbolic GHGE reduction rhetoric (Chapter 13). Grant suggests (Chapter 12) that business is less well able to provide cognitive leadership, but typically tried to avoid onerous climate change policy measures.

Interaction between different types and styles of leadership

More than one type of leadership is required to achieve integrative institutional bargaining success (Young 1991). The sole use of structural leadership by the EU and/or its largest Member States (or even by the world's most powerful states such as the USA and China) cannot deal successfully with a highly complex, long-term, cross-border and cross-sectoral policy problem such as climate change. Conversely cognitive or entrepreneurial leadership on their own will also not suffice. Young (1991: 304) attributes the USA's inability to avert the 1920s world economic crises to its failure to accompany its considerable structural powers with intellectual leadership; while Grubb and Gupta (2000: 19), who perceive hegemony as the extreme of structural leadership, argue that '[t]he global and long-term nature of the climate change problem means that pure hegemony is not relevant to climate change'.

The timing and sequencing of different types of leadership is important because cognitive leadership operates on a different timescale to structural and entrepreneurial leadership. Cognitive leadership (in Young's terminology, intellectual leadership)

> is a deliberative process; it is difficult to articulate coherent systems of thought in the midst of the fast-paced negotiations associated with institutional bargaining. It is also in part due to the fact that new ideas generally have to triumph over the entrenched mindsets or worldviews held by policymakers. (Young 1991: 298)

The preceding chapters have shown that it has taken considerable time to reframe climate change so that it is now widely perceived not only as a threat but also as an opportunity to increase the EU's energy security and to modernise its economy through ecological modernisation. In addition to analysing different leadership types the preceding chapters have also assessed different leadership styles, namely heroic versus humdrum and transformational versus transactional styles. Heroic and transformational leadership styles are closely related because the former relies on long-term objectives, strong policy coordination and the ambitious assertion of political will while the latter leads to history-changing events. Humdrum and transactional leadership styles are also related because the former is incremental, short-term and without the ambitious assertion of political will, while the latter leads to incremental policy change (see Chapter 1). In the early 1990s the EU aspired to a heroic and transformational leadership style, but often defaulted in practice to a humdrum and transactional leadership style because of the wide gap between its rhetorical ambition in international climate change politics and its lack of specific domestic implementation measures (Chapter 5). The climate policy measures which the EU adopted to implement its obligations under the Kyoto Protocol has helped it to close the 'credibility gap' (Chapter 5) which had opened up between its heroic/transformational leadership style in its external climate change policies and its humdrum/ transactional leadership style in its internal climate change policies.

The distribution of power amongst a wide range of EU institutional, Member State and societal actors, and the consensual style of EU decision-making which often produces unanimous decisions even under QMV rule (Börzel 2002; Hayward 2008; Héritier 1996; Wurzel 2002), encourages the adoption of a humdrum/transactional leadership style that can occasionally be punctuated by heroic/transformational outbursts. Amongst EU institutional actors it has been DG Environment, the Environmental Council and in particular the EP which have most often adopted a heroic/transformational style. Amongst Member States it was the environmental leaders (e.g. Germany and the Netherlands)[4] but also France and the UK who have most frequently made use of a heroic/transformational leadership style. There has even been competition amongst these four Member States over the adoption of the most ambitious domestic GHGE reduction targets, although Liefferink and Birkel (Chapter 9) caution that 'cost-free leadership' in the form of ambitious targets which are not backed by implementation measures amounts to merely symbolic leadership. ENGOs have most frequently adopted a heroic/ transformational leadership style, although in their practical day-to-day involvement in the EU climate policy-making they often had to fall back on a humdrum/transactional style.

Ecological modernisation

The concept of ecological modernisation assumes that ambitious environmental policy measures can be beneficial for both the environment and the economy (Chapter 1; Jänicke 1993; Weale 1992). From this perspective, climate change poses not only an environmental threat but also as an opportunity to modernise the economy while moving towards a low carbon future. However, the preceding chapters clearly show that some EU institutional, Member State and societal climate policy actors advocated the concept of ecological modernisation much earlier and more strongly than others.

The EP and ENGOs (Chapters 4 and 13) were the earliest, strongest and most consistent proponents of ecological modernisation. But the accession of the poorer Eastern European states in 2004/2007, together with the 2008 credit crunch, created doubts over the commitment to ecological modernisation even within the EP, widely regarded as the 'greenest' of the EU's institutions. Broadly speaking, members of the EP (MEPs) from the poorer Eastern (and Southern) European Member States and/or the political right are less supportive of ecological modernisation than MEPs from more affluent Northern European Member States and/or the political left (including Green Parties).

During the economic turbulence which followed the credit crunch, key proponents of ecological modernisation demanding a strong EU leadership role in international climate change found themselves having to prevent the Commission's climate change and energy proposals from being significantly weakened or vetoed, rather than pushing for anything more ambitious. These proponents included EU institutional actors (EP, the Commission's DG for Environment and the Environmental Council), Member States (Germany, the Netherlands and UK) and societal actors (ENGOs and renewable energy producers).

Commission President Barroso (a late convert to the view that ambitious EU climate change policy was also beneficial for the economy (Wurzel 2008a)), defended the EU's leadership role in the run up to the 2009 Copenhagen climate conference by arguing that the climate and energy package provided a 'win-win' strategy (Chapter 3). Since 2005, the European Council has dealt more frequently with climate change issues while coming to accept a pale version of ecological modernisation. The European Council and in particular the Environmental Council have paid increasing attention not only to the threat of climate change but also to the opportunities which ambitious climate change policies provide for modernising Europe's economy and improving energy security (Chapter 5).

Germany's strong endorsement of ecological modernisation is partly related to the influence of the Green Party and its participation in two consecutive Red-Green coalition governments (1998–2005). There is, however, also a long-standing German tradition of industrial policy which was transformed into ecological industrial policy (*ökologische Industriepolitik*) by taking up key features of ecological modernisation. Germany's interpretation of ecological modernisation is characterised by Jänicke (Chapter 8) as 'leadership by example', which is not to say that it is always in the forefront. Germany's coal and automobile industries have often acted as a brake on the support given by German Chancellors for ecological modernisation. But ecological modernisation was applied when an ecological tax reform was adopted. Germany has developed a rapidly growing 'climate protection industry' which has created a significant number of jobs (Chapter 8).

Although ecological modernisation has also been important in Dutch environmental policy, the exposed competitive position of energy intensive domestic industries (e.g. oil refineries and horticulture) have loomed large in Dutch governments' perception of the 'national interest' (Chapter 9). In the UK the rubric and principles of ecological modernisation have been invoked as a form of cognitive leadership, although it took the British government a long while to achieve this. Despite a slow start, the UK increasingly adopted ecological modernisation as a guiding principle – sometimes even at the instigation of industry (Chapter 6). France's slow endorsement of ecological modernisation has hindered its ability to exercise cognitive leadership in EU climate change policy. Its awkward relationship with ecological modernisation results from its heavy reliance on nuclear power, the promotion of which has not been linked to ecological modernisation (Chapter 7).

Ecological modernisation does not play a significant role in Poland and Spain. Costa (Chapter 11) argues that Spanish industry rejects the central premise of ecological modernisation. Active support for ecological modernisation and EU climate change policy has therefore been left to generally weak

Spanish ENGOs, minor political parties, a few maverick MPs, and the Environment Ministry. There are signs of change, as seen in the passing of a Sustainable Economy law in late 2009, although this has been portrayed as symbolic leadership.

Dai and Diao (Chapter 15) show that China's heavy reliance on coal-fired power stations for electricity production has slowed tentative moves towards ecological modernisation. For the time being ecological modernisation in China is likely to be limited to the adoption of innovative end-of-pipe technologies (e.g. carbon capture and storage (CCS)). Bang and Schreurs (Chapter 14) explain that in the USA ecological modernisation is not widely supported, although something akin to it was invoked by President Obama's 'green new deal'.

As argued by Grant (Chapter 12), the consent of business is essential in devising and implementing EU climate change policies. The danger is that the need for business consent risks diluting EU climate change policy to the point where it no longer reflects the idea of ecological modernisation. Industry perceptions of the potential benefits of ecological modernisation vary widely, with, for example, some airlines seeking to moderate the impact of the aviation industry on the world's climate, while others aggressively denying either the existence of the problem or their responsibility for it.

Brussels-based ENGOs are in favour of making use of ecological modernisation to avert (or at least mitigate) climate change and to move towards a low-carbon economy in Europe. In the early twenty-first century they formed advocacy coalitions with development NGOs to promote ecological modernisation not only in Europe but also in the developing world. There have been loose coalitions between ENGOs and environmentally progressive businesses (e.g. renewable energy producers) who have also endorsed ecological modernisation (Chapter 12).

At least since the late 1990s, ecological modernisation has constituted a central plank for the EU's cognitive leadership strategy in international climate change policy. However, the EU's cognitive leadership ambitions have been hampered by the fact some EU institutional actors, Member States and societal actors have either accepted a weak version of ecological modernisation belatedly (e.g. European Council), or have remained less than fully convinced about the claim that ambitious climate change policy measures are beneficial for both the environment and economy (e.g. Poland and Spain as well as large parts of business).

Policy instruments

The employment of new environmental policy instruments (NEPIs) (such as eco-taxes and emissions trading) is a typical but not a necessary concomitant of ecological modernisation. As we have seen in the German case, a generally pro-ecological modernisation standpoint can co-exist with a hostile attitude to certain types of NEPIs, such as emissions trading (Chapter 8).

Typically it is easier to secure political agreement for some NEPIs than others. The Commission's 1992 proposal for an EU-wide CO_2/energy tax was vetoed by the UK (Chapter 6), whereas its proposal for an EU ETS was adopted speedily with only relatively minor changes by the Council and EP, although it had initially been opposed by Germany (Chapter 8). Clearly the EU's differing decision-making rules – unanimity requirement for EU-wide environmental taxes and QMV for the EU ETS – played an important role. Encouraged by early American ETS experiments and frustrated by the stalled EU-wide CO_2/energy tax proposal, the Commission (and DG Environment in particular) showed considerable entrepreneurial leadership when it put forward its EU ETS proposal. The EP often still retains a preference for traditional regulation and environmental taxes although it has also accepted the EU ETS as a useful instrument.

Individual Member States vary considerably in their enthusiasm for different types of NEPIs (Jordan, Wurzel and Zito 2005). The UK vetoed the Commission's CO_2/energy tax proposal but later adopted a national ETS for CO_2 emissions which it then advocated as a model for the planned EU ETS (Chapter 6). However, as the UK discovered, the uploading of domestic policy instruments to the EU level is difficult and rarely takes place without significant alternations (Héritier 1996).

France's unease with ecological modernisation extends to certain NEPIs. Due to its heavy reliance on nuclear power, France lobbied (unsuccessfully) for an EU-wide CO_2 tax instead of the Commission's CO_2/energy tax proposal. Szarka (Chapter 7) suggests that French resistance to the implementation of the EU ETS evaporated because its apparent poor institutional fit was less threatening than originally feared: in practice the methodology of the EU ETS broadly fitted with existing domestic institutional arrangements so that adaptation requirements were moderate, with the result that this policy instrument was simply 'accommodated'.

In line with the corporatist Dutch tradition, which emphasises negotiation and consensus, voluntary agreements between industry and the government in addition to eco-taxes gained in importance at the expense of traditional 'command-and-control' regulation' in the Netherlands from the 1980s onwards. The Netherlands also became one of the EU's eco-taxes pioneer. It has pleaded for the wide use of the Kyoto Protocol's flexible instruments (i.e. CDM and Joint Implementation (JI)) to be able to fulfil its EU burden/effort-sharing agreement obligations.

Spain has been slow in adopting NEPIs on the domestic level while finding it difficult to implement the EU ETS (Chapter 11). Perhaps surprisingly, Jankowska (Chapter 10) argues that Poland exhibits preference for market-based instruments (at least in domestic climate change policy) which she explains with Polish policy makers' distrust for 'command-and-control' regulations that are still associated with the Communist past. Poland has, however, clashed with the Commission about its implementation of the EU ETS which was charitable towards its domestic coal industry and industrial high energy users.

For a long time Brussels-based ENGOs favoured traditional regulation and environmental taxes; they were initially opposed to emissions trading, suspicious of voluntary agreements and considered informational tools merely as supplementary policy instruments. Despite their pragmatic acceptance of the EU ETS, Brussels-based ENGOs continue to campaign for the tightening of its rules. This constitutes a considerable shift in ENGOs' attitudes. At least up to the late 1980s, almost all European ENGOs rejected emissions trading on ethical grounds, while comparing it with the sale of indulgences. ENGOs still favour ambitious GHGE reduction targets, deadlines and monitoring requirements in legally binding EU (and national) regulations and international treaties (Chapter 13).

Businesses have generally favoured voluntary agreements and market-based instruments (and emissions trading in particular) over 'command-and-control' regulations (Chapter 12). Since about the late 1990s, the main differences about policy instruments between Brussels-based ENGOs and businesses have shifted from advocating different policy instrument types – voluntary agreements and emissions trading (business) versus stringent regulations and eco-taxes (ENGOs) – to the strictness of the rules for one particular type of policy instrument. For example, most European businesses favoured the free allocation of allowances under the EU ETS while most Brussels-based ENGOs campaigned for the full auctioning of allowances.

Bang and Schreurs (Chapter 14) point out that the USA have been an emissions trading pioneer but not for GHGE, although some American states (e.g. California) have now set up GHG ETSs. Importantly, it was largely due to the American insistence on the inclusion of emissions trading in the Kyoto Protocol that the EU became a reluctant GHG emissions trading pioneer (Wurzel 2008b). Dai and Diao (Chapter 15) flag up that Chinese climate change policy still relies largely on traditional regulations, central government planning and government-sponsored programmes.

The adoption of ('new' and/or 'old') policy instruments is essential for the implementation of policy objectives regardless of the governance level (e.g. Member State, EU and/or international). Any actor offering climate change policy leadership therefore needs to adopt some policy instruments. Innovative market-based policy instruments (e.g. eco-taxes and emissions trading) require considerable cognitive leadership because they constitute a departure from tried-and-tested traditional 'command-and-control' regulation. A heroic/transformational leadership style can help to overcome resistance against the adoption of innovative policy instruments, although a more humdrum/transactional leadership style often emerges during the implementation phase of NEPIs.

Multi-level governance

Jänicke (Chapter 8) identifies what he calls 'enforced leadership' in which the EU provides the policy arena for the 'uploading' of ambitious German climate change targets which are then protected against domestic backlashes by EU institutional actors (e.g. the Commission). This example shows that under certain circumstances EU institutional actors can use the multi-level governance structures to force Member States to live up to their self-adopted EU (and international) climate change leadership ambitions. In other words, within the EU it has become difficult to get away with what Liefferink and Birkel (Chapter 9) have called 'cost-free leadership' that amounts to little more than symbolic politics.

A similar argument can be made for the EU itself, which adopted a heroic leadership style for the UNFCCC and in particular the Kyoto Protocol negotiations, although it had adopted very few internal climate policy measures to back up its ambitious transformational rhetoric (Chapters 2 and 5). It was only during the Protocol's implementation phase when the EU adopted the internal policy measures which were necessary to comply with its relatively ambitious Kyoto Protocol targets.

In its campaign for a follow-up Kyoto Protocol the EU employed a different leadership strategy by maintaining a 'leader by example' position in international climate change politics. One year before the 2009 Copenhagen climate conference the EU adopted a climate and energy package which consisted of the internal policy measures necessary to implement the 20 per cent GHGE reduction offer which it offered on a unilateral basis in Copenhagen. Oberthür and Dupont (Chapter 5) argue that this changed in strategy enhanced the EU's credibility but failed to increase its political influence at the 2009 Copenhagen climate conference, where it was excluded from the crucial negotiations between Brazil, South Africa, India and China (so-called BASIC states) and the USA who hammered out the Copenhagen Accord without any (would-be) European leader present.

Whether a unilateral (instead of a conditional) 30 per cent GHGE emissions reduction offer, and greater financial support for climate adaptation measures in developing countries, would have increased the EU's influence in Copenhagen, as was argued by ENGOs (Chapter 13), remains contested. What is uncontested is that there is a 'constantly evolving dynamic' between the supranational and international (as well as the national) climate change policy decision-making levels which 'is crucial to a fuller understanding of both EU and international climate politics' (Jordan *et al.* 2010b: 189; similar Oberthür and Pallemaerts 2010b: 52). The different leadership types and styles which EU institutional actors, Member States and societal actors have exhibited in EU internal and external climate change policies can therefore be explained only with reference to the multi-level governance structures within which these actors have to operate.

Conclusion

Young (1991: 285) has pointed out '[b]y themselves, the actions of leaders are not sufficient to guarantee that institutional bargaining will yield positive results . . . Yet leadership does raise the probability of success'. Political scientists have shown considerable research interest in political leadership issue since Burns (1978: 1) argued that 'we know far too little about *leadership*' and Young (1991: 281) claimed that leadership is 'a complex phenomenon, ill-defined, poorly understood, and subject to recurrent controversy'. The division of political science into international relations and comparative politics has, however, created an 'intellectual apartheid' (Bulmer 1994: 355) which discouraged an analytically fruitful dialogue between the two sub-disciplines on leadership issues in Member States, EU and international climate change politics. The analytical leadership framework put forward in Chapter 1 does not pretend to offer a new leadership theory; rather, its more modest ambition was to encourage the chapter authors to generate new analytical insights and empirical findings while drawing on a reasonably robust analytical framework.

At first sight the differentiation into structural, entrepreneurial and cognitive leadership types seems to deepen further old theoretical divides, because the analysis of structural leadership resembles the main analytical focus of realists/neorealists, entrepreneurial leadership is most closely related to pluralist/neofunctionalist theory and cognitive leadership fits constructivist approaches well. However, our typology of different leadership types and styles as conceptualised in Chapter 1 and applied in the actor-centred chapters which follow, show that the relationship is not necessarily disjunctive. On the contrary different types of leadership can be mutually enhancing for the facilitation of integrative bargains. As we have argued above (while drawing on Young (1991)), more than one type of leadership is usually required to achieve integrative bargaining success and thus also an enhanced likelihood of successful and long-standing problem-solving.

Overall the EU has a positive record in working towards substantive internal and external climate change policies which stipulate relatively ambitious GHGE reduction targets, clear deadlines and explicit monitoring mechanisms. How, then, is it possible to explain that the EU had only a moderate impact on the vague 1992 UNFCCC and no discernible impact on the even vaguer 2009 Copenhagen Accord? One possible answer, in line with realist/neorealist international relations theory, would be to argue that the EU lacked sufficient 'hard' power (i.e. structural power) and was therefore unable to provide structural leadership in international climate change politics. The EU's overreliance on 'soft' power (i.e. entrepreneurial and cognitive leadership) was insufficient to persuade powerful countries (such as the USA and China) to accept the EU's preference.

Making use of our leadership typologies, a more differentiated picture becomes apparent, which shows that the EU has exhibited more entrepreneurial and, in particular, cognitive leadership than structural leadership. To theorise this a little further by drawing on Peterson's (1995) three-fold differentiation of EU policy-making between (1) super-systemic *history-making*, (2) systemic *policy-setting* and (3) sub-systemic/meso-level *policy-shaping* decisions. Here one could argue that the EU provided more successful leadership in between the 'history making' 1992 UN Rio conference (which adopted the UNFCCC) and the 2009 UN Copenhagen climate conference (which adopted the Copenhagen Accord) than at these two conferences where it has punched below its weight (i.e. its putative economic structural powers). At the 2009 Copenhagen climate conference the EU was excluded from the crucial negotiations between the BASIC states, which hammered out the Copenhagen Accord without any European leader present (Chapters 2 and 5).

This reveals the following important insights about leadership and the EU. The first is that successful integrative bargaining is unlikely to occur if one particular type of leadership (e.g. cognitive) is not accompanied by at least one other particular type of leadership (e.g. structural). Nye (2008: x) makes a similar point when he argues that 'effective leadership requires a mixture of soft and hard powers skills' which he calls 'smart power'. Importantly, [h]ard and soft power sometimes reinforce and sometimes interfere with each other' (Nye 2008: 41).

It does not follow that the absence of EU structural leadership at one point (e.g. 2009 Copenhagen climate conference) negates the often influential cognitive and/or entrepreneurial leadership seen at an earlier stage. It might indeed be argued that without cognitive and entrepreneurial leadership, the 'history-making' negotiations would not have taken place at all. Credit should be given where it is due, and for what it is due, rather than withheld because of a lack of visible influence on 'high politics' decisions which are taken at high-profile international conferences. We therefore agree with Underal (1994: 194), who argued that 'processes of searching, learning, innovation, and support building tend to be harder to grasp and model then the logic of incentive manipulation and rational choice', and hope that this book will make a contribution to the better understanding of the EU's different types and styles of leadership in international climate change politics, which would merit further research.

The EU still seems to be grappling to find the right mix between different types and styles of leadership (drawing on both its hard and soft power capabilities). Its future influence in international climate change politics is likely to depend on finding the right balance within a rapidly changing multi-level governance context in which the EU's internal and external climate change policies are inextricably linked.

Notes

1 We are grateful to Tanja Börzel for her extremely useful comments on an earlier draft. All remaining errors remain our responsibility.
2 The tasks of the rotating Presidency (e.g. Wurzel 1996) are similar to what Young (1991: 294–95) lists as the main tasks of entrepreneurial leaders.
3 Austria, Denmark, Finland and Sweden also form part of the 'green sextet' (Wurzel 2008b).

Bibliography

Börzel, T. (2002) 'Pace-Setting, Foot-Dragging and Fence-Sitting. Member State Responses to Europeanization', *Journal of Common Market Studies*, 40(2), 193–214.

Brenton, T. (1994) *The Greening of Machiavelli*, London: Earthscan.

Bulmer, S. (1994) 'The Governance of the European Union: A New Institutionalist Approach', *Journal of European Public Policy*, 7(1), 351–80.

Burns, J. M. (1978) *Leadership*, New York: Harper & Row.

Compston, H. and Bailey, I. (eds) (2008) *Turning Down the Heat*, Basingstoke: Palgrave/Macmillan.

Egenhofer, C. and Georgiev, A. (2009) *The Copenhagen Accord*, Brussels: Centre for European Policy Studies.

Grubb, M. and Gupta, J. (2000) 'Leadership', in J. Gupta and M. Grubb (eds), *Climate Change and European Leadership. A Sustainable Role for Europe?* Dordrecht: Kluwer Publishers, 15–24.

Gupta, J. and Grubb, M. (eds) (2000) *Climate Change and European Leadership. A Sustainable Role for Europe?* Dordrecht: Kluwer Publishers.

Harris, P. (ed.) (2007) *Europe and Global Climate Change*, Cheltenham: Edward Elgar.

Hayward, J. (2008) *Leaderless Europe*, Oxford: Oxford University Press.

Hèritier, A. (1996) 'The Accommodation of Diversity in European Policy Making and its Outcomes: Regulatory Policy as a Patchwork', *Journal of European Public Policy*, 3(2), 149–67.

Jänicke, M. (1993) 'Über ökologische und politische Modernisierungen', *Zeitschrift für Umweltpolitik und Umweltrecht*, 16, 159–75.

Jordan, A. and Liefferink, D. (eds) (2004) *Environmental Policy in Europe*, London: Routledge.

Jordan, A., Liefferink, D., Wurzel, R. K. W. and Zito, A. (2005) 'The Rise of "New" Policy Instruments in Comparative Perspective: Has Governance Eclipsed Government?', *Political Studies*, 53, 477–96.

Jordan, A. and Rayner, T. (2010) 'The Evolution of Climate Change Policy in the European Union: An Historical Overview', in A. Jordan, *et al.* (eds), *Climate Change Policy in the European Union. Confronting Dilemmas of Mitigation and Adaptation?* Cambridge: Cambridge University Press, 52–80.

Manners, I. (2002) 'Normative Power Europe: A Contradiction in Terms?', *Journal of Common Market Studies*, 40(2), 235–58.

Moravcsik, A. (1999) 'A New Statecraft? Supranational Entrepreneurs and International Cooperation', *International Organization*, 53(2), 267–306.

Nicolaidis, K. and Howse, R. (2002) ' "This is my EUtopia . . .": Narrative as Power', *Journal of Common Market Studies*, 40(4), 767–92.

Nye, J. (2008) *The Powers to Lead*, Oxford: Oxford University Press.

Oberthür, S. and Roche Kelly, C. (2008) 'EU Leadership in International Climate Policy: Achievements and Challenges', *The International Spectator*, 43(2), 35–50.

Oberthür, S., Roche Kelly, C. and Pallemaerts, M. (eds) (2010a) *The New Climate Policies of the European Union: Internal Legislation and Climate Diplomacy*, Brussels: Academic Scientific Publishers.

Oberthür, S., Roche Kelly, C. and Pallemaerts, M. (2010b) 'The EU's Internal and External Climate Policies: An Historical Overview', in S. Oberthür and M. Pallemaerts (eds), *The New Climate Policies of the European Union: Internal Legislation and Climate Diplomacy*, Brussels: Academic Scientific Publishers, 27–63.

Peterson, J. (1995) 'Decision-making in the European Union: Towards a Framework for Analysis', *Journal of European Public Policy*, 2(1): 69–93.

Schmidt, J. R. (2008) 'Why Europe Leads on Climate Change', *Survival*, 50(4), 83–96.

Schreurs, M. and Tiberghien, Y. (2007) 'Multi-level Reinforcement: Explaining European Union Leadership in Climate Change Mitigation', *Global Environmental Politics*, 7(4), 19–46.

Stern, N. (2007) *The Economics of Climate Change*, Cambridge: Cambridge University Press.

Underdal, A. (1998) 'Leadership in International Environmental Negotiations: Designing Feasible Solutions', in A. Underdal (ed.), *The Politics of International Environment Management*, Dordrecht: Kluwer, 101–27.

Weale, A. (1992) *The New Politics of Pollution*, Manchester: Manchester University Press.

Wurzel, R. K. W. (1996) 'The Role of the EU Presidency in the Environmental Field: Does It Make a Difference Which Member State Runs the Presidency?', *Journal of European Public Policy*, 3(2), 272–91.

Wurzel, R. K. W. (2002) *Environmental Policy Making in Britain, Germany and the EU*, Manchester: Manchester University Press.

Wurzel, R. K. W. (2008a) 'Environmental Policy: EU Actors, Leader and Laggard States', in J. Hayward (ed.), *Leaderless Europe*, Oxford: Oxford University Press, 66–88.

Wurzel, R. K. W. (2008b) *The Politics of Emissions Trading in Britain and Germany*, London: Anglo-German Foundation.

Young, O. R. (1991), 'Political Leadership and Regime Formation: On the Development of Institutions in International Society', *International Organisation*, 45(3), 349–75.

Index